NEUHAUS

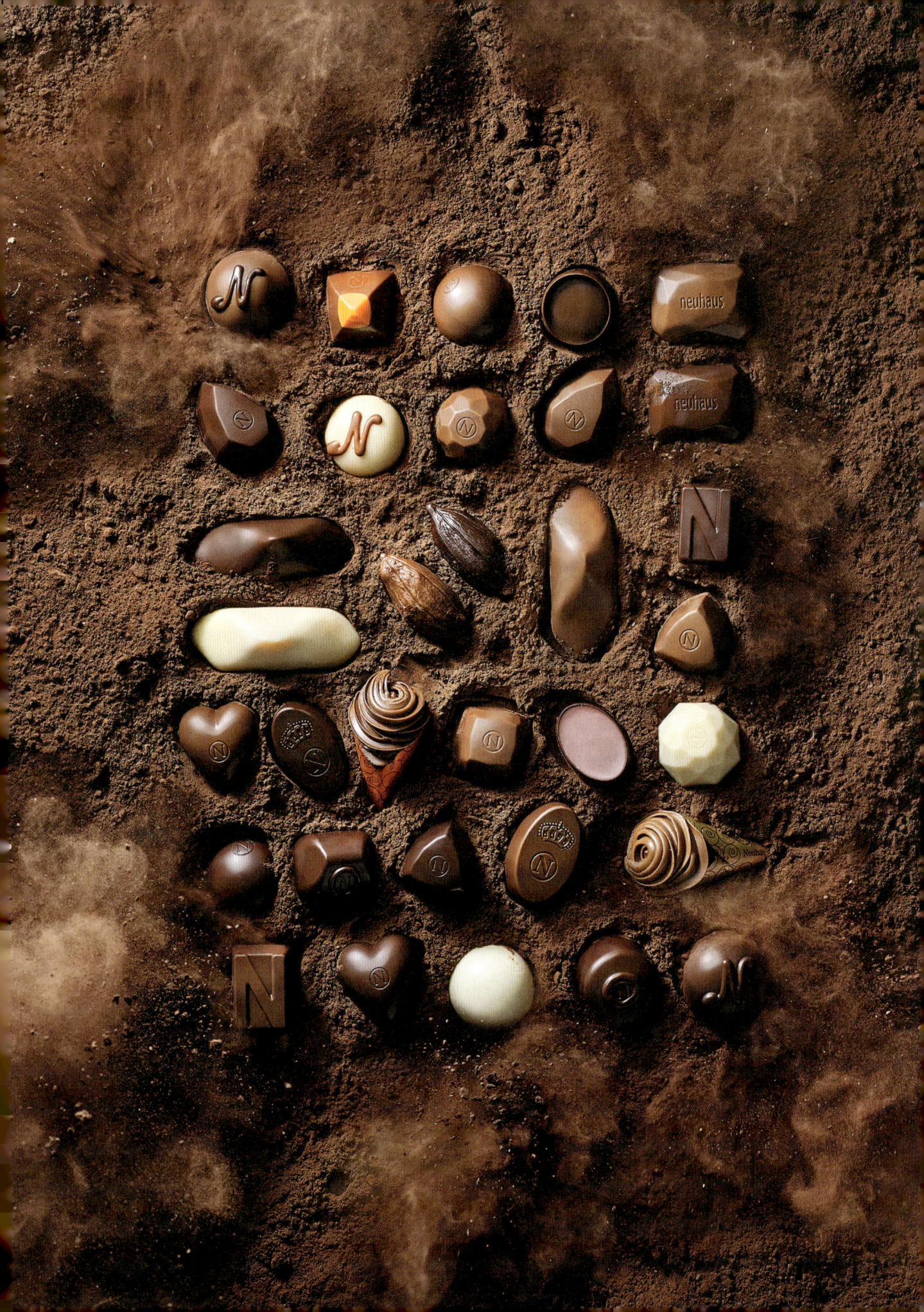

NEUHAUS

CONTENTS

P.6 — FROM A BITTER BEVERAGE TO A BITE-SIZED DELICACY

P.21 — AND THEN CAME NEUHAUS

P.40 — ICONS AND CREATIONS

P.72 — ARTISANS AND FANS

P.98 — BEHIND THE SCENES

P.114 — RECIPES

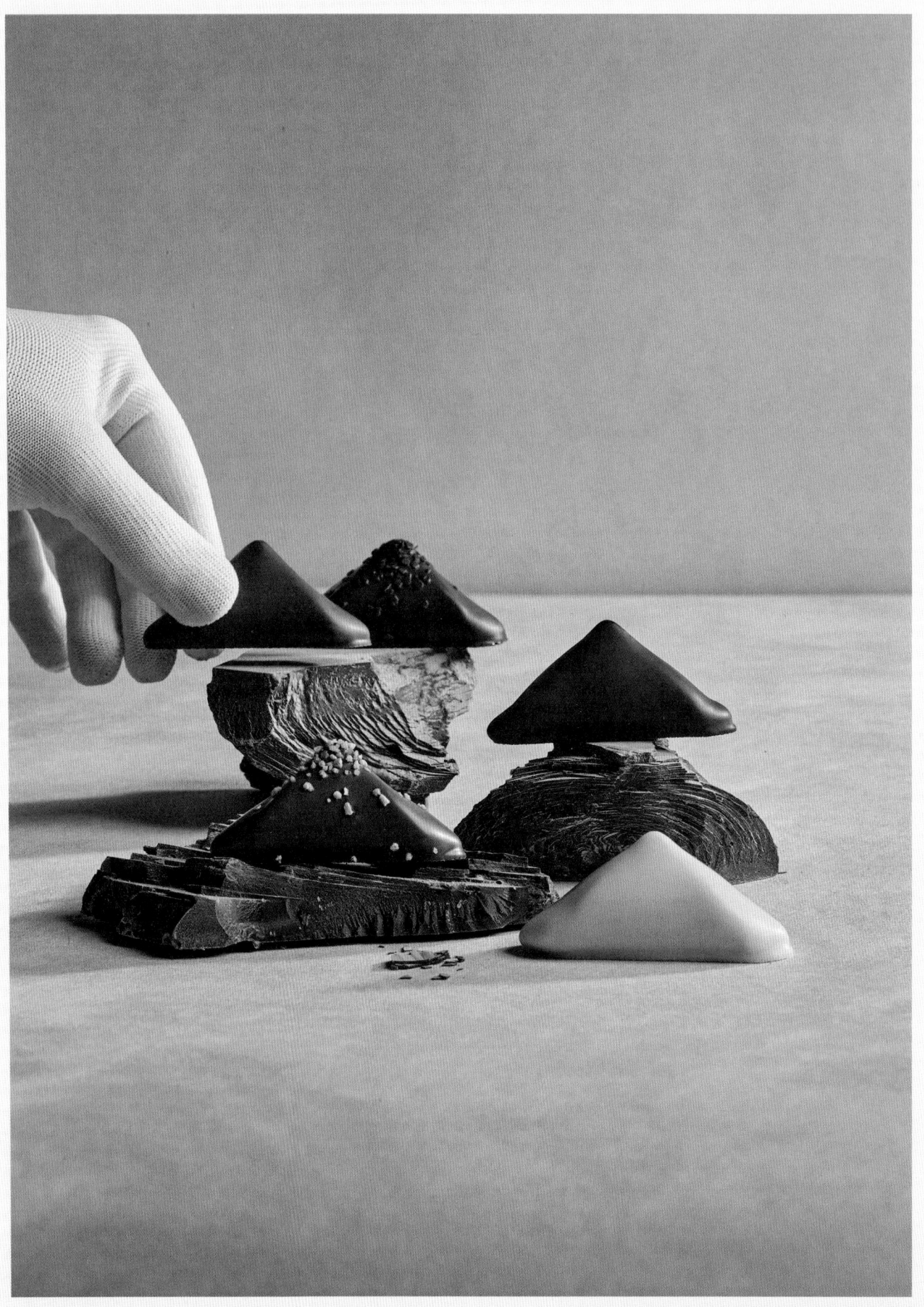

NEUHAUS
HEART-MELTING EXCELLENCE FROM BELGIUM

Why write a book about Neuhaus today? The story of a company like Neuhaus is conveyed through its iconic pralines, the connections it forges, the memories it embodies, and the excellence it perpetuates. For over 160 years, Neuhaus has produced more than just chocolate; it also evokes emotions, creates memories, and instils a unique concept of gourmet sharing.

It is time to pay tribute to this history. From the invention of the praline in 1912, which revolutionised the world of chocolate, to contemporary innovations, 'Neuhaus' has always been more than just a name.

It is a living heritage, cherished in the hearts of Belgians and chocolate lovers worldwide. This book provides a glimpse into the world of Neuhaus, where craftsmanship, the pursuit of perfection, and a passion for taste converge.

But it is not just a nostalgic look in the rear-view mirror. Each exquisite mouthful results from a journey undertaken by experts who select the finest beans, artisans who meticulously execute their creative tasks, and enthusiastic salespeople in the boutique who passionately uphold the heritage. These behind-the-scenes contributors, often unsung talents, infuse Neuhaus with its soul and uphold its high standards.

This book celebrates exceptional expertise and a unique talent for caring for others through stories, images, portraits, and exclusive recipes. It also invites readers to enthusiastically rediscover Neuhaus and understand its influence on chocolate culture, experiencing, page after page, the emotions that make Neuhaus a treasured, one-of-a-kind gourmet heritage.

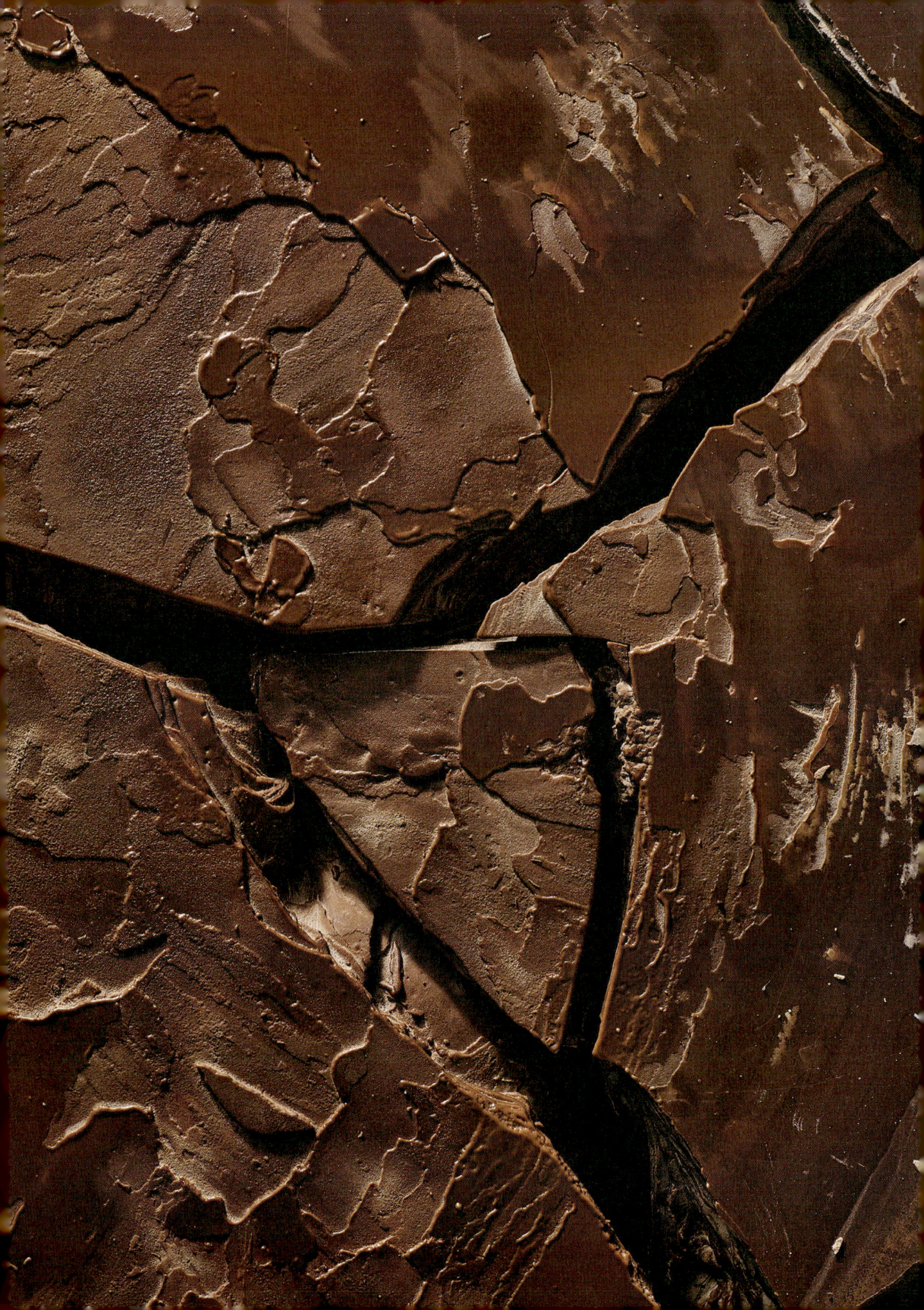

FROM A BITTER BEVERAGE TO A BITE-SIZED DELICACY

Once regarded as the sustenance of gods, chocolate has evolved significantly. Its captivating history is marked by transformations: from sacred to utterly hedonistic, from a hot beverage to a delicate bite-sized delight and from a luxury for the elite to an accessible indulgence for everyone.

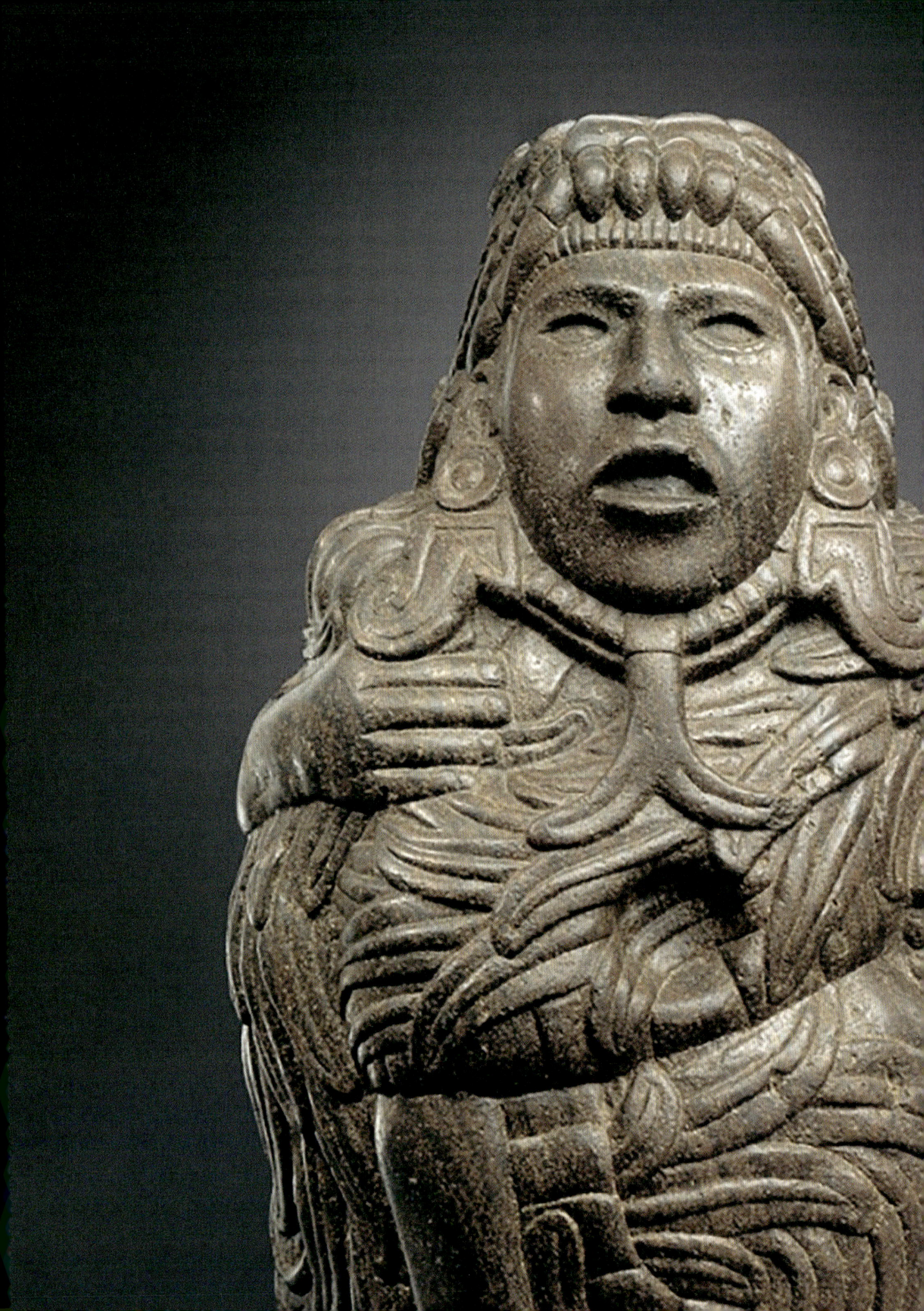

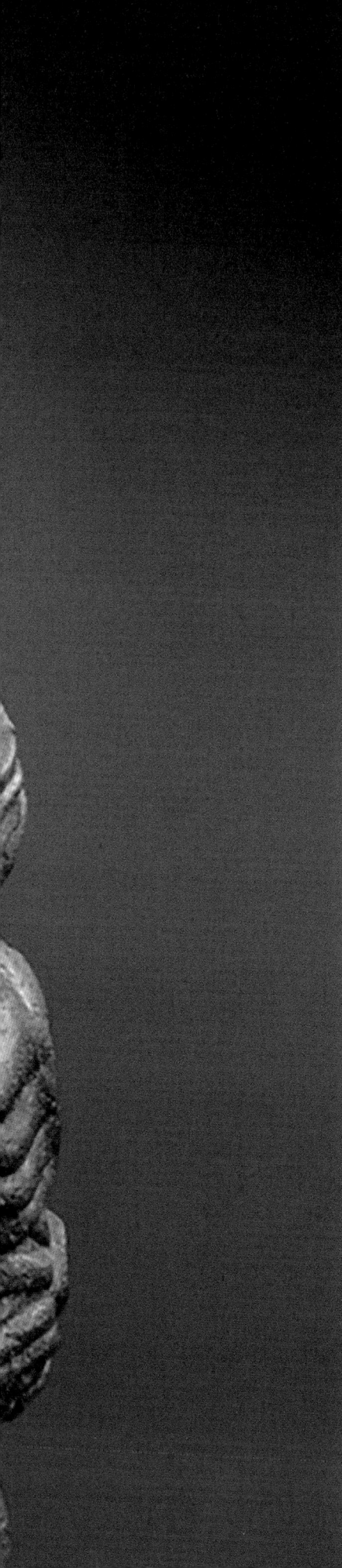

A BEAN GIFTED BY THE GODS

The history of chocolate stretches back several millennia to a period long before its introduction in Europe, where it was initially transformed into a luxury item. According to author Sophie D. Coe [1], the earliest evidence of chocolate consumption, dating back more than 3,000 years, was discovered in the jungles of Mexico and Central America. Mesoamerican civilisations regarded cacao as a sacred gift, a divine food bestowed upon them by the gods. Before them, the Mayas, the Aztecs, and the Olmecs believed the cacao tree's colourful pods and bitter beans held a divine essence.

These ancient peoples believed cacao beans were a gift from the feathered serpent god Quetzalcóatl. Cacao, scientifically named 'Theobroma cacao', was anything but a simple food resource: it possessed a cosmic symbolism. Cacao embodied sacred wisdom and energy gifted by the gods to humankind to strengthen humanity's connection with the forces of nature.

Anthropo-zoomorphic sculpture of the serpent god Quetzalcóatl (Quai Branly Museum, Paris)

THE OLMECS AND THE RITUAL CULTIVATION OF CACAO

(1500 - 400 BC)

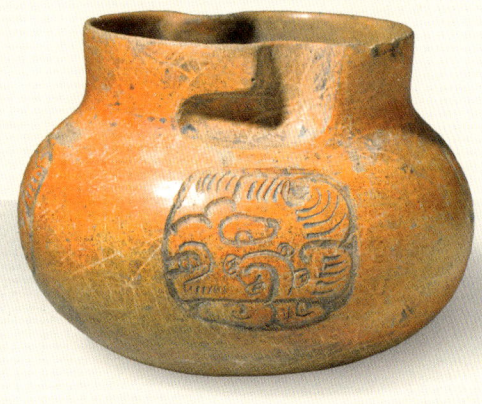

Short, wide pot with screw-on, lockable lid for holding chocolate (MIA, Minnesota)

The earliest evidence of cocoa cultivation emerges with the Olmec civilisation, one of the oldest in Central America, established in the tropical lowlands of south-eastern Mexico. Around 1500 BC, the Olmecs developed agricultural techniques for growing cacao. The beans were extracted from the pods, fermented, ground, and transformed into a beverage reserved for the elite and religious ceremonies. Archaeological studies of Olmec pottery have uncovered residues of theobromine, an alkaloid found in cacao, confirming the active consumption of this product dating back to this period at the latest. Sacred rituals may have accompanied the preparation of this bitter beverage, although details remain elusive.

To the Olmecs, each cocoa pod symbolised fertility and prosperity. Cacao trees represented the sacred links between people and spirits. These beliefs contributed to the popularity of cacao as a mystical ingredient capable of providing strength and clairvoyance. The Olmecs thought cultivating cacao trees made them part of a sacred cycle of life and renewal, a cycle that would, in turn, also influence later civilisations such as the Mayas and Aztecs.

THE MAYAS AND CHOCOLATE AS A SACRED ELIXIR AND AS CURRENCY

(300 BC – 9th century)

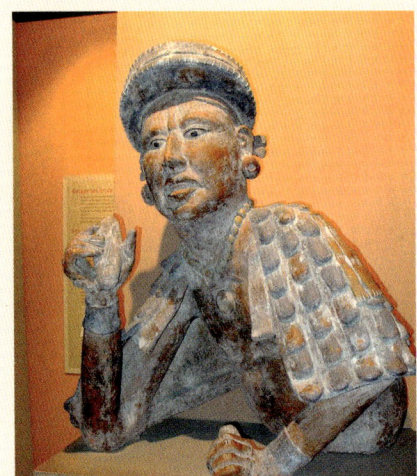

Noble Maya offering cocoa paste (Chocolate Museum, Bruges)

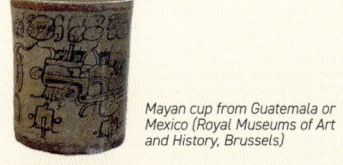

Mayan cup from Guatemala or Mexico (Royal Museums of Art and History, Brussels)

From 300 BC onwards, the Mayas, an advanced civilisation in Central America, perfected cacao cultivation and made it a central part of their economy and religious rites. They fermented cocoa beans, ground them and mixed them with water, corn flour and sometimes chilli pepper, transforming them into a thick, spicy infusion, a bitter, frothy drink called 'chocolhaa'. Priests and nobles consumed it during ceremonies in homage to the gods. Chocolhaa was considered a sacred elixir, a source of vitality and spiritual power.

Cocoa also played a significant role in the Maya economy as a form of currency. The beans became a symbol of wealth and prosperity, serving as a means of payment throughout the territory. A handful of beans bought you a turkey, a length of cloth or a certain quantity of corn; for a couple of hundred, you could buy a slave or some jewellery.

Cocoa beans were weighed and traded in the markets, proving their great value in Mayan society.

According to the Popol Vuh, the K'iche Maya's sacred text, the gods used cocoa to create the first humans. Cocoa trees, which grow in the shade of tall jungle trees, represented much more to the Maya than just food: they embodied life itself. Cocoa symbolised perpetual renewal and the strong connection between nature and divinity.

The True History of Chocolate, London, Thames & Hudson, 2013.

THE AZTECS AND THEIR RITUAL CACAO USAGE

The Aztecs, a warrior civilisation established between the 14th and 16th centuries, adopted cocoa in a more codified form. Their cocoa was referred to as 'xocolatl' in the Aztec language, meaning 'bitter water', which perfectly describes the taste of this beverage. Emperor Moctezuma II, who reigned in the early 16th century, consumed several cups of chocolate daily, convinced of its energising and aphrodisiac properties. The chocolate drink also served as a tonic for Aztec warriors before they went into battle.

Unlike the Mayans, the Aztec Empire lacked tropical territories suitable for growing cocoa. Beans had to be imported from warmer regions, primarily Chiapas and Yucatán. Consequently, the Aztecs instituted a tribute system: conquered peoples were required to deliver shipments of cocoa beans as taxes. Their reliance on imported cocoa reinforced its status as a valuable substance, reserved for the elite and utilised as currency in the Aztec markets.

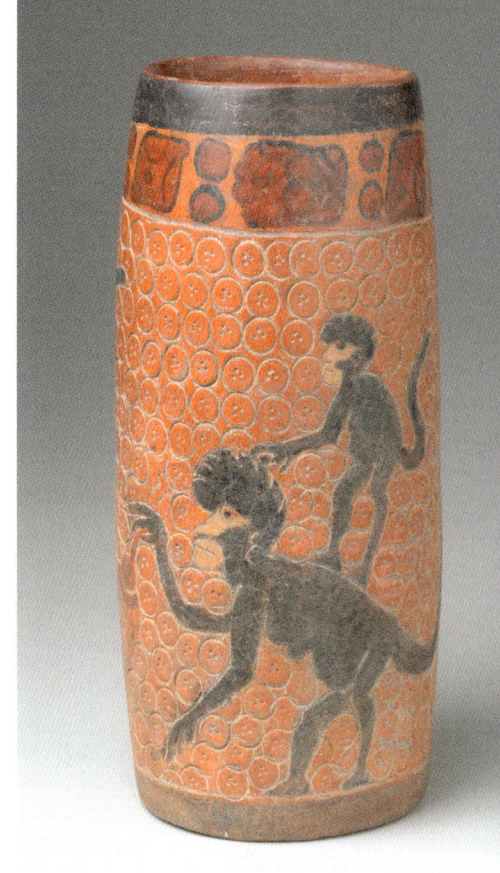

Vase depicting monkeys from the Mayan region of Isometric, these animals played an essential role in the spread of cocoa. The ancient Mayans combined chocolate, water and chillies in this type of vase (MIA, Minnesota).

As a sacred drink, cocoa was consumed during religious ceremonies and offered to the gods. The Aztecs associated cocoa with blood, which they viewed as a vital energy source. They added rocou, an earthy, peppery-tasting spice derived from the seeds of a tropical shrub (rocouyer) that also served as a natural red-orange colouring agent. The result was an amber-coloured, blood-like concoction used during sacrificial ceremonies to obtain divine protection.

For the Mayans and Aztecs, preparing cocoa was not merely food preparation but a proper ritual. They traditionally poured the drink from one container to another from a specific height, creating a dense, frothy liquid that they regarded as the essence of the sacred beverage. The accompanying noise, rhythm, and dexterity required for this technique were mastered by the initiated, who performed it as a ceremonial act. Additional ingredients such as chilli peppers and corn flour were selected according to the occasion, symbolising strength and vitality for warriors, or blessings for religious ceremonies. This preparatory process contributed to the recognition of chocolate's status as a cosmic and divine substance in these cultures.

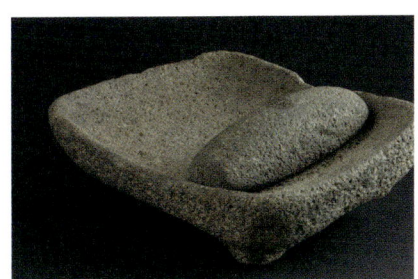

Metate e mano, in English respectively 'the largest stone surface' and 'the hand', used by the Mayans to grind cocoa beans. (Royal Museums of Art and History, Brussels)

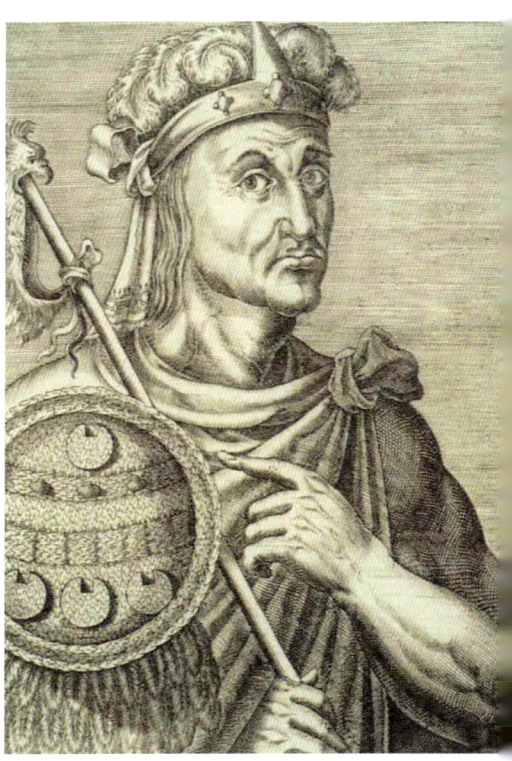

Emperor Moctezuma II (Royal Library of Belgium, Brussels)

THE ENCOUNTER

Christopher Columbus encountered Mayan merchants carrying cocoa beans on his fourth voyage in 1502. When the Spaniards saw cocoa beans for the first time, they were astonished and confused. To understand their reaction, let's time travel back to 1502 and join Columbus on his fourth and final voyage to the New World. As he approached the coast of Central America, he and his crew spotted some Mayan merchants in canoes. The Spaniards searched their merchandise, hoping to find gold or precious stones.

Instead, they found quantities of seemingly worthless dark, oval beans they had never seen before. They did notice, however, how meticulously the natives handled these beans. Whenever the Maya merchants dropped a bean, they rushed to pick it up reverently, as if it held some sacred importance. This attitude intrigued the Spaniards, who were unaware of the significance of these beans in Mesoamerican culture.

Though Columbus noted the existence of these strange seeds, his obsession with gold and spices remained paramount. The bitterness and unremarkable appearance of the cocoa beans did not capture the explorer's attention. Eager for more apparent riches, he regarded them as just an exotic curiosity devoid of value.

First landing of Christopher Columbus in America in 1492 (Prado National Museum, Madrid)

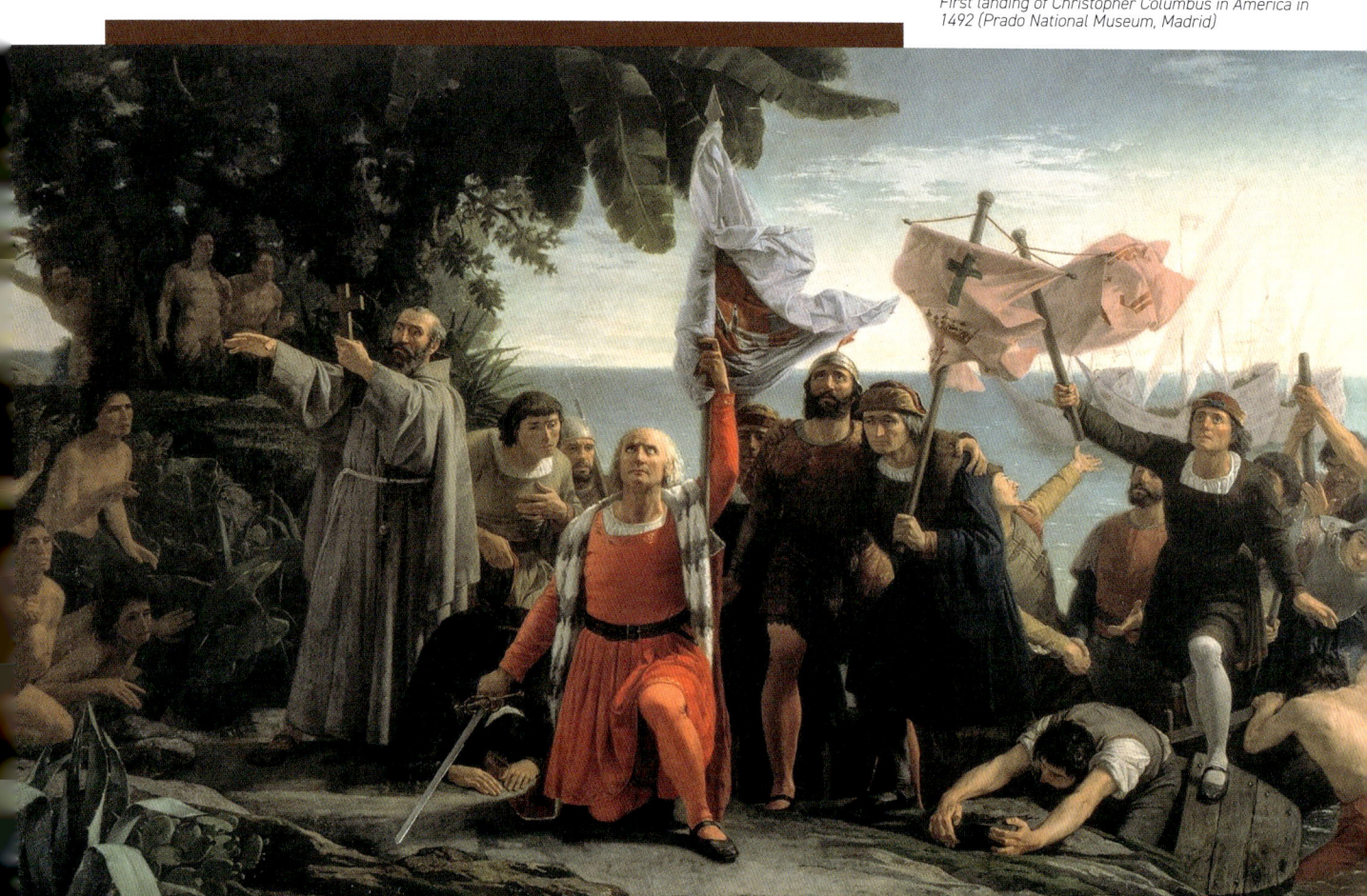

It was not until the arrival of Hernán Cortés in Mexico in 1519 that Europeans began to understand the true importance of cocoa in Aztec society. Cortés discovered that the beans were used as currency and transformed into an energy drink consumed by nobles and warriors. Fascinated by this unique culture, the Spaniards finally took a serious interest in this 'bitter water' and its beans, an interest that eventually led to cocoa crossing the Atlantic to conquer European palates.

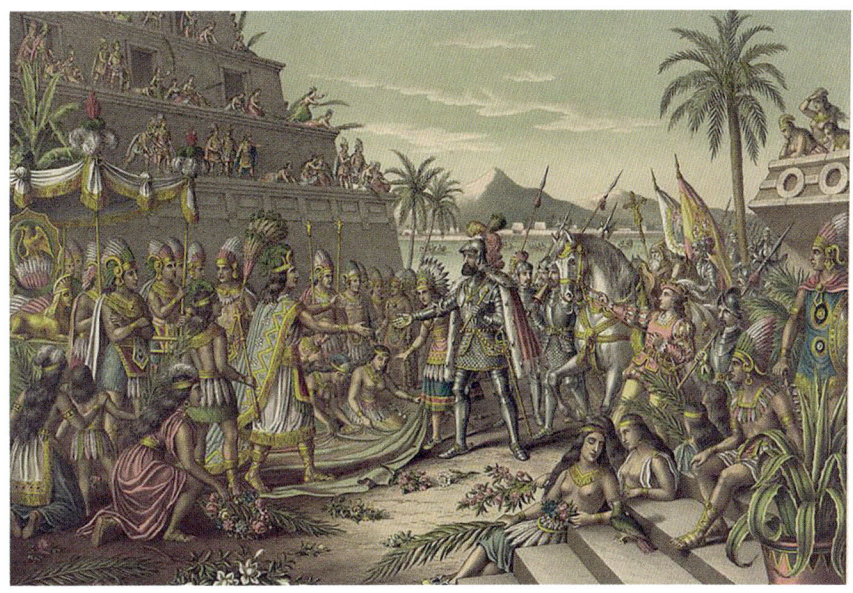

Hernán Cortés meets the Aztec emperor Moctezuma II, a great lover of chocolate (Library of Congress, Washington)

When cocoa crossed the Atlantic in the early 16th century, it entered the aristocratic salons of Spain under a seal of secrecy. At the Spanish court, chocolate was initially reserved for the elite. For decades, it remained a privilege shrouded in mystery. Served hot, this beverage from another world intrigued and seduced the Spanish nobles, who cherished its rarity as much as its stimulating properties. Hot chocolate became a luxury elixir, and the nobles exchanged recipes as if they were jealously guarded treasures. Eventually, all of Europe succumbed, but the first chocolate lovers savoured each sip with a mixture of fascination and fear, convinced that it contained the strength, energy, and mystery of 'the Americas'.

A couple of culinary adjustments helped to coax the seduction. By adding sugar and cinnamon, cooks sweetened the flavour, transforming the beverage and giving it an exotic touch that swiftly seduced European nobility. Hot chocolate became a luxury product first in Spain, then in Italy and France, where it was consumed in aristocratic salons.

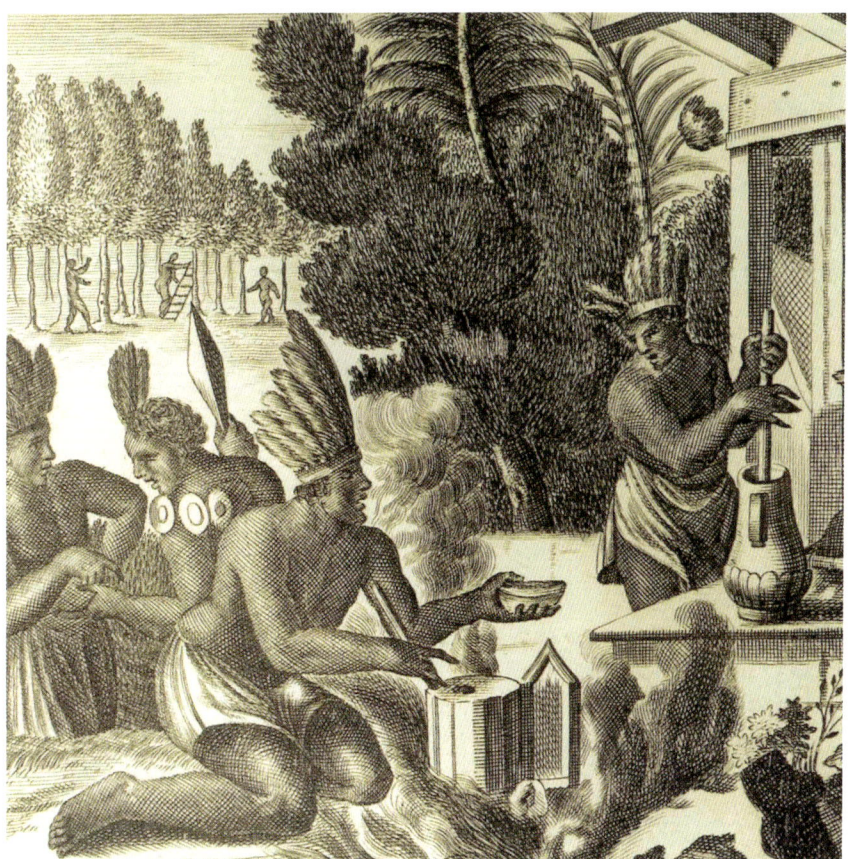

The inhabitants of New Spain preparing cocoa for chocolate (Royal Library of Belgium, Brussels)

THE DISTRIBUTION OF CHOCOLATE IN EUROPE AND INDUSTRIAL INNOVATION

In the 17th century, chocolate conquered the European courts and became a symbol of refinement. Anne of Austria introduced it in France, while in England, so-called 'chocolate houses' flourished, where the nobility gathered in private lounges. Chocolate, once reserved for sacred ceremonies, evolved from a highly prized pleasure to a more widespread consumer product, thanks to the advances of the Industrial Revolution.

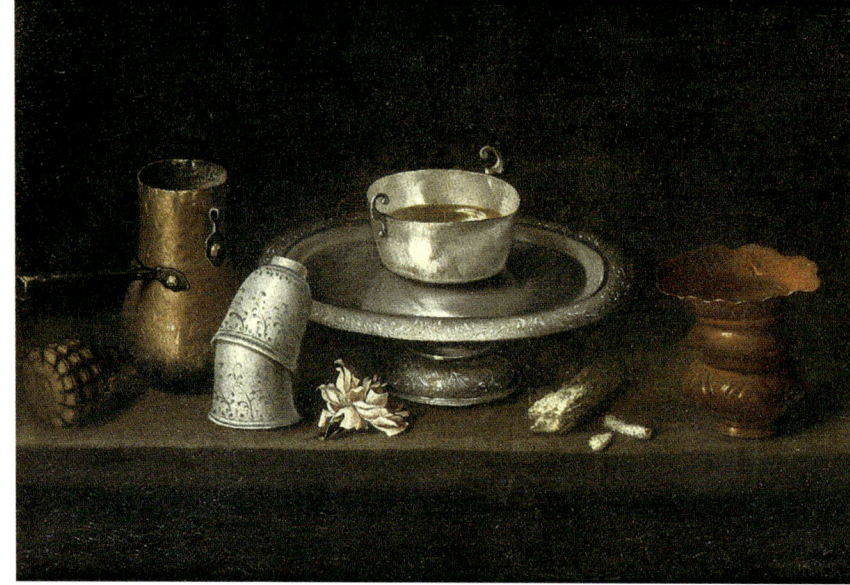

Still Life with a Bowl of Chocolate, *painted around 1640 (Museum of Fine Arts and Archaeology, Besançon*

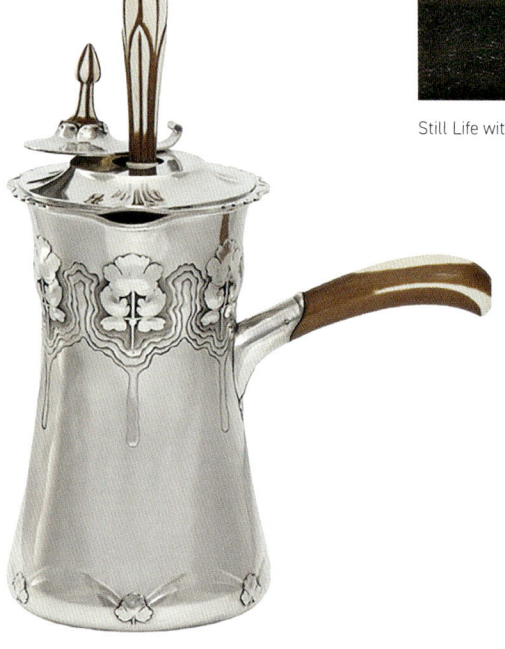

Silver chocolate pot, circa 1900
(Musée des Arts Décoratifs, Paris)

In 1847, British chocolatier Joseph Fry invented the first solid chocolate bar by mixing cocoa butter and sugar. This format made mass production of chocolate feasible, making the product accessible to all social classes. Numerous brands - Cadbury, Lindt, Nestlé, and others - contributed to the democratisation of chocolate, which became a popular product throughout Europe and beyond.

Over the centuries, cocoa farming has evolved in response to the producing countries' economic demands and social standards. From the 19th century onwards, cocoa growing, once the domain of small-scale farmers, gradually became a global industry dominated by large plantations in Latin America and West Africa.

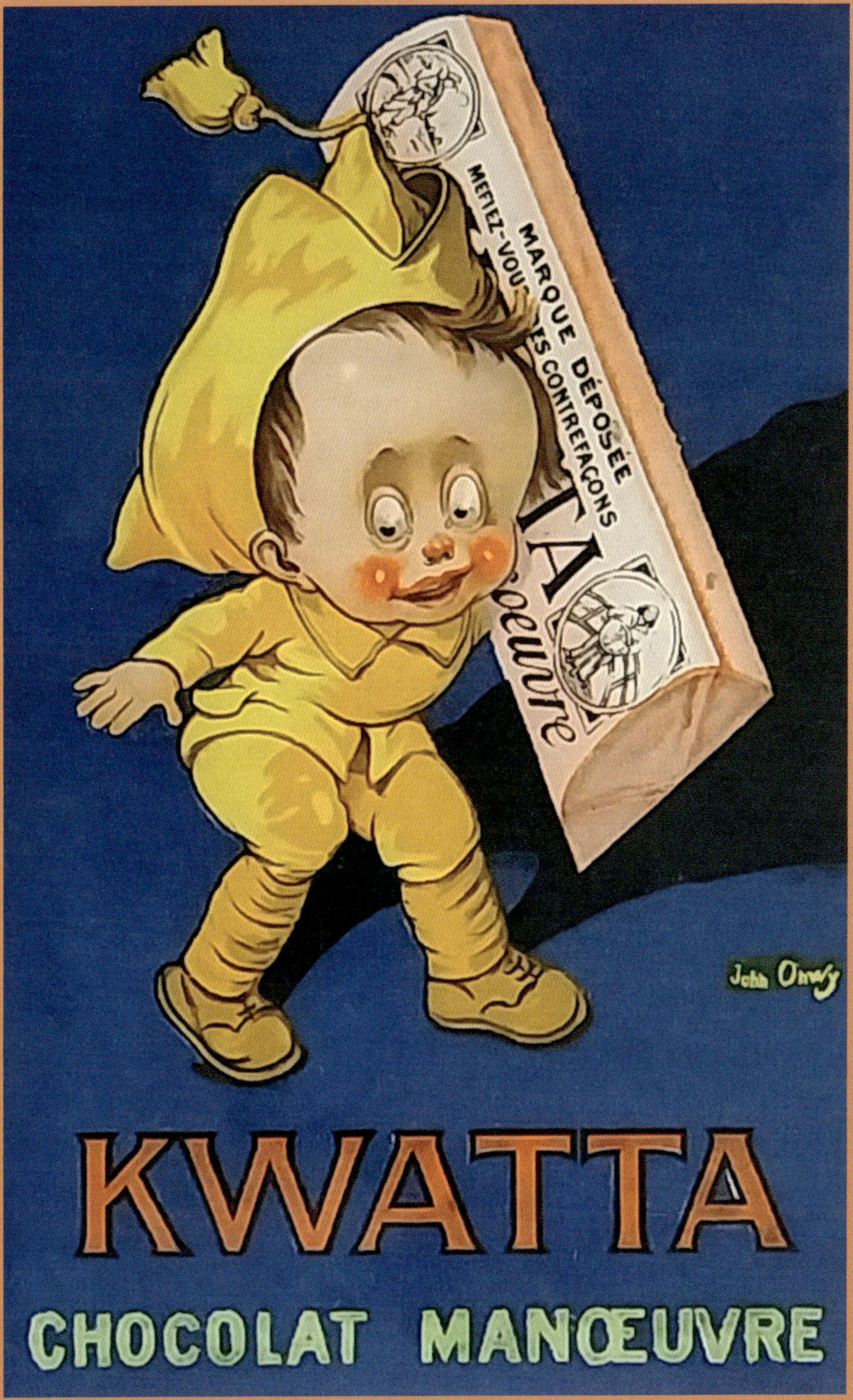

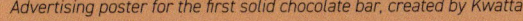
Advertising poster for the first solid chocolate bar, created by Kwatta

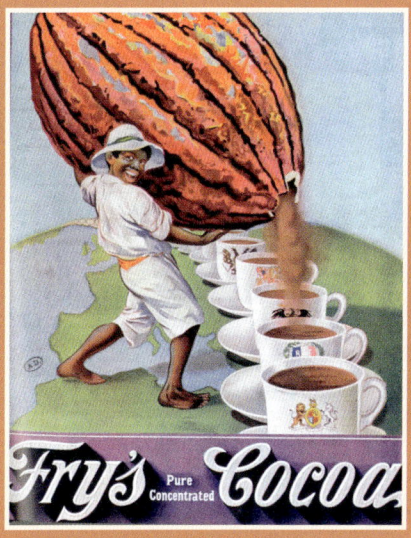
Advertising poster for Fry's cocoa powder, 1906

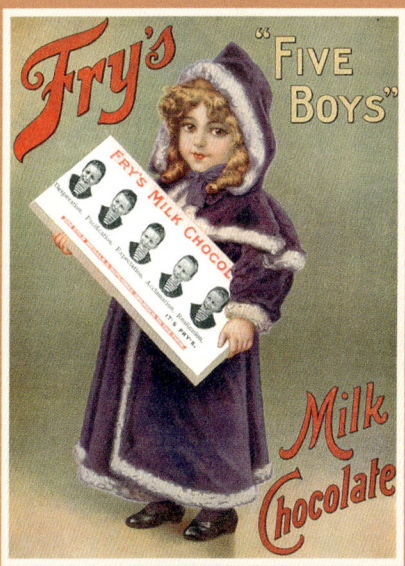
Early 20th-century advertisement for Fry's "Five Boys" milk chocolate in the UK (Private collection)

With the rise of modern pastry-making in the 20th century, chocolate broke free from its restraints to establish itself as an essential ingredient in many recipes. French pastry chefs Auguste Escoffier and Gaston Lenôtre explored chocolate in all its forms, from ganaches to mousses, and popularised complex preparations that highlighted cocoa's unique texture and flavours. This diversification created iconic specialities like truffles, chocolate éclairs, and sophisticated chocolate desserts. It transformed chocolate into a crucial ingredient in world gastronomy. The transformation spread rapidly, establishing chocolate as a staple in pastry culture and leading to a growing demand for original, aesthetically pleasing creations.

THE ORIGINS OF
INTERNATIONAL FAME

'Belgian chocolate'. The expression has gained traction. This may seem surprising, given that you'd be hard-pressed to find cocoa trees anywhere in the Low Countries. In reality, the term is used to describe a unique know-how. Its story began in the 17th century when chocolate was introduced to the Southern Netherlands, where it was first used as a medicinal remedy. However, in the 19th century, at the height of the Industrial Revolution, Belgium started making its mark on the European scene. Two significant assets contributed to this: the expansion of the ports of Antwerp and Amsterdam, which had become hubs for the cocoa trade, and a couple of technical innovations that transformed the quality of the product.

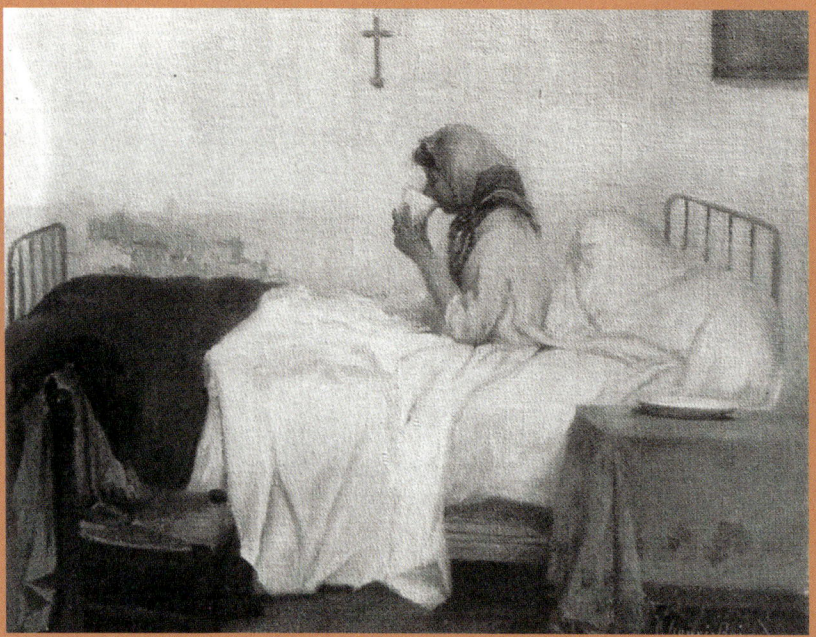

The Cup of Chocolate *by Henri Georges Bréard, circa 1912*

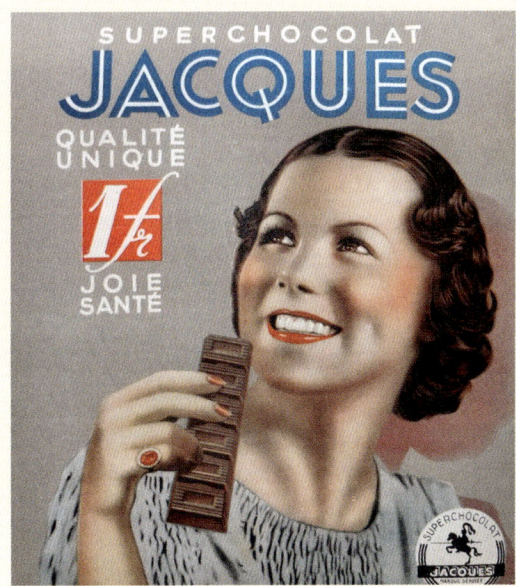

Advertising poster for chocolatier Jacques

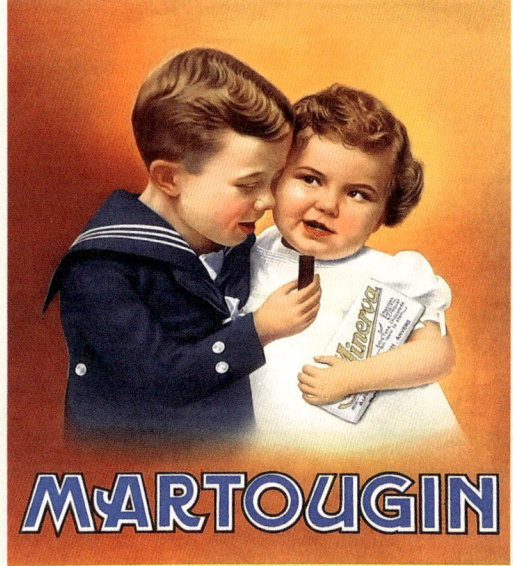

Advertising poster for chocolatier Martougin

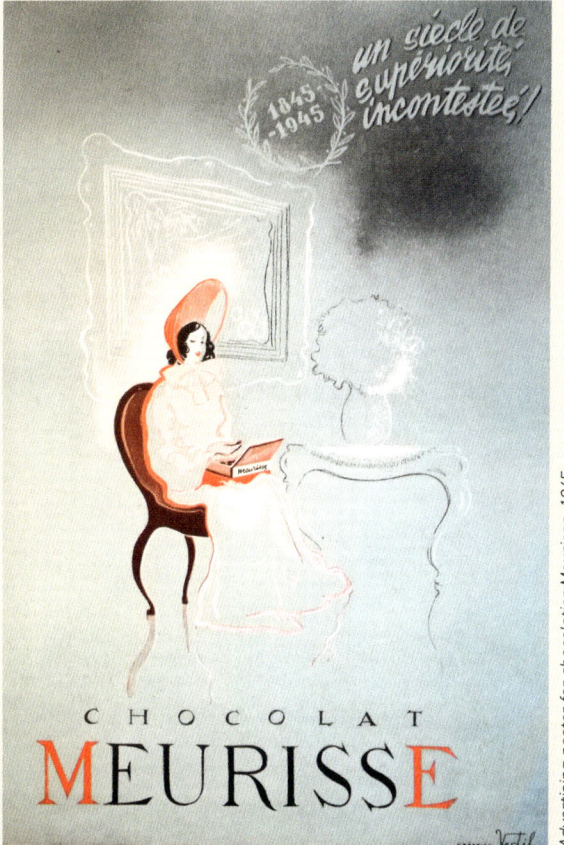

Advertising poster for chocolatier Meurisse, 1945

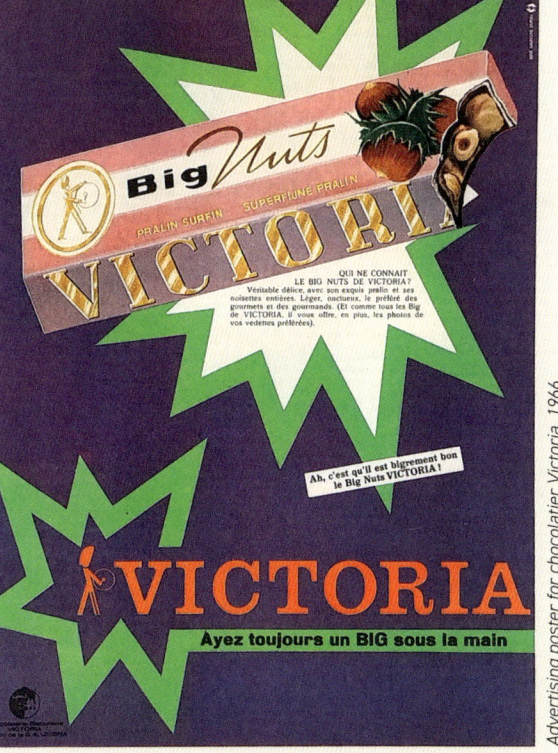

Advertising poster for chocolatier Victoria, 1966

Chocolate makers in Belgium excelled in the art of grinding and refining. While other nations settled for a grind of around 24 microns, Belgian artisans employed powerful presses and unique expertise to reduce the particle size to barely 12 microns. This level of finesse revolutionised the taste experience: the finer the cocoa is ground, the more aromas it releases, and the silkier its texture becomes. From the 19th century onwards, this technical mastery allowed chocolatiers to produce a more refined and aromatic chocolate, solidifying Belgium's reputation.

Besides their technical know-how, the particular care with which these chocolatiers selected their beans was essential. The Belgian chocolate makers travelled the world searching for the best origins, monitoring the harvests, and guaranteeing a high-quality supply. This respect for the raw material is also evident in the rigorous selectivity with which they chose other ingredients, such as sugar, produced in Belgium for centuries.

The Belgians' strong attachment to this traditional craft explains the high concentration of chocolate makers in their territory. By the early 20th century, dozens of master chocolatiers worked in and around the capital, perfecting their art. According to recent figures, the country is now home to nearly 500 chocolate makers and 2,000 shops, resulting in a ratio of one shop for every 5,500 inhabitants. At Brussels National Airport, a veritable global showcase, two tonnes of chocolate are sold daily. This figure indeed confirms the worldwide appeal of this excellent product.

Belgian chocolate's reputation is attributed to its high standards exceeding current norms. For example, its cocoa percentage in the composition of dark chocolate often surpasses 43%., while the legal minimum is 35%. This commitment to quality and a long-standing passion for chocolate enables us to produce consistently high-quality chocolate, from the most modest artisan to the most prestigious houses.

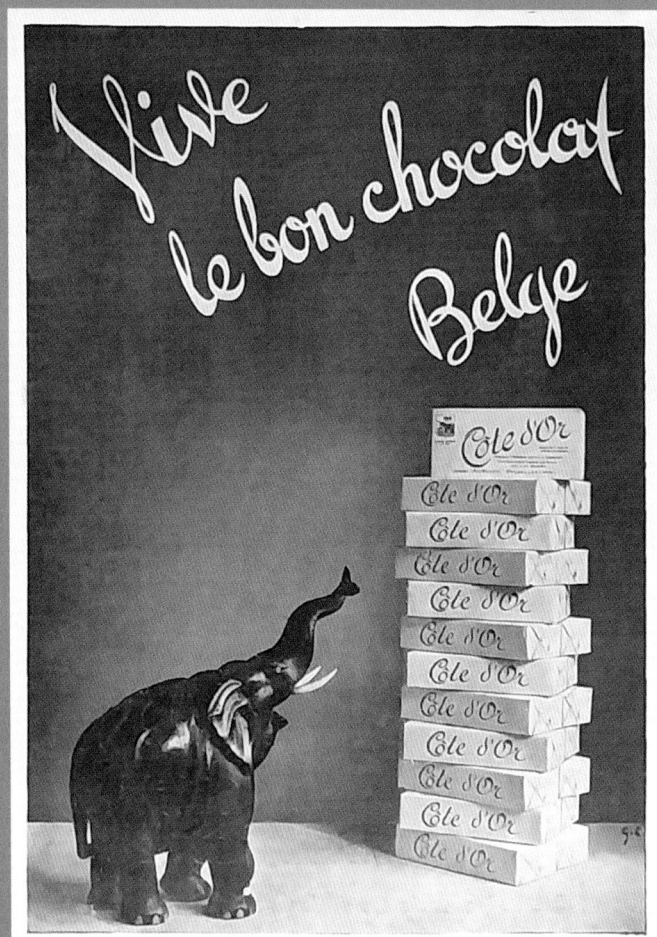

Advertising poster for Côte d'Or, 1930

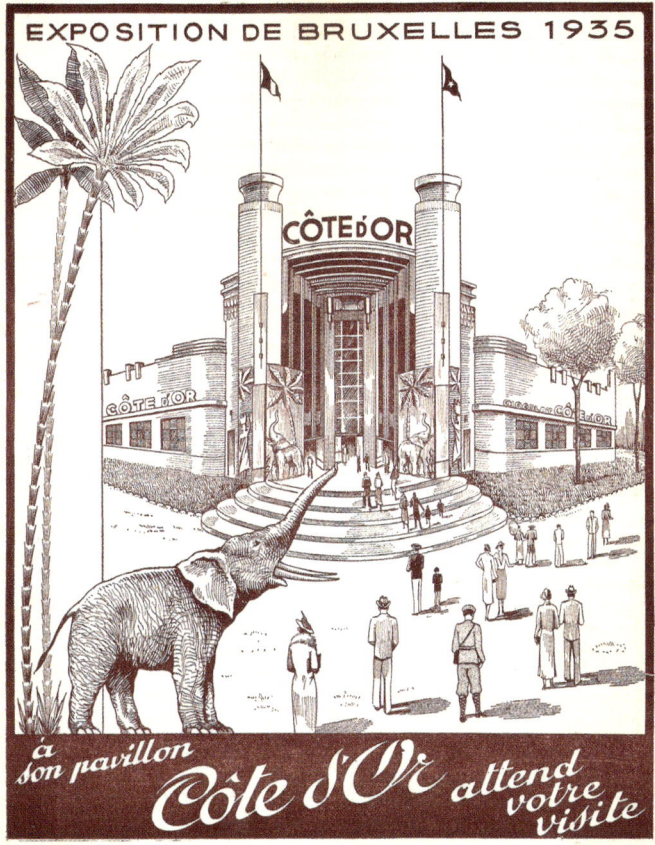

Advertising poster for Côte d'Or, 1935

This excellence extends beyond the country's borders. According to the Belgian Foreign Trade Office, in 2018, over 70% of the country's production was exported, reflecting a remarkable 51% increase over ten years compared to 2008. The primary market for Belgian chocolate remains the Netherlands (27% of exports), followed by France, Germany, the UK, and the USA. Even more surprisingly, distant markets such as Japan are showing a sustained interest in this symbol of Belgian excellence.

In Belgium, chocolate is not merely a product; it is heritage, an art, almost a religion. Belgian artisans have perfected a unique know-how to transform exotic raw materials into exceptional products for generations. A subtle balance of technological innovation, rigorous craftsmanship and passion has firmly established Belgian chocolate as a global icon. It is a confection that never ceases to captivate gourmets and connoisseurs worldwide.

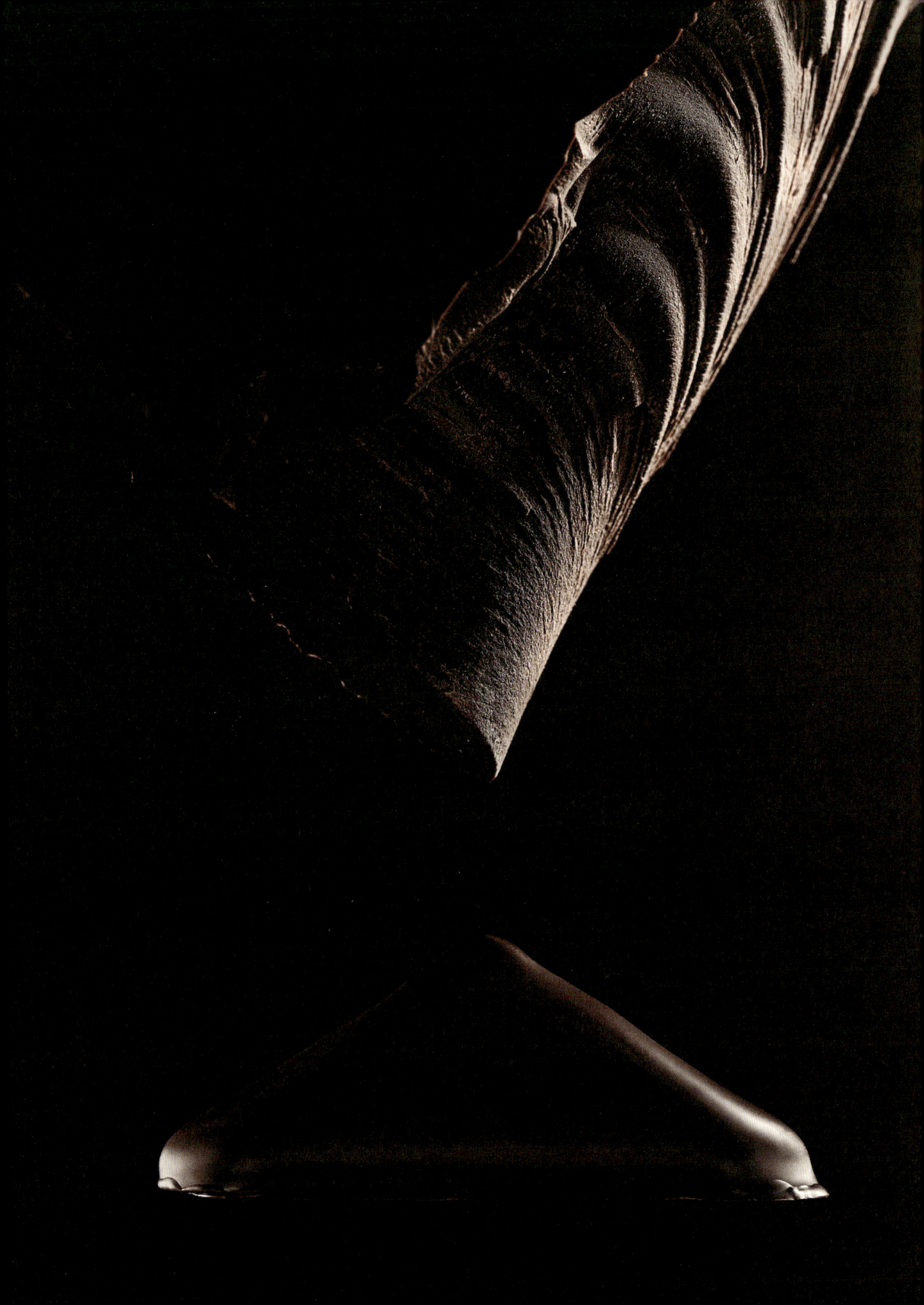

AND THEN CAME NEUHAUS

The story begins with a pharmacist who couldn't stand the sight of blood. It continues in a Brussels gallery and eventually expands beyond borders. This is how a family-run business helped shape the fate of Belgian chocolate.

CHOCOLATE-COATED MEDICINE

In 1857, Jean Neuhaus, a Swiss pharmacist who had abandoned his chosen career as a doctor due to his sensitivity to the sight of blood, moved to Brussels. He opened a shop in the Galeries Royales Saint-Hubert. The establishment, soberly named 'Confiserie et pharmacie Neuhaus', sold medicine coated in chocolate to soften the taste of the active ingredients. Chocolate was still regarded as a medicinal product in its own right, used to treat coughs, soothe the stomach, or added to make medicines more palatable.

The idea of coating medicines in chocolate was a great success, and Jean Neuhaus's shop soon attracted a loyal clientele. Capitalising on his growing reputation, Neuhaus increasingly focused on selling chocolate confectionery, making his shop an absolute must for chocolate lovers. What had begun as a simple pharmacist's gimmick gradually evolved into a chocolate-oriented business.

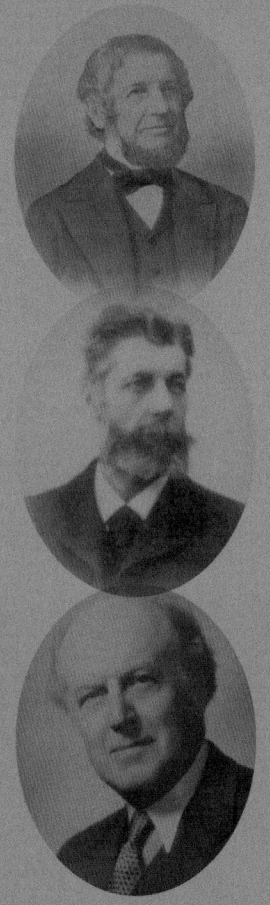

From top to bottom: Jean Neuhaus, Frédéric Neuhaus, and Jean Neuhaus Jr.

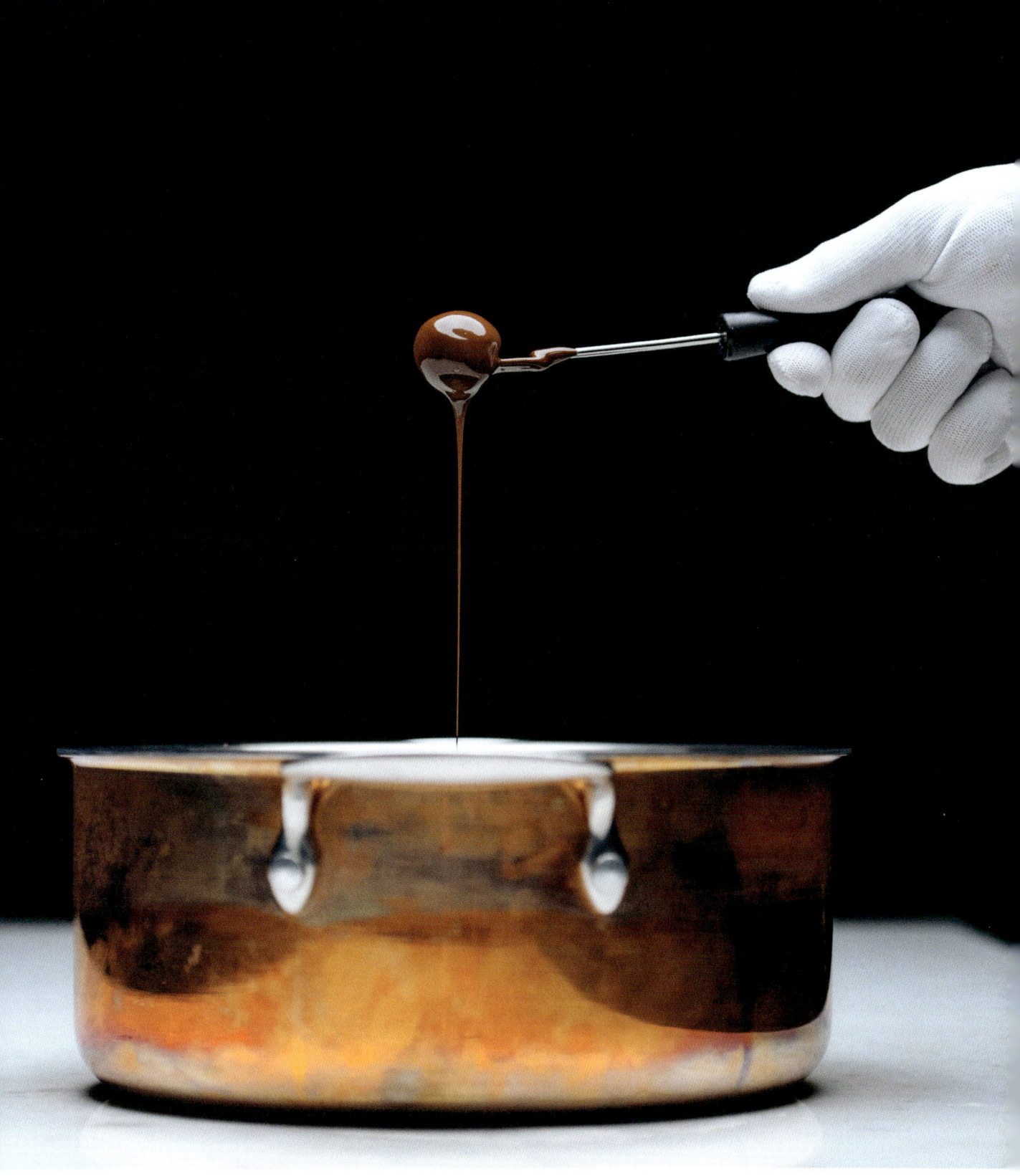

Though sometimes relegated to a secondary role, Frédéric Neuhaus, the founder's son, also played a vital part in the continued growth of the family business. He quickly recognised the gourmet potential of chocolate as a fully-fledged product in its own right. Under his leadership, the shop gradually transformed into a confectionery, slowly abandoning its medicinal purpose in favour of sweet chocolate treats. Driven by customers' growing enthusiasm, this shift profoundly transformed Neuhaus and established the foundations for its future role as a key player in the Belgian chocolate industry.

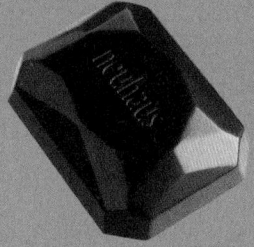

THE INVENTION OF THE PRALINE BY JEAN NEUHAUS JR. MARKS THE CREATION OF THE VERY FIRST CHOCOLATE BONBON IN 1912

In 1912, Jean Neuhaus Jr., the founder's grandson, advanced innovation by creating a revolutionary confection: the filled praline. Inspired by the idea of incorporating creams and ganaches into enticing, visually appealing shells, he envisioned a bonbon with a melting centre, enclosed in a delicate layer of chocolate. This invention marked a pivotal moment in the history of chocolate worldwide and established Neuhaus as a pioneer in the industry.

The first praline was celebrated as a triumph by the shop's customers. Neuhaus continued to innovate by offering an array of fillings: creamy ganaches, crunchy pralines, and even candied fruit. The praline thus became a multi-sensory experience—a refined sweet that revealed new flavours with each bite. This invention enabled Neuhaus to establish a Belgian tradition of filled chocolate, which other chocolatiers later embraced and continually reimagined.

The praline embodies the essence of chocolate, taking on a refined form that allows texture and flavour to reach their peak within just two bites. Far more than a mere confection, it is a jewel of precision and expertise, a miniature vessel enclosing a world of sensations. The praline transforms chocolate into a multi-sensory experience, with the crunchiness of its shell preceding the melting of ganache or the crispness of a praliné. Each praline is crafted as a work of art, combining noble, exotic, or spicy ingredients to create an exquisitely unique taste experience with every tasting.

Besides being a delicacy, the praline is also a symbol of elegance and luxury. Its emblematic case, the ballotin, elevates chocolate tasting to a hedonistic ritual. Transformed into a praline, chocolate becomes the ultimate delicacy, reconciling tradition with modernity, simplicity with sophistication. It is the culmination of centuries of gourmet evolution, a tribute to craftsmanship. This treat transcends everyday life and affirms chocolate as a transcendent experience, a luxury accessible to all.

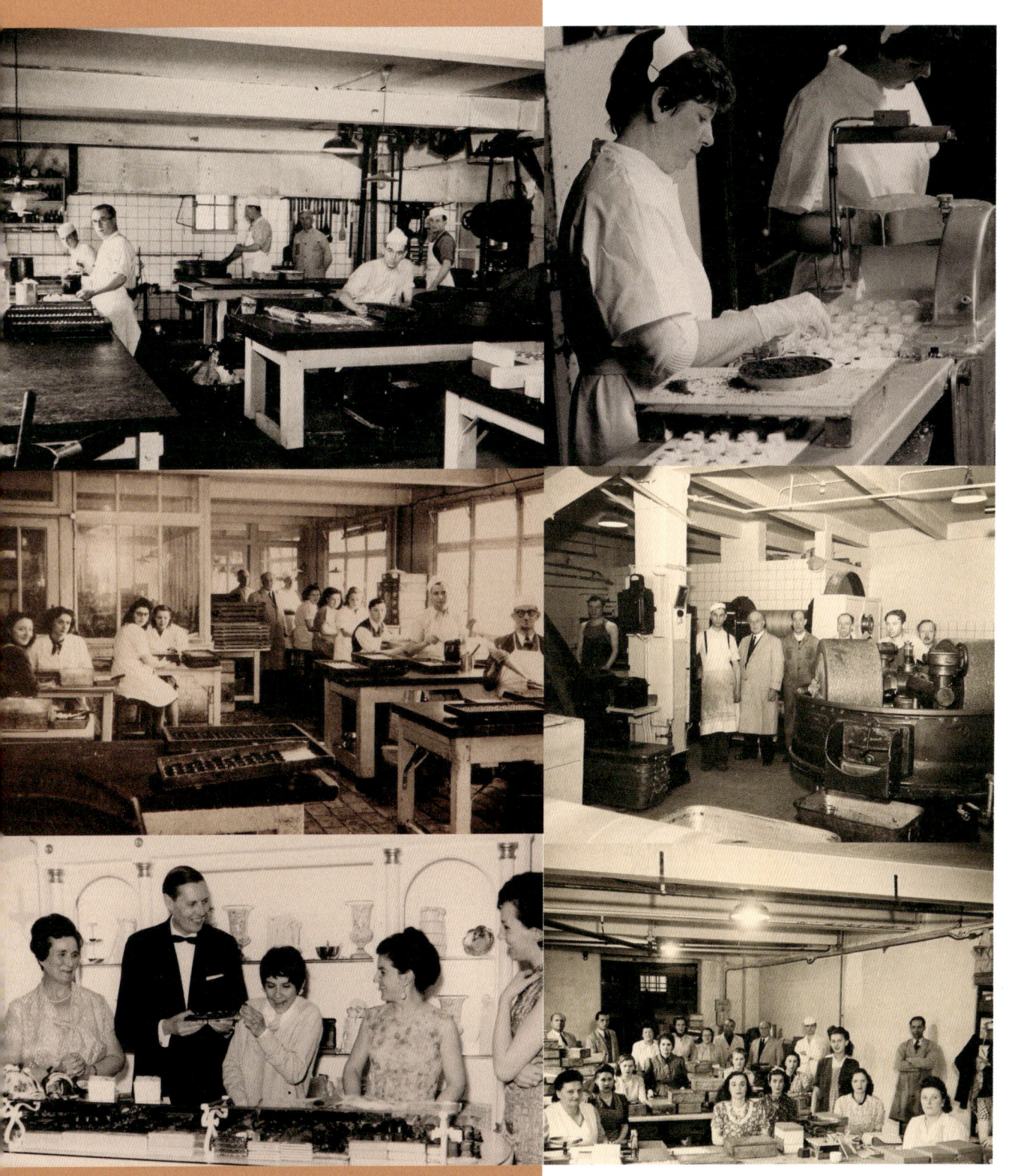

Neuhaus workshops around 1940. Bottom left: opening of a Neuhaus shop, circa 1950

THE INVENTION OF THE BALLOTIN:
THE ART OF PACKAGING

Reproduction of the first Neuhaus box invented by Louise Agostini in 1915

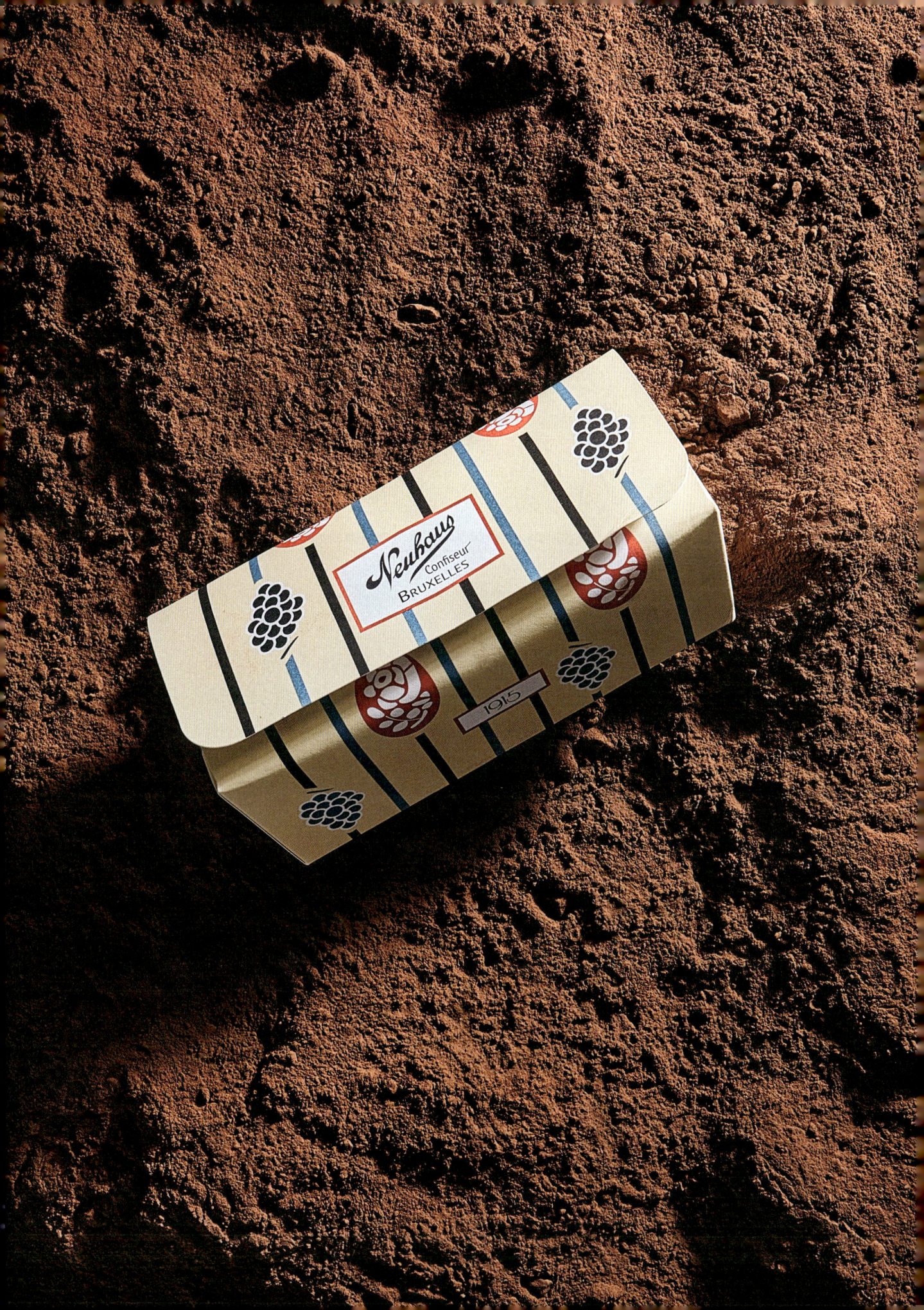

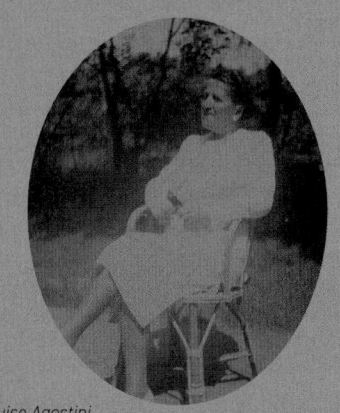

Louise Agostini

In 1915, Louise Agostini, wife of Jean Neuhaus Jr., came up with an innovative packaging idea to support the success of the praline: the ballotin. This cardboard box, meticulously designed to protect the delicate pralines, became a presentation case that was both functional and elegant. At a time when chocolates were often sold in rudimentary packaging that was ill-suited to their finesse, Louise Agostini realised the added value a carefully designed box could bring to the gourmet experience. She believed her husband's pralines deserved a nicer container than a simple paper cone, so she conceived refined packaging inspired by jewellery boxes that combined aesthetics and practicality. Her acute sense of detail and innovation transformed a delicious product into a precious gift, with the container design rivalling the contents.

This visionary move marked a turning point in the world of chocolate. The elegantly decorated ballotin soon became a symbol of quality and refinement, reinforcing the perception of Belgian chocolate as an exceptional product.

This concept, which transformed a simple delicacy into an object of desire, inspired the profession and became the standard. It should be noted that Neuhaus registered the patent for the ballotin, thereby recognising its innovative nature, but chose not to prohibit other chocolate makers from using it. This open approach allowed the ballotin to spread freely and become the standard in chocolate-making, benefiting the entire profession. Even today, these precisely crafted boxes with thoughtful designs, some adorned with subtle patterns, evoke a sense of accessible luxury and meticulous attention to detail, celebrating artisanal expertise. Each ballotin tells a story and enhances the pleasure of chocolate beyond mere tasting, adding an emotional and sensory dimension to the gourmet ritual.

With this invention, Louise Agostini did more than satisfy a practical need: she created a veritable art de vivre, where chocolate is offered, shared, and savoured like a jewel. Visionary and timeless, her creation perfectly embodies the elegance of Belgian

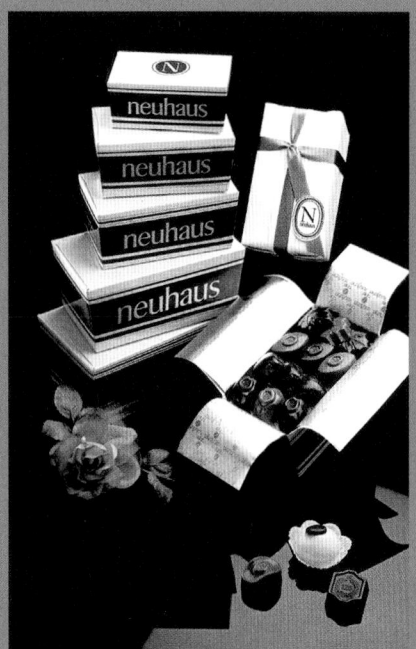

Advertisement created in the 1970s

Copy of the original ballotin registration report by Jean Neuhaus Jr., dated August 16, 1915

chocolate, transforming every bite into an unparalleled moment of pleasure. The invention of the ballotin revolutionised the way chocolate was presented in Belgium. Henceforth, customers could offer pralines in a container worthy of their refinement. The ballotin thus became a symbol of luxury and elegance, inseparable from the Neuhaus image. Even today, this box is used by many chocolate makers and remains an essential reference in the Belgian chocolate world.

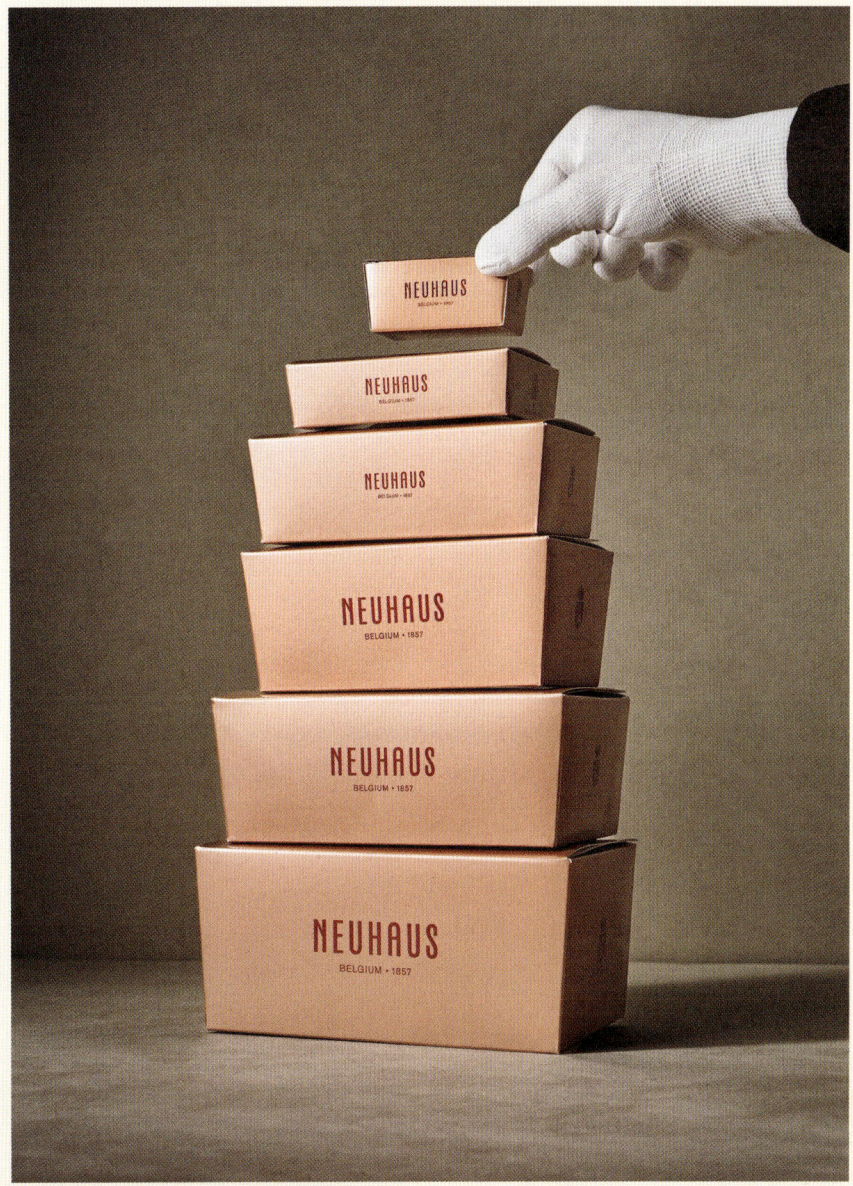

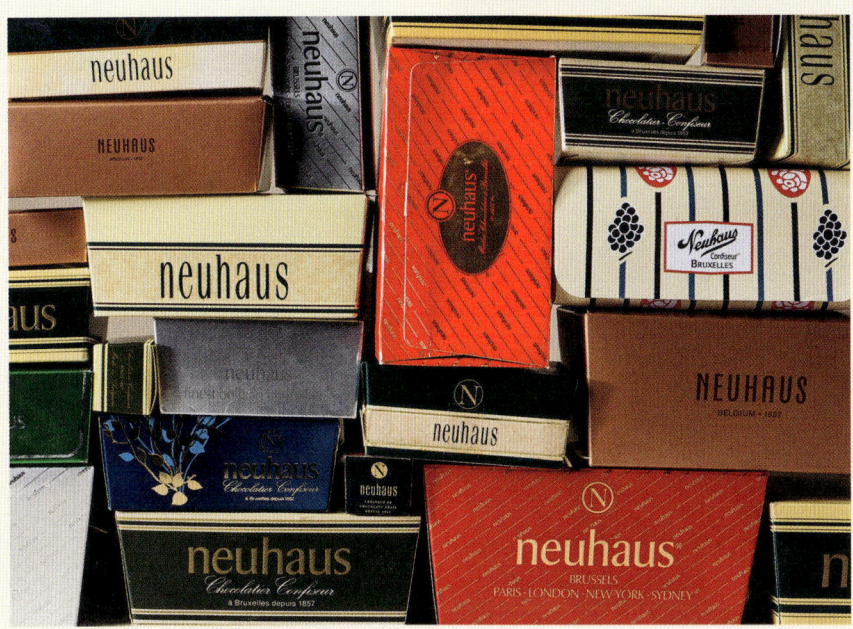

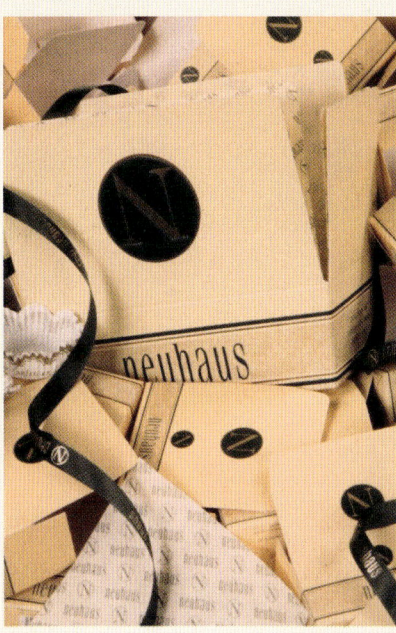

PLAYING TO THE GALLERY

It is no coincidence that Jean Neuhaus set up shop in the prestigious Galeries Royales Saint-Hubert. On the contrary, it was a wise decision that reflected a clear ambition: to position his boutique at the heart of Brussels' cultural and commercial activity. 'Passage Saint-Hubert', as it was known then, is a 200-metre-long gallery covered by an elegant glass roof, hailed by the press as 'the brightest passageway in the world'.

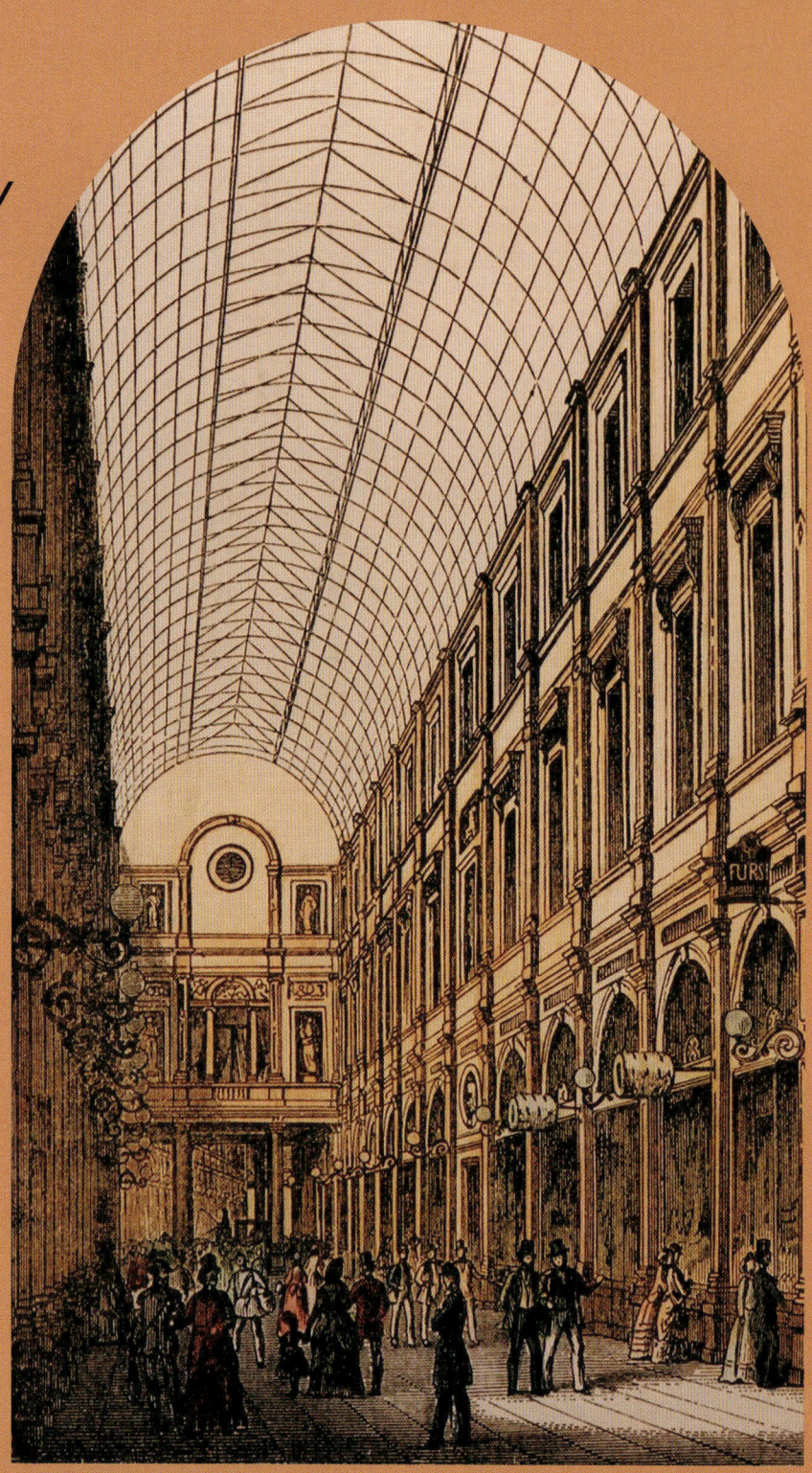

Lithograph of a lively view of the Galerie de la Reine in Brussels in the 19th century

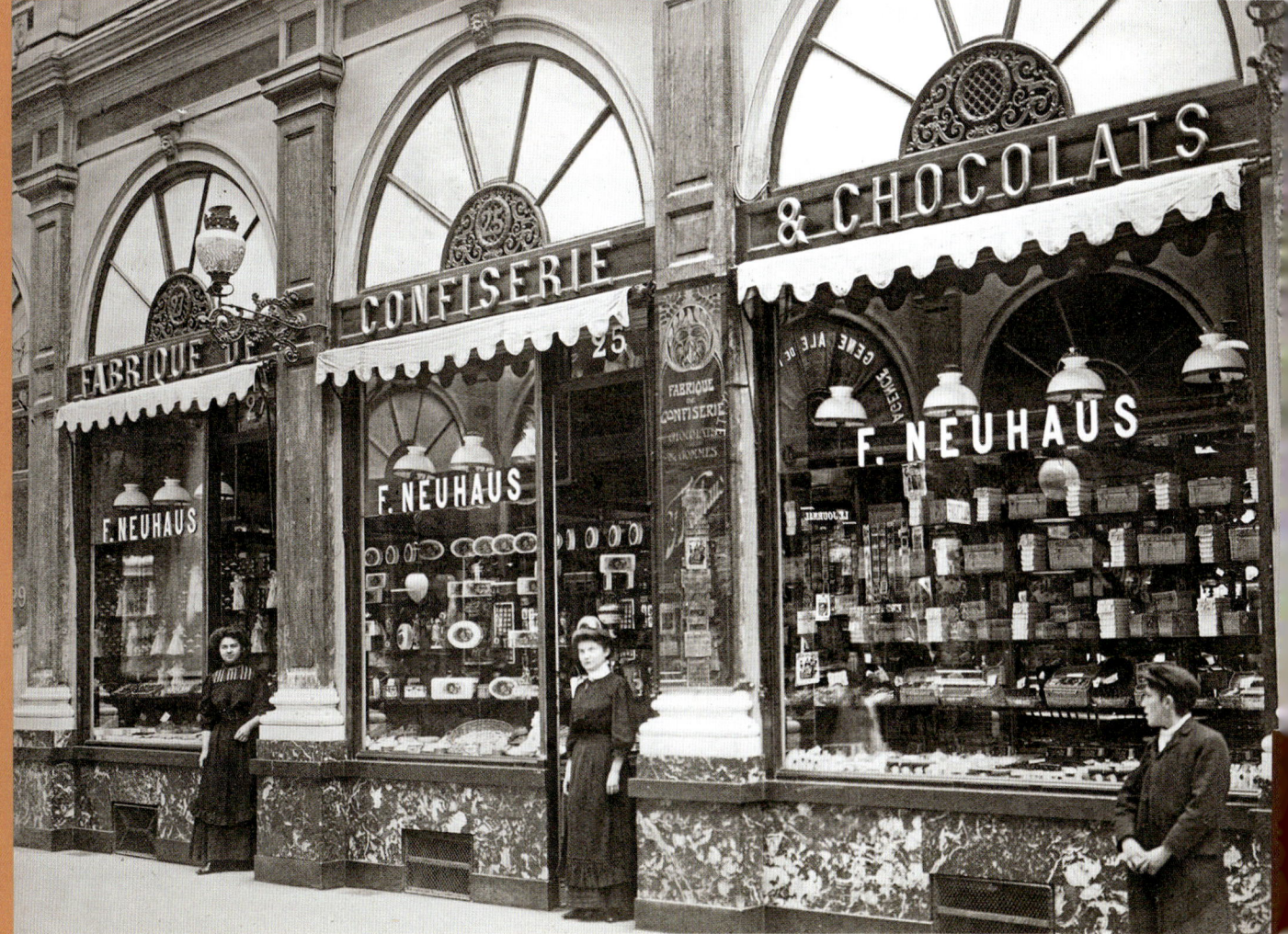

The Neuhaus shop in its early days, in the Galerie de la Reine (circa 1900)

Ideally located near the Grand Place, this gallery is a favourite spot for Brussels residents to stroll and a must-see attraction for visitors. As a gathering place, it has consistently drawn a wealthy and cultured clientele. Notable figures such as Baudelaire, Victor Hugo, and Alexandre Dumas frequented the cafés and literary salons that enlivened the area, particularly the 'Café de la Renaissance', now known as 'Taverne du Passage'.

This choice of location could not have been more appropriate from Jean Neuhaus's point of view. The Galeries Royales offered an ideal showcase for his expertise and benefited from a constant flow of passers-by, which enhanced its visibility. This apex of elegance and life perfectly embodied the image he wanted for his boutique, where quality and refinement were key to the experience.

NEUHAUS AND ITS INTERNATIONAL EXPANSION

During the 20th century, Neuhaus became a major player in the Belgian chocolate market. The reputation of its pralines spread beyond Belgium's borders, and the brand gained international recognition. Neuhaus's creations at the Universal Exhibition in Brussels in 1958 attracted visitors worldwide. The chocolates, presented in decorated ballotins, were immensely successful and established Neuhaus's global reputation.

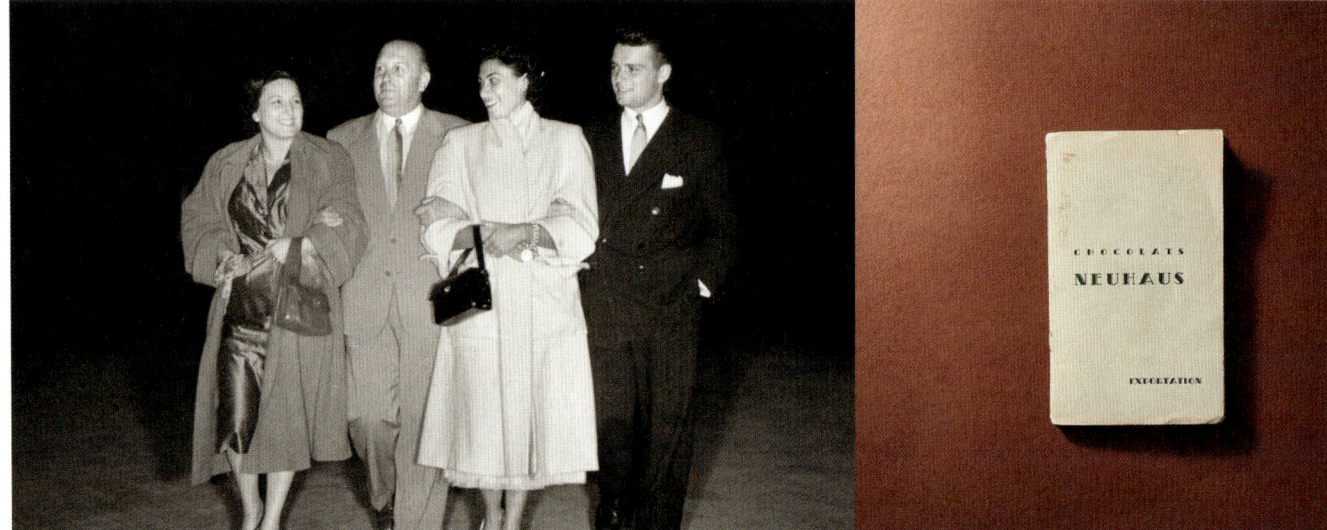

From left to right: Suzanne Neuhaus, Adelson De Gavre, their daughter-in-law Fernande Müller, and their son Pierre De Gavre

Exhibition catalogue, circa 1950

Two exceptional morsels embody the perfect blend of creativity and refinement, entirely in harmony with the spirit of the house: a duo of pralines crafted by Adelson de Gavre, master chocolatier at Neuhaus and husband of Suzanne Neuhaus (daughter of Jean Neuhaus Jr.). The cult film 'Et Dieu… créa la femme' (1956) by Roger Vadim, featuring a sensual and audacious Brigitte Bardot in the title role, inspired de Gavre to create two pralines that celebrated femininity and elegance: Caprice and Tentation. This duo, the forerunners of a collection destined to become iconic, captivates with its subtle interplay of textures and rich flavours. Named Irrésistibles, this collection attests to Neuhaus's art of transforming cultural references into timeless chocolaty treasures—a touch of glamour honouring Belgian heritage.

After the world exhibition, Neuhaus began exporting its pralines and opened shops internationally. The brand became a symbol of Belgian chocolate-making artistry and a benchmark for luxury. Whether in France, the United States, or Japan, Neuhaus chocolates captivated chocolate lovers with their subtlety and creativity. Neuhaus now embodies a tradition of excellence intricately linked to the sophistication of Belgian chocolate.

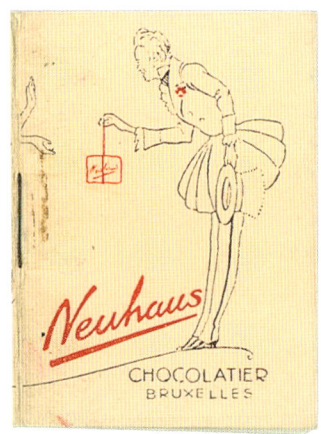 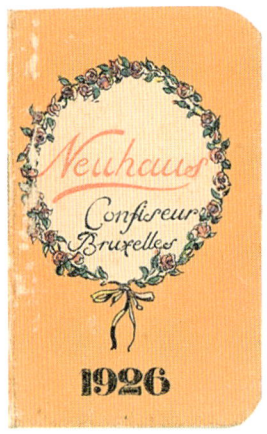 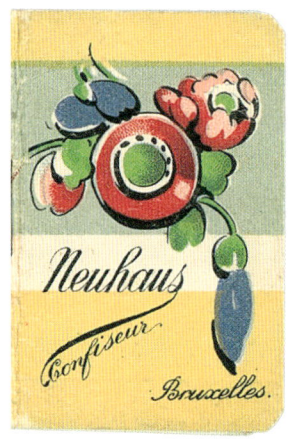 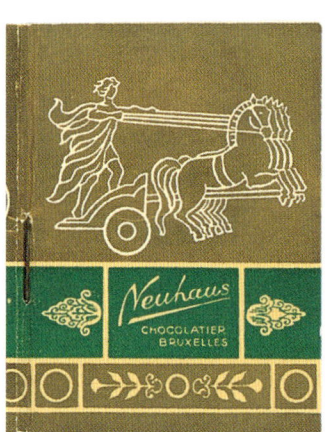

Catalogues (between 1920 and 1940)

NEUHAUS' CONTINUOUS MODERNISATION AND INNOVATION

Over the decades, Neuhaus has consistently innovated to meet the evolving expectations of consumer tastes, which are at the vibrant heart of the brand's creations, while maintaining traditional methods. The brand develops seasonal collections and limited editions, collaborating with chefs and artisan chocolatiers to offer new flavours. Classics, such as Manon and Caprice pralines, remain staples, but Neuhaus also explores new flavour combinations by incorporating spices, citrus fruits, and exotic ingredients.

Neuhaus also favours quality raw materials, selecting cocoa beans grown sustainably in Latin America, a region where the Maître Chocolatier has invested, and West Africa. The brand is committed to ensuring supply chain traceability to guarantee its chocolate is ethical and of high quality. Thus, the Neuhaus master chocolatiers preserve the traditional art of praline-making while adapting it to modern requirements.

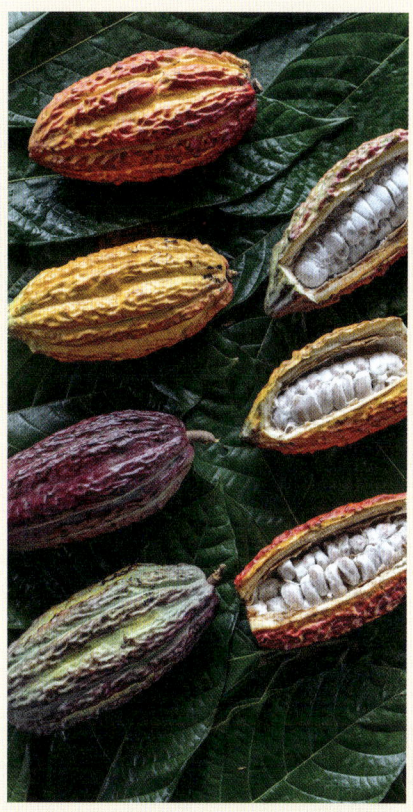

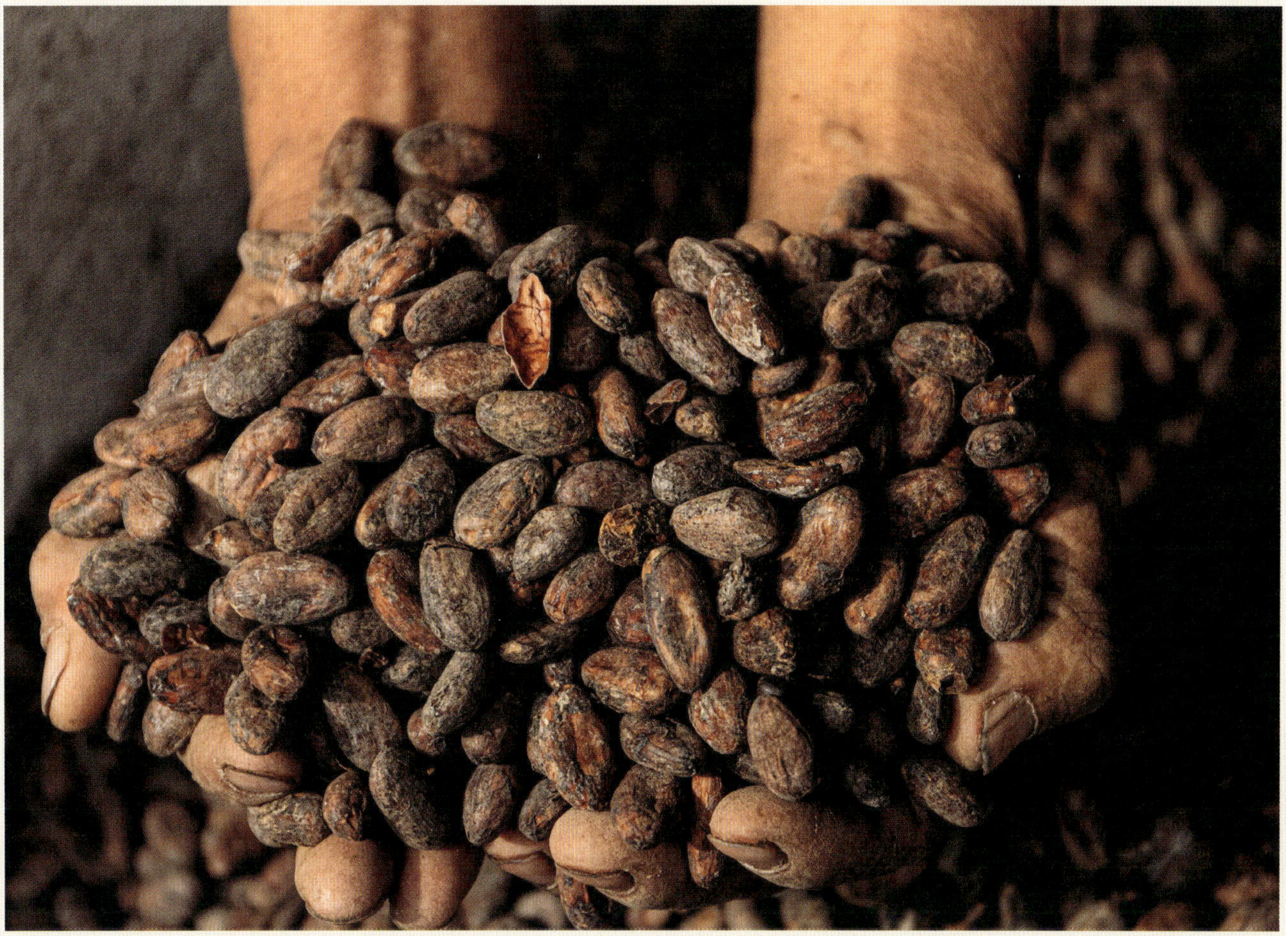

Cocoa from the plantation in which Neuhaus (Bois Sauvage) invested in Guayaquil, Ecuador

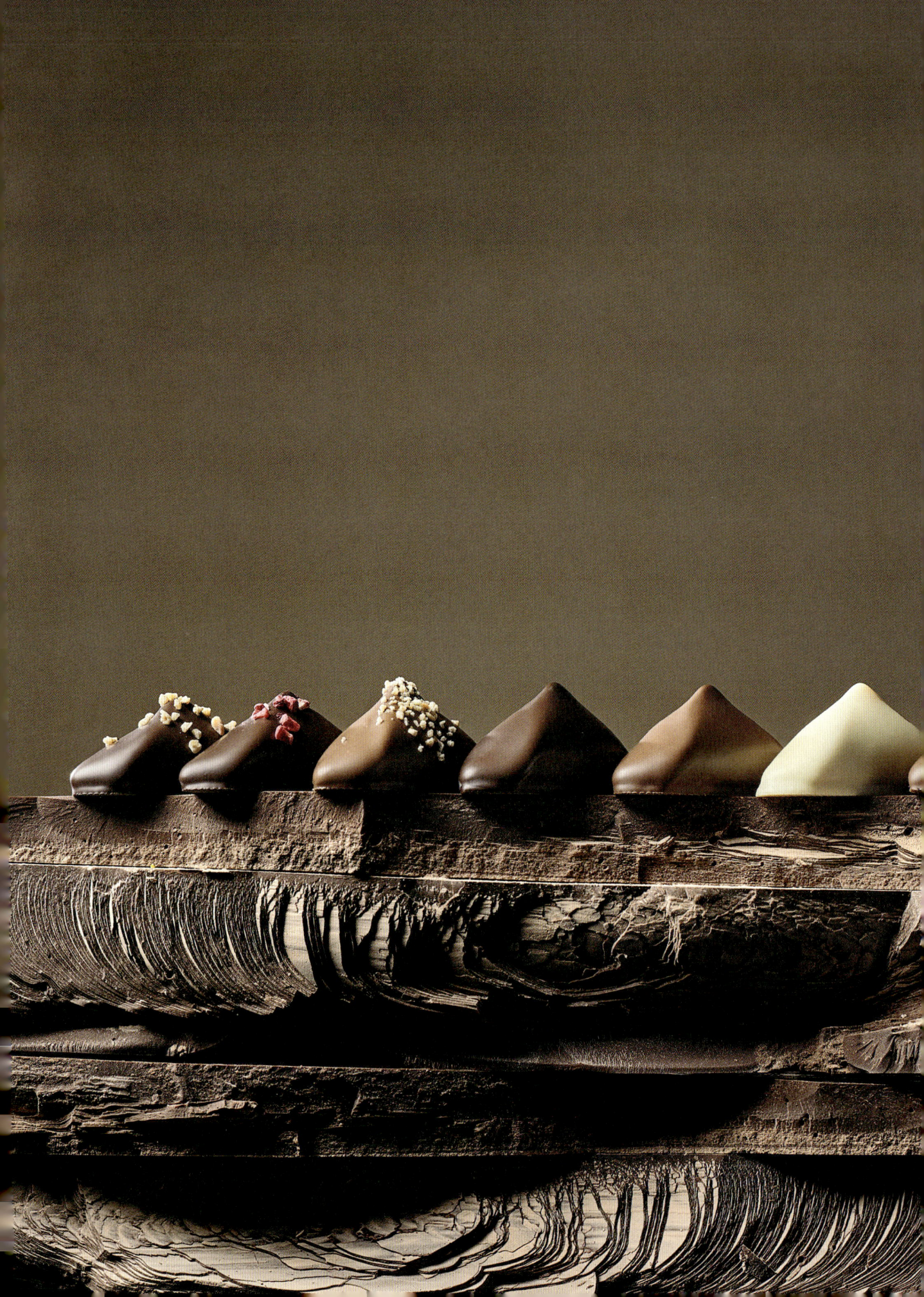

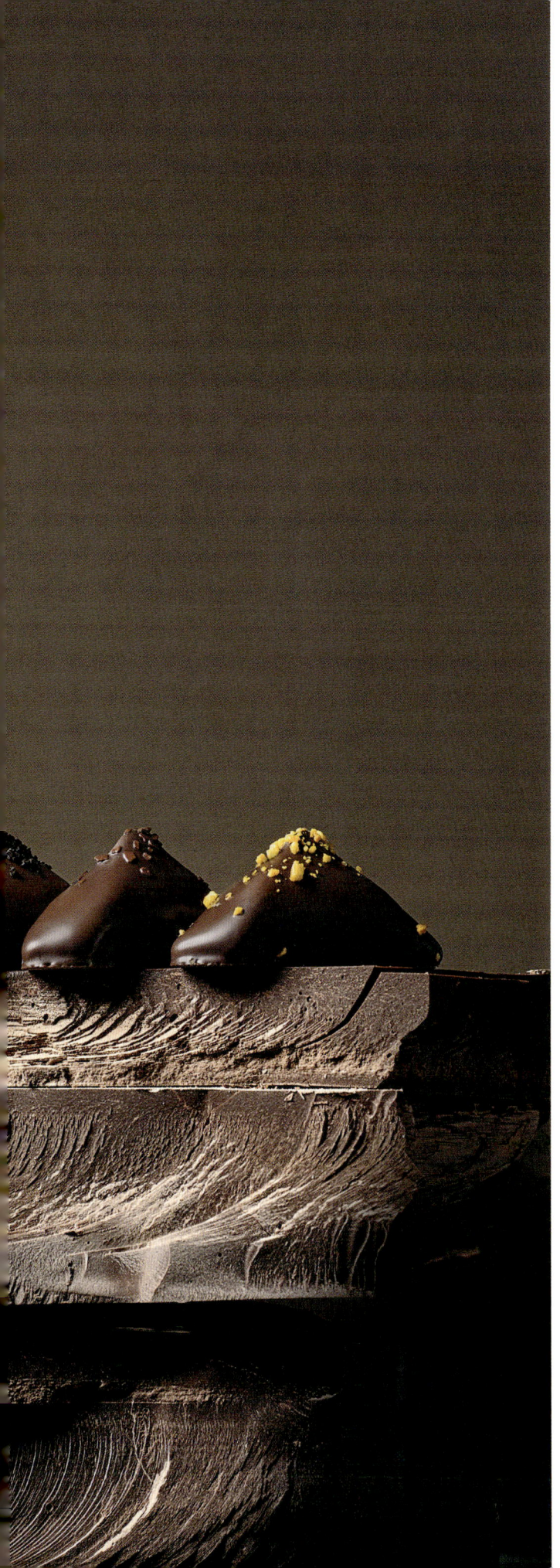

NEUHAUS NOW: A CONSTANTLY EVOLVING HERITAGE

Today, Neuhaus remains a leader in luxury chocolate in Belgium and worldwide. Proud of its heritage, the company continues to promote the Belgian art of chocolate-making by upholding its high quality standards. Neuhaus pralines, elegantly presented in a variety of boxes, embody tradition and innovation, offering customers a unique gourmet experience.

Each Neuhaus praline tells the story of know-how passed down for 150 years, reflecting a blend of passion, creativity, and respect for the product. By merging traditional techniques with contemporary innovations, Neuhaus preserves the heritage of Belgian chocolate, transforming each creation into an explosion of flavour.

NEUHAUS, THE AUTHENTIC ESSENCE OF BELGIAN CHOCOLATE

From its sacred roots to the most modern creations, the history of chocolate narrates a fascinating journey through the ages and across cultures. What was once a bitter-tasting sacred beverage reserved for the gods and the elite has become a universal delight in the form of refined pralines elegantly packaged in ballotins. As a pioneer and guardian of Belgian tradition, Neuhaus continues to preserve this heritage by producing creations that combine excellence with inventiveness.

Today, every Neuhaus praline is conceived as a celebration of chocolate, honouring ancient civilisations and modern artisans. Neuhaus embodies the connection between past and present, culture and gastronomy, offering customers an immersive experience infused with the essence of Belgian chocolate. Each praline represents a journey, a narrative and a passion - a totem that has become an icon of indulgence.

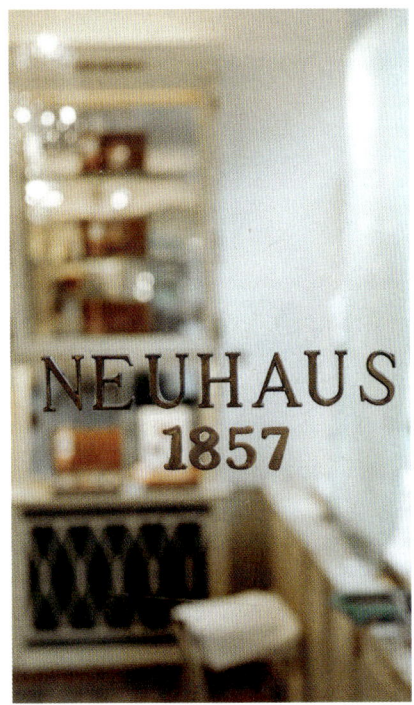 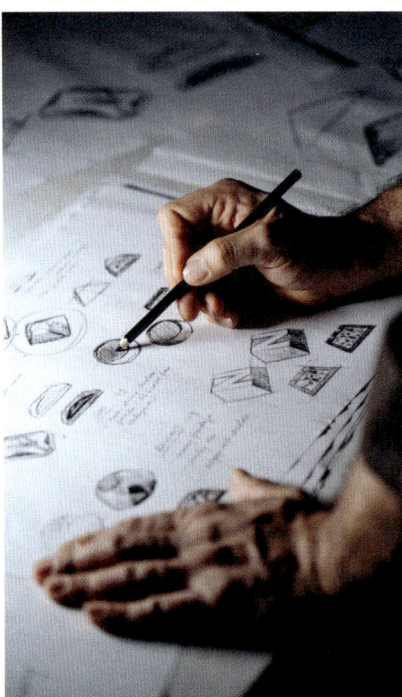 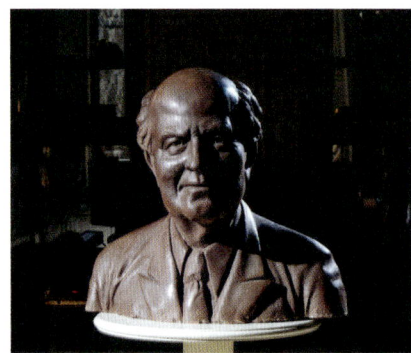 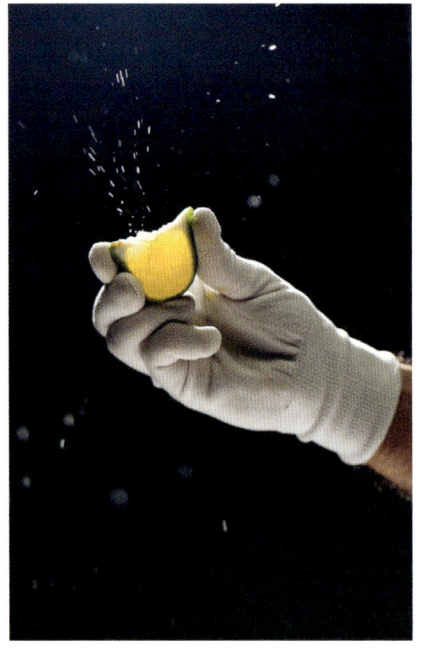

Center: process of designing pralines (2023); top right: chocolate bust of Jean Neuhaus Jr.

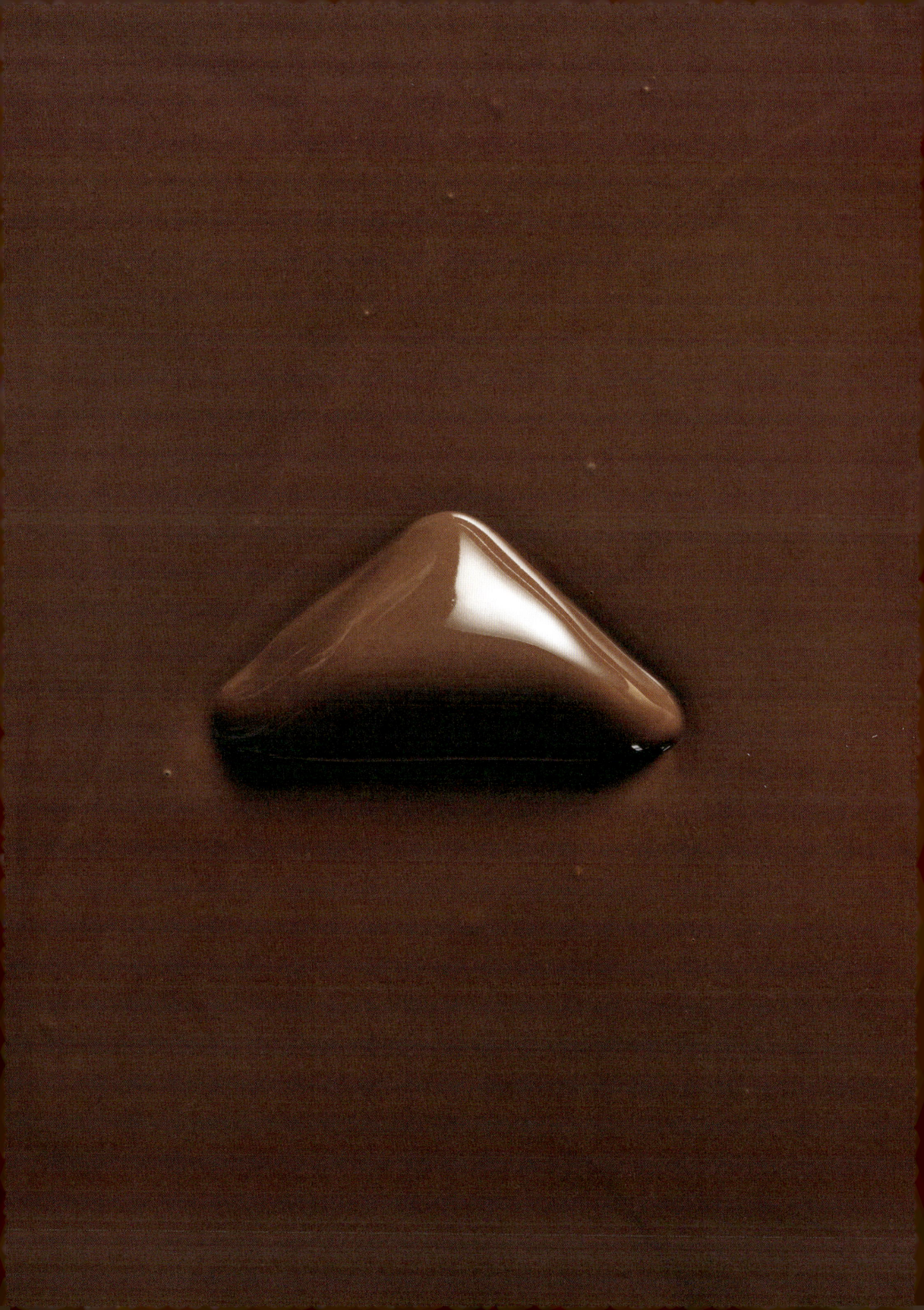

PATRICIA DE GAVRE

IN SEARCH OF LOST TIME

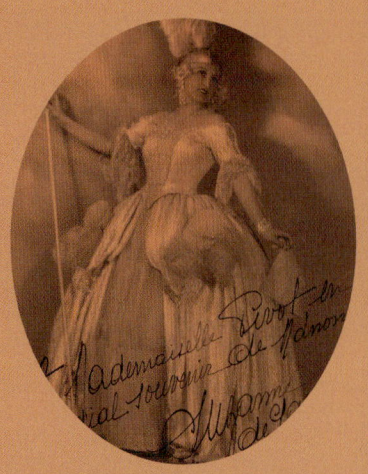

Suzanne Neuhaus at the time when she performed at La Monnaie

A traveller's desk steeped in history stands out on the first floor of Patricia De Gavre's Brussels home. It belonged to her grandmother, Suzanne Neuhaus, first light soprano at the Théâtre de la Monnaie, where she sang leading roles in Verdi, Puccini, Mozart and other composers before transitioning to a completely different vocation: managing the boutique ensemble.

It was not unusual for Suzanne to get out of bed at night and sit in front of the small piece of furniture to jot down her nocturnal musings, create sketches for window decorations, and add various stylistic annotations.

From her creative grandmother, the elegant sixty-year-old has inherited a taste for beauty and harmony. 'Suzanne Neuhaus was an artist', she says with unabashed admiration. Suzanne created meticulous window displays, combining shimmering silks with objects she'd picked up on her travels. 'Her shop windows were always splendid', recalls her granddaughter. 'There were silk ribbons and pastels in spring and hushed atmospheres in winter. She had an innate sense of style.'

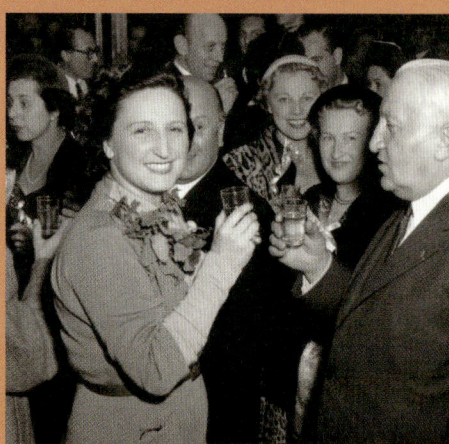

Suzanne Neuhaus in the foreground during a Neuhaus celeb

'My grandmother used to go to Venice as if she were on a mission: with a keen eye and an empty suitcase', says Patricia. She would buy glassware, ribbons and small refined objects to embellish the windows of the Neuhaus boutiques. She used to say that beauty is in the details. In the heart of the Serenissima, she rediscovered the baroque lightness she loved so much. There was nothing frivolous about these trips; they fed her imagination and nourished her vision of beauty applied to the world of pralines.'

'Neuhaus runs in my veins, it's part of my DNA,' says Patricia De Gavre. Various elements of her luminous interior evoke this carnal and emotional link with the saga of the creator of pralines. Two armchairs in the living room once furnished the family flat above the Galeries Saint-Hubert boutique, occupied by her great-grandparents, Jean and Louise Neuhaus-Agostini. As a child, she would go there for lunch with her family. 'A place of life, a refuge from time,' she recalls. Near the seats, four jars stand next to a window. Today, they are filled with sand and shells; Patricia remembers seeing them filled with colourful sugared almonds, chocolate, coffee beans and barley sugar. 'The trays on which the fruit jellies were presented were a mixture of colours and flavours: green for apples, red for raspberries, violet for blackberries... it was deliciously beautiful.'

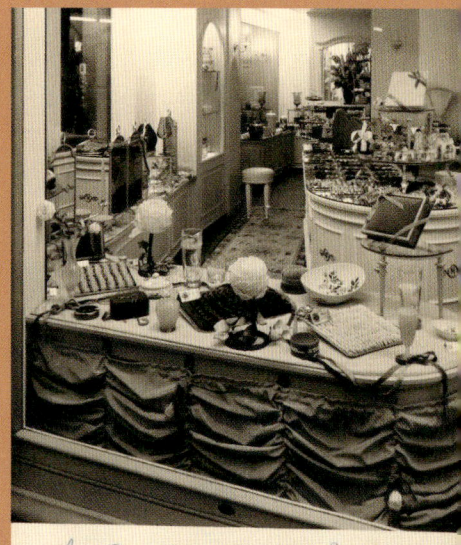

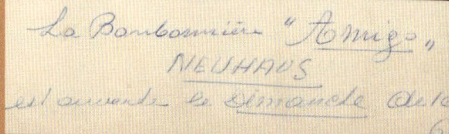

Patricia is the keeper of these memories: 'I feel like the writer Marcel Proust and his legendary madeleines, but in my case it is the flavours of pralines I'm searching for', she confides. Her palate retains traces of recipes that have vanished, of the sweets of yesteryear. She remembers the scent of cocoa, walnuts, hazelnuts, and roasted almonds wafting through the Anderlecht factory, the hum of the machines, and the chocolate-makers' precise movements. As a little girl, she dipped her finger into the intense flavours of hot chocolate under the indulgent gaze of the workers.

Born in 1957, the centenary year of the founding of the house of Neuhaus, Patricia grew up on the family estate in Dilbeek, surrounded by three generations of Neuhaus. Her family heritage is rich with objects, stories, and expertise passed down through the generations—a privilege she shares with her sister Dominique. 'We were known as the chocolatiers' daughters, the "girls of the castle", as people out there in the Pajottenland used to call us', she smiles.

Patricia De Gavre speaks movingly about the Galeries Saint-Hubert shop and the workshop beneath the boutique where it all began in 1857, before the factory was relocated. As a teenager and student, she learnt the art of handling boxes in the workshop below the boutique. With delicate, precise gestures, she folded the packaging paper of each box into three neat folds, 'like pleats in a woman's blouse', before sealing the gift ballotin with a green ribbon and its gold label, 'In the colours of Napoleon', she still remembers.

From an early age, Patricia was introduced to the aesthetics and demands of the trade, and her grandmother, Suzanne De Gavre-Neuhaus, prepared her to take over the management of the shops. She would show us how to arrange knick-knacks and play with heights and colours to decorate shop windows. It was all about balance and harmony. However, this destiny never materialised. When Neuhaus was sold, the transmission was interrupted, depriving Patricia of a dream future.

Today, she treasures this memory, offering a personal perspective on the history of the House of Neuhaus. As a proud descendant of a dynasty of chocolate-makers and confectioners, she is eager to demonstrate that Neuhaus represents much more than just a company; it encompasses a world of artists, visionaries, creators, and indelible fragrances. 'I remember when my parents used to supply the Belgian royal family for events like christenings', says Patricia De Gavre.

Patricia De Gavre recalls her father, Pierre, who was trained as a chocolatier by his beloved grandfather, Jean Neuhaus, and his father, Adelson De Gavre. He once said to her: 'If you want to give up your studies to work in the factory, I'll agree to it on the condition that you learn the trade from the ground up. You'll carry the bags of coal and the bags of cocoa, and you'll learn our skills.'

Pierre De Gavre chose this path and achieved his goal with determination, humility, and courage, learning every gesture and each step in transforming a cocoa bean into a delicious praline. 'He had the intelligence of the hand', Patricia clarifies. Highly appreciated by his workers, he knew how to repair the machines, could replace absent staff members, and was always present in the workshops, at their side: 'He was a true craftsman, passionate about his job as a creator.'

She recalls how the workers moulded the chocolate by hand and carefully assembled the boxes. At the heart of this nostalgia lies an unshakeable pride in belonging to a lineage of creators with unique know-how. She recognises that Neuhaus remains a reference point. Patricia serves as a guide, passing on the family history of the House of Neuhaus.

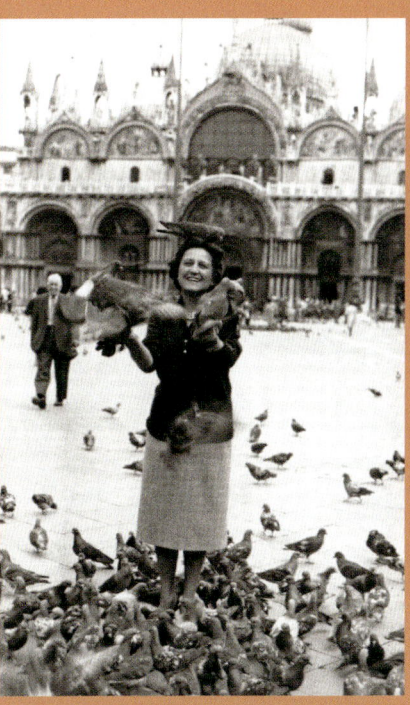
Suzanne Neuhaus in Venice, a city dear to her heart

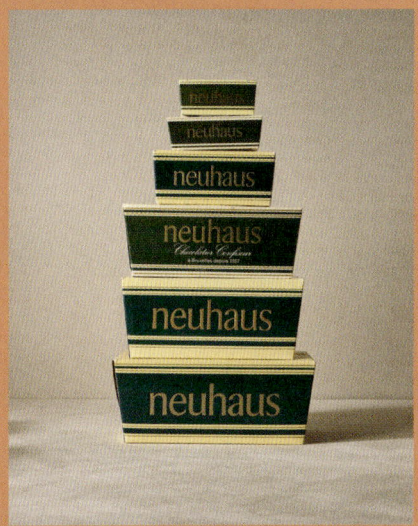
Tower of ballotins (circa 1965)

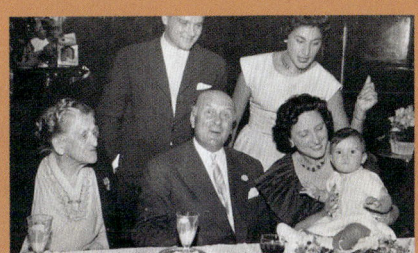
Four generations of Neuhaus: Louise Neuhaus-Agostini, Adelson De Gavre, Suzanne Neuhaus-De Gavre and Patricia De Gavre; behind them, Pierre and Fernande De Gavre

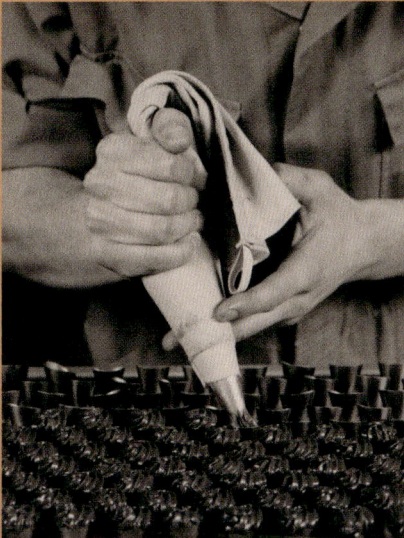
Hand-piping of Neuhaus cones (circa 1965)

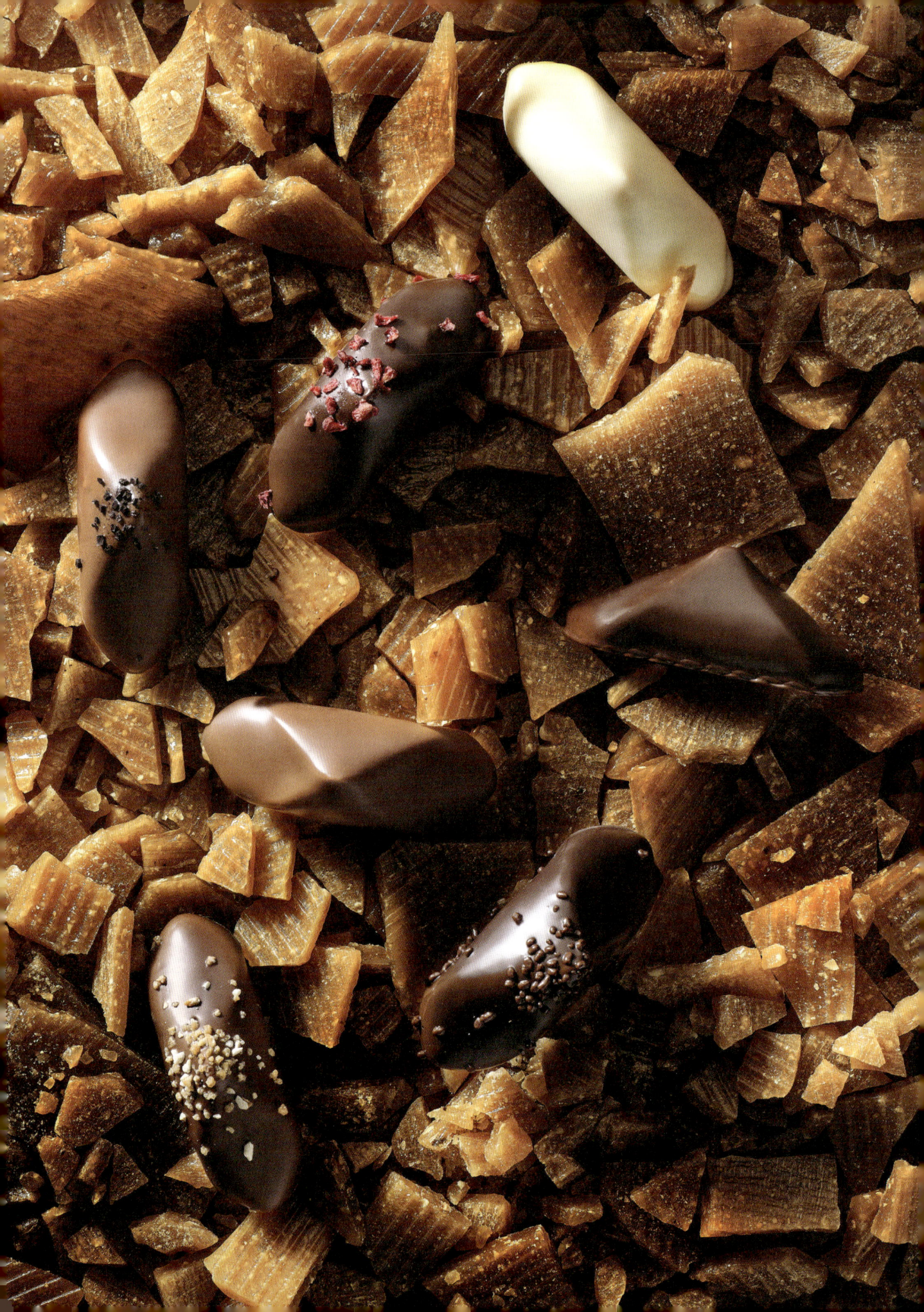

ICONS AND CREATIONS

As the inventor of the Belgian praline, Neuhaus conjures textures and flavours with virtuosity. Each creation outlines a delicate cartography encompassing heritage, innovation, and refinement.

For over 160 years, Neuhaus has focused on the excellence of Belgian chocolate-making, elevating this craft into an unforgettable taste experience. Through its creations, the company has far transcended the realm of gourmet delights: each of its pralines offers a hedonistic journey, resembling an alchemical potion whose textures and flavours narrate a unique story. Consequently, they are much more than chocolate bonbons; they represent the ultimate expression of this noble product from the tropics, the culmination of an expertise that enhances their ingredients and exceeds expectations.

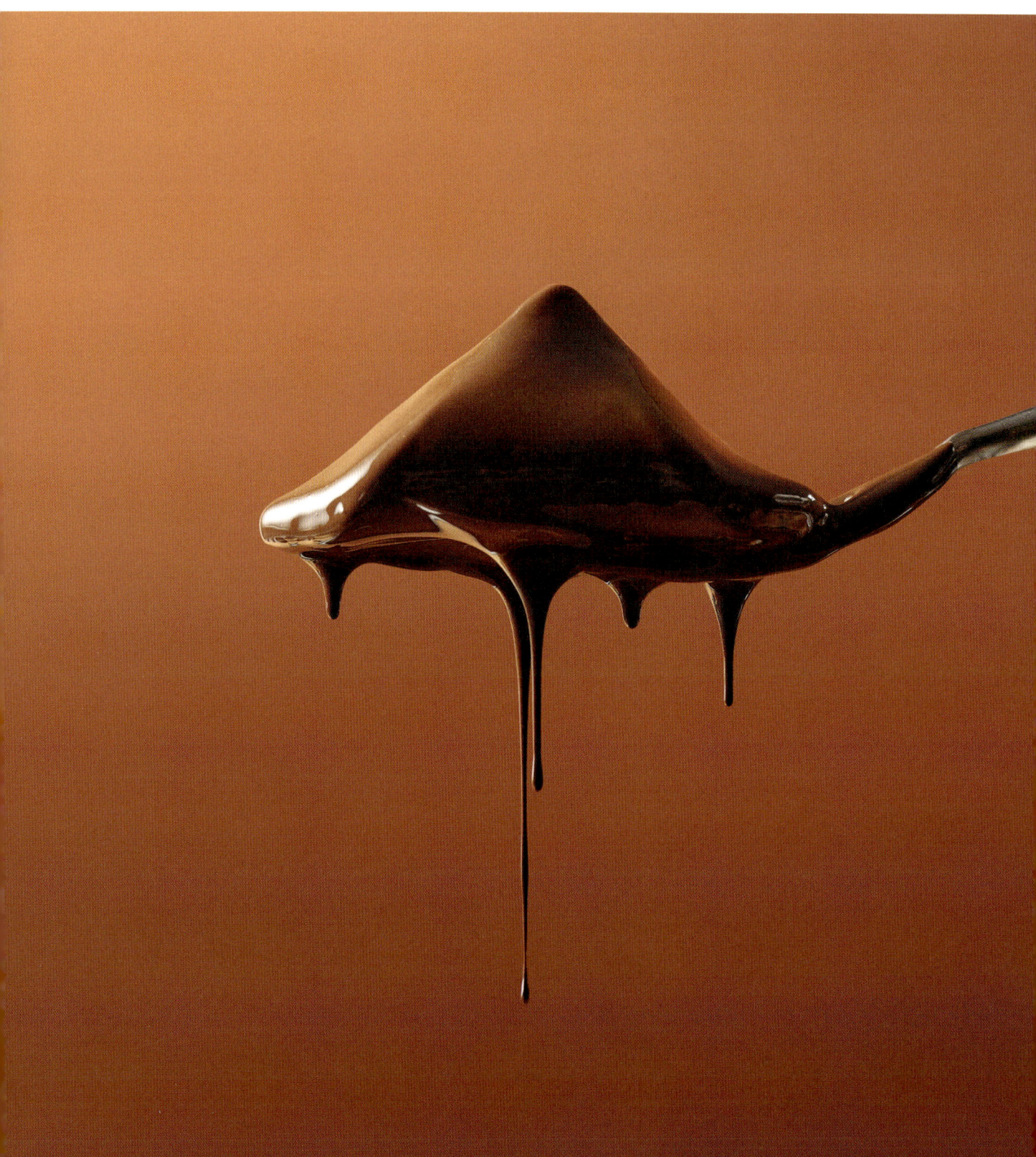

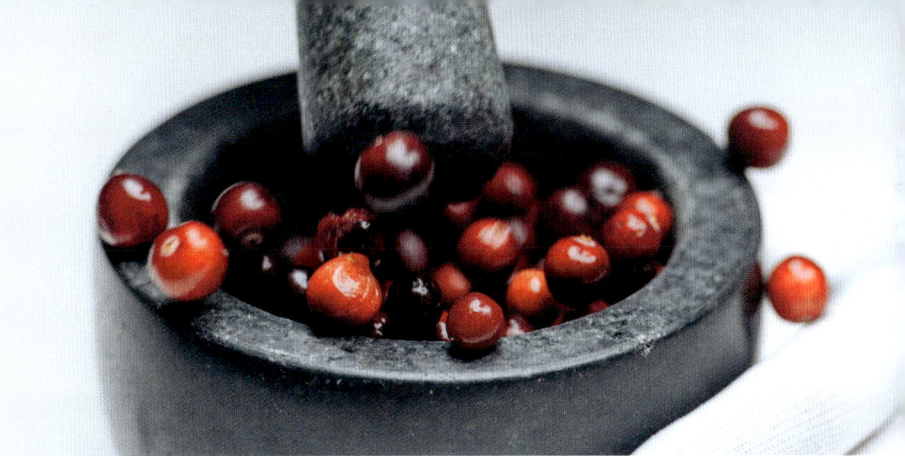

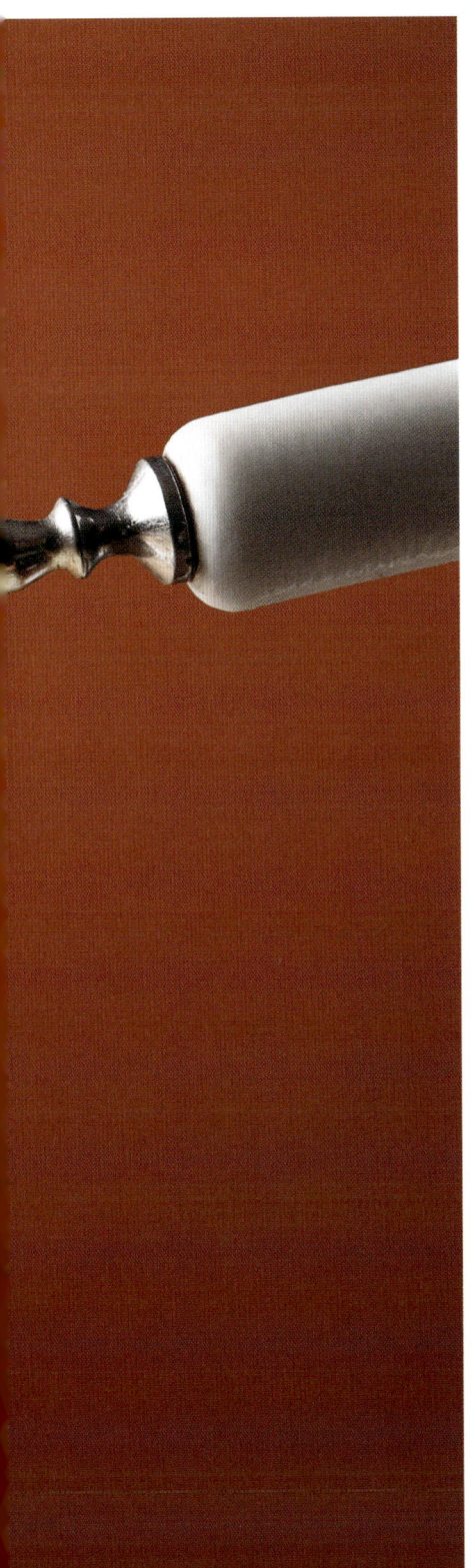

This format, invented by Jean Neuhaus in 1912, was revolutionary. The technique devised by the visionary chocolatier of enclosing delicate fillings within a thin shell of chocolate unlocked an infinite array of possibilities. A crunchy couverture could henceforth envelop the softness of ganache. The intense flavour of praliné could contrast freely with smooth cream. Tender milk chocolate could counterbalance the spicy warmth of Belgian speculoos. These texture-rich encounters, combined with a palette of flavours ranging from caramelised notes to fruity nuances, transformed each praline into a dazzling, unique experience.

Some Neuhaus creations beautifully express this quest for balance and emotion. For instance, the beloved Caprice, with its heart of fresh cream encased in a nougatine shell coated in dark chocolate, is a masterpiece of contrast, crunchy yet melting in the mouth. Likewise, Jean, a tribute to the creator's son, exemplifies sophistication, with its intense, creamy bite elevated by rich dark chocolate. The entire range results from a tireless pursuit of perfection and reflects exceptional expertise, ensuring that every detail, from composition to contours, enhances the sensory experience.

Having passed through the hands of Neuhaus, these pralines exceed the simple pleasure of ordinary confections. By maintaining the subtlest balance between technique and inspiration, as well as tradition and innovation, they embody the essence of chocolate. Tasting these exceptional creations allows one to experience the harmony of an age-old gesture nourished by constantly renewing creativity. When savouring these marvels, chocolate lovers will discover the richness and complexity of chocolate in its most exquisite forms.

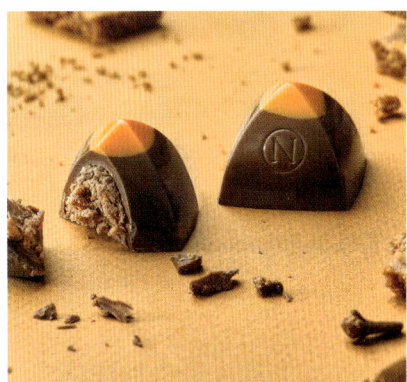

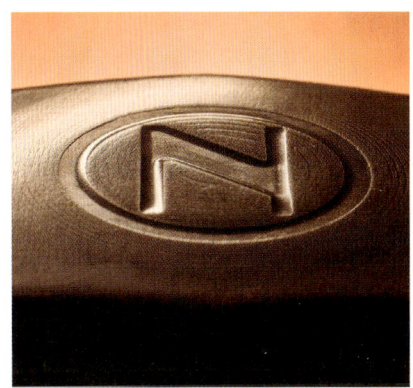

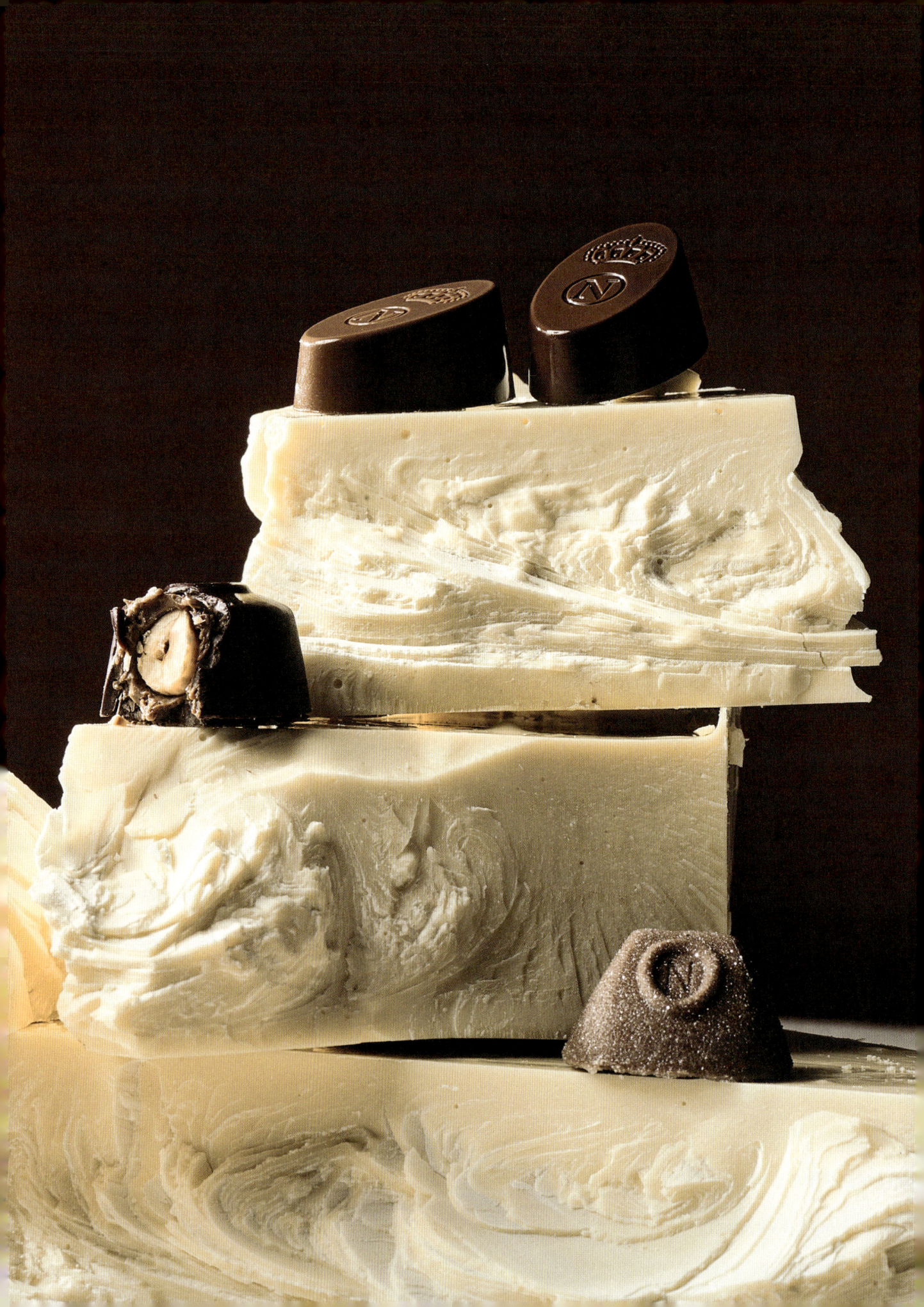

ICONS

Behind the shiny nougatine of Caprice, the crunchy gianduja of the golden Cornet, or the raspberry ganache of Suzanne, a whole world of indulgent imagination surfaces. Through its iconic creations, Neuhaus celebrates its connection to Belgium, a passion for opera, and the architecture of the capital. These are powerful narratives, that have forever shaped its DNA.

ALBERT

Neuhaus has a special relationship with the Belgian royal family, demonstrating its deep attachment to their values and history. As a licensed supplier to the Belgian Court since 1883, the company celebrates the elegance and prestige associated with the monarchy. A perfect illustration of this connection is the Albert praline, a tribute to King Albert II, created in 1959 to mark the wedding of the then-future king Albert and doña Paola Ruffo di Calabria, heiress of a prestigious Italian lineage.

This praline aligns with the Neuhaus tradition of creating treats in tribute to royal family members, such as those dedicated to King Baudouin, Queen Fabiola, King Philippe, Queen Mathilde and Princess Astrid. Within its delicate chocolate shell, the Albert praline unveils a generous heart of hazelnut praliné, symbolising refinement. A whole, finely caramelised Piedmont hazelnut serves as its core, honouring Queen Paola's Cisalpine origins. This crunchy, sweet and delicately contrasting blend of textures has become an emblematic piece in the Neuhaus range that merges history with chocolate excellence.

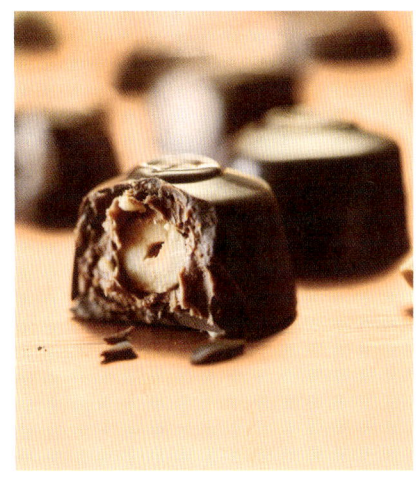

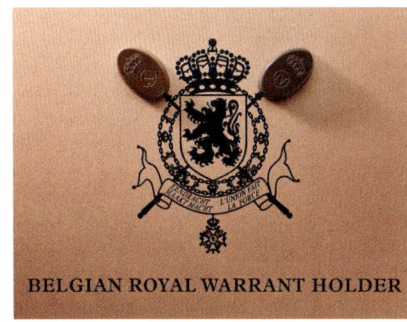

BELGIAN ROYAL WARRANT HOLDER

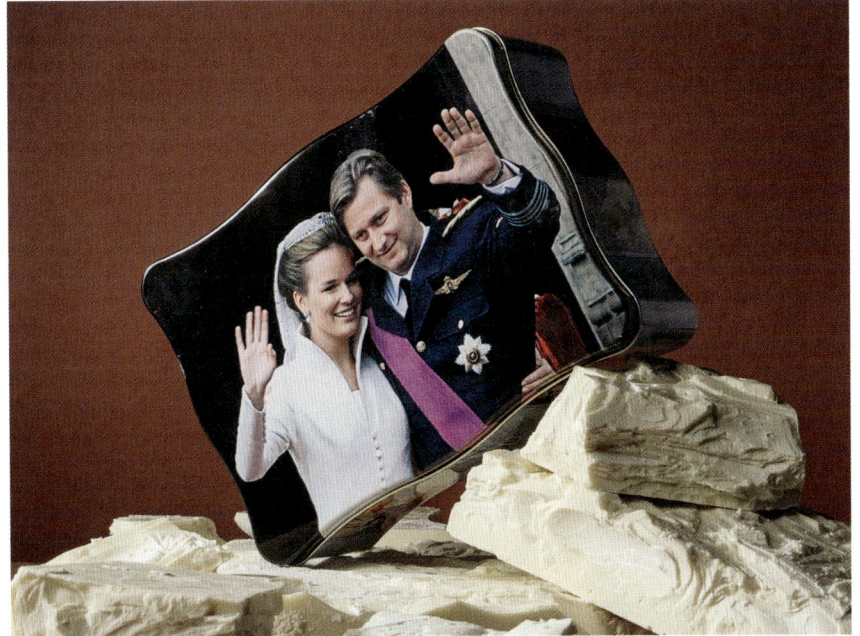

Neuhaus box, special edition created for the royal wedding of Philippe and Mathilde

45

ART NOUVEAU

Neuhaus regards the rich heritage of Belgian art and ornamentation as an inexhaustible source of inspiration. Its Art Nouveau praline pays tribute to Belgium's golden age of design. Within its diamond-shaped shell, inspired by the jewellery industry, lies a delectable surprise that matches its aestheticism: a Peruvian chocolate ganache with roasted hazelnuts.

A similar tribute is paid to Art Deco (see box), which the Maître Chocolatier honours with an architectural design for its dark chocolate casing filled with Californian almond praliné and nougat slivers.

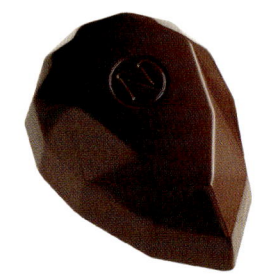

CAPRICE AND TENTATION

With Tentation, Caprice forms a duo of Irrésistibles - a title coined in 2010 to designate an evolving family of creations consisting of ten delightful pralines, developed from these two. How do you tell them apart at a glance? Caprice has a dark chocolate coating; Tentation has a milk chocolate coating. All the chocolates in this range are marked by a distinctive triangular shape that has established them in the national imagination and earned them various nicknames: 'Napoleon's hats', 'bicorns' or simply 'triangles'.

This duo of pralines was crafted with remarkable precision in 1958 to coincide with the Brussels Universal Exhibition. Caprice is a thin nougatine filled with smooth Madagascar vanilla fresh cream and coated in intense Belgian dark chocolate. Tentation features nougatine filled with Arabica coffee ganache and coated in fine Belgian milk chocolate. Together, they offer a contrasting experience, as the intensity of Caprice's dark chocolate meets the sweetness of Tentation's milk chocolate. Their respective ganaches, meanwhile, provide complementary flavours.

These emblematic chocolates derive their name from the cinephilia of Adelson de Gavre, son-in-law of Jean Neuhaus Jr. Deeply influenced by Brigitte Bardot's charisma - the French actress often portrayed characters that were as liberated as they were provocative - he chose the names Caprice and Tentation for two of his creations. These names reflect the sensuality and audacity permeating this cinematic reference, consecrated by posterity. This duo, deeply rooted in the elegance and spirit of that era, remains a powerful symbol of the creativity and daring that have shaped Neuhaus's reputation. It also reflects the company's connection to its history.

In the wake of this fantastic twosome, the Maître Chocolatier created new versions inspired by today's tastes, named in the same semantic vein: Désir 64% Cocoa (nougatine topped with a dark Peruvian chocolate ganache); Plaisir (nougatine, hand-filled with a Piedmont hazelnut ganache and coated in fine Belgian milk chocolate); Séduction (nougatine topped with a raspberry cream); Délice (nougatine topped with salted butter caramel); Emotion (nougatine, hand-filled with fresh cream made of 100% Arabica coffee beans and coated in creamy white chocolate); Folie (nougatine hand-filled with a hazelnut ganache, coated in intense Belgian dark chocolate, and sprinkled with crispy hazelnut pieces); Frisson (a yuzu, sweet mango, and lemony coriander blend in a creamy white chocolate ganache, enrobed with dark chocolate, and sprinkled with orange biscuit crumble).

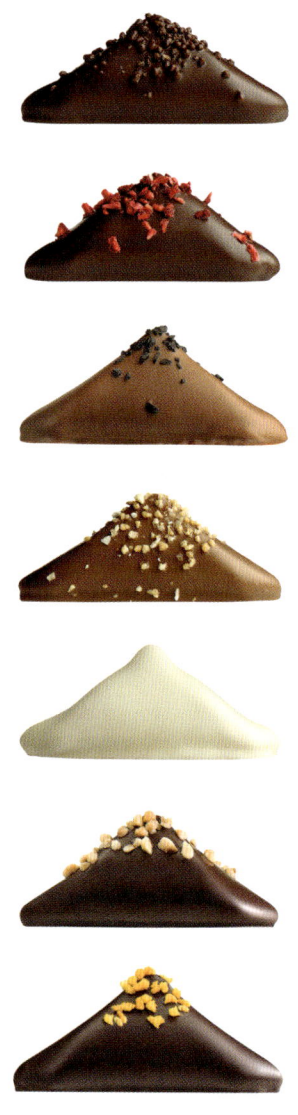

From top to bottom: Désir, Séduction, Délice, Plaisir, Émotion, Folie and Frisson

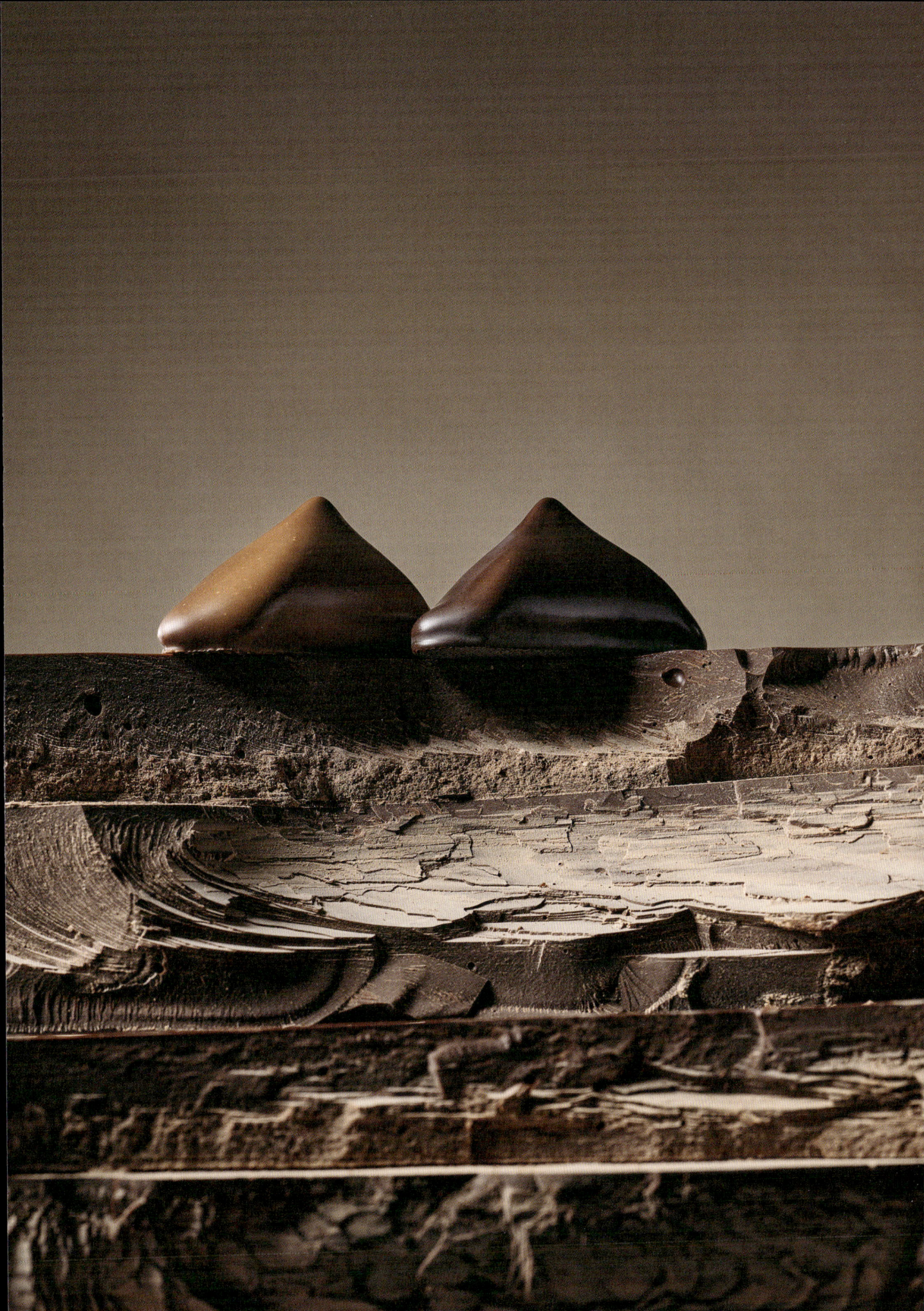

LES CORNETS

The Germanic-sounding name 'Neuhaus' conceals the Italian roots of the family that gave rise to the Belgian praline. When Jean Neuhaus's ancestors emigrated to Switzerland, they changed their surname from 'Casanova' to 'Neuhaus', which means 'new house' in German.

In 1970, Neuhaus referred to this ancestry by presenting a gianduja-based creation as a gustatory hint: the velvety preparation made from cocoa and hazelnut paste originated in the land of Dante. A true jewel in the Neuhaus range, the Cornet Doré is renowned for its elegant shape and deliciously melting hazelnut praliné. The design of this timeless classic was purportedly inspired by the paper cones in which pralines were initially served.

The Cornet Doré's little sister, the Cornet Fondant, is characterised by its softness and roundness. This hazelnut praline, enhanced with a milder touch of dairy, will appeal to fans of softer chocolates. Its emblematic cornet shape aligns this praline with the house's history.

Beneath its delicate chocolate shell, the Cornet Noisettes conceals a secret weapon: a creamy gianduja-based filling infused with finely roasted hazelnut chips. It is truly awe-inspiring.

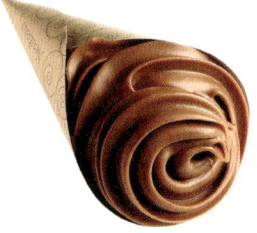

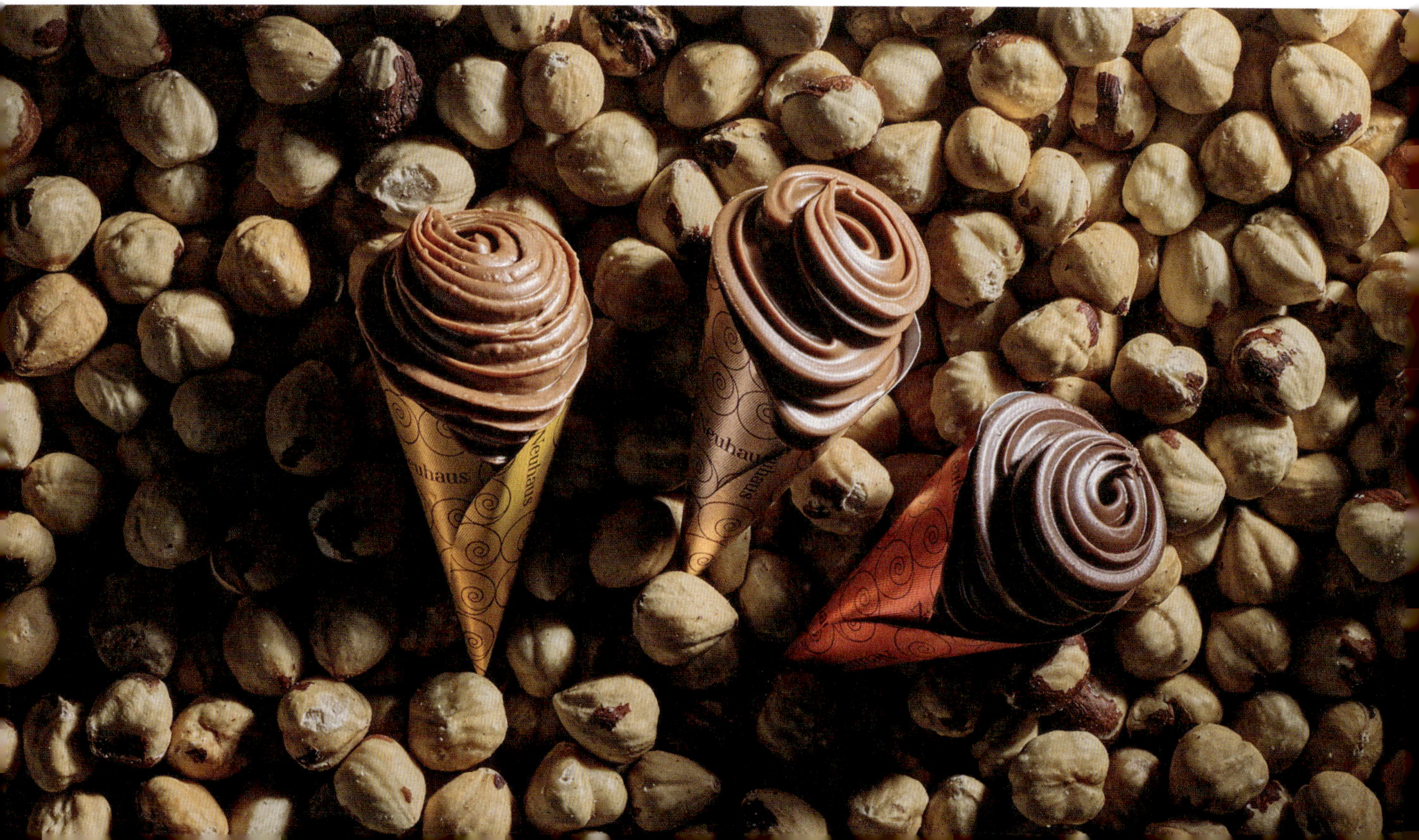

DIVINE

For the 100th anniversary of the Belgian praline in 2012, the Master Chocolatier was determined not to miss a trick. No fewer than five celebratory pralines were created for the occasion. These included the Divine, a treat everyone agrees is most aptly named. Its combination of milk chocolate and soft caramel is certainly unbeatable, and let's not forget the little touch that makes all the difference: its chopped Piedmont hazelnuts.

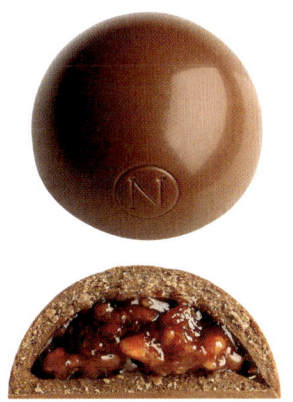

GALERIE

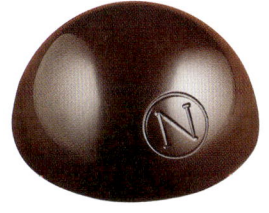
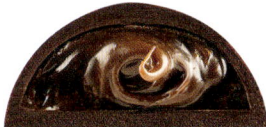

When Jean Neuhaus, a Swiss citizen originally from Neuchâtel, moved to Brussels in 1857, he chose the prestigious Galerie de la Reine as the location for his shop. This covered passageway, an architectural jewel in the heart of the capital, was to become the birthplace of one of the world's most famous chocolate brands. The Galerie de la Reine remains home to this emblematic boutique, a proud witness to the enduring, intimate link between the house of Neuhaus and this history-steeped site.

To celebrate this historic connection, Neuhaus crafted the Galerie, a praline meant to be savoured as a tribute to the refinement and elegance of a location distinguished by its 200-meters-long glass roof. Beneath its intensely dark chocolate coating, this creation conceals a dark caramel with a melting texture and a subtle yet robust flavour. In all simplicity, it evokes the charm of the Galerie de la Reine, a location that has stood the test of time while ultimately retaining its soul.

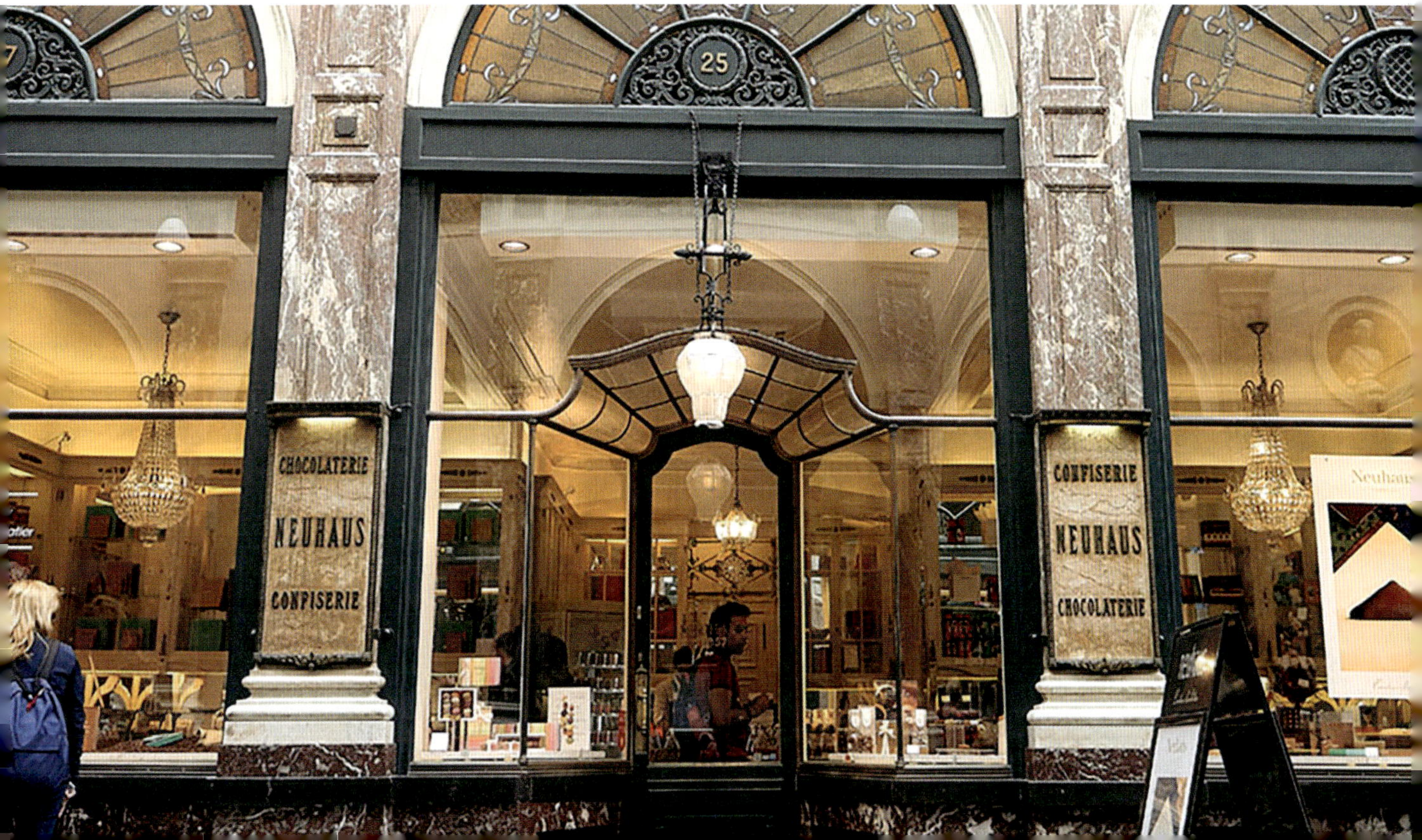

JEAN 72 %

In 1912, Jean Neuhaus Jr. revolutionised the confectionery world by creating one of Belgium's finest specialities. The 'praline', as Neuhaus named it, enjoyed immediate success. His invention was more than just a simple chocolate-coated bite-sized treat; it made culinary history by providing a radically new taste experience, delivering surprising contrasts and sweet harmonies.

Among the contemporary creations of a Master Chocolatier who enjoys revisiting his history (Pierre, Louise, Suzanne...), the Jean 72% praline stands out. It is a tribute to Jean Neuhaus' visionary spirit and heritage. An intense 72% dark chocolate layer with subtle bitterness envelops its core, a smooth ganache made from exceptional Madagascar cocoa. This cocoa, renowned for its rich, complex flavours, adds fruity, slightly acidic notes that fully reveal the finesse of this creation.

Jean 72% entices and delights dark chocolate aficionados while narrating a tale of passion for authentic taste and a pursuit of perfection. Savouring this praline is akin to diving into the unique realm of Neuhaus, where tradition and modernity converge to create an extraordinary sensory experience. It pays homage to a Belgian invention that, more than a century later, continues to delight palates across the globe.

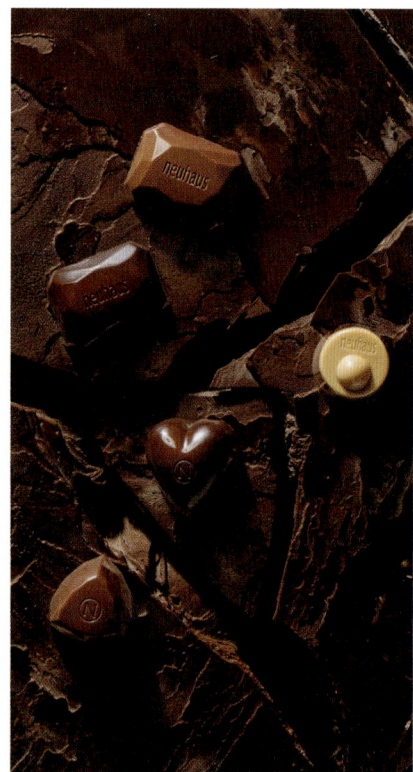

The Neuhaus family as pralines! At the top, Jean and Louise, the heart in the middle is Suzanne, Frédéric is at the bottom left, and finally Pierre, the last generation, on the right

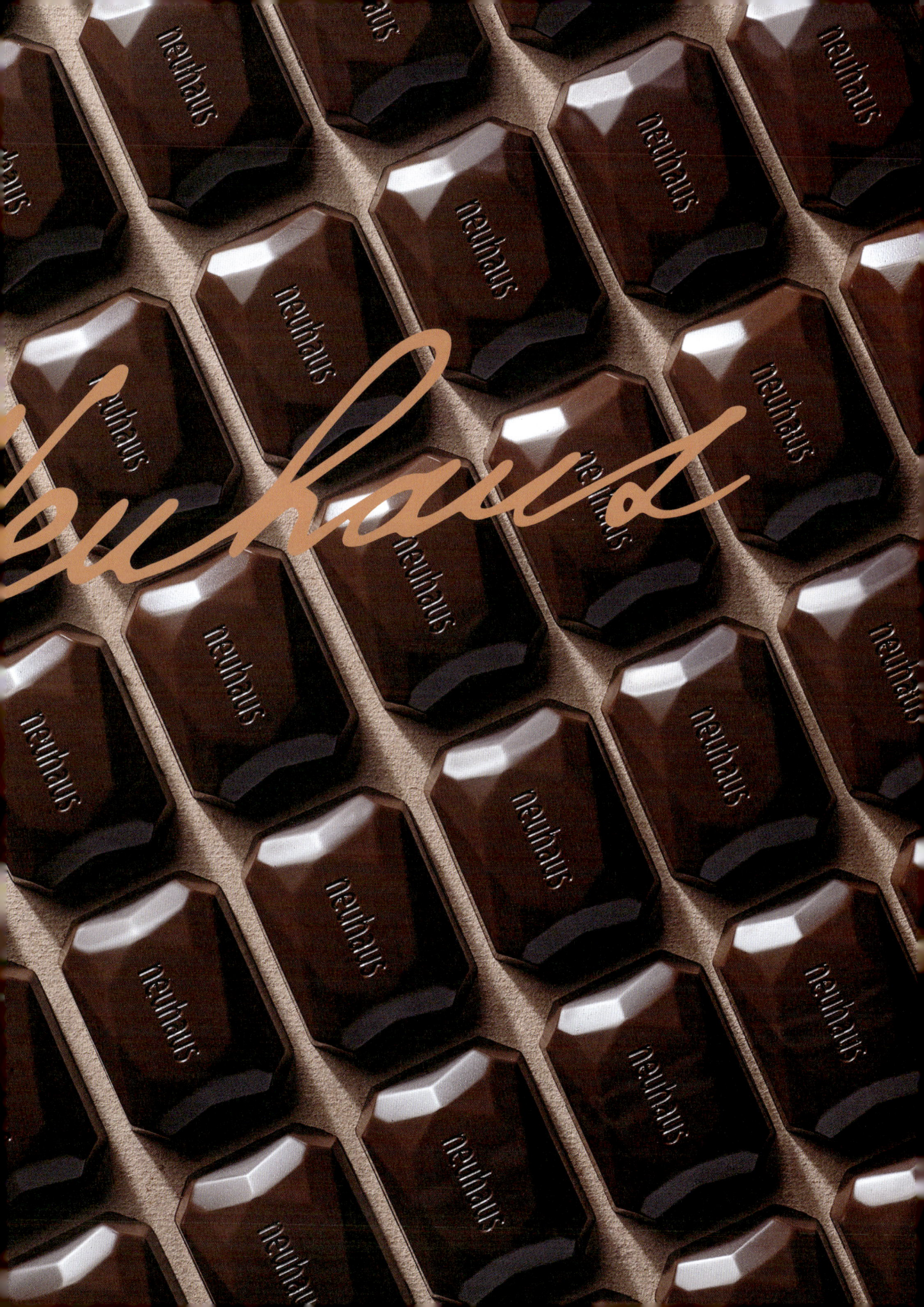

LOUISE

Louise Agostini conceived the ballotin to replace the traditional paper cornet with better protective packaging for the precious Neuhaus pralines. She was also an indispensable support to Jean Neuhaus Jr. Her contributions were vital to the success of the house, both as a partner and as an inspiration in the family business. Her active role merited being highlighted through a soft praline that combines a smooth ganache and sweet Venezuelan milk chocolate.

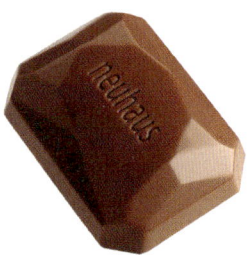

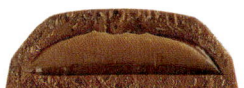

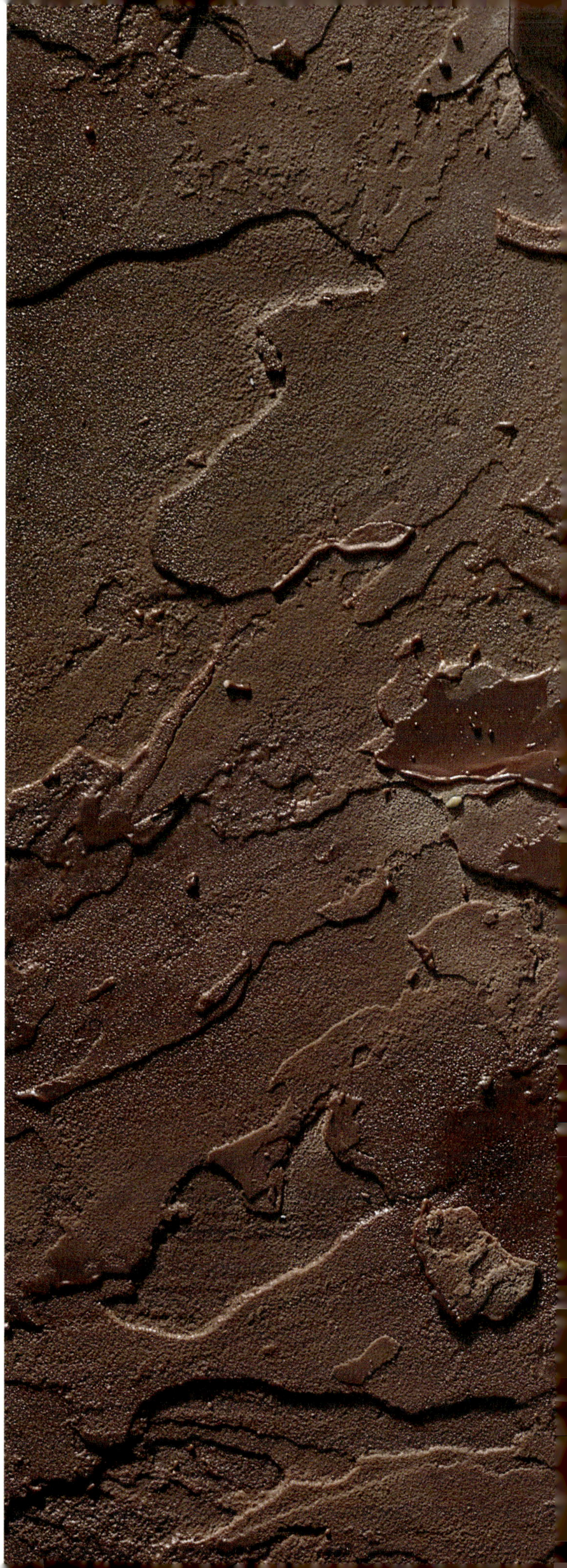

The founding couple: Jean and Louise

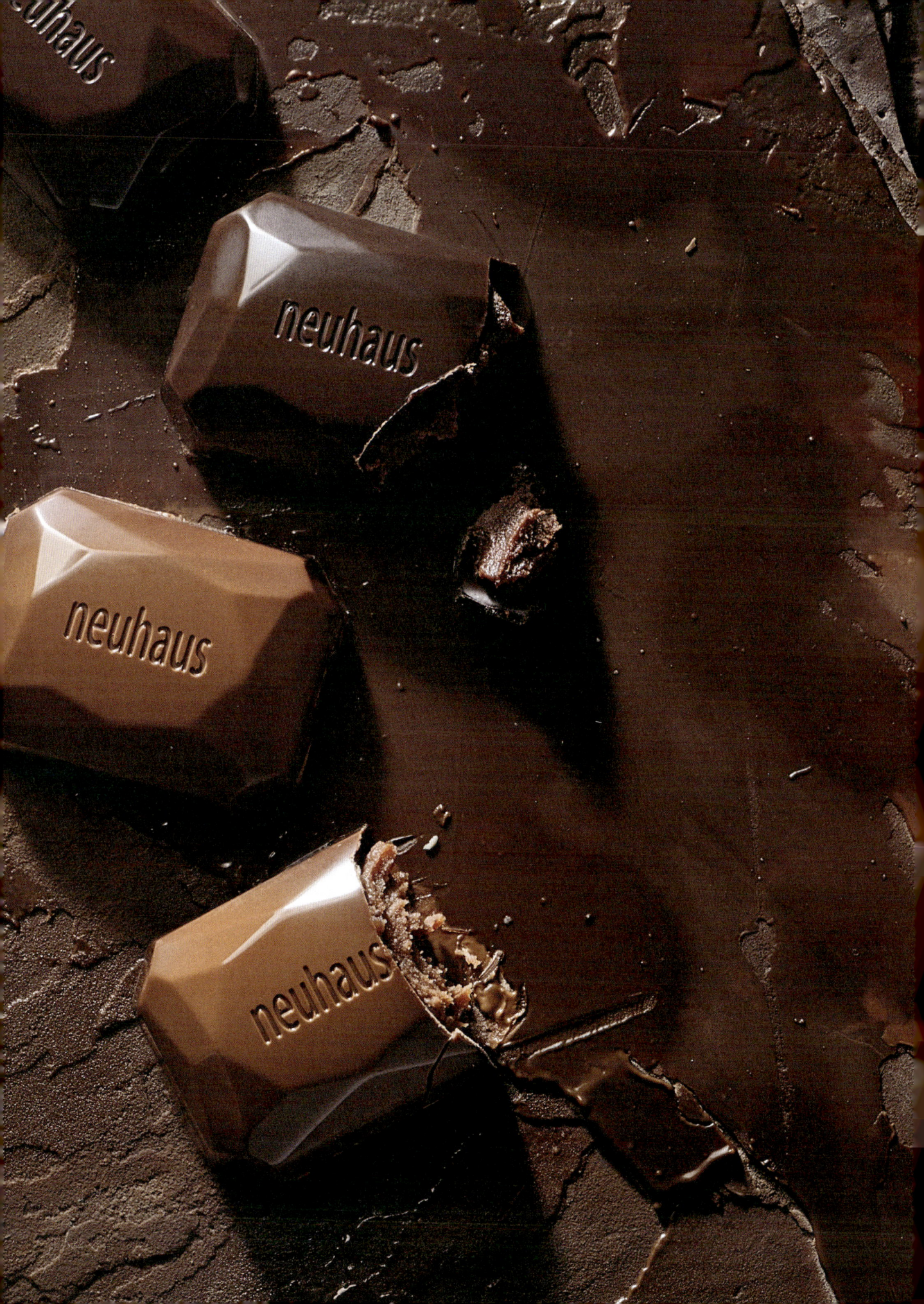

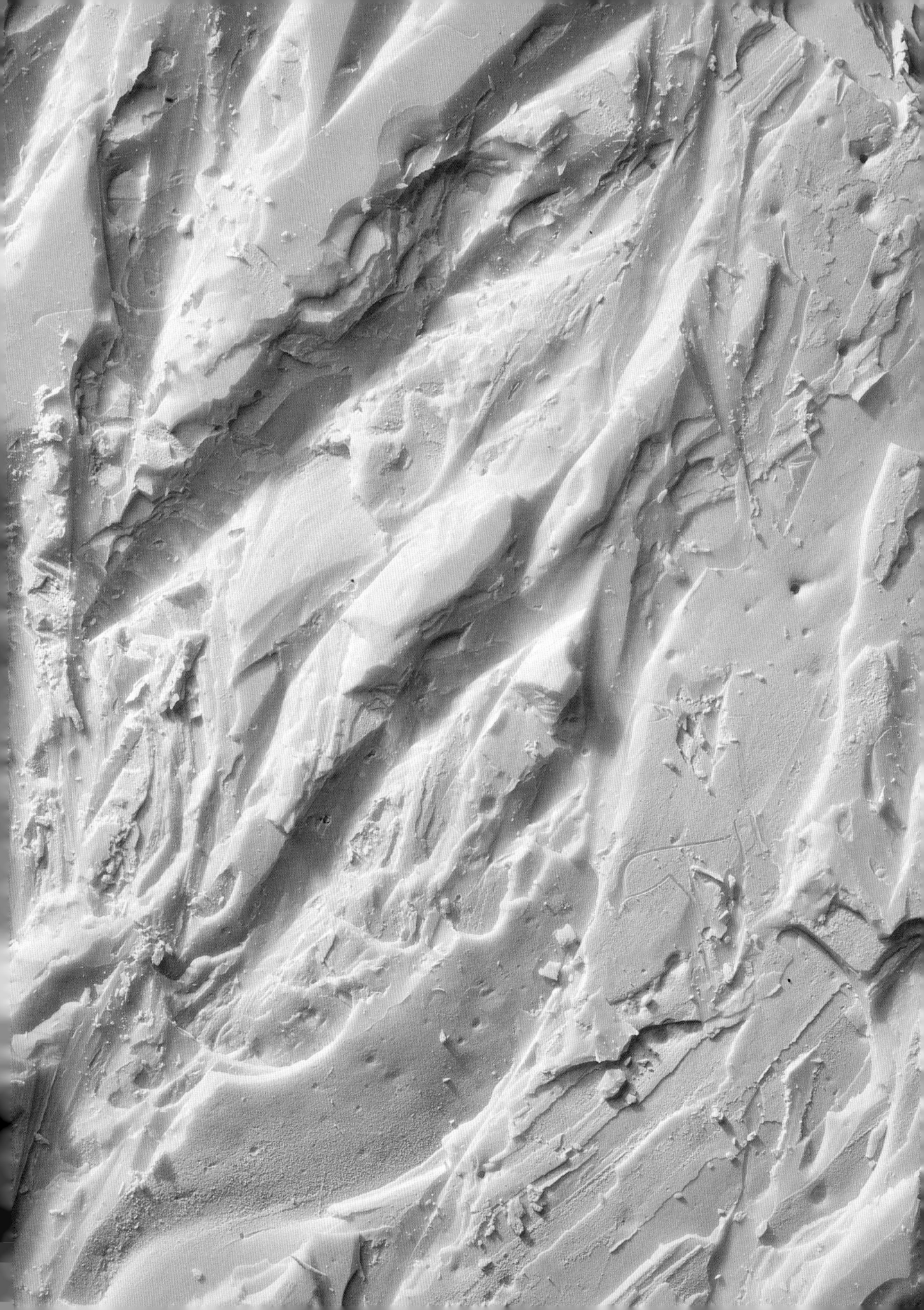

LES MANONS

The Manon occupies a special place among the most emblematic chocolates made in Belgium. Yet its exact origins remain uncertain, as they are shared between several prestigious houses, including Neuhaus and Corné Port-Royal, each of which has contributed to its development and reputation.

The history of the Manon appears to be intertwined with a particular context: the cocoa shortages of the 20th century, especially during and after the world wars. These restrictions compelled Belgian chocolatiers to display remarkable ingenuity in offering refined creations while adapting to supply constraints. In this context, they explored the use of alternative ingredients, such as buttercream, coffee, or vanilla, to conceive distinctive and elegant pralines — among them, the Manon.

The Manon Sucre, now often associated with Maurice Corné, founder of Corné Port-Royal, is believed to have originated in this context. Corné would have used a thin layer of sugar paste to encase a filling of buttercream flavoured with coffee or praline, topped with a whole hazelnut. This bold combination of textures and flavours quickly won over sweet lovers and has become a must-have classic.

However, the success of the Manons cannot be attributed to any single company or creator. Other Belgian chocolatiers have experimented with similar recipes, each adding their unique touch to this praline. Still, the Manon name, evocative of delicacy and femininity, quickly became synonymous with indulgence.

At Neuhaus, the interest in Manon is linked to Suzanne De Gavre, an opera singer and the daughter of Jean Neuhaus Jr. In the 1990s, the Master Chocolatier launched a collection of refined chocolates to evoke Suzanne de Gavre's performance in 'Manon', the famous opera by the French composer Jules Massenet.

The Manon range extends from Manon Noir, featuring its intense dark chocolate mousse, to Manon Lait, which has fresh cream with praliné and caramelised hazelnuts, along with Choco Café (fresh coffee cream), Sucre Vanille (vanilla-flavoured fresh cream on nougatine with a pecan nut and vanilla sugar cream), Sucre Café (coffee-flavoured fresh cream on nougatine with a pecan nut and coffee sugar cream), and Choco Vanille (vanilla-flavoured fresh cream from Madagascar topped with a pecan nut).

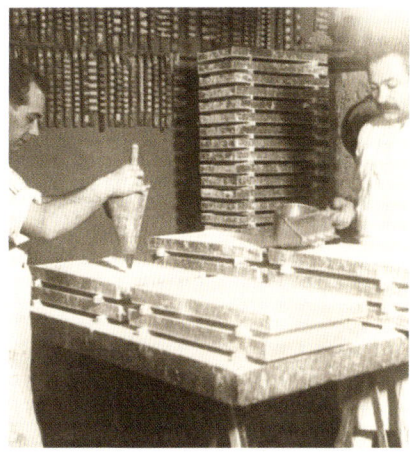
Corné workshops

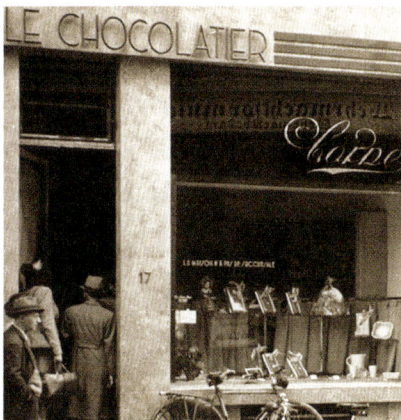
Corné shop

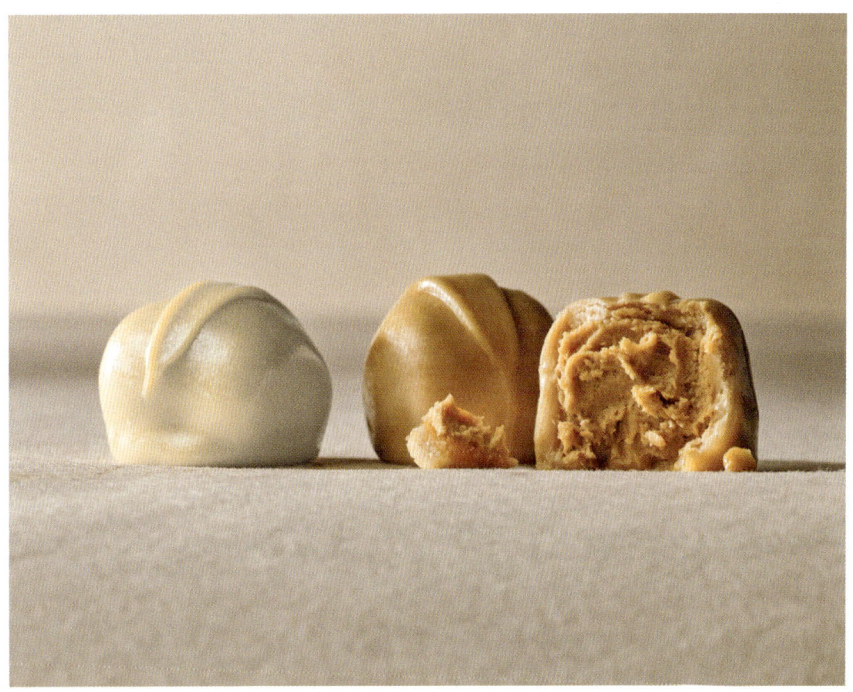

SUZANNE

Ganache is a culinary preparation made with chocolate and cream, often used in patisserie and chocolate-making. It is characterised by its smooth, melting texture, which can be adjusted according to the proportions of its ingredients. Within the Neuhaus range, ganaches form a tempting family, including Bonbon 13 (hazelnut ganache with rum) and the enticing floral flavours of Violetta (a violet-flavoured ganache enriched with French violet crystals). Not to forget Suzanne, created as a tribute to the daughter of Jean Neuhaus Jr. and Louise Agostini. The voice of this mezzo-soprano at the Brussels Théâtre de la Monnaie earned her a melodious tribute in the form of Ecuadorian dark chocolate and raspberry ganache.

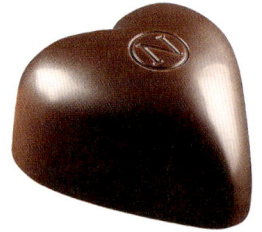

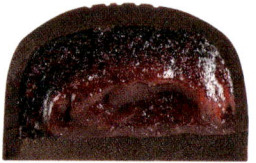

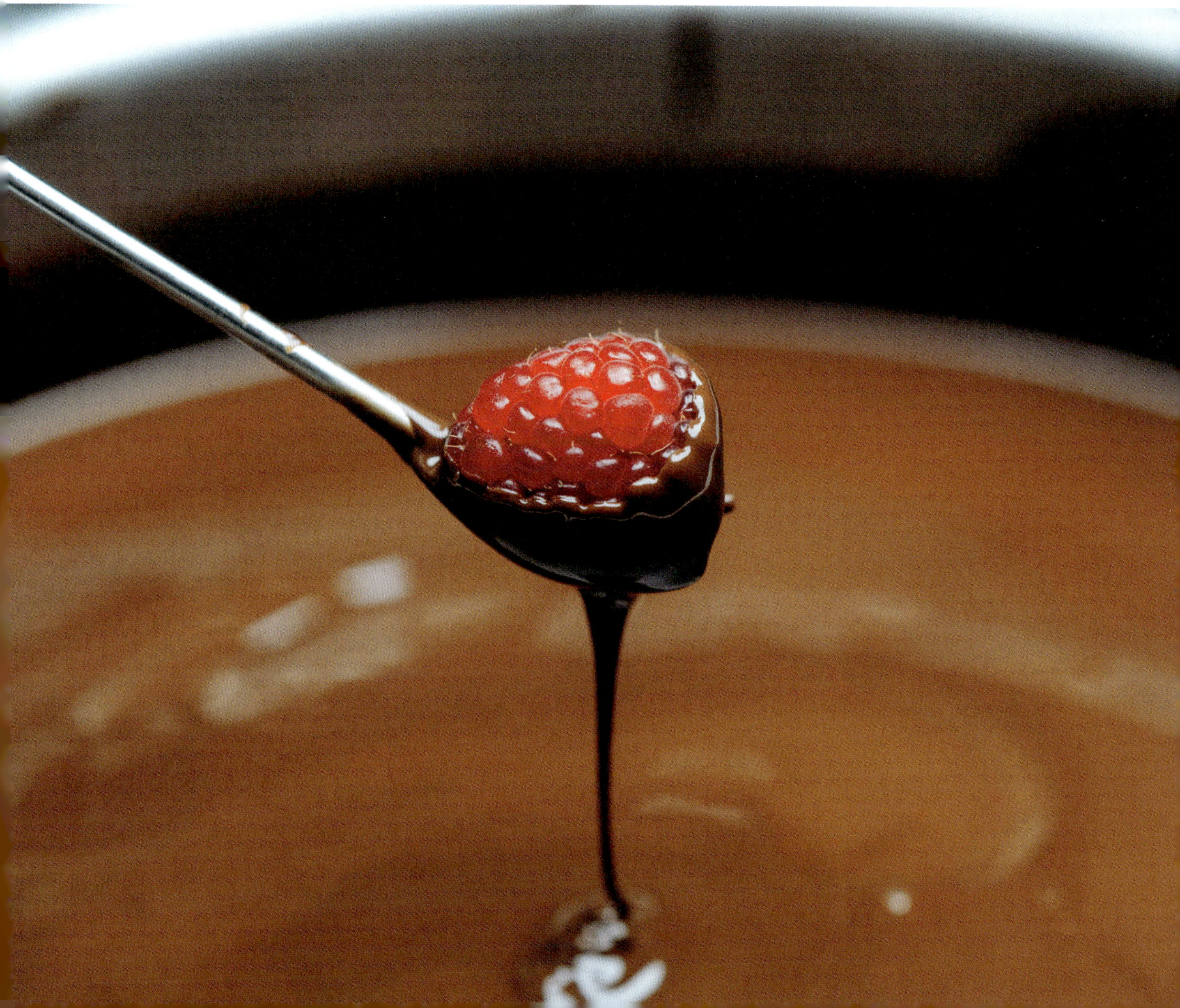

TO OUR DEAR DEPARTED

Like many objects of pleasure, pralines reflect their time. They capture trends, embrace the tastes of an era, and may disappear when fashion changes. Some iconic Neuhaus creations have marked the decades before giving way to more contemporary flavours. This is true for liqueur chocolates, once shop window stars boasting sophisticated flavours such as Cointreau and Grand Marnier, designed to enchant the palate.

Today, these classic flavours have given way to mixology-inspired creations that showcase the elegance of infused gin, the warmth of bourbon, and the floral notes of bitters, reflecting the latest cocktail trends. This evolution testifies to Neuhaus's commitment to the spirit of the time, consistently balancing heritage and innovation, even as some enduring favourites still thrive, such as the amusing Cerisette (a cherry, including stem and stone, macerated in alcohol).

But what remains of the vanished pralines, and what stories did they take with them? Our counters are no longer adorned with the colourful wrappers of the Fraise des Bois (fondant sugar cream with strawberry pulp) or the slightly curved silhouette of the Paillette (candied orange peel coated in chocolate).

The same applies to Baie rose (marzipan with granulated sugar and a pink peppercorn), Passion poire cannelle (pear and cinnamon ganache), and the Snobinettes range (champagne, cappuccino, hazelnut), as well as Euro (praline with nougat chips), Dollar (hazelnut praline), Fruits de mer (hazelnut praline), and various crème fraîche pralines, including Aphrodite (vanilla butter topping a gianduja base), Black & White (vanilla butter with hazelnuts), and even Satan and Méphisto (hazelnut and almond cream with finely chopped roasted nuts with sugar, in dark chocolate and milk chocolate versions).

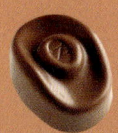 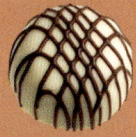 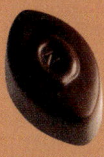 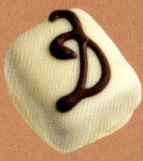 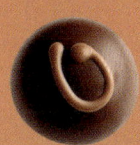 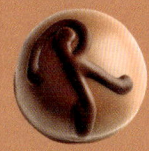

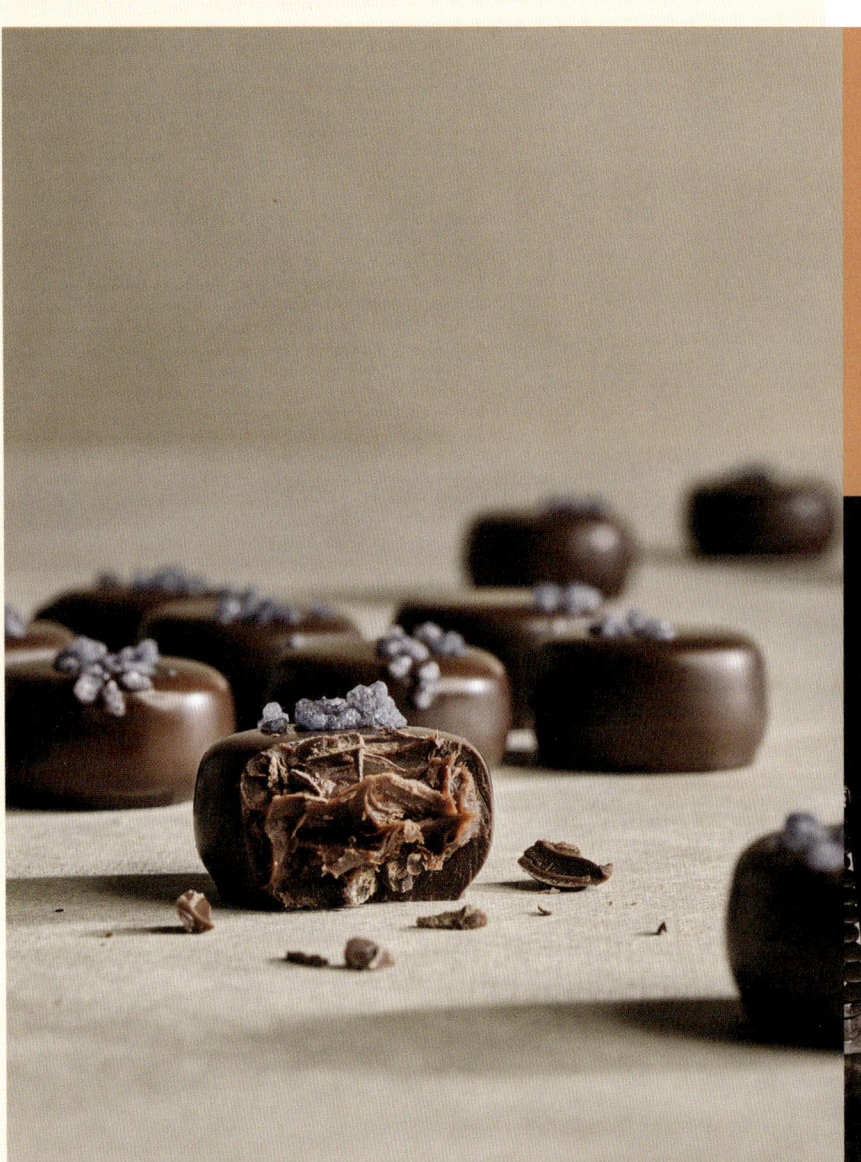

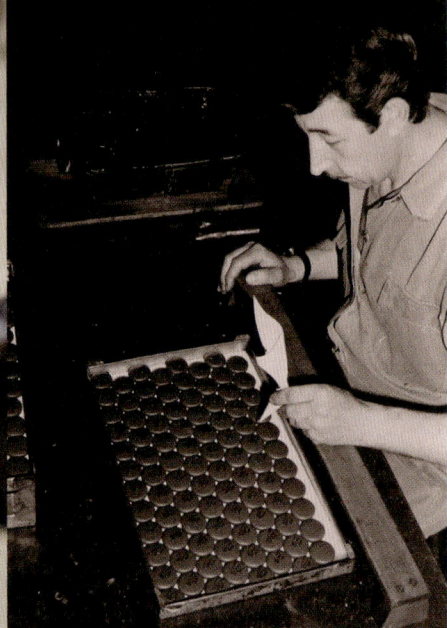

Nature abhors a vacuum but is not above working miracles. Two emblematic chocolates that had once been retired, Violetta and Bonbon 13, inspired such a wave of nostalgia among their loyal fans, quick to express their attachment, that they were allowed a triumphant return to the range. Violetta, characterised by its milk chocolate ganache, subtly scented with violet and coated in a thin layer of dark chocolate, captivates with its refined floral balance.

Bonbon 13 is a tribute to tradition: a crunchy hazelnut praline coated in intense dark chocolate that showcases seductive contrasting textures and timeless indulgence.

Fun fact: the number '13' on the praline was most likely initially a capital 'B', the graphic evidence of which has been lost over time. In light of the public's enthusiasm, the Maître Chocolatier had to reinstate these two must-haves. This proves that certain flavours transcend all trends and capture chocolate lovers' hearts.

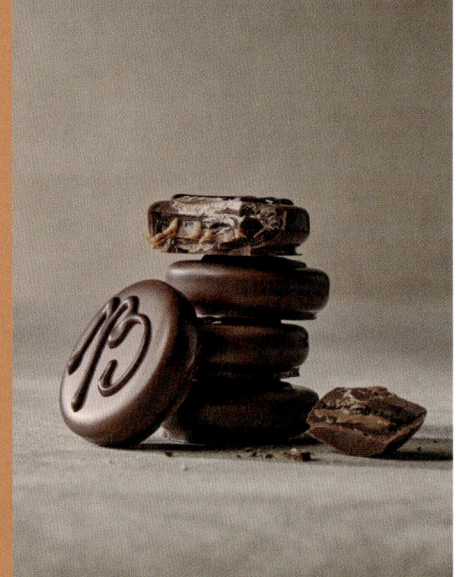

Violetta at the top and Bonbon 13 at the bottom

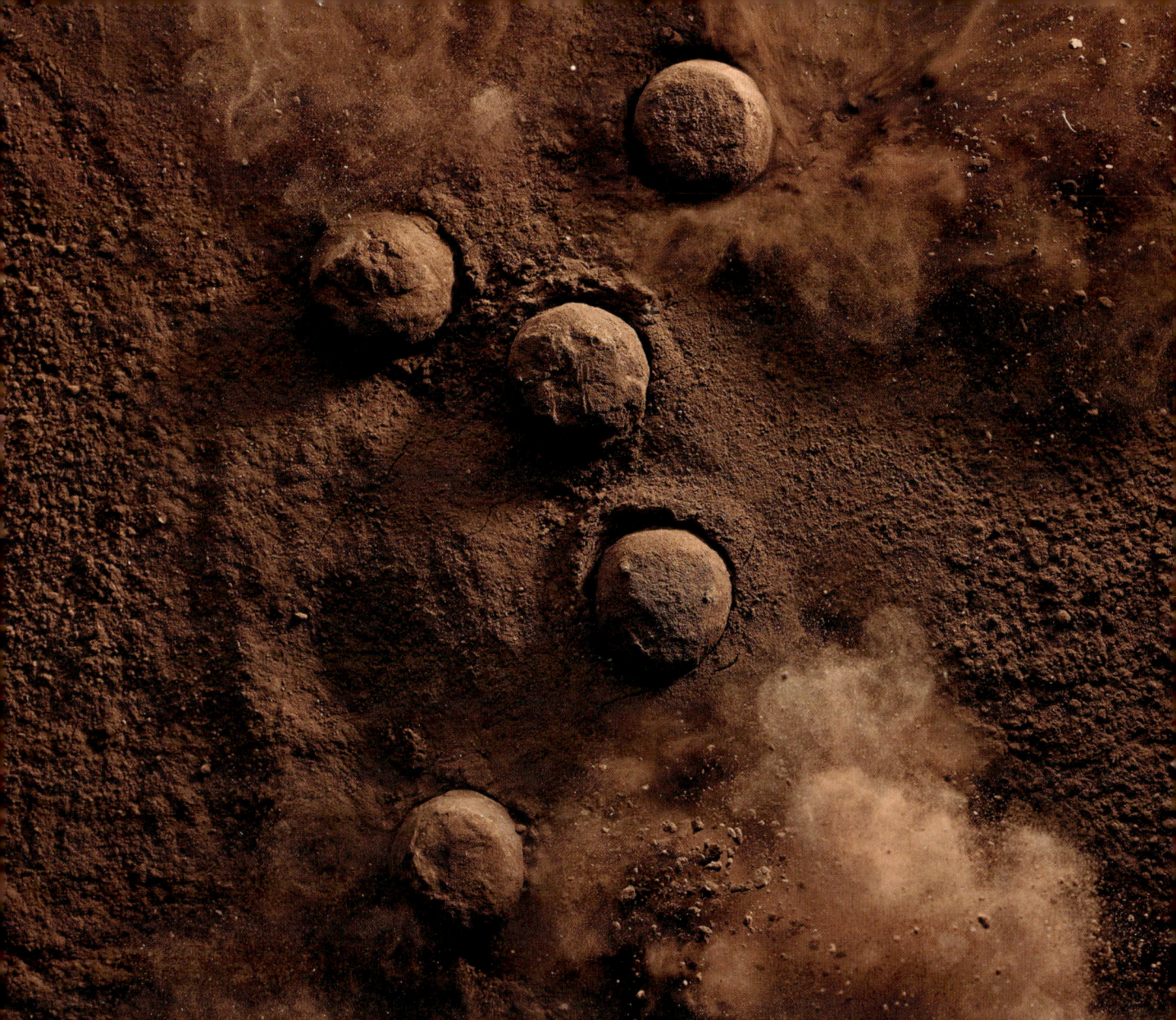

THE BEST TRUFFLE IN THE WORLD

ACCORDING TO BLOOMBERG

In 2017, Bloomberg declared Neuhaus truffles the best in the world and ranked the 16-piece Prestige ballotin first in its category. Journalist and culinary critic Kristen Krader described these creations as a one-of-a-kind experience, a mix of refinement and mastery of chocolate techniques.'Oh, my God, I feel like I just fell into a chocolate-filled swimming pool', she wrote, impressed with the charm of these generous yet delicate creations.

Their soft coating reveals an exquisitely unctuous and frothy core from which flavours unfold in successive waves. 'It makes you realise how many old or mediocre chocolates you may have eaten in your life', she added, emphasising the exceptional freshness of the Neuhaus products, which seem 'to have been manufactured right at that moment'.

The journalist was also very taken with the case containing these chocolaty treasures. The bright red box, adorned with elegant gold-embossed trim, promises quality in its own right. 'Just looking at it, you know what you are holding is special', she specified. This acknowledgement, among many others, speaks to Neuhaus's savoir-faire and its ability to elevate Belgian chocolate to a world-class level of excellence, confirming its place among the undisputed references in chocolate.

ART DECO AS SIGNATURE

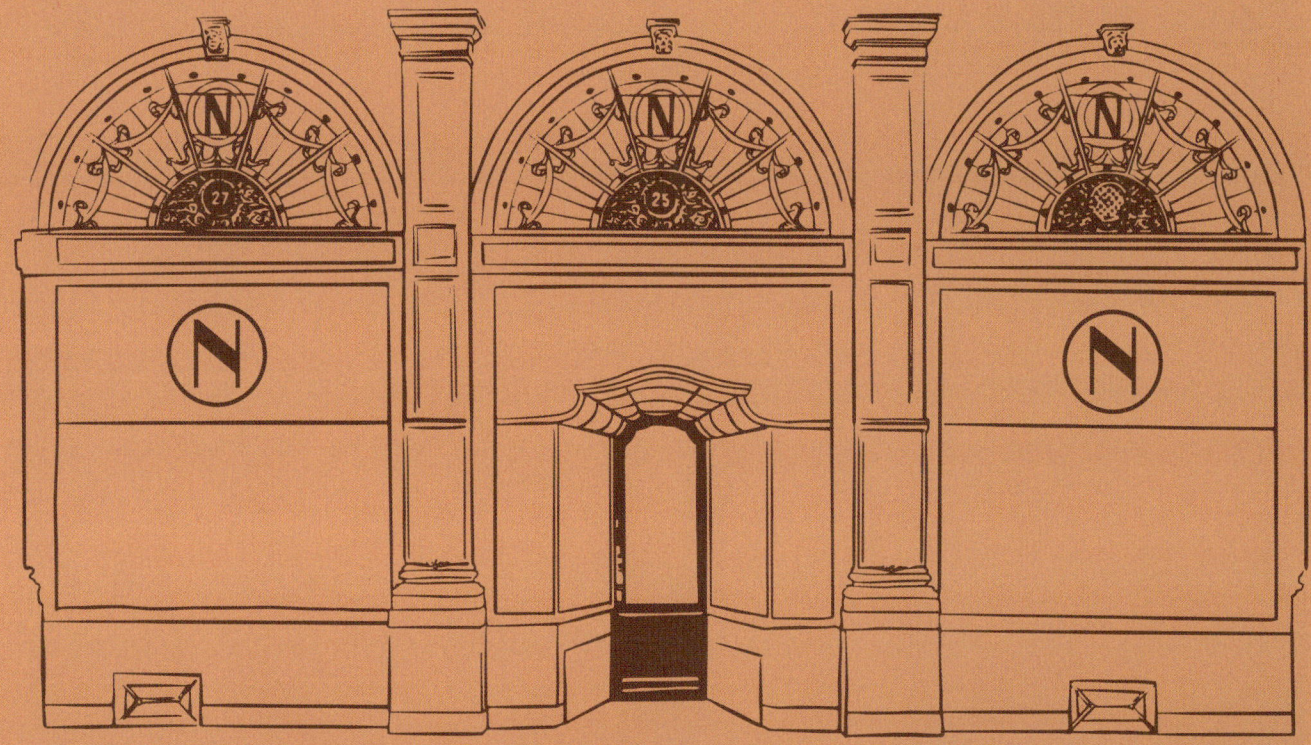

Art Deco, the architectural and decorative movement that emerged in the interbellum, made its mark with geometric elegance and structural lines. In Belgium, this style has been particularly prominent in emblematic buildings such as the old Hôtel Plaza in Brussels, the Villa Empain, and the Palais des Beaux-Arts, designed by Victor Horta. These buildings exemplify a modernity where the interplay of edges and shapes achieves a harmonious balance between splendour and rigour.

Neuhaus is fully committed to this heritage. More than just a style, Art Deco serves as a visual signature that weaves through the company's history. Inspired by the iconic façade of its historic boutique, with arches and curves that convey the essence of this movement, the brand has revived this aesthetic in its creations. In 2018, the visual identity of the Maître Chocolatier was reinterpreted through this lens, and its influence resonates throughout the boutiques, particularly in the display units, which reflect the graphic fluidity characteristic of the 1920s.

This imprint extends to the intricate details of the boxes, particularly the History box, whose motifs and interplay of lines pay homage to the movement's emblematic patterns. Moreover, we must not forget the chiselled geometric shapes of the famous Art Deco praline, which reflect this appreciation for elegant sobriety. This delicate harmony should be savoured without moderation.

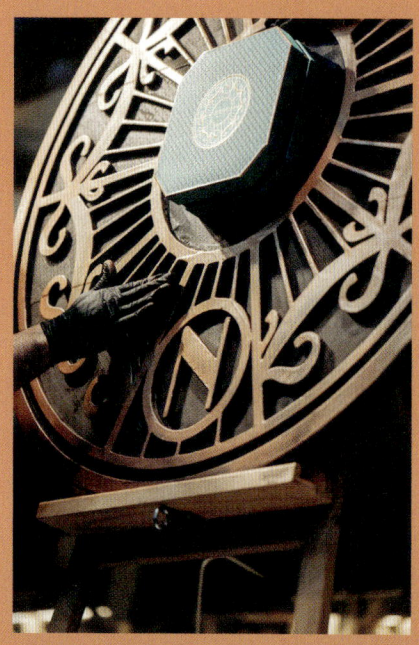

THE COLLABORATIONS

Neuhaus stands out in the world of chocolate for its bubbling creativity and ability to push the frontiers of traditional know-how. This Master Chocolatier has thrived through the ages by constantly renewing itself. As befits this innovative spirit, Neuhaus has always engaged in daring collaborations with designers, top chefs and other visionary artists to create fruitful partnerships. Each new creation is conceived as a sensory experience, reflecting a dialogue between our chocolate heritage and the aspirations of the times. Isn't that the role of a pioneer, a visionary?

Isn't this a value inscribed in the brand's very DNA? There's every reason to think so, considering the extent to which pralines and their ballotins - those precious objects of indisputable refinement - manage to achieve a seamless fusion of timeless elegance and contemporary hedonistic codes. Indeed, there is no shortage of examples of this.

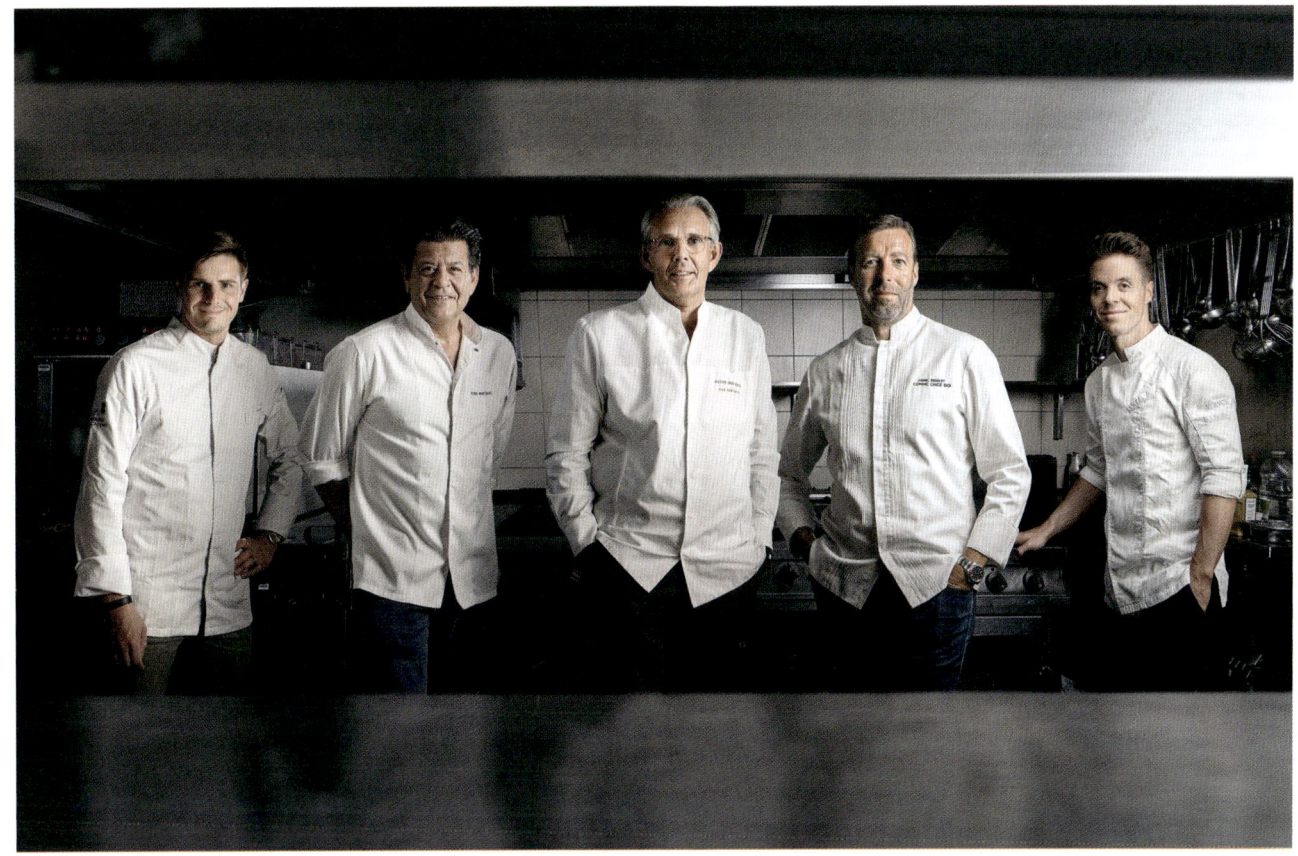

From left to right: Tim Boury, Yves Mattagne, Peter Goossens, Lionel Rigolet, and Thierry Theys

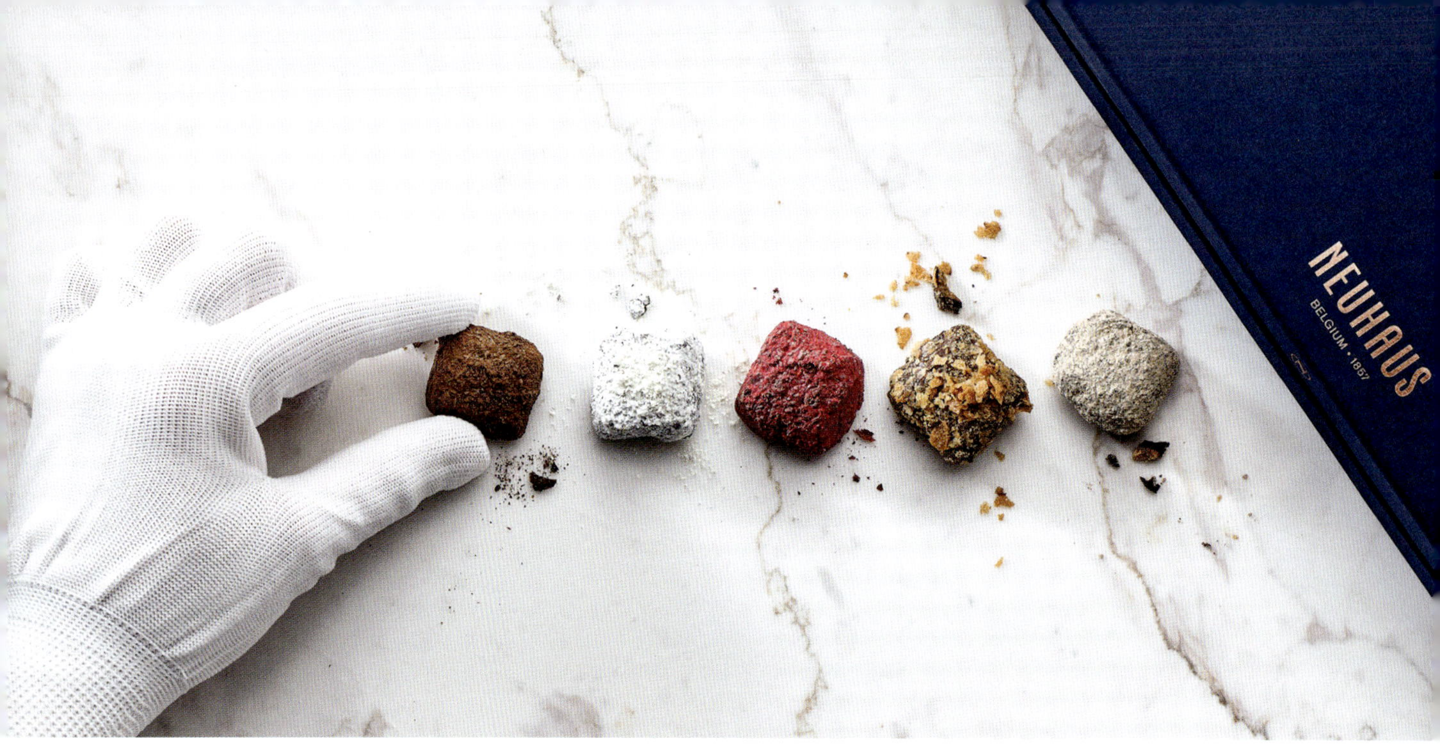

LES TRÉSORS: AS REGARDS GASTRONOMY

With Trésors, Neuhaus aims to reinvent a classic: the truffle. Presented in an elegant midnight blue box, these creations seek to please the most discerning chocolate lovers, enabling them to elevate a dinner or give someone an unforgettable gift.

The collection features five unique pralines, each embodying a perfect balance of textures and flavours. Lionel Rigolet from the Comme Chez Soi restaurant in Brussels combined intensely dark chocolate from Vietnam with the spicy notes of candied ginger, softened by slivers of white chocolate. This bold combination creates an immersive tasting experience with a subtle finish.

Thierry Theys from restaurant Nuance in Duffel crafts his treasure with creamy hazelnut praline and blond chocolate, enhanced by an exotic hint of passion fruit. Toasted hazelnut oil adds delicate depth to the composition, while the tanginess of the passion fruit counterbalances its sweetness, resulting in an irresistibly light praline.

Peter Goossens, the renowned chef of Hof van Cleve, the top restaurant in Kruisem, set out to explore the richness of pecan nuts by combining them with caramel chips and a touch of Guérande salt. This praline, elevated by a delicate hint of raspberry, plays on contrasts that captivate the finest palates.

Tim Boury from restaurant Boury (Roulers) proposes a reinterpretation of caramel. His caramelised chocolate ganache, infused with caramel vinegar and enriched with Isigny caramel, sprinkled with muscovado sugar, combines acidic and creamy notes to soften the powerful impact of dark chocolate, providing a deliciously surprising experience.

Finally, Yves Mattagne from La Villa Lorraine (Brussels) showcases the Piedmontese hazelnut in a praline made with praliné, white gianduja, and Venezuelan milk chocolate. Coated in dark chocolate and crispy feuilletine, this creation highlights the truffle's gastronomic purity and the richness of its chocolate heritage.

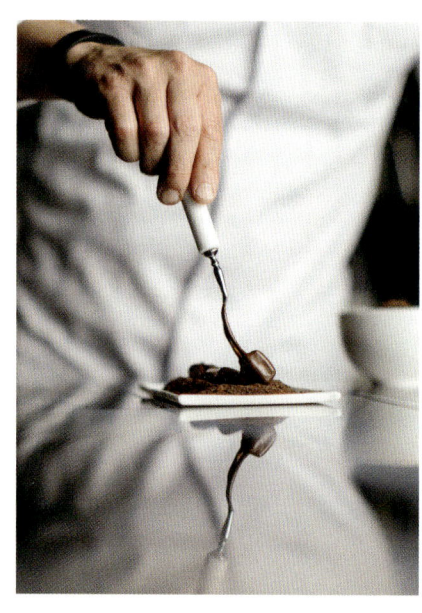

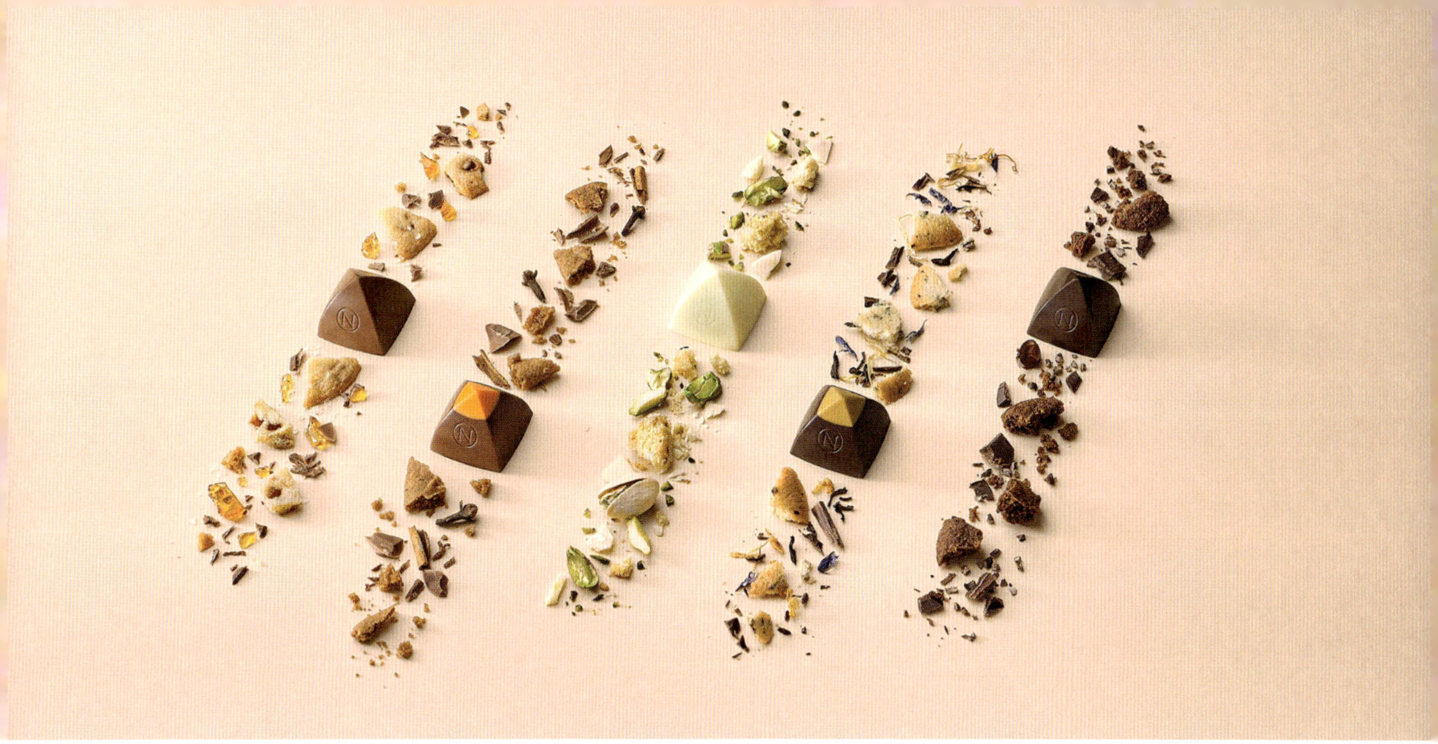

LES GOURMANDS: LET IT CRACKLE

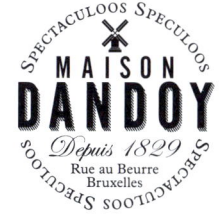

True to its quest for excellence, Neuhaus enjoys collaborations with key figures and institutions from Belgium's gastronomic heritage. One such collaborator is Maison Dandoy, a renowned traditional biscuit maker founded in 1829. The two emblematic houses celebrate Belgian know-how through various creations that combine chocolate and a crunchy biscuit.

The resulting Gourmand collection is a delightful fusion of expertise, where tradition and innovation intertwine. Neuhaus designed the chocolate for the filling and coating, ensuring perfect harmony of intensity and creaminess. The filling is a skilful blend of Neuhaus chocolate and finely ground Maison Dandoy biscuits, producing a subtly crunchy texture with warm speculoos or shortbread notes. Each bite of this gourmet fusion reveals the best of both worlds. Note: the use of Maison Dandoy's discarded 'imperfect' biscuits also reflects a commitment to act responsibly and sustainably by reinventing these treasures in an even more gourmet form.

This collection celebrates the gourmet heritage of five emblematic Dandoy biscuits, reinterpreted through Neuhaus's chocolate-making expertise. One of its pieces, the 1857 praline, is a praliné with speculoos coated in milk chocolate. It is not a novelty, as it has already been part of the existing Neuhaus range, reflecting the enduring relationship between the two houses. Four new creations have been added to the range.

The Gourmand Pistache is a seasonal favourite for the Neuhaus team, delighting with its soft and creamy praliné and pistachio shortbread enrobed in sweet white chocolate. The Gourmand Caramel Salé, a biscuit caramel and milk chocolate blend, charms with its generous crunch and comforting notes. The Gourmand Earl Grey, coated in dark chocolate, reveals the subtlety of bergamot, enhanced by an elegant aromatic touch. Lastly, the Gourmand Chocolat Noir, a Maison Dandoy favourite, combines a dark chocolate biscuit with a hint of Guérande salt, offering a deep, balanced intensity.

These pralines represent the latest chapter in a long-standing collaboration celebrating Neuhaus and Maison Dandoy's shared heritage. Apart from the 1857 praline, this joint effort has already produced the famous Belgian Thins, a series of addictive creations designed to commemorate the meeting of nougatine and speculoos. Les Gourmands, presented in an elegant tin box reminiscent of our grandmothers' sweet boxes and featuring a terrazzo design that evokes biscuit slivers, now elevates the art of Belgian confectionery to new heights.

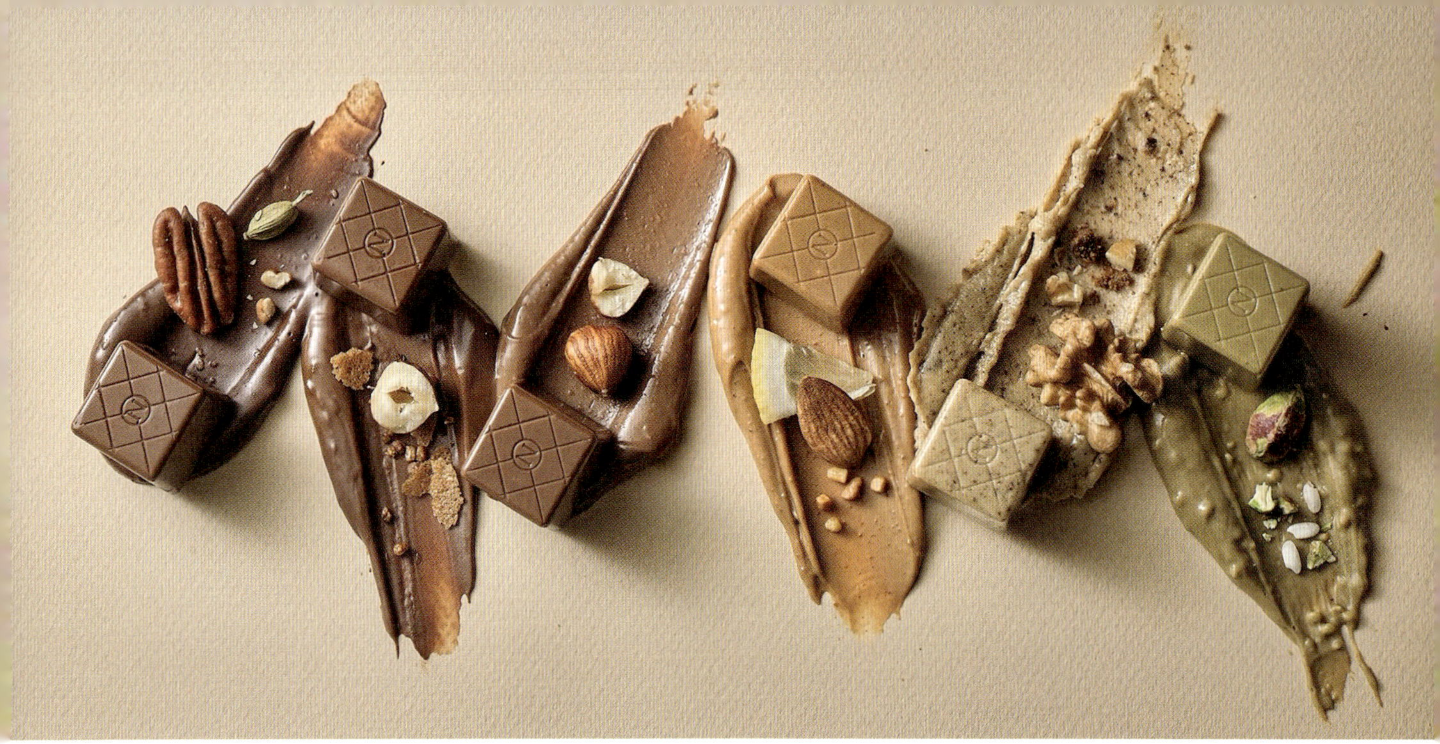

LES SAVOUREUX: WHEN GIANDUJA ADOPTS NEW SHADES

Some recipes endure the test of time with grace. Gianduja is one such creation. Born from the union of chocolate and hazelnuts, it embodies a melt-in-the-mouth sweetness that is both comforting and instinctive. However, when a tried-and-true tradition like this one meets bold innovation, something extraordinary unfolds... This is precisely the spirit behind Les Savoureux—a collection that reimagines one of the great classics of fine chocolate-making.

To create Les Savoureux, master chocolatiers have drawn on their rich heritage while embracing a fresh, creative impulse, guided by the vision of Michelin-starred chef Tim Boury. Together, they have crafted a series of remarkably smooth pralines, allowing each nut to showcase its unique character in a refined interplay of textures and flavours.

The tone is established from the very first bite with Walnut Vanilla—a silky blend of blonde chocolate and walnut, enhanced by a hint of vanilla and muscovado sugar—creating a praline that is as soft and rounded as velvet.

Next, we have Hazelnut Sobacha, which features a more distinct personality. Roasted hazelnuts combine with milk chocolate and the surprising richness of sobacha—an infusion of roasted buckwheat—resulting in toasted notes accentuated by a drizzle of honey.

Almond Yuzu offers a brighter, more vibrant contrast. In this creation, white chocolate blends with crunchy caramelised almonds, enhanced by a zesty hint of yuzu. It provides a perfect balance that evokes the sweetness of memory and ignites a sensory awakening.

Pecan Cardamom conveys an air of understated sophistication. The richness of the pecan harmonises beautifully with milk chocolate, enhanced by a hint of cardamom and a subtle note of apple—a plush, warm, and refined combination.

Finally, Pistachio Puffed Rice evokes childhood nostalgia with a contemporary twist. The creamy pistachio beautifully contrasts with the crisp texture of puffed rice, enhanced by a touch of Guérande sea salt and a hint of cherry. A praline that is both playful and sophisticated.

Les Savoureux narrates the story of a reinvented classic, a cherished memory reimagined, and a heritage celebrated from a fresh perspective. Through these five creations, gianduja becomes a delicate canvas for the imagination of taste. This collection invites you to rediscover pure pleasure.

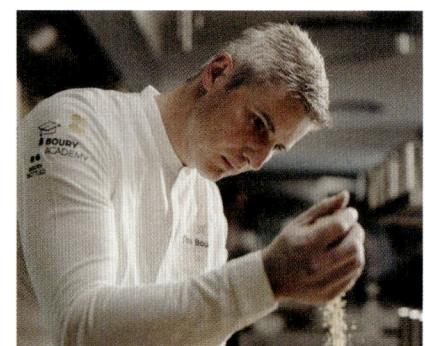

Tim Boury reinvents gianduja in collaboration with Neuhaus for the Les Savoureux collection

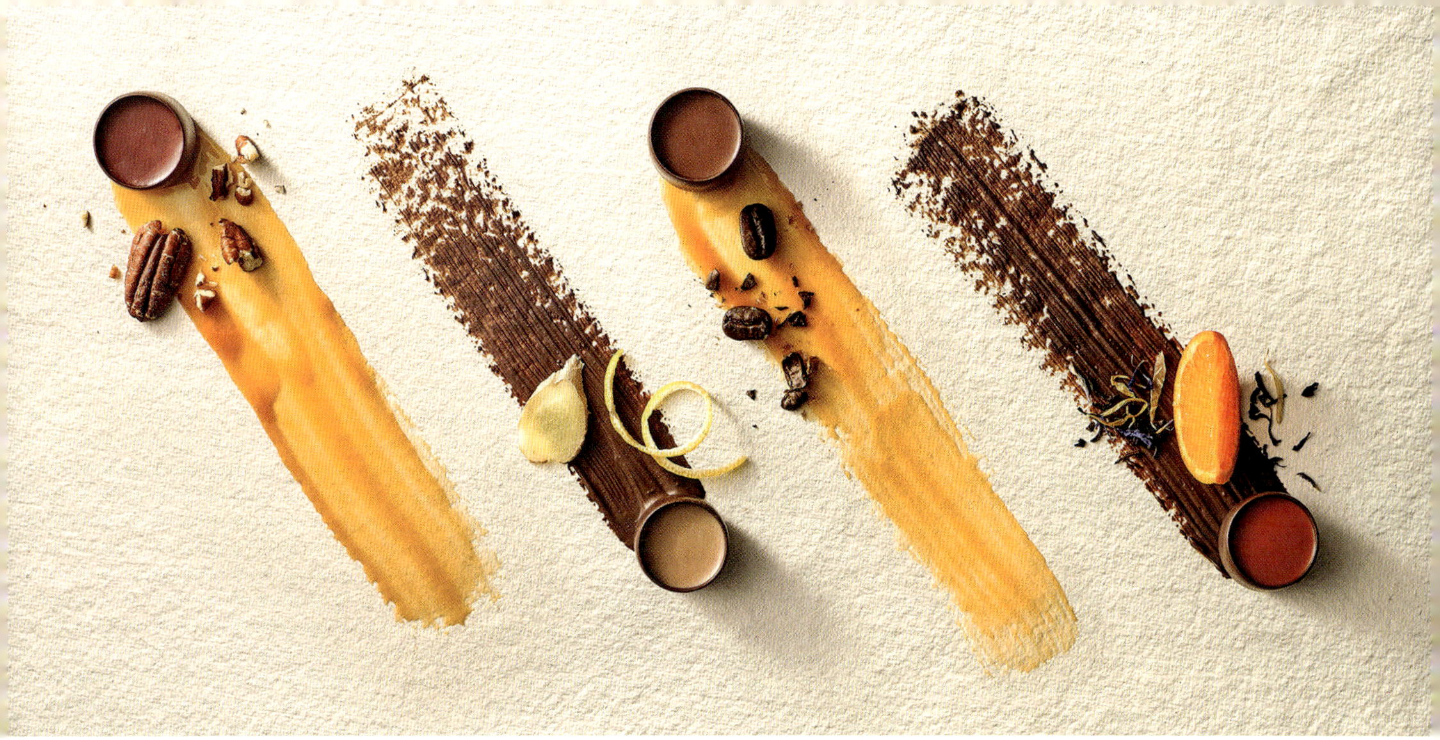

THE VEGAN COLLECTION: A GOURMET REVOLUTION

Always at the forefront of innovation, Neuhaus is one of the first Belgian chocolatiers to offer a collection of vegan pralines. By inventing the Belgian praline, the company revolutionised chocolate; this latest collection takes things a step further, addressing contemporary demands without compromising quality or enjoyment.

The range is available in four refined recipes that celebrate the creamy textures and complex flavours for which Neuhaus is renowned. Tart ganaches with yuzu and ginger, combined with intense dark chocolate, Earl Grey tea, and mandarin ganaches, wrapped in elegantly coloured shells, broaden the taste spectrum. The caramel pralines feature notes of aromatic coffee and crunchy pecans, enhanced by mouth-melting, beautiful coatings.

The innovation doesn't stop at flavour: every ingredient has been carefully reconsidered. Traditional chocolate has been replaced by Peruvian dark chocolate (64% cocoa) without any dairy fat. Chickpea protein substitutes for the conventional milk powder to recreate the velvety texture of milk or white chocolate. Even for caramel fillings, vegetable alternatives like coconut fat or pea protein are used to ensure a sensory experience identical to classic pralines.

Presented in an elegant box, they reinforce the house's commitment to delivering unlimited pleasure to everyone, whether vegan or a chocolate lover.

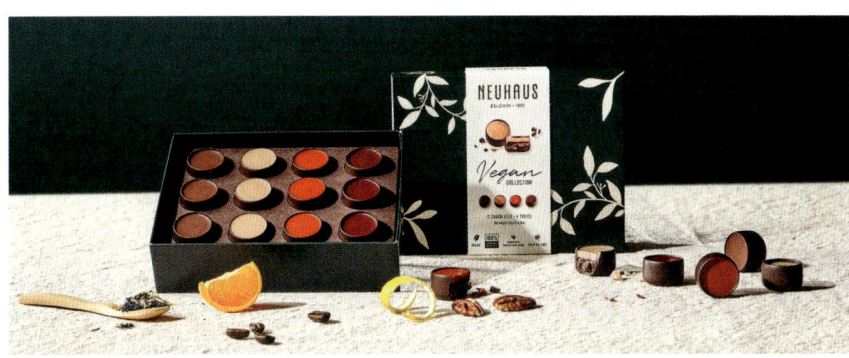

Vegan collection

NEUHAUS

A PIONEER IN ONLINE CHOCOLATE EXPERIENCES

Since 2025, Neuhaus has taken innovation a step further by launching a new service: customers can now assemble a custom gift box online. Wherever they are in Europe, they can choose from 38 varieties of emblematic pralines and have their selection delivered to their home or sent to a loved one.

This innovation continues a transformation that began five years earlier during the 2020 pandemic. This pivotal period accelerated Neuhaus' online sales, which increased sixfold in just a few months, revealing a real craze for remotely ordered chocolate. 'Since then, our online sales have continued to grow, becoming a perfect complement to our worldwide network of 750 stores', says Isabel Baert, CEO of the brand.

True to its 160-year history and visionary spirit, Neuhaus has always sought to combine tradition and innovation. With this service, the company meets the expectations of today's consumers by recreating online the unique experience of in-store choice. 'Nothing will replace the pleasure of in-shop browsing and tasting, but we can now offer an elegant, practical alternative to those who choose to order from the comfort of their homes', adds Isabel Baer.

This project marks a new stage in the evolution of the Maître Chocolatier in 2025, affirming its position as a pioneer in the world of exceptional chocolate and demonstrating its commitment to enhancing the customer experience.

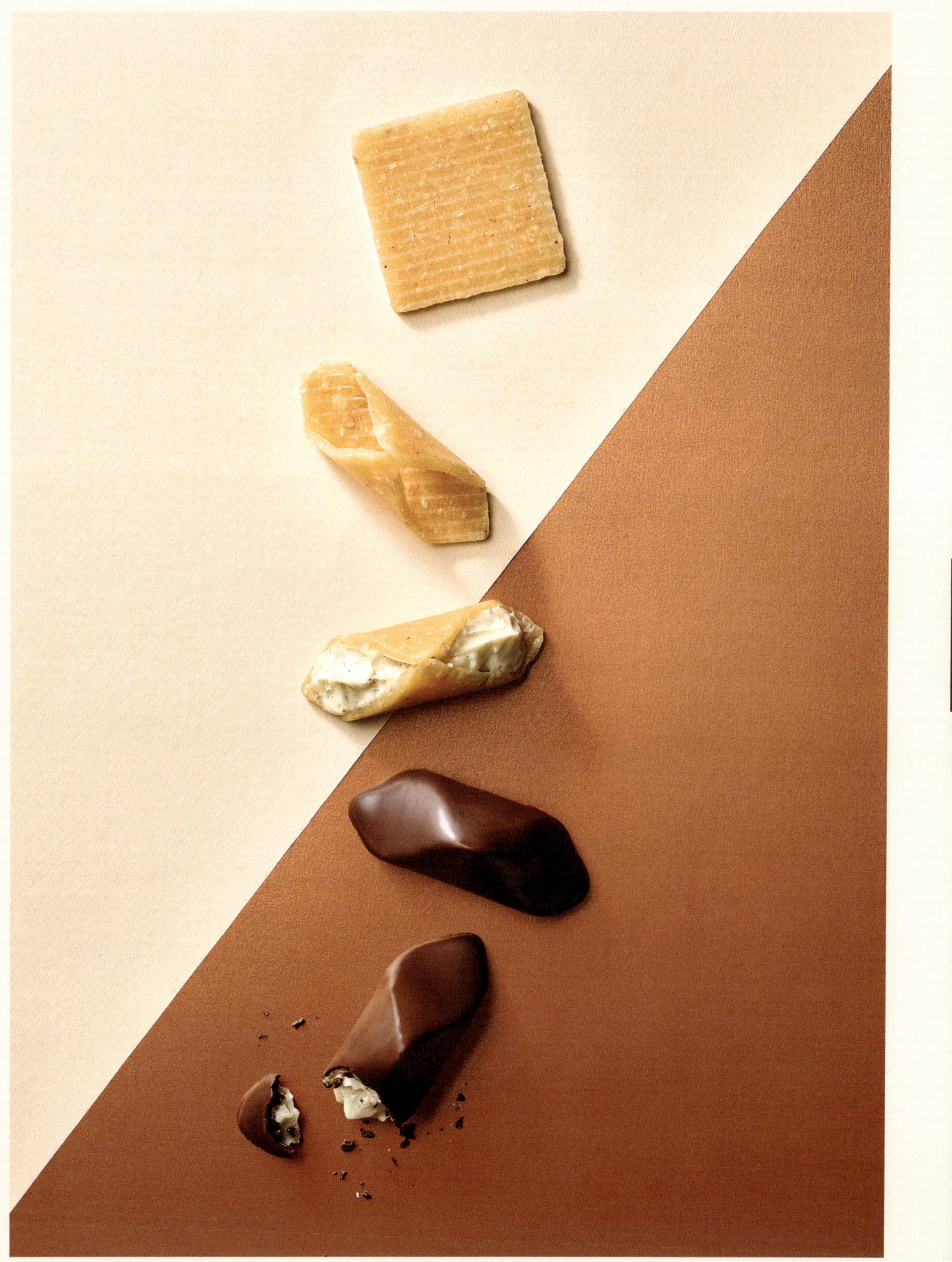

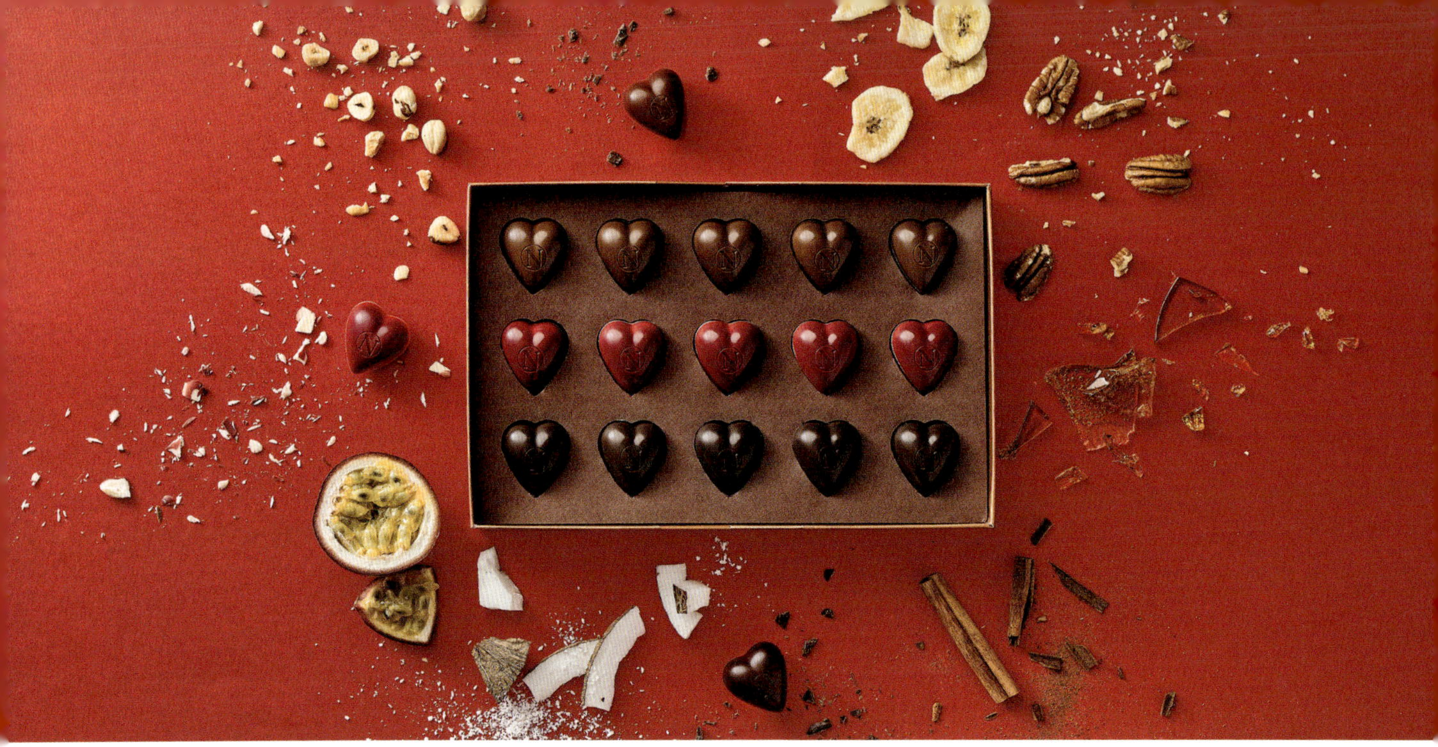

OPPOSITES ATTRACT: THE MAGNETIC ALLURE OF YOUTHFUL TALENT

Always ready to break new ground, Neuhaus has teamed up with Belgian Michelin-starred chef Mallory Gabsi to reinvent Valentine's Day in a daringly gourmet manner. They have co-designed a limited edition collection, Opposites Attract, which celebrates the concept that contrasts attract and balance each other. This irresistible principle could not fail to appeal to Neuhaus, a brand with a rich history of embracing complementarity. After all, Caprice, the long-standing Neuhaus signature creation, combines the crunch of an intense dark chocolate shell with the creamy softness of a vanilla buttercream.

Mallory Gabsi, who sees Neuhaus as a kind of Proust madeleine, says: 'There were always Manon pralines at my grandmother's. She would hide them so we didn't gobble up her whole stash, but she would sneak us a little praline occasionally'. His intimate relationship with the Maître Chocolatier didn't stop there: 'At home, it was simple: it was always Neuhaus. And to us, that meant quality and special moments'.

The Opposites Attract collection, stemming from this special affinity, explores the workings of opposition: 'Contrasts are the secret to achieving real balance, whether for a recipe or in a couple. For me, it's crucial,' the chef divulges. Each praline tells a story through its complementary flavours and textures: a milk chocolate heart combines the liveliness of passion fruit with the sweetness of salted butter caramel spiced up with cinnamon. A white chocolate heart merges a hazelnut ganache with crunchy gianduja and coconut chips. Finally, the dark chocolate reveals a sensual black banana and pecan praline duo.

'My favourite item in this collection is the coconut praline. I'm a coconut fan, so as soon as we discussed this, it was a no-brainer', confides this star chef, to whom every detail of this collaboration matters. For instance, the box shaped like a love letter and the tiny decorated boxes that serve as extensions of the meticulously assembled alchemies of taste they enclose.

This alliance of tradition and innovation also celebrates love. The man, still in the early stages of his rise to gastronomic greatness, puts it poetically: 'In a box of pralines, there's always one you eat first and one you save for last. The same goes for love: save the best for last.'

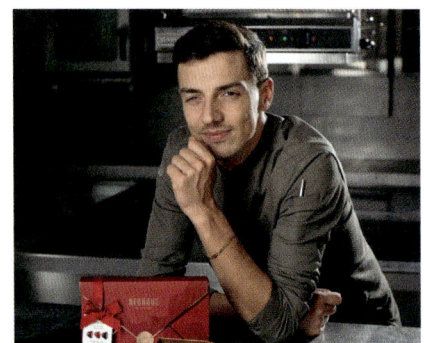

Mallory Gabsi in collaboration with Neuhaus for Valentine's Day 2025

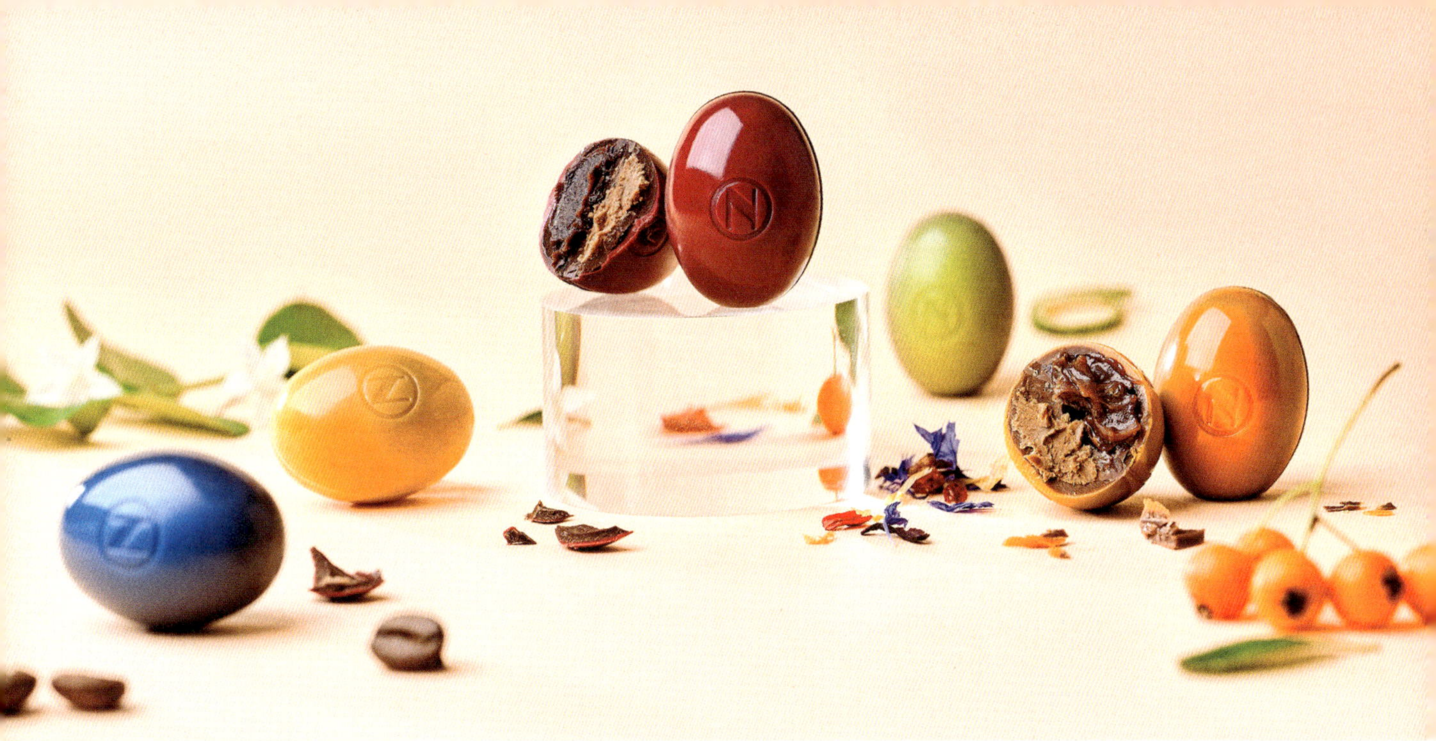

BOTANICALS: NATURE SPEAKS

For this limited Easter edition, Neuhaus has partnered with Gert De Mangeleer, the Belgian chef of the Hertog Jan restaurant. Inspired by the treasures of his botanical garden at the Botanic Sanctuary Antwerp hotel - an establishment with which Neuhaus shares a long history of collaborations - De Mangeleer has created original chocolate creations that blend the freshness of plants with the comforting roundness of Belgian chocolate.

This collection showcases five refined Easter eggs, vibrantly coloured to symbolise spring. Each egg offers a unique tasting experience, enhanced by bold aromatic combinations.

Thé Samba Canneberges forms a fruity alliance of ganache with cranberries, Samba tea, and gianduja with chia seeds. This dark chocolate egg captivates with its invigorating, slightly tangy notes.

Lovers of sweetness and light will appreciate the finesse and freshness of Thé Vert Jasmin. Its white chocolate shell reveals two ganaches: one infused with jasmine and green tea, sprinkled with cocoa nibs, and the other with mandarin, creating a perfect balance of floral sweetness and liveliness.

The bright green, glowing Yuzu Poivré combines milk chocolate with a zesty yuzu ganache and an almond praline, enhanced by Espelette chilli and Timut pepper. This creation stands out for its contrast of acidity and spice with the sweetness of chocolate.

Finally, Café Anis appeals to lovers of intense sensations. This dark chocolate praline features a ristretto ganache enriched with passion fruit, aniseed, and ginger gianduja. Its subtle blend of roasted aromas and spicy notes offers an energising, refined experience.

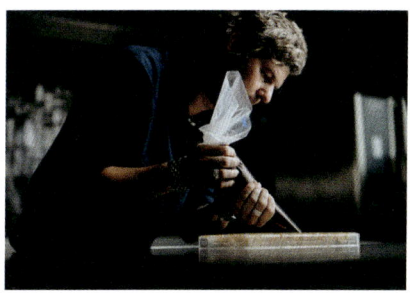

Gert De Mangeleer in collaboration with Neuhaus for the 2023 spring limited edition

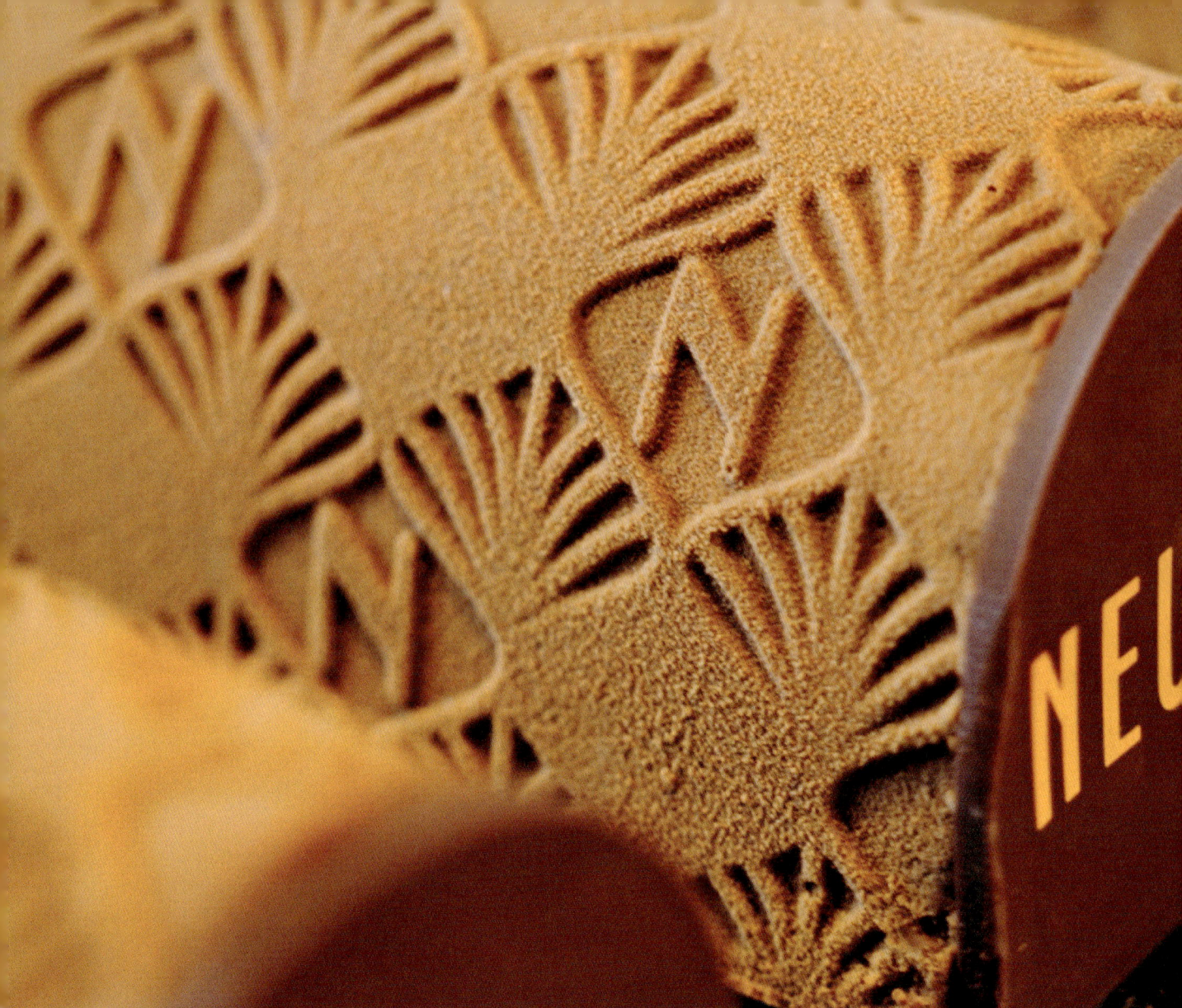

THE YULE LOG: JINGLE BELLGIAN

To add sparkle to the 2024 festive season, Neuhaus has collaborated with the two-star Belgian chef Yves Mattagne (La Villa Lorraine, Brussels) to redesign the traditional Yule log. The result is a dessert that is both classic and innovative, crafted to amaze even the most discerning palates.

This exceptional log brilliantly blends exotic flavours and refined textures. Its crunchy shell, made from finely ground buckwheat praline and Maison Dandoy chocolate biscuits, encases a generous multilayered heart. An intensely dark chocolate mousse (80% cocoa), combined with delicately flavoured passion fruit buttercream, sits atop an almond sponge cake soaked in pineapple coulis, all resting on a dark chocolate base for a perfect balance of lightness and intensity.

Thanks to its daring combinations, this creation offers gustatory pleasures that transport the dinner guests to far-flung destinations. Yves Mattagne, renowned for his meticulous approach to flavours, has crafted a refined, whimsical interpretation of an emblematic end-of-year dessert here. Or how to transform a tradition into an unforgettable experience.

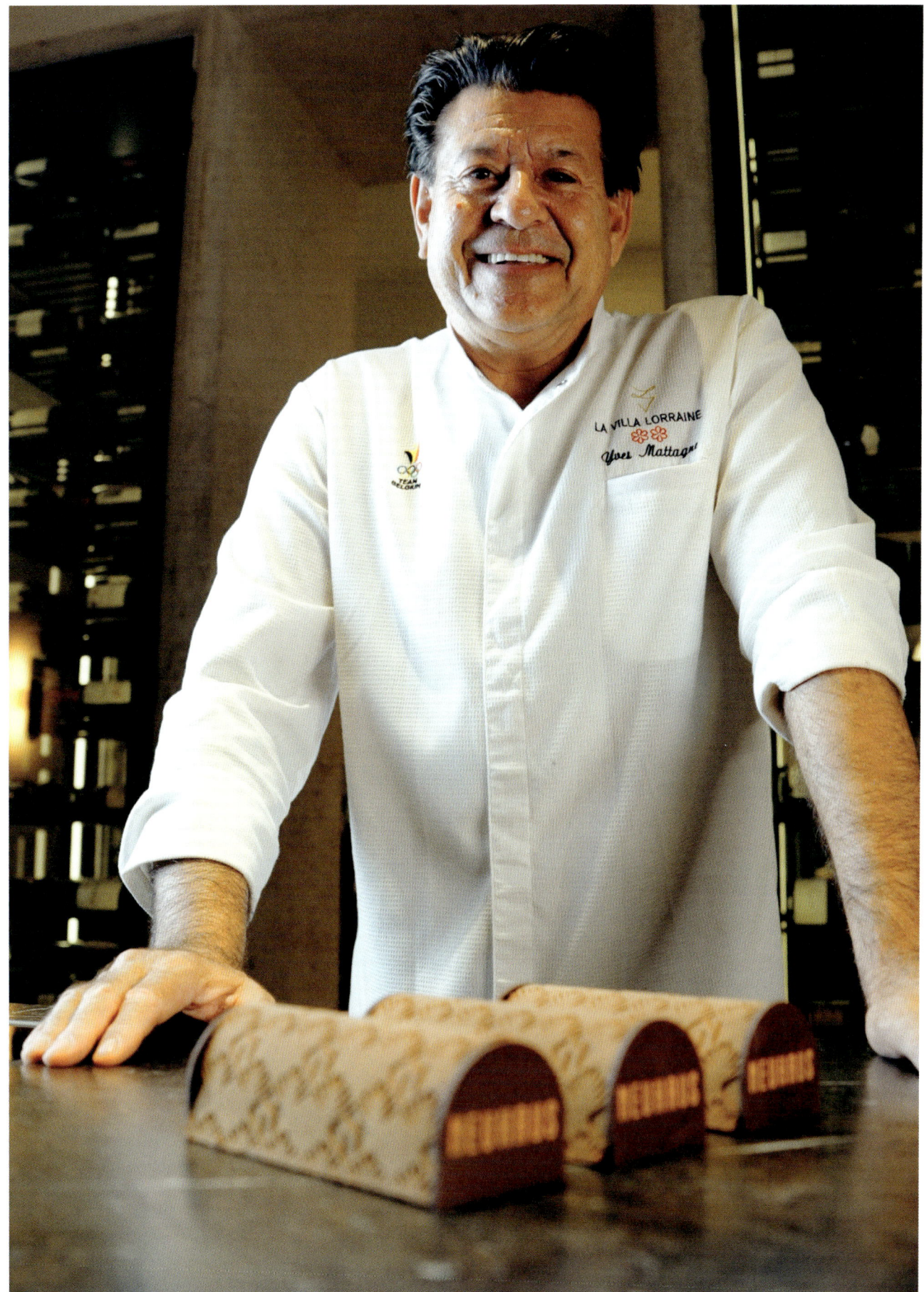

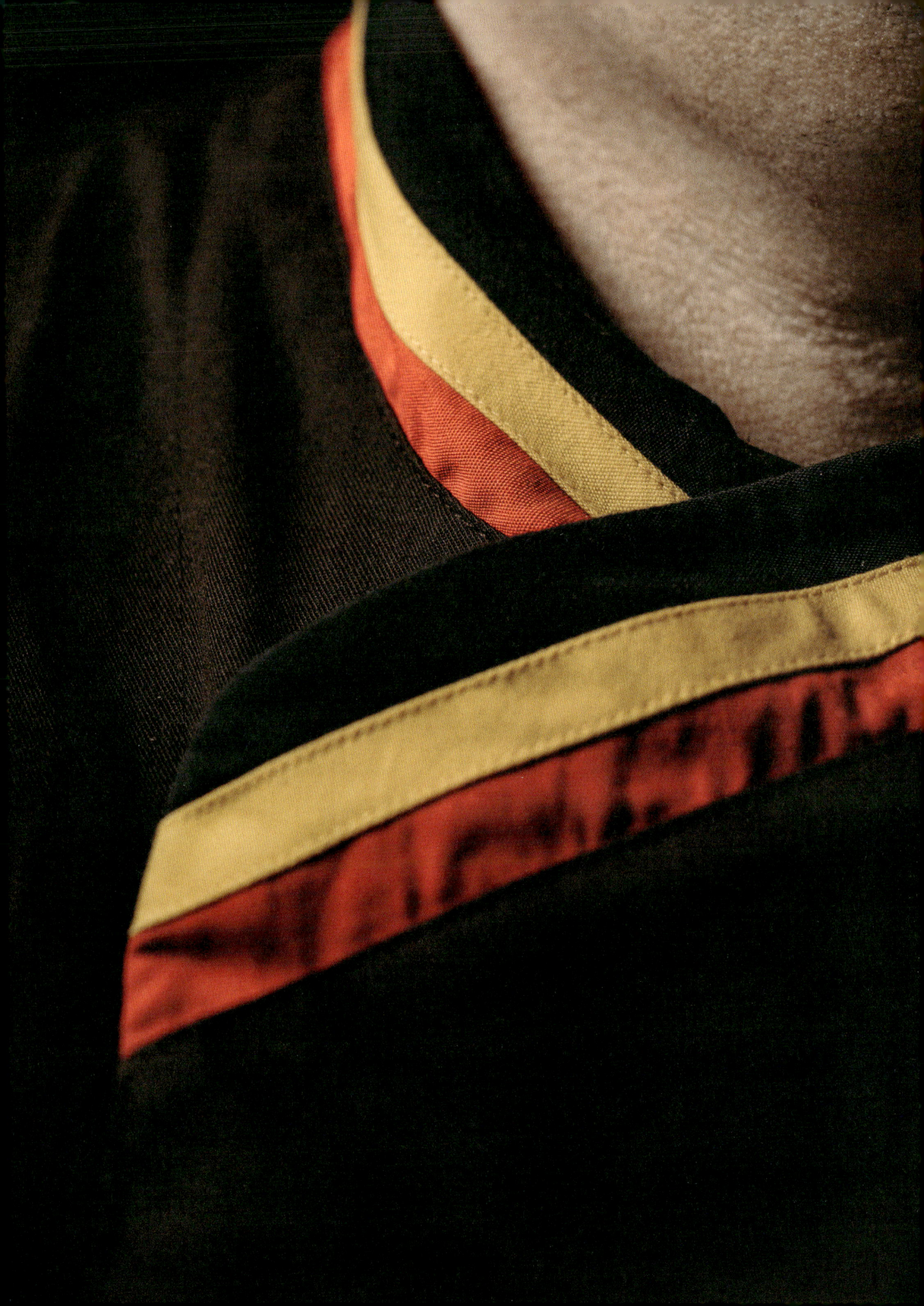

ARTISANS AND FANS

Chocolate is a living material that doesn't like to be fixed in place. It requires precision in every movement, careful listening, and adaptability. At Neuhaus, this subtle know-how is passed down from craftsman to craftsman through observation, example, and experience. We embrace this heritage to develop it further; some preserve it, some innovate, while others add a personal touch. A shared commitment unites us: never to betray the substance but to serve it to its fullest potential.

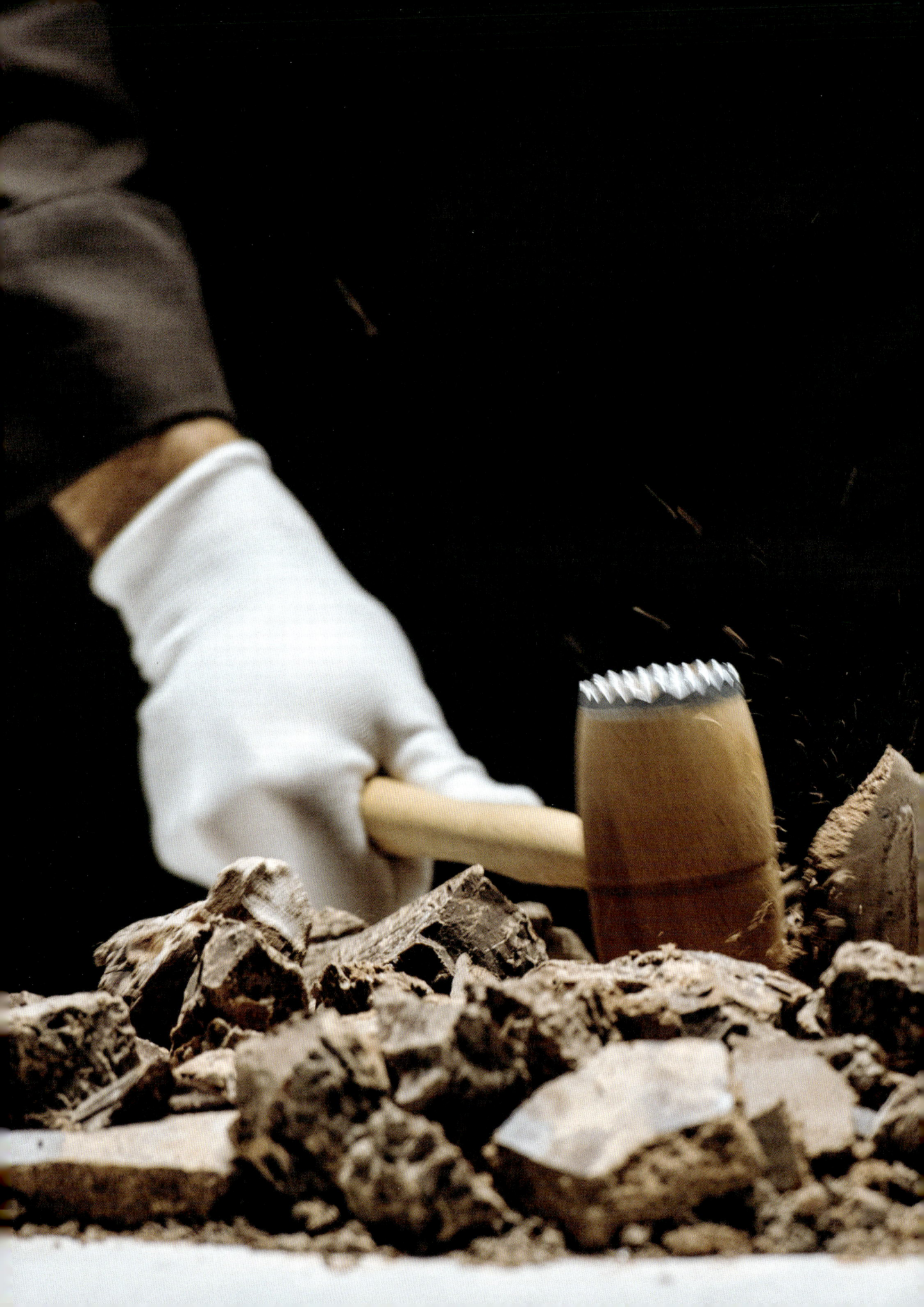

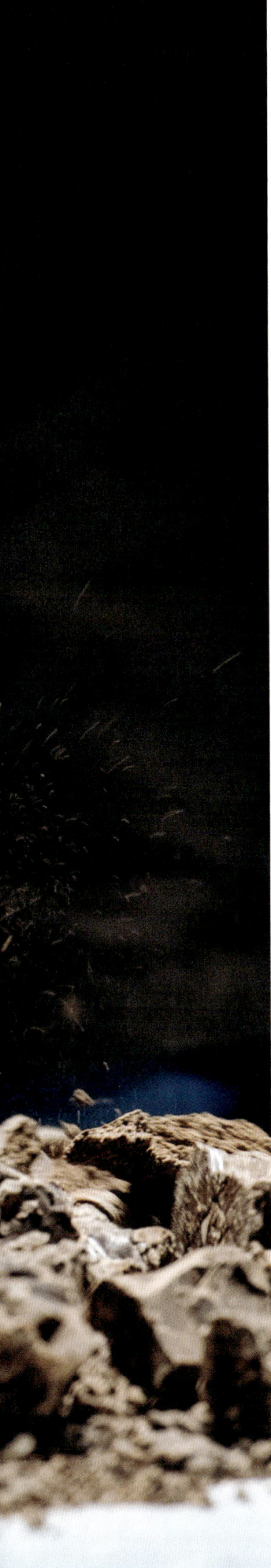

THE INTELLIGENCE OF THE HAND

The praline results from this intimate relationship with the material: an accomplished, concentrated, and almost idealised form of chocolate. It serves as chocolate's double, its refined mirror, an enhanced version. This condensed expression comes to life in the flavours and aromas, as well as in the gesture - the meticulous, repetitive act of transforming a noble raw material into a moment of enjoyment. Without this firm intentionality, the savoir-faire would be mere technical knowledge, a series of mechanical, soulless instructions. With it, expertise becomes true mastery, where instinct mingles with will and movement with idea.

This gesture, repeated a thousand times, becomes second nature. It becomes anchored in the body like a reflex, a knowledge refined through experience. There's nothing cerebral about it. It is almost autonomous, like breathing or a heartbeat. It is sometimes called the 'intelligence of the hand', but it is much more than intelligence: it is an intimate dialogue between the craftsman and the material. It is a conversation born of observation, feeling, and attentively listening to the textures under the fingers, the aromas escaping from the ingredients, and the almost imperceptible sound of ganache smoothly dissolving or chocolate crackling.

At Neuhaus, this concrete intelligence is evident in every movement, every cut, and every coating. For over twenty-eight years, it has flourished under the guidance of a master chocolatier like Olivier Demol. At 55 years old, this guardian of flavours embodies both the rigour of gesture and the intuition of taste. 'My passion for chocolate originated in my grandmother's kitchen', confides Olivier. In that modest room where her generous cuisine simmered, he discovered the importance of local ingredients and the demands of a job well done. He continues, today, to pursue two pillars of a sensitive approach with the same fervour. From those early days, he remembers the Koetjesreep, a humble chocolate bar from the Netherlands, which inspired his first mousse. This childhood memory, a blend of tenderness and greed, set him on the path to a demanding craft.

He began his career in bakeries, pastry shops, and ice cream parlours. These apprenticeships provided him with a solid technical foundation. However, his thirst for knowledge and perfection compelled him to train with the best: Lenôtre in Paris and Bajard in Perpignan. 'You can't simply improvise the title of master chocolatier; you must earn it. It is proven over time, over decades, through patient precision and relentless curiosity',

Olivier recalls with emotion the presentation of a Neuhaus dessert in Tokyo, alongside that year's 'Meilleur Ouvrier de France', and his participation in major world exhibitions—so many milestones, and each one an opportunity to showcase Belgian chocolate to the world. Yet, beyond these prestigious moments, an intimate creation best captures his commitment: the Irrésistibles, a collection of fine chocolates celebrating nougatine and lightness. 'This creation, brought to life using the finest raw materials from around the globe, is my signature achievement at Neuhaus',

His quest for perfection is also reflected in bolder collections. Among these, the vegan line occupies a unique position. Crafted to the same rigorous standards as the classic ranges, it showcases the company's ability to evolve without compromising its essence. The pralinés made from hazelnuts and almonds exude pure aromas while preserving taste and texture perfectly. 'It wasn't just about modifying an existing recipe by eliminating all animal ingredients. We aimed to achieve a new concept that features a distinct balance, textures, and flavour identity in its own right. This requires a degree of simplicity, indeed, but it is designed to enhance the purity of the flavours', shares Olivier.

It is important to emphasise the 'we' aspect because, at Neuhaus, creativity is not a solitary pursuit. It results from a collective effort where engineers, marketers, and buyers all contribute to perfecting a balance. Creating a product involves consultation just as much as conviction. Olivier will always ensure that each praline conveys a story true to the Neuhaus DNA—not a frozen past but a living, evolving heritage.

This appetite for co-creation aligns closely with a deep desire to share knowledge. Olivier envisions establishing a Neuhaus Academy, as he firmly believes in the importance of passing on excellence. 'Expertise is gained through experience. Transmitting it requires patience, adaptation, and attentive listening',

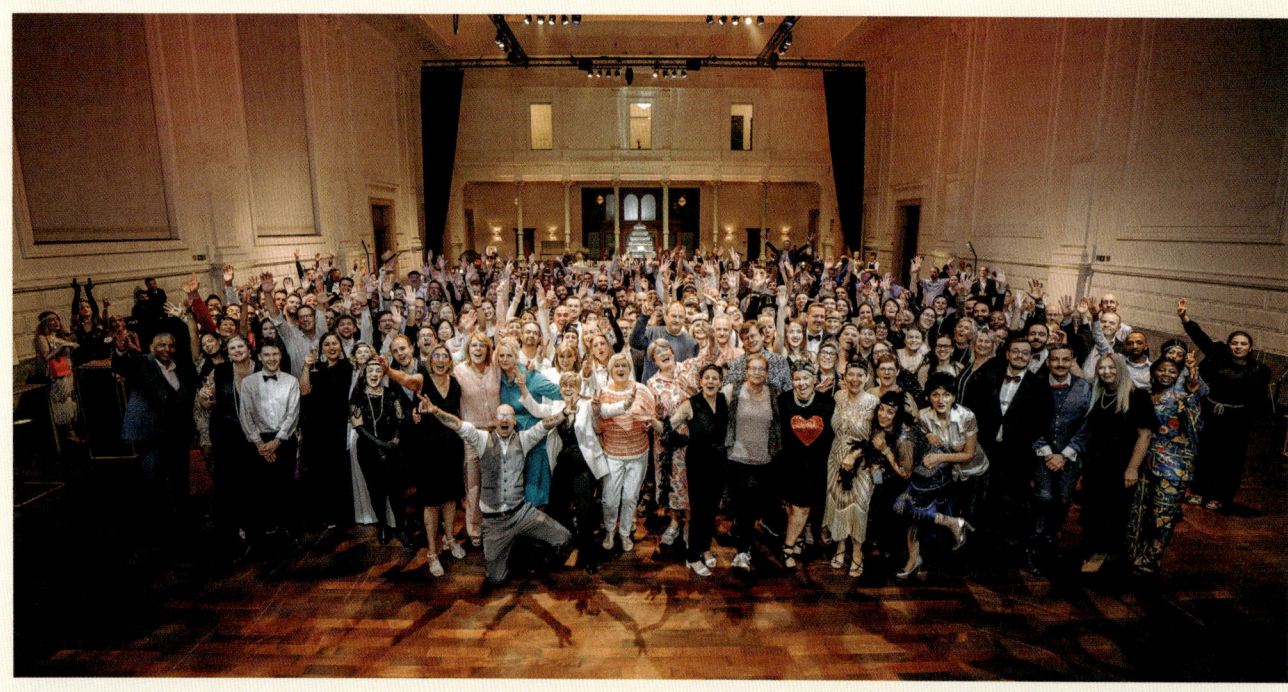

The Belgian Neuhaus team at the staff party in 2024

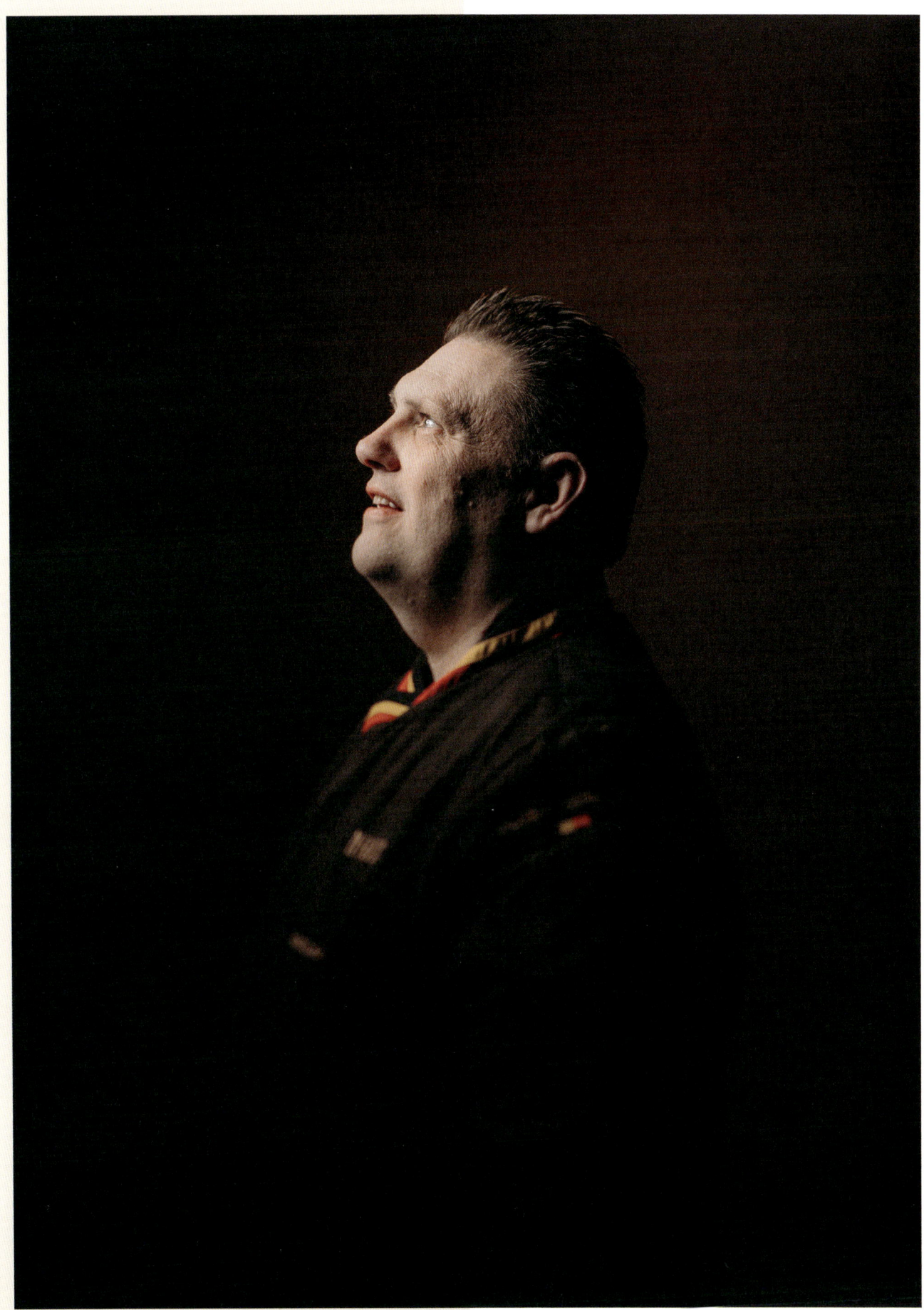

Olivier Demol, Maître Chocolatier

TRANSMISSION, THE LINKS IN A CHAIN

Olivier Demol is convinced of this, but he's not the only one in the workshop: the belief that expertise is valuable only when passed on is ingrained in Neuhaus's DNA. The Maîtres Chocolatiers share their knowledge through words, hands, dedication and passion. 'Passing on' does not imply duplication; it entails translating knowledge into another hand, another sensibility. What matters is not mere repetition but the ability to make what has been learnt resonate, bringing it to life in another body, another story.

This vision achieves its full significance through the career of Éric Lauwers, the brand's ambassador since 2018. Although his entrance into the world of chocolate was not obvious, it quickly transformed into a vocation. 'Working with cocoa presents so many fascinating challenges that I chose to make it my profession', he says. His first enduring memory? A chocolate figurine he received at seven has remained etched forever in his gustatory memory.

After completing his education at the PIVA catering school in Antwerp, he and his wife opened a shop before he decided to join Neuhaus. In the workshop of The Loft, located in the Brussels Airlines Business Lounge at Zaventem Airport, truly a window on the world, he shares his expertise with travellers from around the globe. His teaching style is impressive: 'Chocolate is alive; it demands total dedication', During his international demonstrations, the talented teacher evokes the precision required to temper chocolate to 31.5°C, the patience necessary at each stage, and the constraints such as humidity or temperature fluctuations.

He never ceases to demonstrate his commitment to transmitting knowledge and has trained several recruits poised to emerge as the next generation. 'Some of them continue to call me 'master', he says with a smile. In Vlezenbeek, he has introduced young souls to all the nuances of the trade, as he is convinced that training should be based on example and passion. Paraphrasing the commonly used description of Hendrik Conscience, the writer credited with 'teaching the Dutch-speaking Belgians to read', he adds: 'I teach them to taste chocolate!'

His career has been marked by many memorable moments. He particularly remembers the day when he was giving a presentation in a shop and suddenly noticed that a Cuban guitarist on the street had stopped in front of the shop window to scrutinise a music score that had been carefully engraved on a chocolate bar. Intrigued, the guitarist took out his guitar, tuned it by ear, and played 'Douce Nuit' from the score in front of the astonished onlookers. Eric recounts this memory with undiminished emotion. It is a perfect illustration of the breadth of his profession.

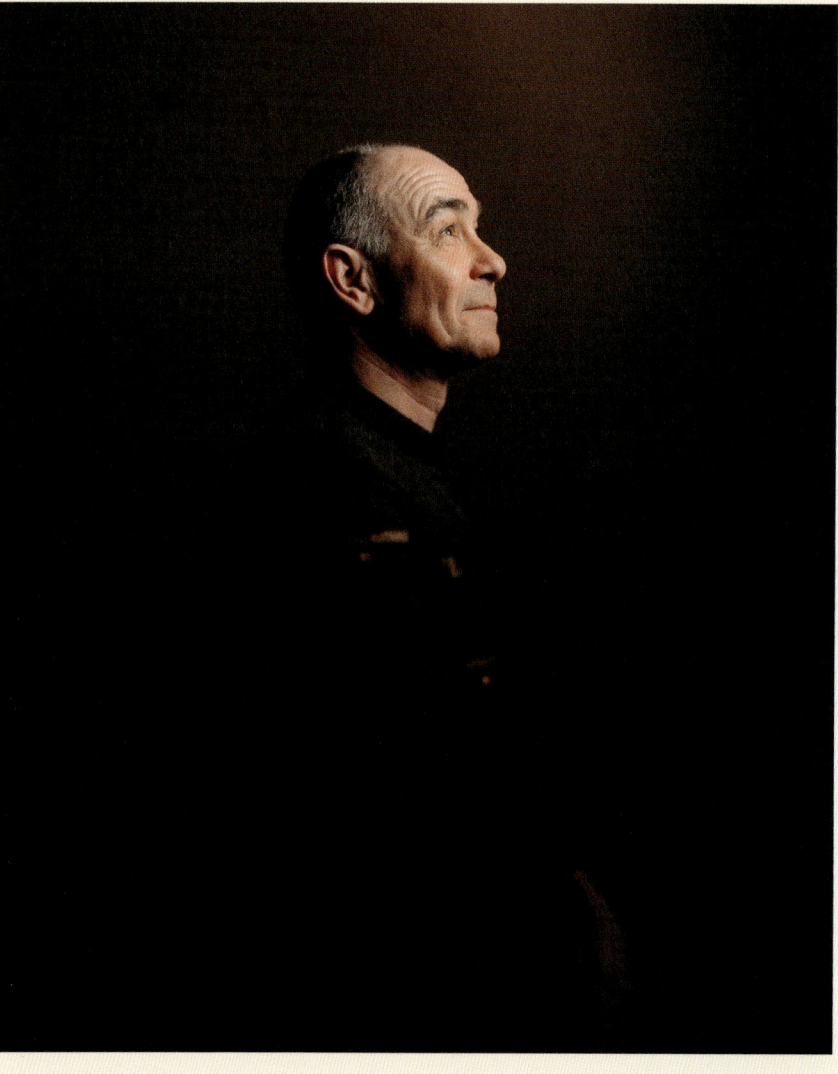

Éric Lauwers, Maître Chocolatier and brand ambassador

THE CREATIVE IMPULSE

Cocoa may have a long history, but also symbolises an ongoing call for innovation. Neuhaus cultivates this dynamic tension, much like Tom Vangal, who embodies this creative drive perfectly. Born in 1978 into a family of bakers, he has been surrounded by the aromas of fresh bread and melted chocolate since childhood. Working with beans became a form of expression, a personal language. Before joining Neuhaus, he honed his skills in the pastry industry for twelve years, developing a rigour and curiosity that are constantly renewed.

In his view, each praline reveals a story. 'Being a chocolatier is a state of mind', he states. Curiosity, precision, and a rejection of gratuitous exoticism characterise his approach, favouring straightforward flavours and a subtle balance. More specifically, Tom is involved in designing the vegan collection, where he experiments freely: without using dairy products, he must redouble his inventiveness to preserve texture and intensity. 'This has been one of my most rewarding challenges and has revealed new horizons regarding taste',

The creativity of this tireless worker goes hand in hand with a quest for emotion. He fondly recalls running workshops for the children of the royal family. 'What touched me was seeing their eyes light up, as I shared a taste for beauty and goodness with them',

His dream? To create a praline as iconic as Caprice. But ultimately, what matters to Tom is offering pleasure and wonder. He thoroughly understands the value of 'those enchanted little interludes that make life sweeter'.

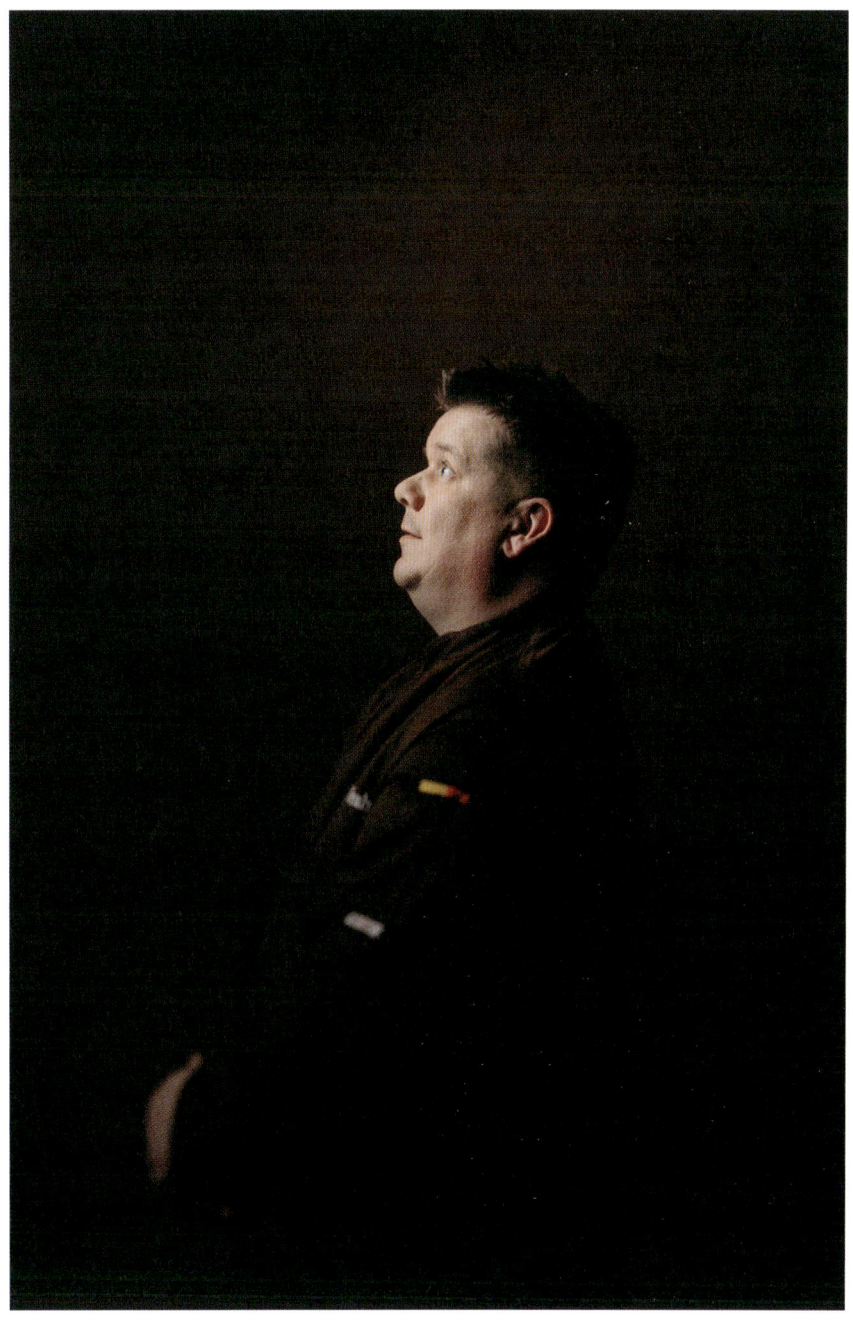

Tom Vangal, Maître Chocolatier

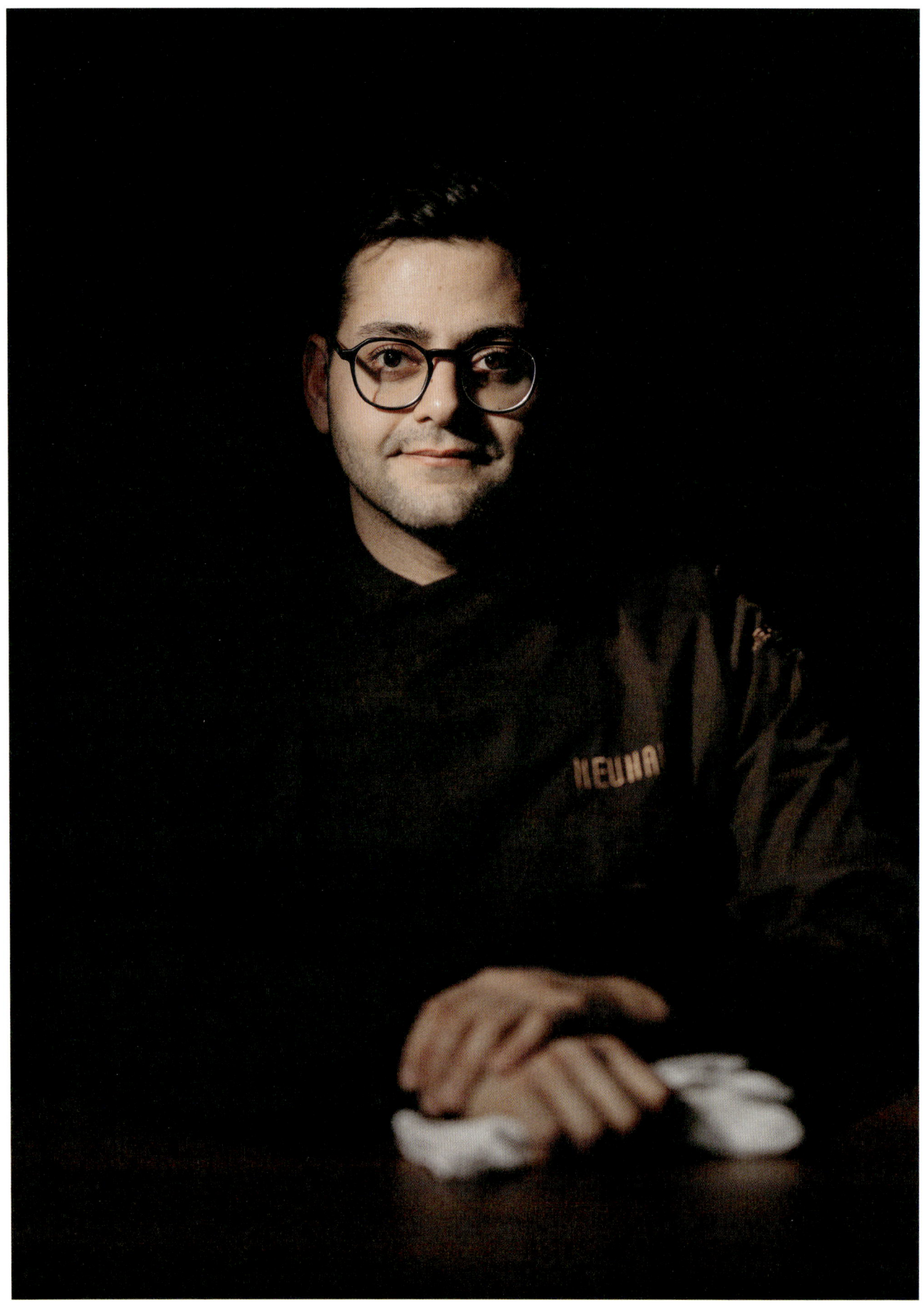

Alim Jetha, Maître Chocolatier

PERSONAL EXPRESSION

While some artisans cherish passing on their craft, others enjoy expressing a more intimate note, a singular sensitivity. This holds true for Alim Jetha, a talented artist who has transformed chocolate sculpture into a medium for personal expression, and of Koen Rombauts, who works alongside him.

Born in 1990 in the Democratic Republic of Congo and of Indian descent, Alim grew up at the intersection of spices and cultures. He moved to Belgium at 17, initially pursuing accountancy before, against the odds, shifting to chocolate making. His first epiphany came from Frédéric Blondeel in Brussels, where he uncovered the expressive potential of the bean and the importance of gesture.

At Neuhaus, where he joined in 2016, this passionate creator cultivates a distinctly sculptural approach to chocolate. The material vibrates under his nimble fingers. He designs monumental pieces - for instance, a 40-kilo boar made for the Durbuy boutique - and masters every stage, from moulding to packaging and transport. 'Sometimes I feel more like an engineer than a chocolatier,' he smiles.

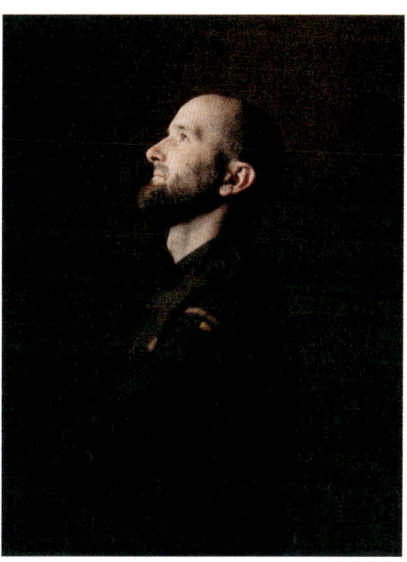

Koen Rombauts, Maître Chocolatier

The creations of Alim and Koen, completely edible, demonstrate a profound respect for the product. Alim emphasises the absence of artifice and the importance of preserving the purity of taste. His approach is almost architectural: patience, anticipation, and attentive listening.

However, emotion is the primary factor that guides his work. He recalls seeing a child captivated by a chocolate Saint-Nicolas in a shop window when he was tired after a lengthy workday and how this reignited his passion for the profession. 'That boy's smile made my day. Never mind how tired I was: in an instant, I was reconnected with the magic of creation'.

Alim dreams of opening his own chocolate factory, possibly in Africa. Meanwhile, he continues to learn, experiment, and share his knowledge in his unique way. His chocolate reflects him: humble, generous, and full of life.

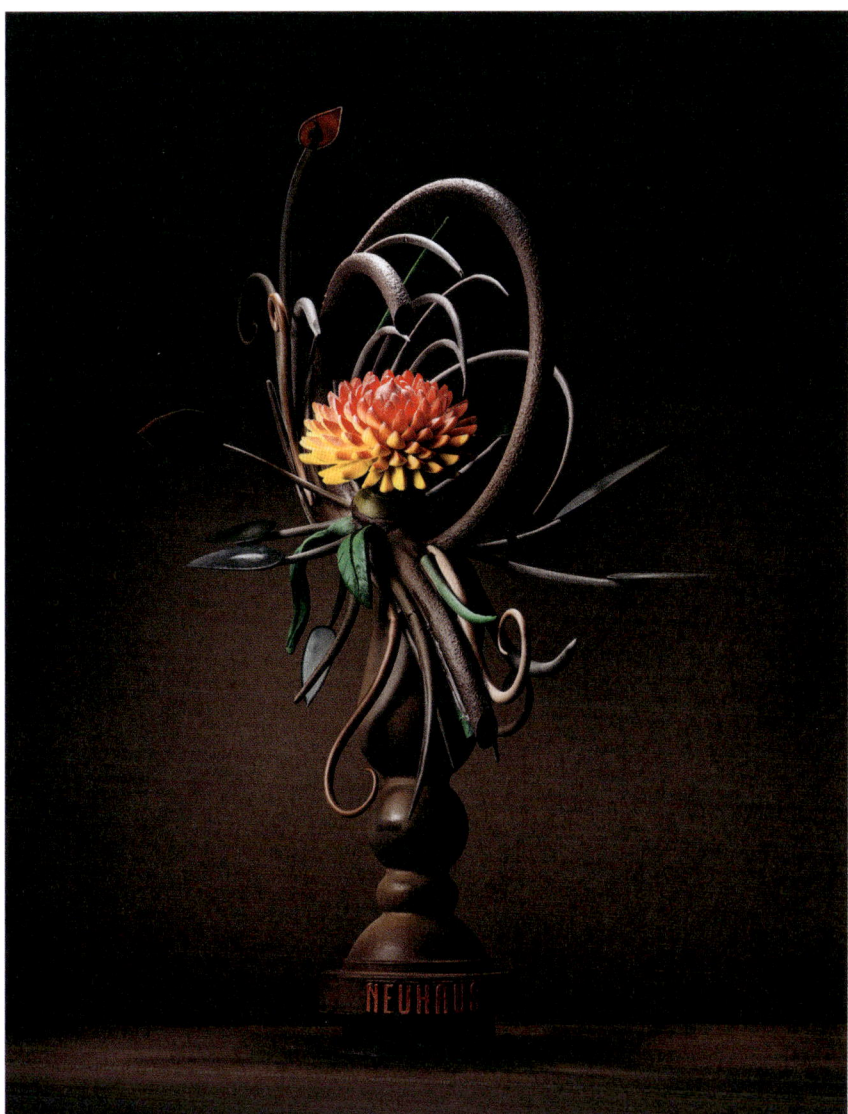

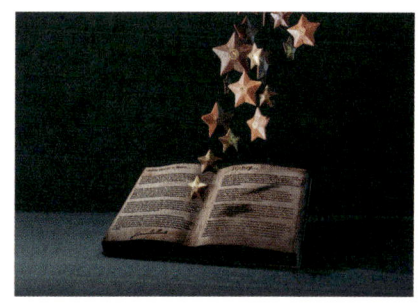

Chocolate sculpture made by Alim Jetha during training with Stéphane Leroux, Meilleur Ouvrier de France

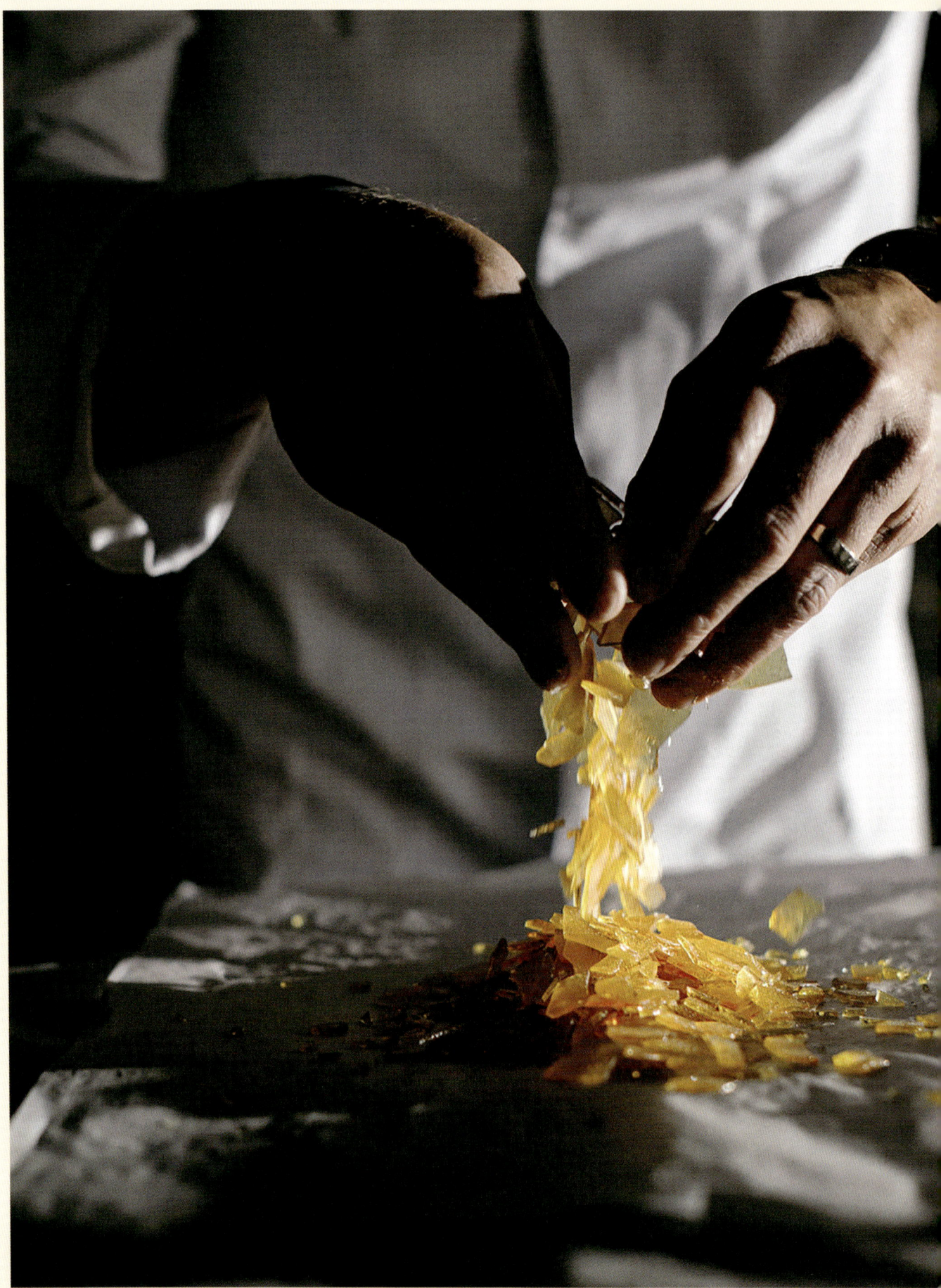

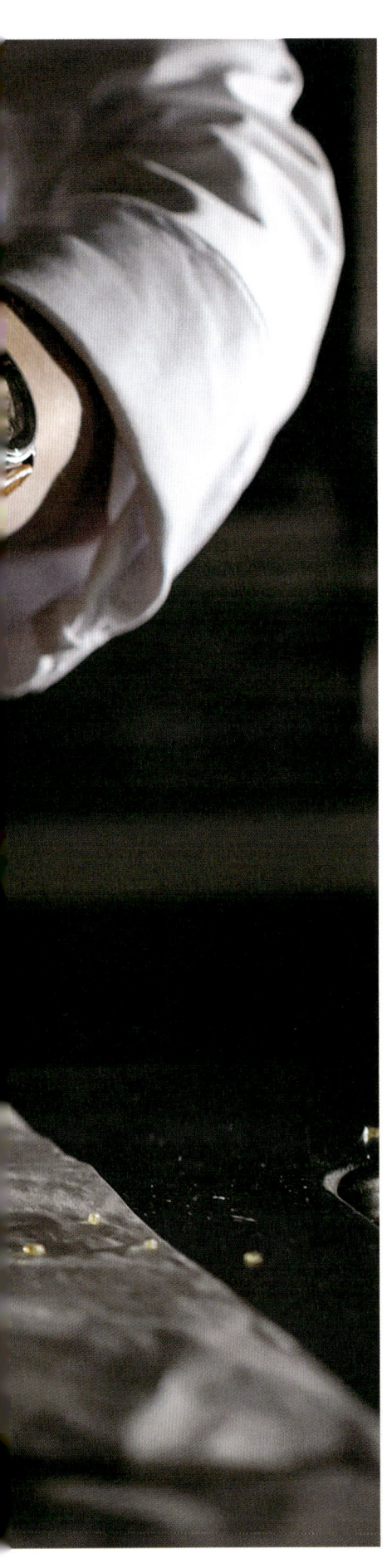

THE FANS AND THE MEMORY OF THE HEART

Some flavours are unforgettable. One bite, and it all comes rushing back: a childhood afternoon, a familiar voice, a parent's smile. Much like in the works of Marcel Proust, chocolate carries an emotional charge and possesses the power to awaken what lies dormant within us. It is no coincidence that chefs and designers feel a connection with Neuhaus with an almost intimate loyalty. They don't just create new pralines; they tell a story- one of their own. Each collaboration is a dialogue between expertise and personal memory, a technical gesture and a reminiscence. Through these ambassadors, the brand forges a bond that transcends simple indulgence. These are shared emotions, contemporary chocolate madeleines in which the pleasure of taste intertwines with the joy of memory.

PETER GOOSSENS
CHEF

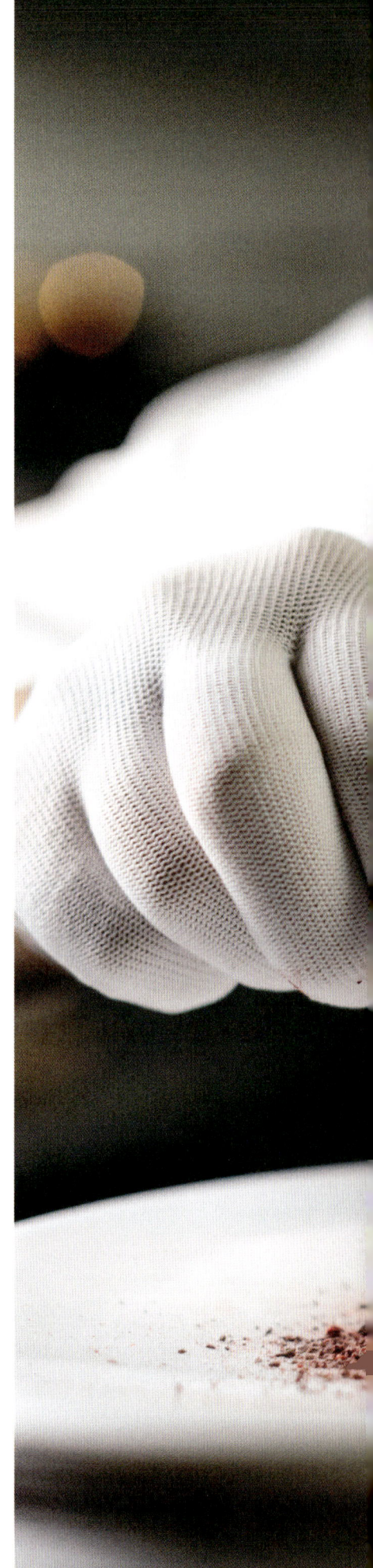

After elevating his restaurant, Hof van Cleve in Kruisem, to the pinnacle of Belgian gastronomy and leading La Rigue in Knokke, Peter Goossens now ranks among the international gastronomic elite. As a key figure in the culinary landscape, he has established a demanding and refined vision. His departure from La Rigue signifies the end of a cycle, but not a decline in influence: at 60, he remains a respected chef whose impact on Belgian haute cuisine is indelible. His career will continue to shape the country's gastronomic excellence.

This highly skilled chef has successfully applied his exacting standards and sense of balance to his collaboration with Neuhaus. He has crafted a subtle truffle in which creamy pecan praline merges with caramelised pecan chips, enhanced by a hint of Guérande salt. The combination is enveloped in a dark chocolate coating, accented by a delicate touch of raspberry.

Peter Goossens remembers his first encounter with the century-old brand: a praline from the Irrésistible range. Thinking back to its crunchy interior and unique mouthfeel makes his mouth water. 'You could say it's a family tradition. The children know that we always buy the same one on certain occasions. At home, we're really into them. This praline contains nougatine, and the sensation is incredible when you take a bite'.

The master has explored this fascination by collaborating with Neuhaus Maîtres Chocolatiers. 'Neuhaus only uses top-quality chocolate and never incorporates any fats other than cacao butter; it truly delivers the pure taste of cacao. I have always made it a priority to respect the original flavours of the raw materials. To me, that is crucial. It is vital to preserve the chocolate flavour in a praline. A praline consists of a chocolate coating and a gourmet heart, so it is essential to express both elements fully'.

For his Neuhaus truffle, Peter Goossens aimed to rediscover this perfect alchemy. 'I have a particular fondness for praliné and, in my opinion, caramelised walnuts combined with chocolate are still the best choice. But I wanted to add a touch of freshness, so the acidity of the raspberry lightens and refreshes the praline'. This creation also reflects his culinary philosophy: 'I attach great importance to proven values, pure and delicious flavours that must be adapted to today's culture. Tastes are changing; we don't eat like we did 50 years ago. Today, we eat lighter, fresher, and more elegantly'.

The truffle reinvented by Peter Goossens for the Les Trésors collection

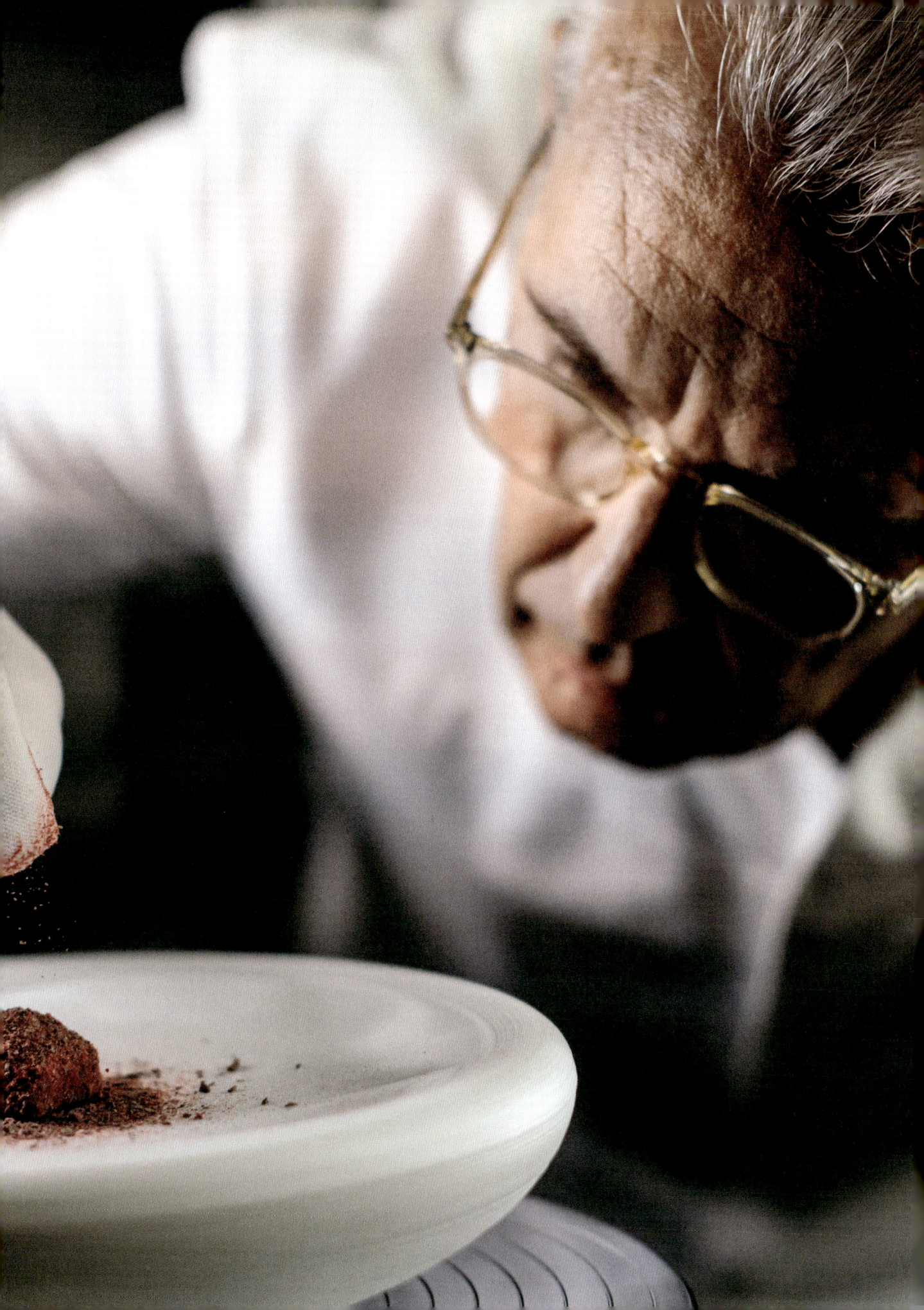

He can already see himself devising other combinations for a new version: 'I would add a vanilla cream, a fruity touch and finely chopped caramelised walnuts to add crunch. The texture in the mouth is important'. Peter Goossens also pays attention to the shapes of the chocolate. The pralines in the Irrésistible range, for instance, have a family resemblance to Napoleon's hat. It's a stroke of genius: 'There is both a reassuring symmetry and a boldness in the volume. It evokes something noble, stable, almost martial... but it remains fine, elegant, never rigid. This contrast touches me.'

When defining Neuhaus, three words come to mind: 'Quality, elegance, flavour'. If he were to give someone a box of pralines as a present, his wife would be the first person he would think of: 'Because she's crazy about them!' What about the future? He encourages Neuhaus to pursue its quest for excellence while exploring new avenues he spontaneously suggests: 'Why not follow the trend for smaller pralines? That would make it possible to enjoy more of them... Also: I'd like to create combinations of ganaches based on green teas or Earl Grey, with a fine chocolate coating... There is no shortage of possibilities.'

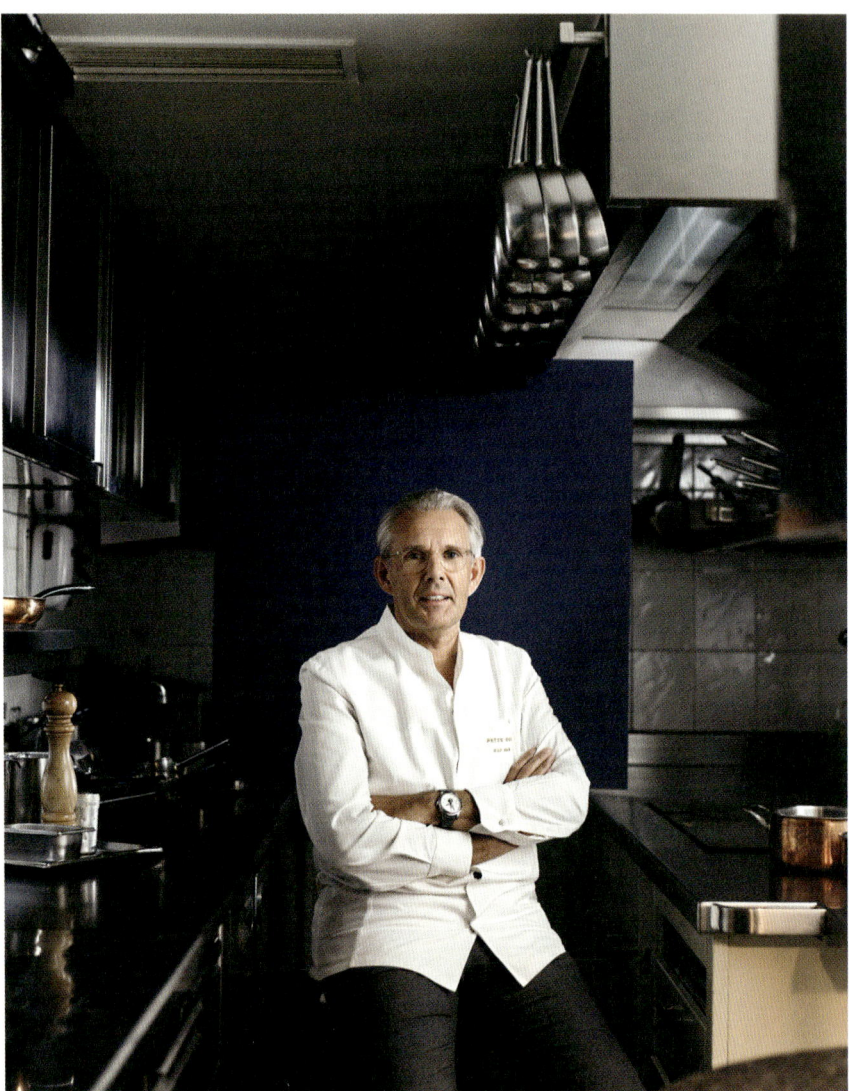

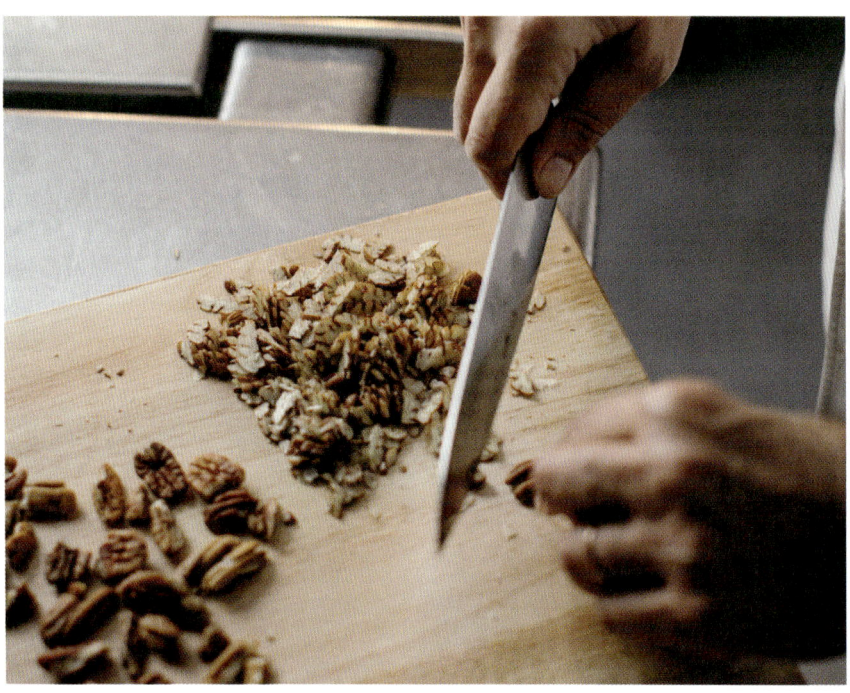

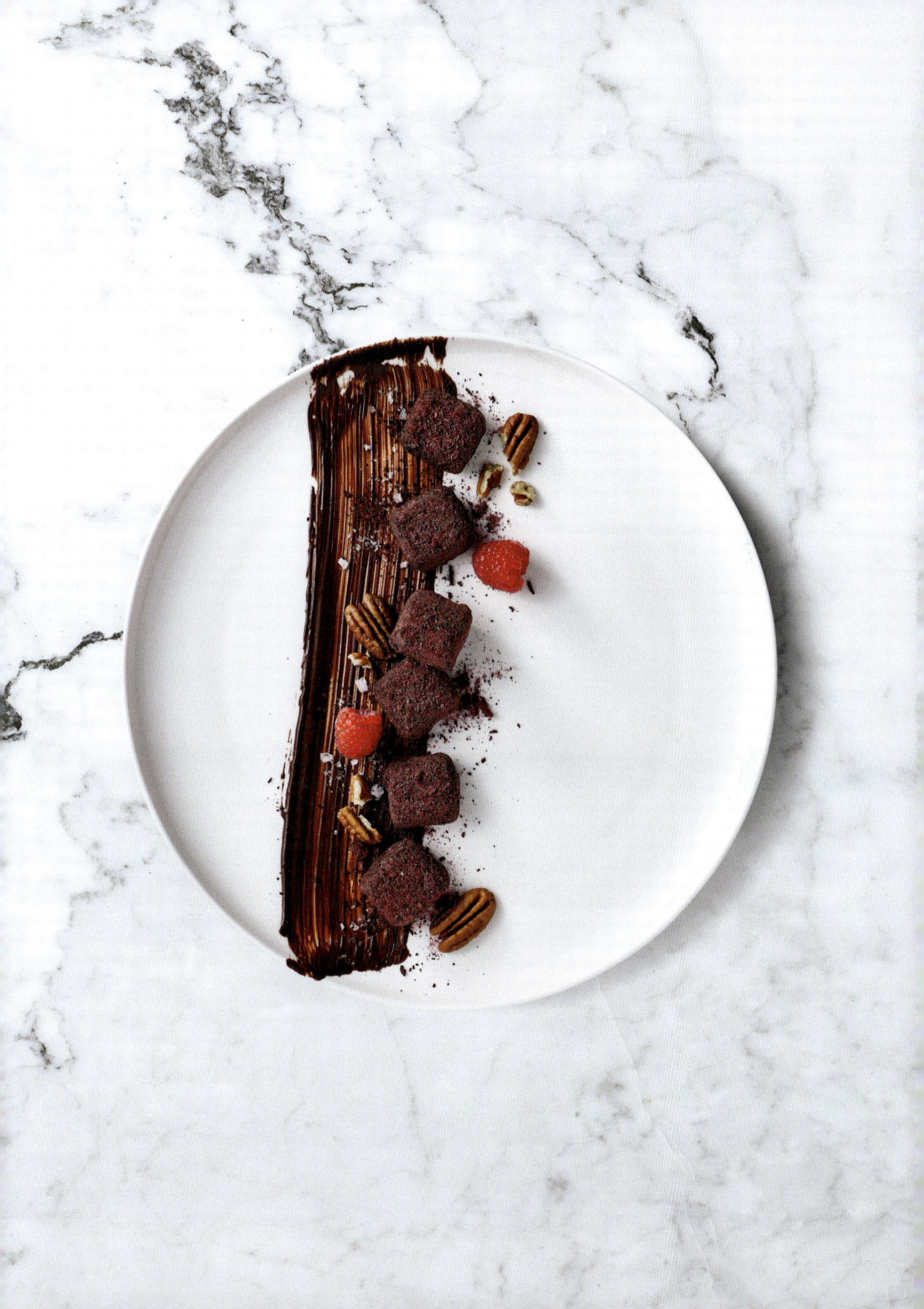

FABIENNE DELVIGNE
FASHION DESIGNER

Fabienne Delvigne embodies the excellence of Belgian craftsmanship. As a renowned milliner and licensed supplier to the Belgian Court since 2001, she creates elegant pieces for crowned heads and connoisseurs of refinement. Her world, characterised by meticulous attention to detail and a pursuit of timeless beauty, naturally resonates with that of Neuhaus, the emblem of exceptional Belgian chocolate.

Neuhaus is an indelible childhood memory for her: 'Neuhaus pralines were the Holy Grail for us. Knowing we had a sweet tooth, our grandmother would show us a few before putting the box away in a hidden spot. Of course, we always managed to find her hiding place and sneak out a couple of extra chocolates to nibble on... but then we had to retie the ribbon around the box into a bow - that was the challenging part'!

Her relationship with Neuhaus deepened over time, culminating in a landmark collaboration. She discovered the Neuhaus stand next to hers in 2001 at the Prestige et Élégance trade show. 'The head chocolatier, noticing my love for his pralines, would regularly come and offer me some on his tray. It was impossible to resist!' This shared sweet tooth inspired an audacious project: creating chocolate hats. 'The idea was to make chocolate hats, but the challenge was immense. We had to strengthen the base and adapt the structure to prevent it from breaking under the catwalk lights'.

Elegance is a common thread between Fabienne Delvigne's creations and the Maître Chocolatier's pralines. 'The Neuhaus shops are lovely, and the packaging is refined. This attention to detail makes all the difference and aligns with my approach'. If the elegant milliner could envision a new praline, she would propose a version of the Caprice in 80% dark chocolate. 'For lovers of intense chocolate, it would be a pure marvel'.

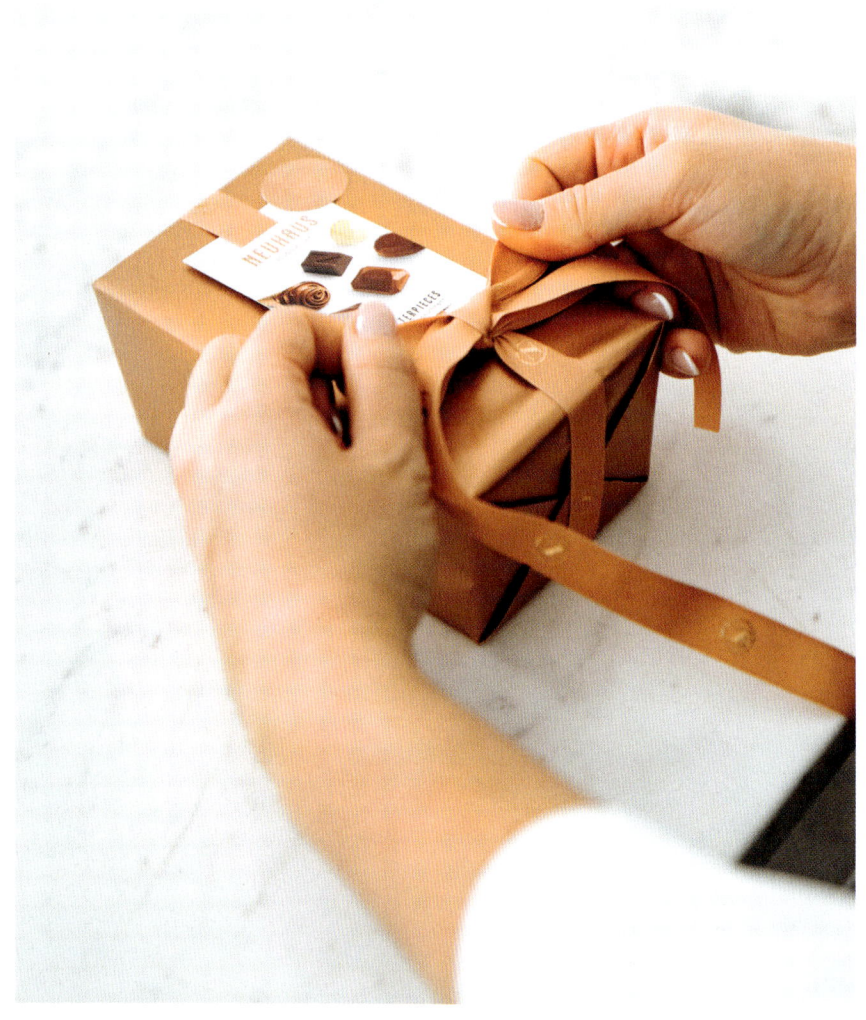

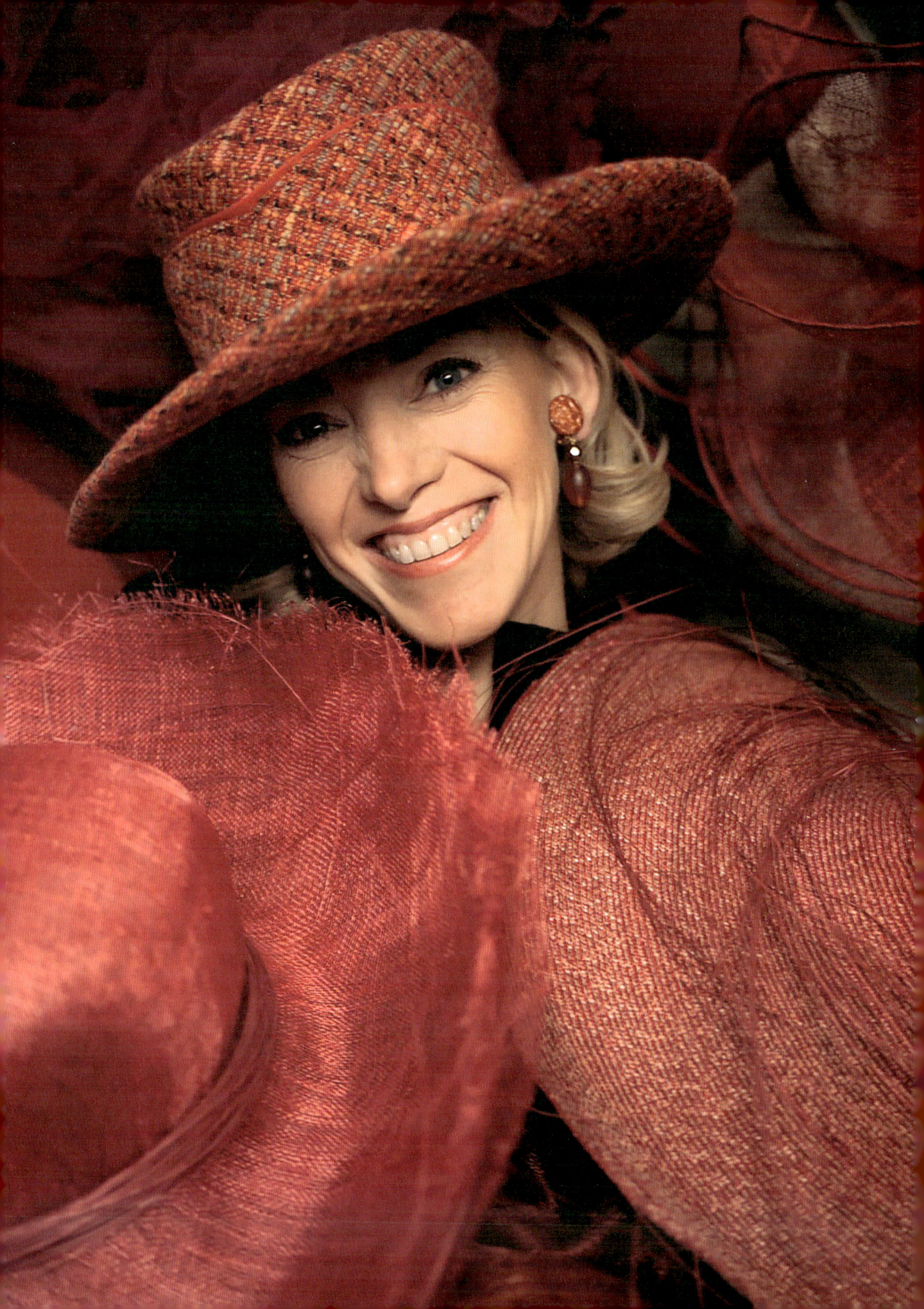

EDOUARD VERMEULEN
FASHION DESIGNER

Édouard Vermeulen has never viewed elegance as a flamboyant display. At the helm of Natan for over forty years, he has consistently embodied a vision of luxury that combines sobriety with exacting standards. Often referred to as 'the couturier to queens', he values a passionate relationship with his profession, where creativity can only be fully realised through a certain serenity. 'Without this inner peace, I can't be creative', he frequently confides, emphasising his deep-rooted need for harmony to sustain his all-consuming inspiration.

This search for harmony extends beyond fashion. It is rooted in an imagination shaped by childhood memories in which taste and transmission play crucial roles. 'My grandparents always had a box of Neuhaus pralines on the table, perpetuating the ritual of enjoying a nice cup of coffee and a praline to conclude a meal. Among these treats, the Caprices held a special place, with their exact combinations of dark chocolate, nougatine, and Madagascan vanilla... For me, a Caprice is a true dessert, a miniature work of art'.

When he had the chance in 2018 to collaborate with the renowned chocolate house on a box containing seventeen Irrésistibles, the couturier aimed to design a box that showcased his expertise. 'I wanted a box of absolute elegance, very pure and simple, in black and white, making it both an object of desire and a gift', he confides. This luxury approach, where the essential takes precedence over ornament, reflects a philosophy he shares with Neuhaus.

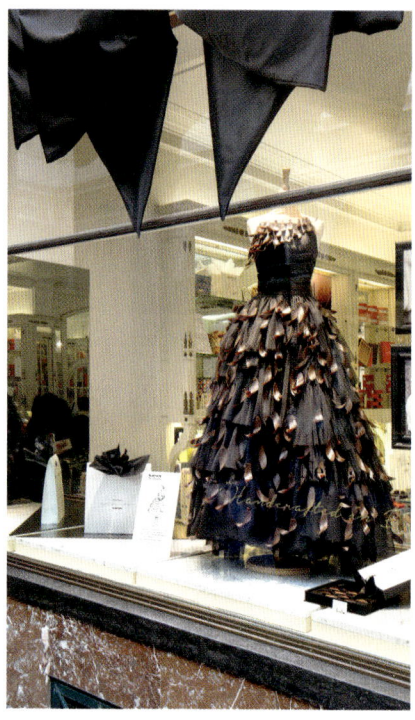

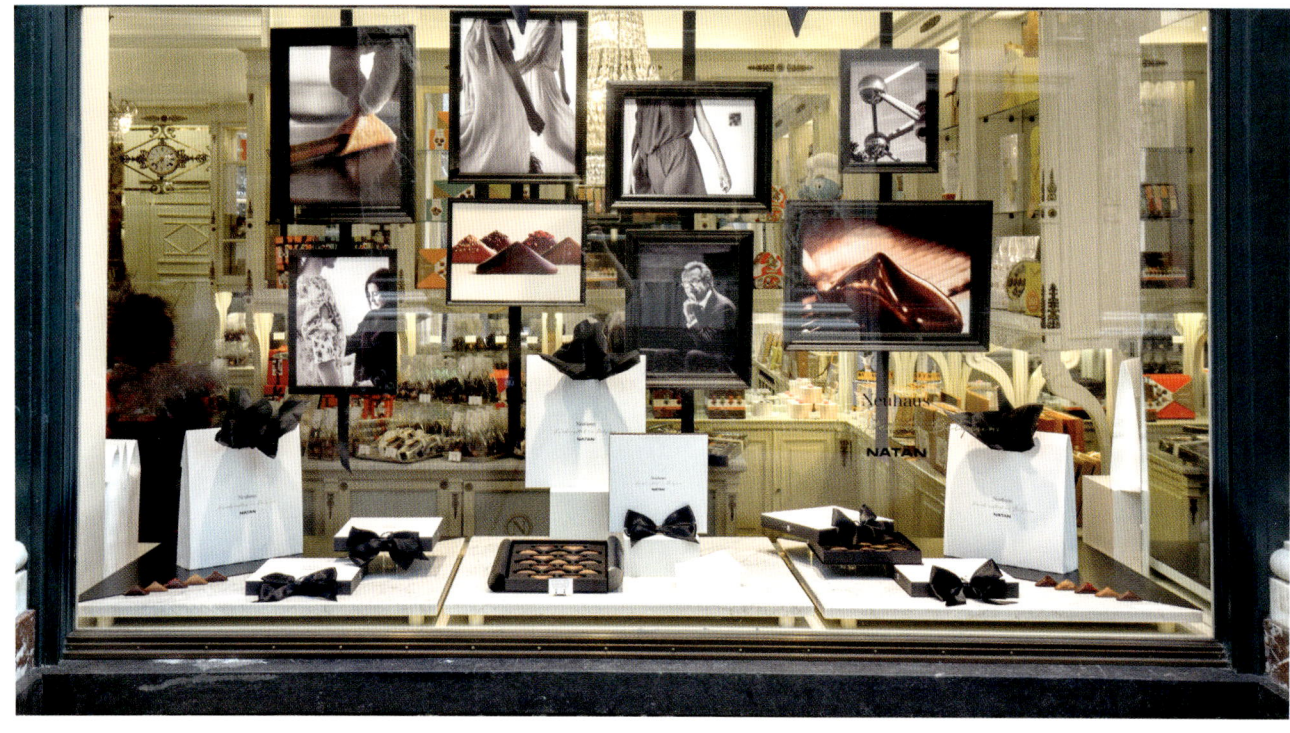

Showcase of the collection created in collaboration with Natan, Galerie de la Reine

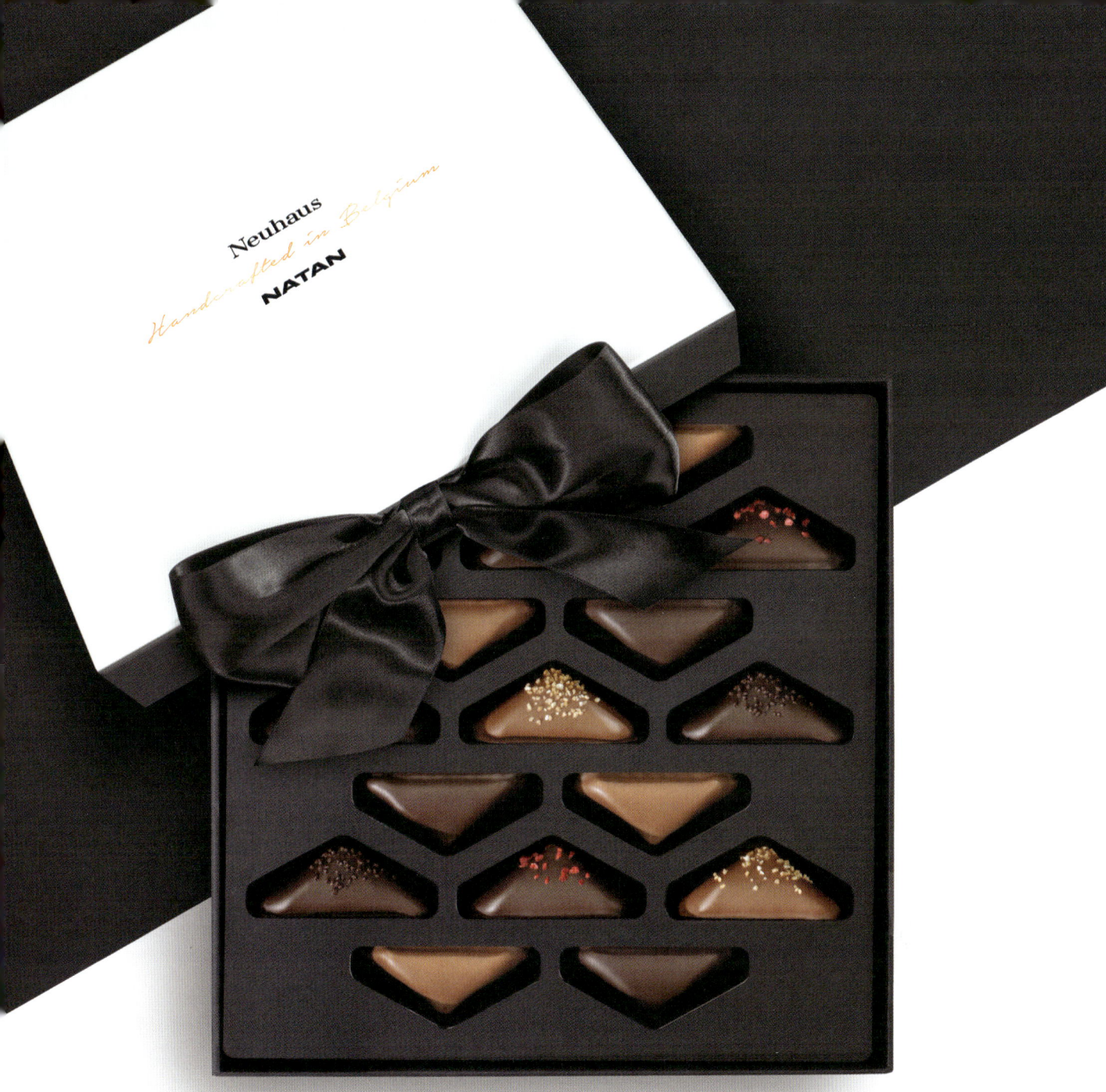

Neuhaus

Handcrafted in Belgium

NATAN

YVES MATTAGNE
AMBASSADOR FOR BELGIAN CHOCOLATE

When Yves Mattagne travels, he never packs his suitcase without slipping in a few boxes of pralines. More than a personal pleasure, this is a thoughtful gesture, almost a diplomatic ritual. Whenever he meets a foreign chef, he presents these Belgian treats, knowing that they symbolise the excellence and reputation of his country's chocolate. 'Belgian chocolate is a benchmark. It's a wonderful way to promote our nation', he confides.

While the head chef at La Villa Lorraine takes pride in his classical approach to gastronomy, he emphasises the importance of training to understand the world of chocolate fully. He admires the work of chocolate makers and the technical skills required to produce this raw material. His own appreciation for chocolate was refined through visits to the Antwerp chocolate museum, Chocolate Nation. 'I learned how to taste chocolate and discover its immense range of aromas, which was truly impressive. I believe everyone should receive a chocolate tasting initiation', explains Mattagne.

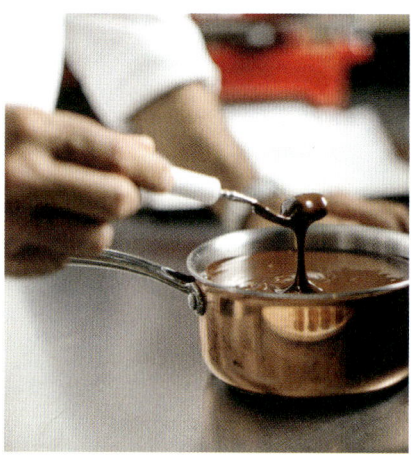

And yet, his attachment to pralines dates back even further. When he was a small child, his grandfather brought him a box of Neuhaus pralines every Sunday. The ritual remained the same: he would rummage around to find the most delicious one, often a milk chocolate praline. 'At the time, nobody preferred the bitter chocolate ones; they were too strong for us', he recalls. Over time, the palate evolves and learns to appreciate the complexity of flavours. Today, the Michelin-starred chef champions the praline as a perfect balance between tradition and indulgence, a pleasure that, far surpassing a simple sweet treat, tells a story while preserving a heritage.

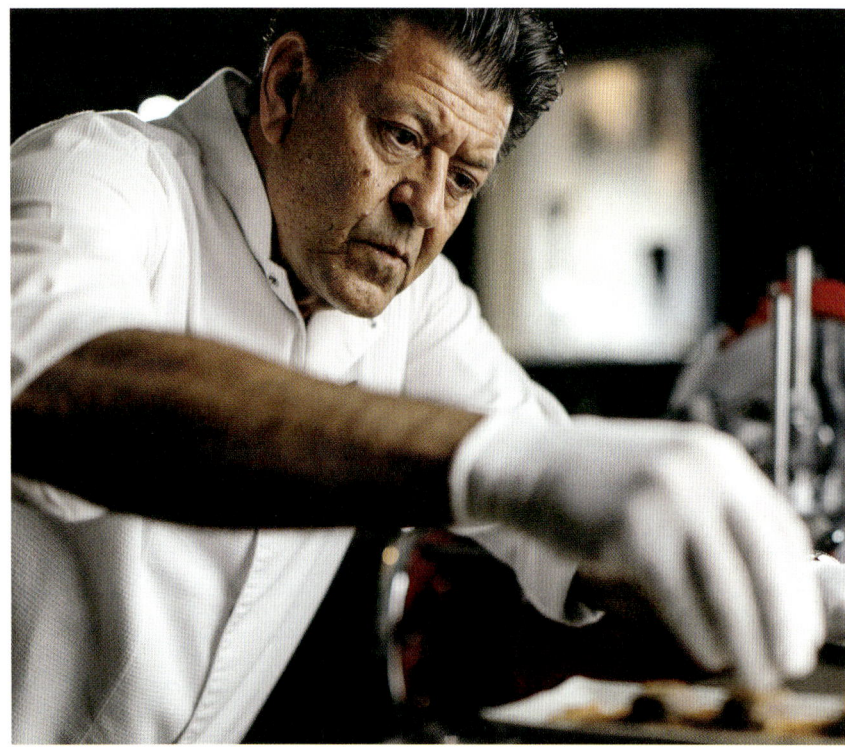

ANNEMIE PEETERS
BELGIAN RADIO AND TELEVISION PRESENTER

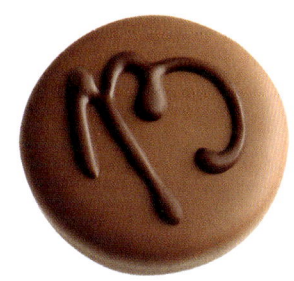

'I grew up in a mining family in Limburg. We never had pralines. Today, when I want to give a gourmet gift, I choose Neuhaus: cocktail chocolates for one of my sons-in-law and vegan chocolates for another son and his partner.

When I feel like treating myself, I hop on my bike and head to the Neuhaus shop in Antwerp. Half an hour later, I'm savouring a coffee with a praline - a moment of pure delight. Their flavours are delightful, and I love their names: Albert, Mathilde, Suzanne, Frédéric, Trillion, Criollo... And then there's my favourite, the rum praline. It's a round, flat milk chocolate praline topped with caramel, enclosing an unmistakable hint of rum. These pralines are so unique that I only buy them for special occasions: a grand celebration... or as a comforting treat.

Since I became a grandmother, summers without my grandson, who splits his time between Flanders and Catalonia, have felt like a painful absence. I've developed a ritual to soften the blow: I buy myself a Neuhaus ballotin of 31 rum pralines, one for each day of a month without him, like a gourmet countdown to his return. Next year, I'll do it again. And perhaps one day he'll have a praline named after him - a 'Carles'. Without any rum - at least for now'.

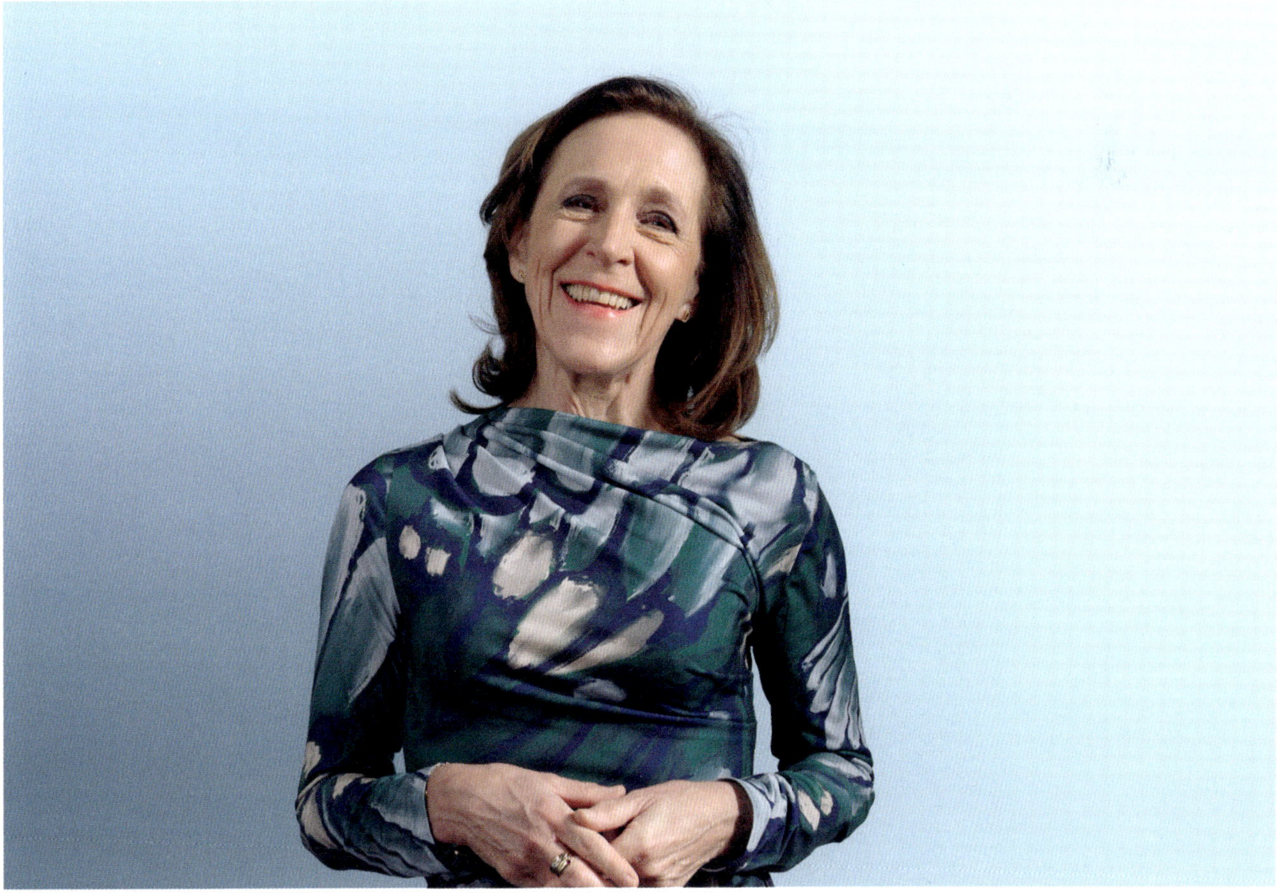

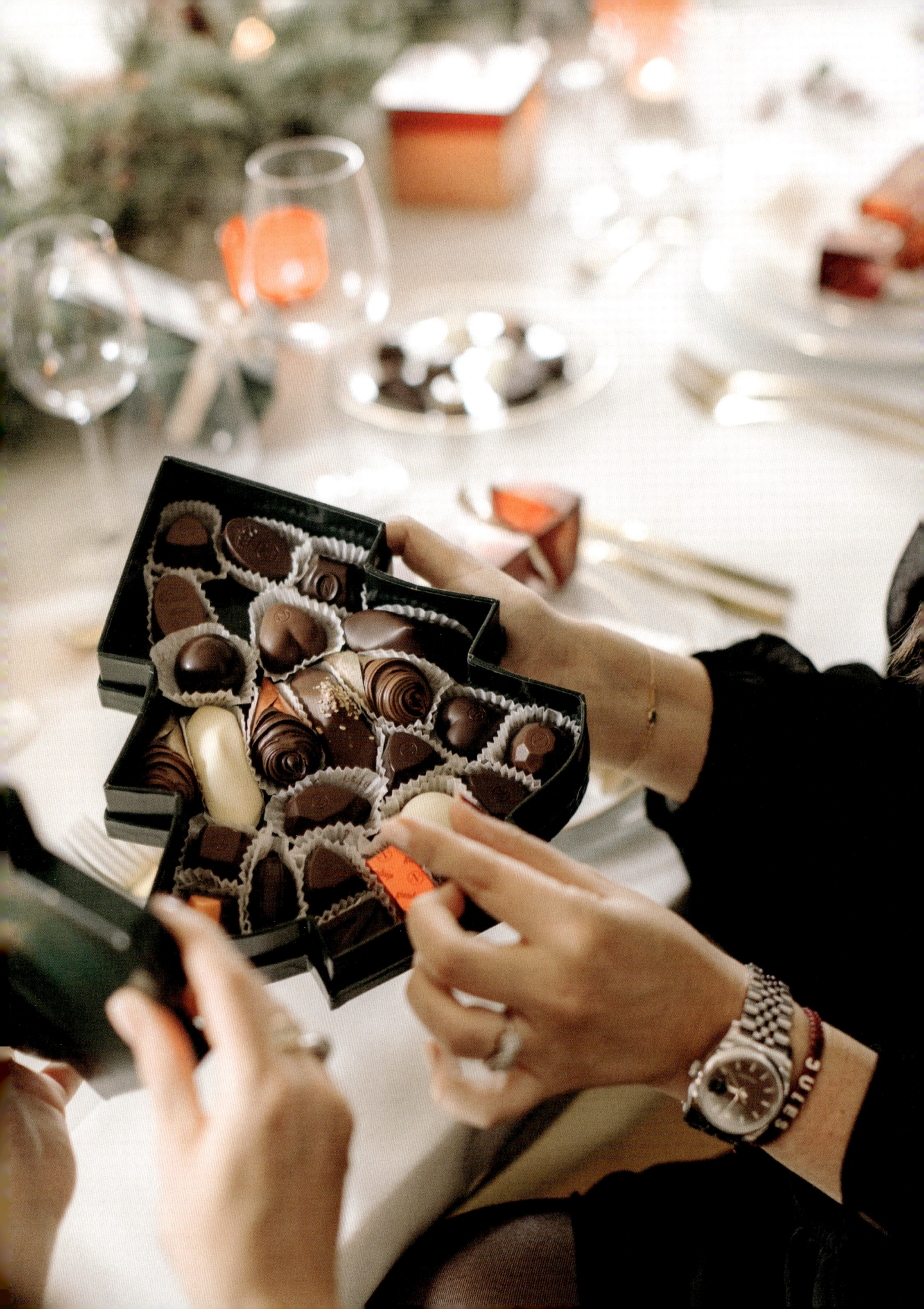

THE INSIDERS AND UNCONDITIONAL LOVE

There is no such thing as chance; only encounters that are meant to be. A tiny detail changes everything in these moments, when a gesture or a thought carries a special meaning. A box of Neuhaus chocolates placed on a table, a box of chocolates slipped into a suitcase, a praline savoured in silence: that's when chocolate becomes more than a pleasure; it becomes a presence. Neuhaus offers some of its loyal customers the status of 'Insiders' and grants them exclusive privileges.

Beyond this inner circle lies a broader circle of unconditional fans: enlightened amateurs or simple gourmets who have formed an equally strong bond with the brand. For them, Neuhaus represents significant moments that embody its refinement and shared ideals. This loyalty is rooted in more than just a preferred taste. It is inspired by chocolate that accompanies without imposing, leaving its mark without flashy brilliance. This chocolate has become an essential element, its presence a repeated, naturally occurring encounter. Some of our devoted Neuhaus fans have enjoyed sharing this experience with us. In their confidences, the praline becomes a common thread and a way to express what truly matters.

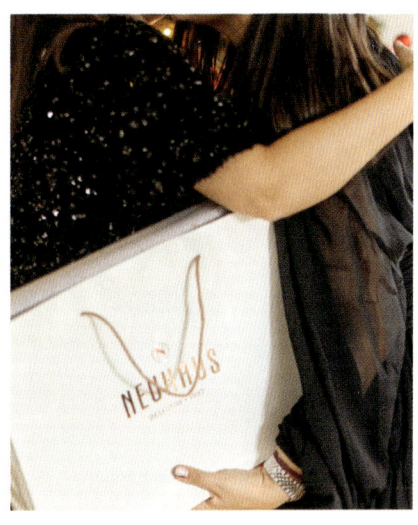

LOVE LETTERS

Over the years, Neuhaus has received numerous messages from enthusiasts - some just passing through, others long-time devotees - who felt the need to share a memory, an anecdote, or a thank-you. These precious words have been sent spontaneously to the brand, often by post or message, much like sending a postcard to someone who has made a difference. What do they all have in common? A Neuhaus praline is always the starting point.

'When my husband brought home a box of Neuhaus chocolates, it felt like a precious gift, a promise of sweetness to share.'

'When my grandmother (a singer at La Monnaie in Brussels) gave me my first taste of a Neuhaus praline, I recognised it as a special moment, a luxury to savour.'

'My first memory of Neuhaus was at a friend's birthday party. She handed me a praline, and I immediately realised this chocolate was different - more refined and intense. Since then, it has become a ritual.'

'I had never tasted Neuhaus chocolate before. When I took my first bite, I was stunned by the balance of flavours- a mixture of sweetness and depth.'

'Every year on Valentine's Day, my husband gives me a heart-shaped box. It's not just chocolate; it's a moment just for us.'

'The beauty of the Neuhaus shop windows has always fascinated me. Each decor is an invitation, a setting that enhances the experience.'

'The opening of a Neuhaus shop near my home was a turning point. Since then, it's unthinkable to walk past it without stopping.'

'One day, my partner ate the Neuhaus chocolate snowman before I even saw it! He swore it was an accident… but I know the temptation was just too strong.'

'A colleague gave me a box of Neuhaus chocolates one day for no reason, on no particular occasion. It's one of the nicest gifts I've ever received.'

'When I arrived in Belgium in 1973, I discovered Neuhaus by chance. Since then, I've never left home without a box. It's become a family tradition.'

BEHIND THE SCENES

They don't sign the boxes, and their names never appear in the credits, yet everything goes through them. A boutique manager who deduces a customer's tastes from a single word. A scientist who analyses the aromas of chocolate, molecule by molecule. A buyer who selects the beans directly at the source. A product manager who arranges the range as if composing a musical score. Their discretion truly deserves a chapter of its own.

THE BOUTIQUES

Entering a Neuhaus boutique resembles a momentary escape from daily life. From the instant you step inside, a subtle scent of cocoa awakens the senses, promising either a suspended moment in time or a nostalgic journey to childhood. The displays unveil a coveted assortment, arranged with the precision of a goldsmith. For over a hundred years, Neuhaus has maintained its heritage while continually reinventing pralines and other chocolate delights with the same creative spirit.

Each boutique is designed as a gourmet theatre, where the boxes await their moment to shine: to be gifted or savoured. It is a place where magic unfolds, bite by bite. This magic would be nothing without those who breathe life into it. Behind the counters, passionate individuals with profound knowledge of flavours and textures guide visitors, sharing advice and stories with infectious enthusiasm.

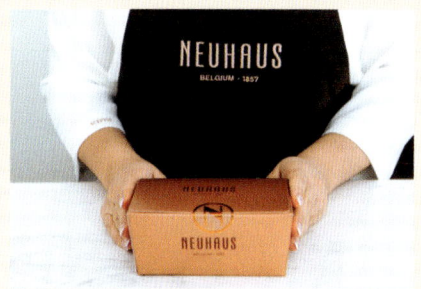

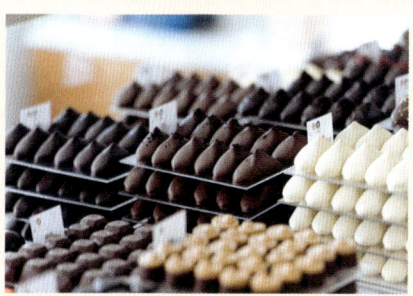

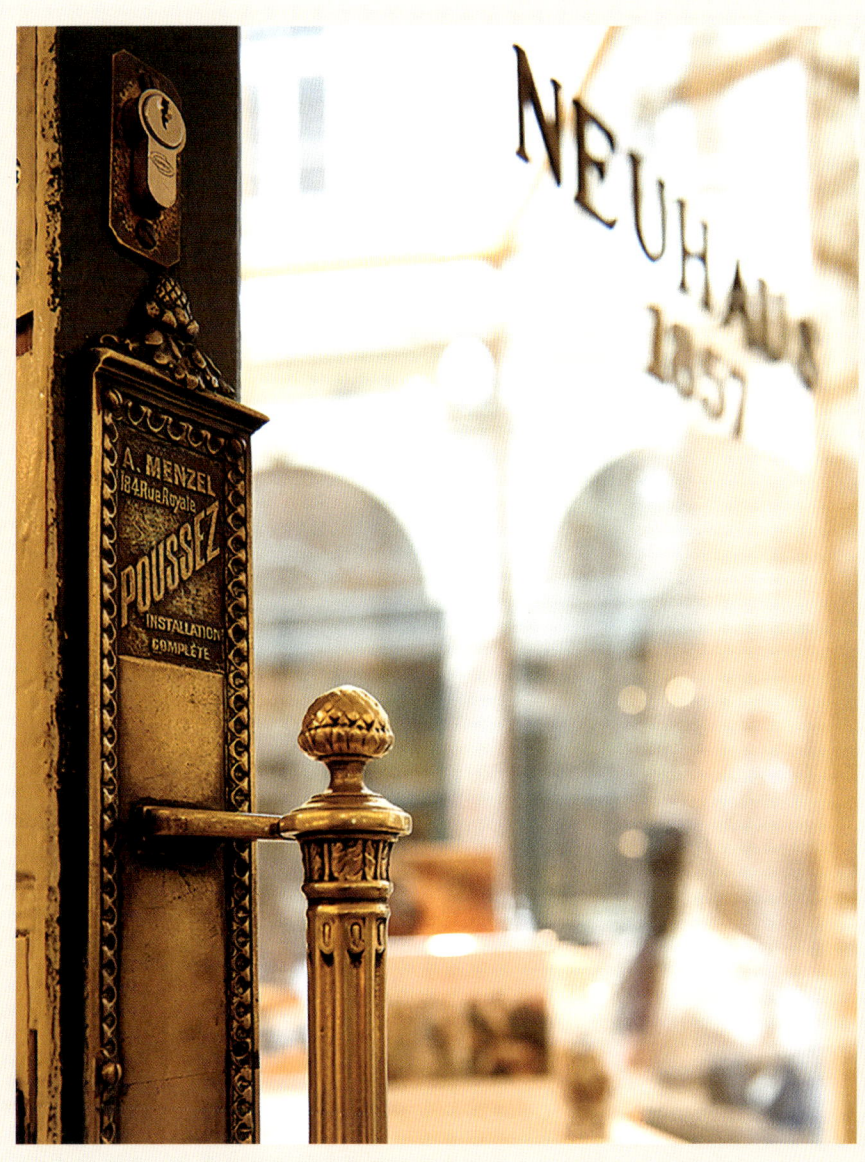

IN LEUVEN:
'A LITTLE JEWEL BOX, A BIG SPIRIT'

When Christine Dewil first walked into a Neuhaus boutique in January 2008, she had no idea that this world would become a second skin to her. Sixteen years later, she remains there, both a witness and a contributor to the evolution of this venerable house. Her story, both personal and emblematic, illustrates her connection to Neuhaus: a blend of passion, expertise, and human connection.

It all began one evening in December 2007. In search of a job, Christine learned that a Neuhaus boutique in Leuven was hiring. After the interview, she secured the position and immediately immersed herself in the brand's chocolate world. On 2 January 2008, she commenced training at the boutique on Avenue de la Toison d'Or—her learning began on the train ride to Brussels, where she diligently memorised the various pralines in the assortment. She needed just three days to grasp the richness of the role, and her enthusiasm grew as she became familiar with the master chocolatier's delightful icons.

Just a few days later, on 14 January, Christine officially joined the Leuven boutique alongside Brigitte Michiels and Walter De Vos. Together, they organised the space and established the store's identity in a spirit of camaraderie that endures to this day. Christine quickly realised that Neuhaus's success depended as much on product quality as on 'the care given to the customer experience'. Every carefully tied box and each piece of advice helps perpetuate the brand's reputation.

Over the years, this passionate employee has cultivated an intimate knowledge of the pralines that have made Neuhaus renowned, including the Caprice, a timeless classic whose story she delights in sharing with customers. By recounting the origins and details of each creation, Christine aims to enhance the narrative dimension of the purchasing experience, transforming a tasting into a memorable occasion.

Another praline dear to her heart is the champagne truffle, often overlooked yet capable of offering a gustatory revelation to those who dare to try it. It is precisely this engagement with customers—those moments when surprise lights up their faces—that makes her work so rewarding.

While Neuhaus chocolate is a universal pleasure, the Leuven boutique stands as living proof of this, drawing a diverse clientele. Some regular customers purchase their weekly box, as do travellers passing through. During the Rock Werchter festival, Christine recognises returning customers from Australia, Brazil, and beyond who remember their previous visits and insist on reliving the experience.

These interactions add a unique flavour to daily life. Each customer brings their own story, preferences, and memories associated with Neuhaus. Behind every purchase lies an intention: a gift, a personal treat, a ritual. That's one of the beauties of the job—the ability to 'make every visit a special moment'.

Although the year has its quieter and busier periods, November and December are an actual endurance test. The boutique becomes overwhelmed with customers seeking festive delights. Christine recalls one customer who, during the first edition of the advent calendars, purchased twenty-five of them. Today, he orders one hundred and forty.

Such a growing demand necessitates precise organisation and seamless teamwork. 'The support from headquarters is invaluable—even the CEO doesn't hesitate to lend a hand in the boutique,' says Christine. In these hectic moments, sometimes all it takes is a shared cake among colleagues to recharge and find the strength to continue.

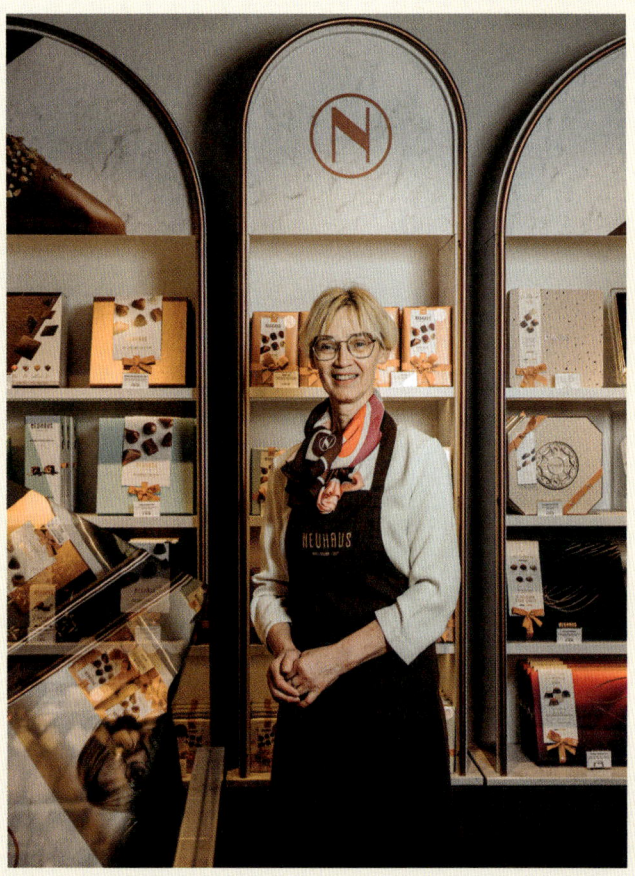

IN BRUSSELS:
'A BOX FULL OF MEMORIES'

When Marilyn van Olst first stepped into a Neuhaus boutique, she never imagined that this world would become her own. Seventeen years later, she has become a fixture, embodying the soul of the Avenue Louise boutique where she works. More than just a job, she has discovered a passion—a way of being that transforms pralines into bridges between people, creating opportunities for connection.

Initially, as a temporary worker, she trained in several boutiques in Brussels before permanently settling on Avenue Louise. There, she found an environment that suited her personality: a loyal yet international clientele, a cosy and elegant atmosphere, and the chance to utilise her language skills. French, Dutch, English, Spanish… Having travelled widely, she can connect effortlessly with international customers who expect excellence and care about every detail.

Among the details that define daily life at Neuhaus, Marilyn mentions with a smile the iconic branded scarf. 'It's almost a rite of passage to learn how to tie it properly', she explains. Each employee develops their unique way of wearing it—some opting for a discreet knot, while others prefer a more voluminous loop.

Some customers are in and out quickly, whilst others take their time, sharing their stories and connections to the brand. Some return weekly, placing the same order each time, while those who discover Neuhaus for the first time have their eyes light up with wonder. Marilyn enjoys watching them hesitate in front of the assortments, offering them a tasting, informing them about each praline's unique traits, and sometimes even anticipating their preferences. Over time, she has learned to read the subtle cues that indicate a taste for bitterness or a love for creamy, vanilla notes.

But no two visits are alike. Over seventeen years, Marilyn has witnessed a procession of celebrities and influential figures, including Jean-Claude Van Damme, Adamo, Maurane, and even the Spanish national football team, whom she instantly recognised as they walked through the door. Some famous clients are chatty and eager to share stories, while others prefer complete discretion. Occasionally, the boutique must close temporarily so that a political figure or VIP can shop in peace. 'When a security team shows up, you know it's not going to be an ordinary visit', she laughs.

Beyond these exceptional encounters, it is the daily attention to each person that drives her. Marilyn often says she could have been a nurse—which is fitting, considering that Jean Neuhaus, the founder, was a pharmacist himself—such is her desire to care for others. She finds this same sense of connection in every day spent at the boutique: in the conversations that arise between tastings and in the subtle gestures that transform a simple transaction into a shared moment.

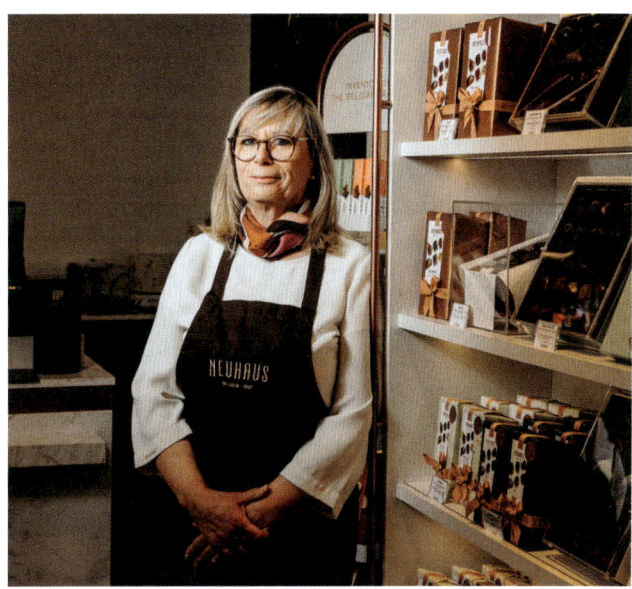

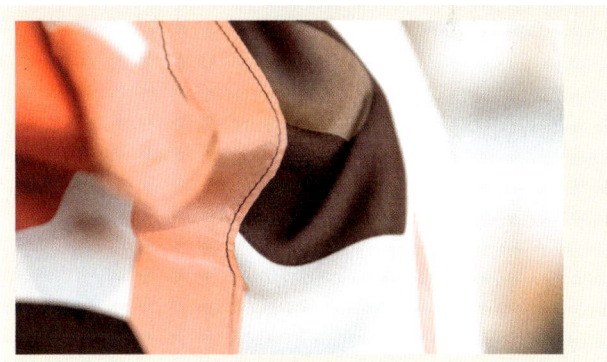

The Neuhaus Scarf, or the Art of Detail
Tied confidently around the neck or wrist, the Neuhaus scarf intrigues as much as it charms. Seemingly modest, its pattern reveals a delicately playful world to those who take the time to observe it. Hidden within the folds of the fabric, one can make out an Irrésistible, accompanied by a stylised mouth ready to bite. This serves as a subtle nod to the brand's gourmet heritage, tucked away like a well-kept secret. Like Neuhaus pralines, this scarf cultivates an elegance of detail—one that unveils itself gradually, with refined understatement.

THE DISCREET ONES

Behind the scenes at Neuhaus—far from the shop windows and workshops—indispensable key figures orchestrate the brand's excellence without seeking the spotlight. From sourcing raw ingredients to product innovation, and from strategic direction to scientific research, these individuals play a vital role in shaping the brand's future. The Chairman of the Board defines the vision; the purchasing manager selects the finest ingredients; the product manager brings new creations to life; and the scientist explores the subtleties of chocolate. These portraits highlight those who, away from the limelight, keep the heart of Neuhaus beating.

VALÉRIE PAQUOT
CHAIRWOMAN OF THE BOARD OF DIRECTORS AT NEUHAUS

Valérie is a board member of Compagnie du Bois Sauvage, a Belgian investment firm founded by her father. Among its various holdings, the company owns the renowned chocolate maker Neuhaus, a symbol of Belgium's gastronomic heritage. However, Valérie's journey is far from typical for a business executive. Before entering the private sector, she dedicated a significant portion of her career to nursing, working to uphold human dignity through her missions with the International Committee of the Red Cross (ICRC).

This humanitarian background profoundly informs her current approach to business. Her focus extends well beyond the end product—she embraces the entire chocolate value chain. Valérie is deeply concerned about working conditions on cocoa plantations, producers' wages, and the long-term sustainability of the economic model. 'I spent a year in Côte d'Ivoire; I saw the cocoa plantations with my own eyes'. She is committed to building a more equitable system—one in which everyone receives their fair share of value.

A globe-trotter with a natural curiosity about others, Valérie is also passionate about sharing her knowledge. Neuhaus is not merely a brand; it is part of Belgian heritage, a house established in 1857 that invented both the praline and the ballotin. Yet she refuses to be confined by nostalgia. 'We're proud of our know-how—we need to carry it into the future'.

Leader, humanitarian, nurse, explorer of humanity—Valérie embodies all these roles simultaneously. She sees no contradiction between her past commitments and her current position. Her driving force is people—whether it's a patient in a hospital bed, a cocoa farmer in Africa, or an employee in a Belgian company. What matters is giving them space, listening to them, and providing them with the means to stand tall. And remain standing.

Alongside her, another female figure is leaving her mark on the Neuhaus landscape: trained in various disciplines yet equally committed to high standards and the sharing of knowledge, Isabel Baert epitomises a new generation of leadership. Her carefully honed trajectory combines international vision with deep Belgian roots.

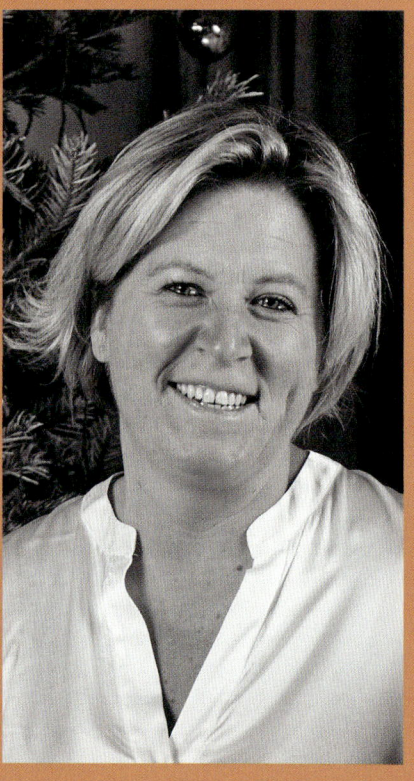

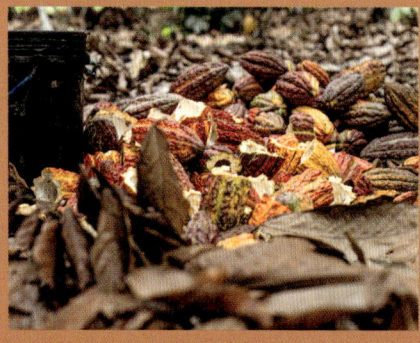

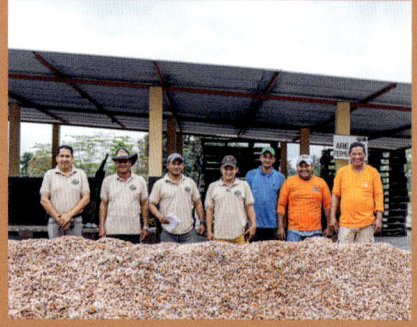

ISABEL BAERT
THE CHISELLED TRAJECTORY OF A VISIONARY LEADER

Born in Roeselare in 1986, Isabel Baert embodies a generation of female managers who think internationally while never losing sight of their roots. She hails from a home where hard work is taken for granted: her mother is a general practitioner, and her father is a leading figure in Belgian finance. The 'keep going, come what may' mentality was instilled in her from childhood. After studying law at KULeuven, Isabel branched out into fashion, studying at Polimoda in Florence and beginning her career at Hugo Boss.

These were the initial steps in a cosmopolitan career, encompassing Germany, the United States, and the United Kingdom, in the realm of top-of-the-range textiles (Van de Velde, Intimacy). Today, this international journey has enriched her strategic vision—an asset for Neuhaus as it continues to extend beyond Belgium's borders.

As a perfectionist, she consistently refines her rigorous approach to products and retail assets, which she will leverage effectively for Neuhaus. One of her mantras is often repeated: 'Stay close to your core'. Neuhaus produces chocolates, and the CEO is dedicated to keeping this at the heart of the business.

Her style? Clear, clean, ambitious: 'If we decide to go somewhere, we do it well', she often repeats. Dubai, Saudi Arabia, and the UK are now central to her strategy, along with the United States, where Neuhaus already has thirteen boutiques. Passionate about sectors prioritising customer satisfaction, she confides that as a child, she dreamed of opening a hotel—a place of hospitality where great care is taken to ensure the customer's experience.

Under her leadership, the brand is making significant investments in its production facilities at Vlezenbeek: a new moulding line will elevate production capacity there by 50%. It's a strong gesture in favour of a Belgian base, and one that the CEO takes pride in. Isabel is as committed to excellence as she is to ethical issues. Faced with European regulations against deforestation (EUDR), she is preparing her company to meet the requirements without compromising on quality.

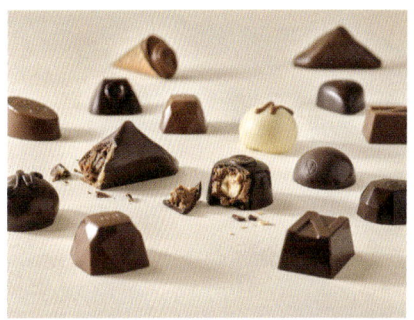

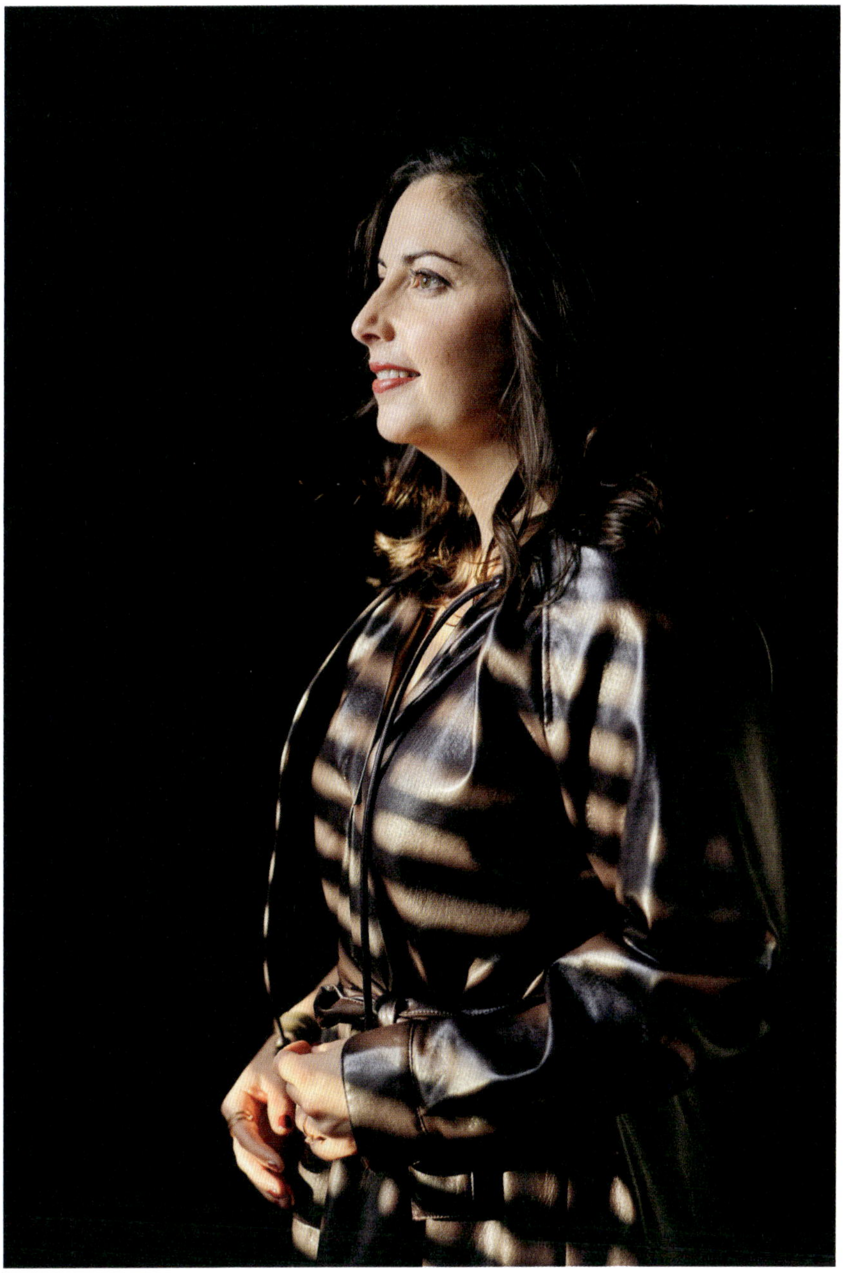

BENOÎT CAHN
HEAD OF PURCHASING

Benoît Cahn joined the Neuhaus team in 2020 and is responsible for purchasing cocoa and raw materials. Passionate about the food industry, he had substantial experience even before joining the Belgian company. He discovered 'a world where each ingredient is unique, defined by its origin, organoleptic qualities and functionalities'.

He believes that at Neuhaus, taste comes first, origin is essential, and prioritising local suppliers is crucial. This commitment translates into 'a constant search for new products and alternative suppliers, as well as close exchanges with Michelin-starred chefs, whose desires must be translated into quality ingredients that are adapted to the production requirements'.

His mission doesn't stop with cocoa. Over time, he has been entrusted with managing the ingredients and packaging purchasing team, 'a key role where the product experience is as much about the pleasure of tasting as it is about the packaging that contains it'. Each praline must be protected and enhanced by its packaging, 'a delicate balance between aesthetics and functionality'.

Throughout his professional travels, Benoît has developed a profound understanding of cocoa. He recalls visiting a Bois Sauvage plantation in Ecuador, where he discovered 'cocoa cultivation carried out with exemplary rigour', with 'young, vigorous cocoa trees perfectly aligned'. He was particularly impressed by the local biodiversity: 'The teams do their utmost to preserve the indigenous cocoa trees as well as the fruit trees, creating an exceptional ecosystem'.

Another trip to Ghana provided him with a deeper understanding of the realities of cocoa in West Africa. He recalls one of the highlights of this journey: 'We offered chocolate to farmers and their children; for some, it was the first time they had tasted the fruit of their labour. It was a suspended moment, almost unreal.'

For Benoît, '...the quality of a chocolate depends on much more than the origin of the beans. Fermentation, drying, roasting and conching are all key stages in releasing its aromas. At Neuhaus, he regularly tastes exceptional chocolates, a pleasure renewed each time'.

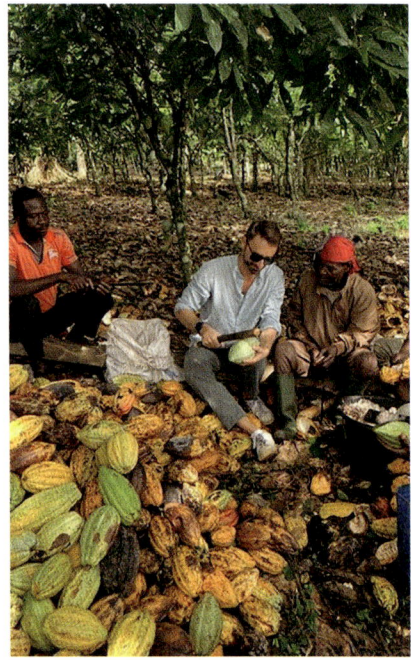
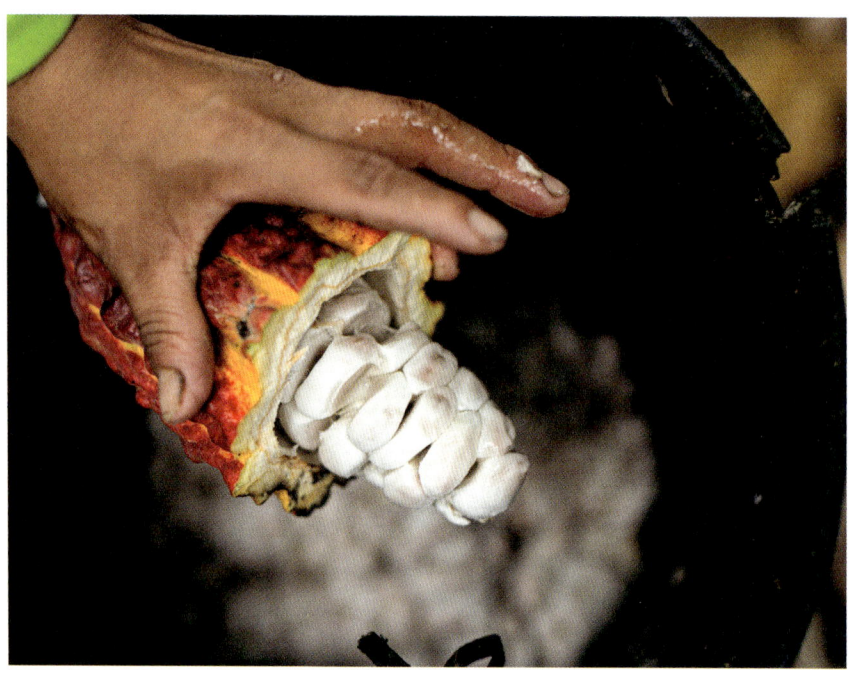

ETHICAL, SUSTAINABLE AND TRACEABLE COCOA

For several years, Neuhaus has committed to producing more responsible cocoa through its Honest Chocolate programme, an initiative based on three pillars: guaranteeing the profitability of farms, ensuring strict social responsibility (respect for human rights), and working to protect the environment through anti-deforestation measures and reforestation programmes.

For Benoît Cahn, who oversees these issues within the company, maintaining a high level of quality while ensuring ethical sourcing remains 'a major challenge', which is overcome through 'rigorous traceability and close collaboration with partner suppliers'. He also emphasises the severe impact of climate change in West Africa. Therefore, Neuhaus is determined to diversify its sources of supply and encourage producers to invest in sustainable adaptations by offering better purchase prices.

Neuhaus is a signatory of the Belgian 'Beyond Chocolate' initiative, an agreement established in 2018 that brings together key players in the sector—public authorities, NGOs, brands, and retailers—to ensure cocoa is sustainable, traceable, and deforestation-free shortly while guaranteeing producers a vital income by 2030.

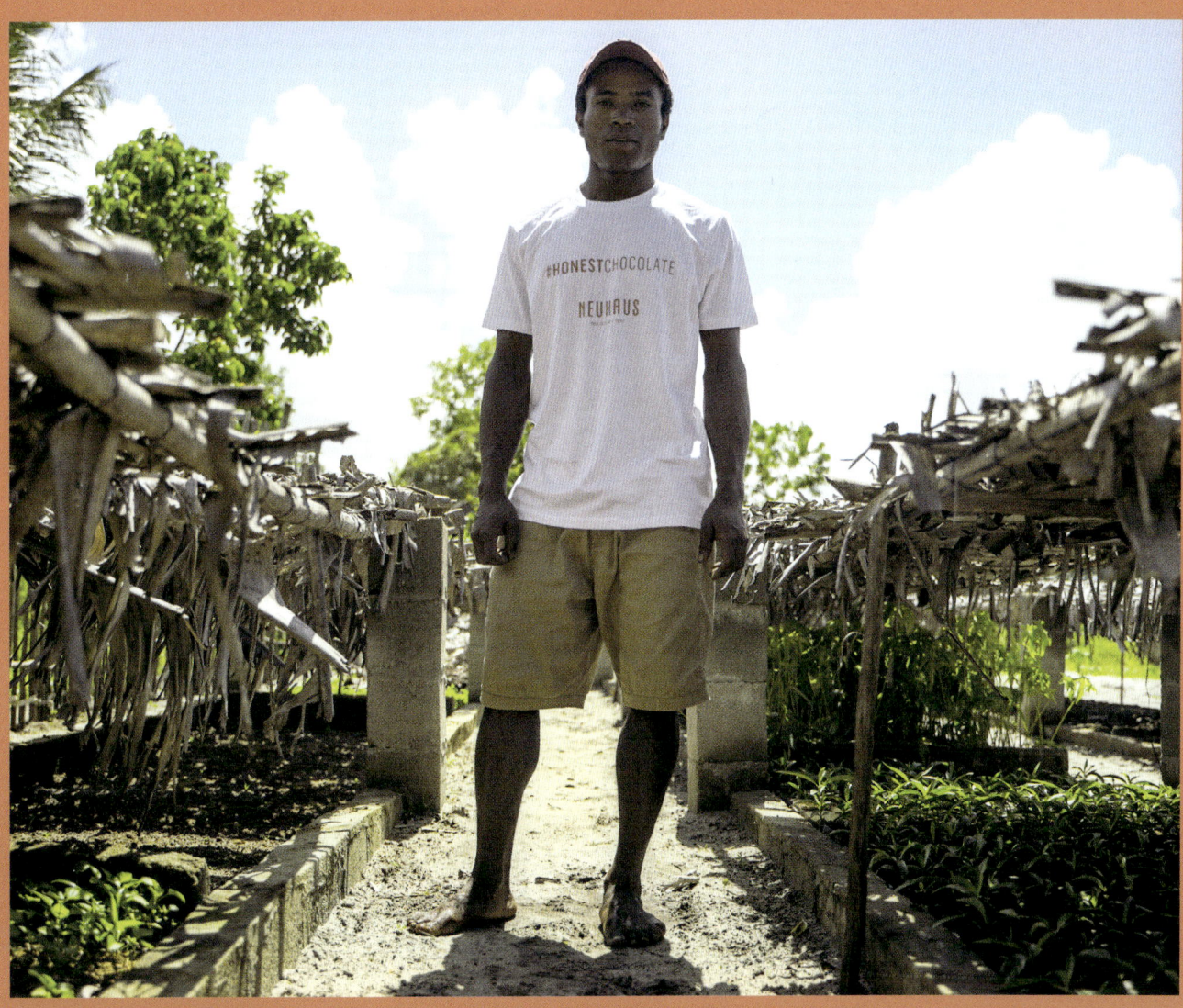

ANNICK BASTIN
SENIOR PRODUCT MANAGER

Behind every box of Neuhaus pralines lies meticulous and passionate craftsmanship. Annick Bastin plays a pivotal role. Her responsibility is not to follow trends or impose her tastes blindly. On the contrary, her mission is to weave each new creation into the brand's DNA, ensuring that every choice has a meaningful reason and contributes to enriching its unique history.

His approach is rooted in a genuine belief: the absolute necessity of a clear and coherent structure for the Neuhaus range. 'It's essential to make our ranges clear. If a customer walks into a shop and sees a profusion of references with no point of reference, they can get lost. The idea is to create 'families' of pralines, to have visual and taste consistency', she insists enthusiastically.

A concern for coherence also permeates the development of the collections. 'It's never simply a question of validating a flavour because it appeals. Each creation is based on a strong concept and a clear intention. We analyse the gaps in the range, identify the underlying trends, and, above all, consider the sensory and emotional experience we wish to offer our customers'.

The 'wow collections'—a term used internally at Neuhaus to refer to projects still in the draft stage but intended to leave a lasting mark on the brand's identity, irrespective of the seasons or holidays—particularly exemplify this approach. These collections require at least two years of work, and occasionally longer if they are immensely popular.

She is particularly passionate about Les Gourmands, the collection developed in collaboration with Maison Dandoy, where the fusion of biscuit-making and chocolate-making was an obvious choice. 'When you think of a biscuit, you immediately think of a metal box, the kind we used to find in our grandparents' homes. We wanted to recreate this comforting and nostalgic image, so we opted for a metal box with a terrazzo-inspired design, subtly reminiscent of biscuit crumbs. These are details that we don't necessarily perceive consciously, but which give a profound coherence to our choices when developing a product'

This rigour is also reflected in the very conception of the recipes. 'You might think, 'Let's just add a little hazelnut flavouring'. But that's not our way at all. We always choose the real hazelnut, the best there is, even if it's more complex and more expensive, because it's an integral part of our identity and our commitment to excellence'.

In this way, Annick Bastin strives with rigour and enthusiasm to bring to life the vision of Neuhaus, a house with a heritage as refined as it is gourmet.

'A real passion drives us and binds the team together, enabling the brand to endure. There's a huge sense of pride in contributing to this heritage, especially as it's Belgian! Many of us grew up with Neuhaus chocolates in our families. To be able, in our turn, to continue this tradition is an honour, both for us and for our loved ones', concludes the senior product manager.

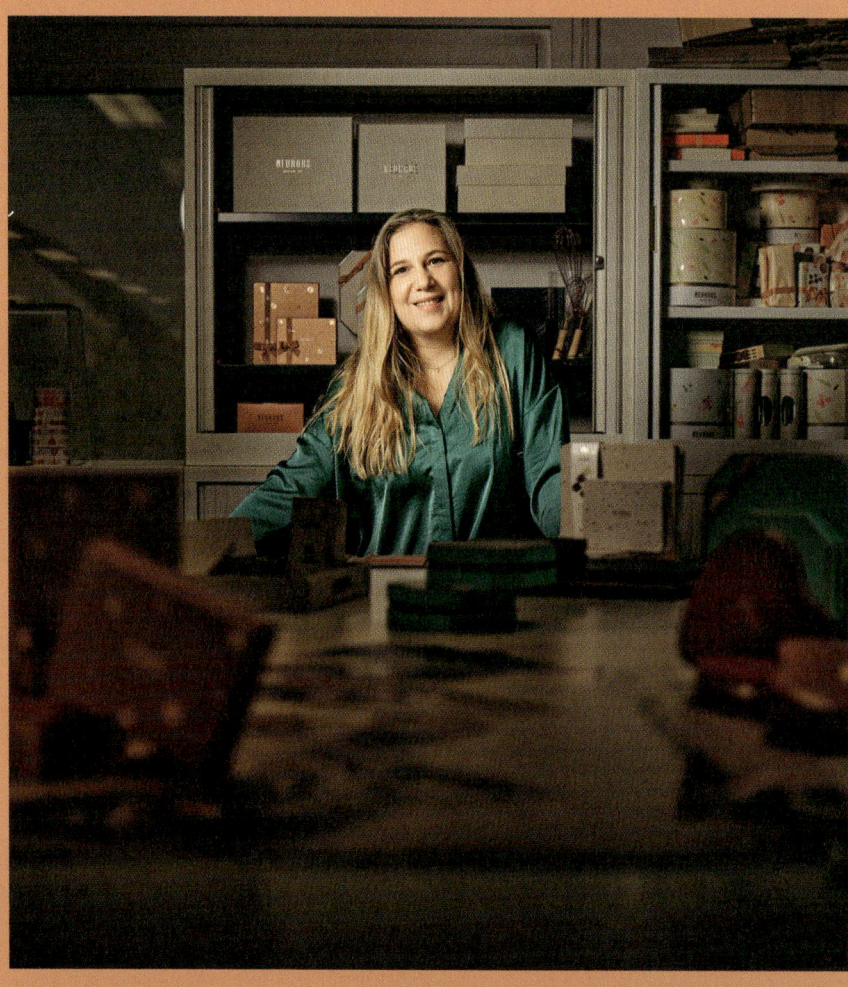

BART VANDEN HOUTE
PRODUCT INNOVATION MANAGER

I fell into a chocolate bath, and since then, I haven't been bored for a moment. Bart Vanden Houte didn't choose chocolate; twenty-five years ago, in the workshops of Neuhaus, he was drawn to it. This bio-engineer with a discerning palate has devoted himself body and soul to chocolate ever since. 'When I think back to my childhood, it's not chocolate that comes to mind first, but my grandmother's rice pudding. We used to fight to scrape the bottom of the dish,' he explains. It's through this simple, gourmet gesture that his obsession with textures, the balance of flavours, and the pursuit of immediate, profound pleasure has been nurtured.

For a quarter of a century, he has orchestrated innovation at Neuhaus with the rigour of a scientist and the sensitivity of an artist. Each praline represents a dialogue between heritage and daring: 'Our chocolates have evolved: they have become lighter, more complex, playing on the contrasts between crunchy and melt-in-the-mouth, between sweetness and bitterness. However, we remain committed to upholding the purity and authenticity of our ingredients.'

Vanden Houte is one of those personalities who advance discreetly yet leave a lasting impression. Under his leadership, the Irrésistibles range has expanded to include subtle new variations. He is also the architect of Thins, thin slabs of chocolate designed to be savoured without expectation, without ritual, simply for the pleasure of the moment. 'Chocolate doesn't have to be ceremonial. It can be a moment to oneself, or a spontaneous sharing.'

Bart is a true explorer of taste. He scours trade fairs, wanders through exotic markets, and observes the work of top chefs with almost amorous attention. He tracks down the spark that will give birth to a new praline, a new balance, and an unsuspected emotion. He dreams of an experience that will engage all the senses: 'A praline that you don't just taste, but see, smell, hear, even... a chocolate that is a total immersion.' A man of both the laboratory and the workshop, he never works alone. Every day, he debates, adjusts, and perfects alongside the master chocolate-makers: 'I'm not the easiest, I'm afraid... But disagreements are often 'good fights'. They push us to go further.'

This attention to detail is also evident in his dealings with consumers: 'A praline can seduce at first sight, intrigue at first bite. But when someone comes back to buy it, you know it's found its place. If chocolate is a story of transmission, Bart is one of those who pass it on. When asked how he would like to be remembered in Neuhaus history, he smiles: 'I hope one day to walk into a Neuhaus shop with my grandchildren and see the joy in their eyes as they discover all these marvels. Then I'll know that my mission has been accomplished.'

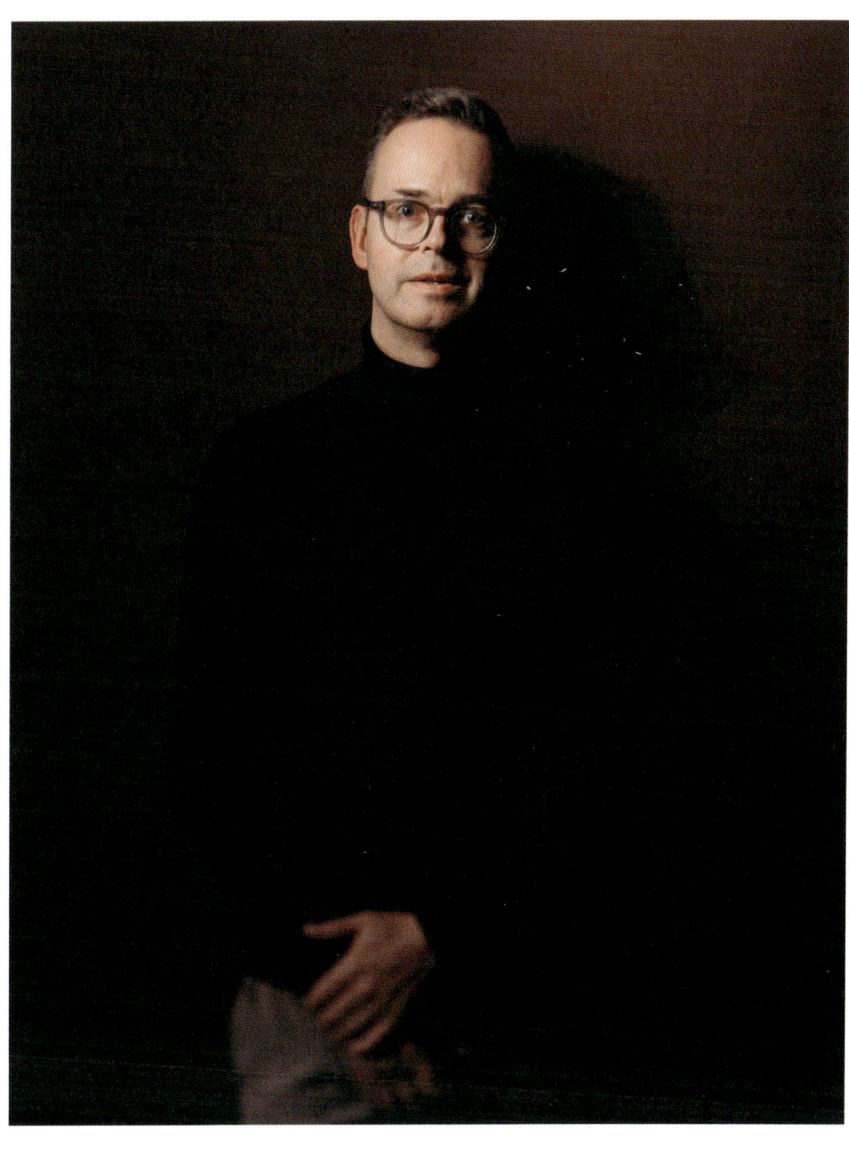

THE ART OF KNOTTING AT NEUHAUS – METICULOUS ARTISANSHIP

At Neuhaus, the knot is more than just packaging: it is a signature. Each box is adorned with a skilfully tied ribbon, designed as the finishing touch to a ritual of elegance.

The origin of this emblematic gesture can be traced back to Brigitte Michiels, a long-serving employee who has become an integral part of the house's memory. It was she who devised this distinctive knot and established this tradition. 'Brigitte knows everything about the history of the brand and makes sure that this type of detail remains true to our identity', explains Annick Bastin.

Specific training is offered in the boutique to ensure flawless execution: the logo must appear precisely on each buckle and at each end. Nothing is left to chance.

In a context where 70% of Neuhaus chocolates are given as gifts, the ribbon serves as the quintessential symbol of gift-giving, a visible sign of the attention bestowed on others and a tangible extension of the Neuhaus experience.

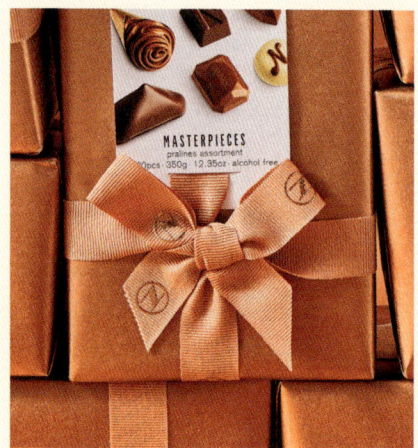

CATHERINE STANDAERT
SCIENCE AND SENSORY EXPERT

At Neuhaus, the pursuit of excellence depends not only on craftsmanship but also on a rigorous scientific approach. Catherine Standaert, a food industry engineer and science and sensory expert at Neuhaus, exemplifies this blend of tradition and innovation. With a foundation established at the Cacaolab, a spin-off from Ghent University specialising in applied chocolate research, she brings invaluable scientific expertise to the refinement of each praline.

'From my very first professional experience, I was fascinated by chocolate', she confides. I was fortunate enough to work on research projects where science directly served industry, providing me with a deeper understanding of the interactions between chocolate's aromatic compounds, the chemical reactions influencing its texture, and the impact of transformation processes on its sensory profile'.

One of his first missions at Neuhaus was to characterise the aromatic profiles of chocolate better using advanced analytical tools. We employ gas chromatography to identify and

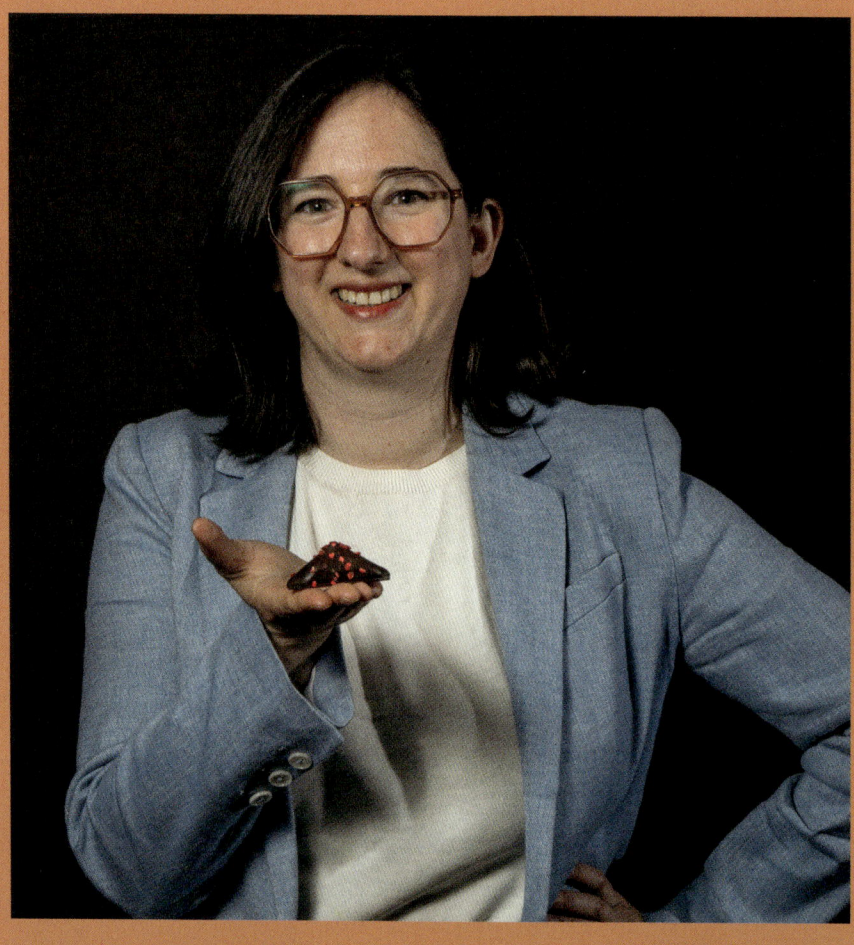

quantify the fragrant compounds present in our chocolates. This enables us to understand why certain flavours dominate and how they interact with other elements', she explains.

However, these analyses are not always adequate. 'A molecule may be very present in a chocolate without being perceived as dominant by the human palate. That's why scientific analysis needs to be supplemented by sensory tests carried out by trained tasters', she explains.

To refine these assessments, Catherine Standaert has established a panel of experts composed of individuals selected for their ability to recognise aromas. 'Our experts have been trained to identify the different notes present in chocolate as objectively as possible. We use reference samples to standardise our tastings and avoid excessive subjectivity.'

Furthermore, an internal panel of untrained employees offers a more spontaneous and subjective perspective on the new creations. They help us understand consumer preferences. For instance, we ask them to compare different recipes, to note the intensity of specific flavours, or to indicate whether they find a particular texture pleasant.

To structure the sensory analysis of chocolate, Catherine Standaert has developed a new tool for Neuhaus: a tasting wheel tailored to the company's specific needs. 'We compared several existing models, including those used for coffee and wine, before adapting our version to chocolate.'

The aim is to provide tasters and consumers with a common terminology. 'Thanks to this reference system, we can express the nuances of a chocolate more accurately and help everyone to identify the dominant aromas. Take vanilla, for example: in many diagrams, it is classified as a spice. But we felt that it shares more similarities with notes of caramel and brown sugar, so we placed it in the 'golden' category (warm, golden notes).'

Far from being an isolated discipline, chocolate tasting has striking parallels with other gastronomic products.

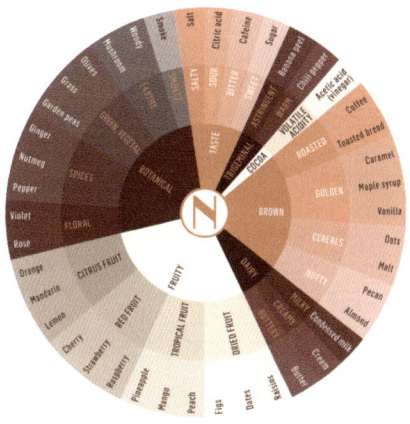

'I think of our experts as 'chocolate sommeliers'. We even use aroma kits originally designed for wine to train our tasters', she confides.

However, the tasting method is slightly different. Unlike wine, which is swirled in the mouth before being expelled, we recommend allowing the chocolate to melt on the tongue. That's when the aromas are fully released. Someone who chews a praline quickly and swallows it immediately would miss out on the full complexity of the flavours.

According to Catherine Standaert, the world of chocolate is constantly evolving, influenced by shifting taste trends and advancements in science. Consumer preferences change over time, and perceptions of sweet, bitter, and savoury evolve depending on culture and generations.

The research suggests new ways to adjust the perception of flavours. 'One of the avenues being explored is the 3D printing of sugar on the surface of chocolate. The idea would be to place the sugar strategically so that it is perceived more intensely at the start of tasting, which would make it possible to reduce the total quantity of sugar without altering the sensation of sweetness. However, these technologies are still a long way from being applied in the industry.'

Finally, the role of colour in taste perception also intrigues researchers. 'At Neuhaus, we only use natural colours, derived from paprika, spirulina or radish. But the visual impact of a praline can unconsciously influence the perceived taste. This remains a fascinating area to explore.'

To fully enjoy a Neuhaus praline, Catherine Standaert recommends taking your time. Ideally, begin by observing the praline, smelling it, and then letting it melt slowly on your tongue. Take note of the first flavours that emerge, the changing textures, and the lingering aromas. A good tasting is a journey.'

Thanks to her scientific approach and expertise, Catherine Standaert is refining the art of tasting. Behind each praline lies not only Neuhaus's historic know-how but also a nuanced and rigorous understanding of what makes chocolate magical.

However, she is not the only one who views this pursuit of equilibrium between scientific precision and gustatory emotion as her mission. Another key figure embodying this long-term need and passion is Bart Vanden Houte, a discreet yet fundamentally significant pioneer of innovation at Neuhaus for more than a quarter of a century.

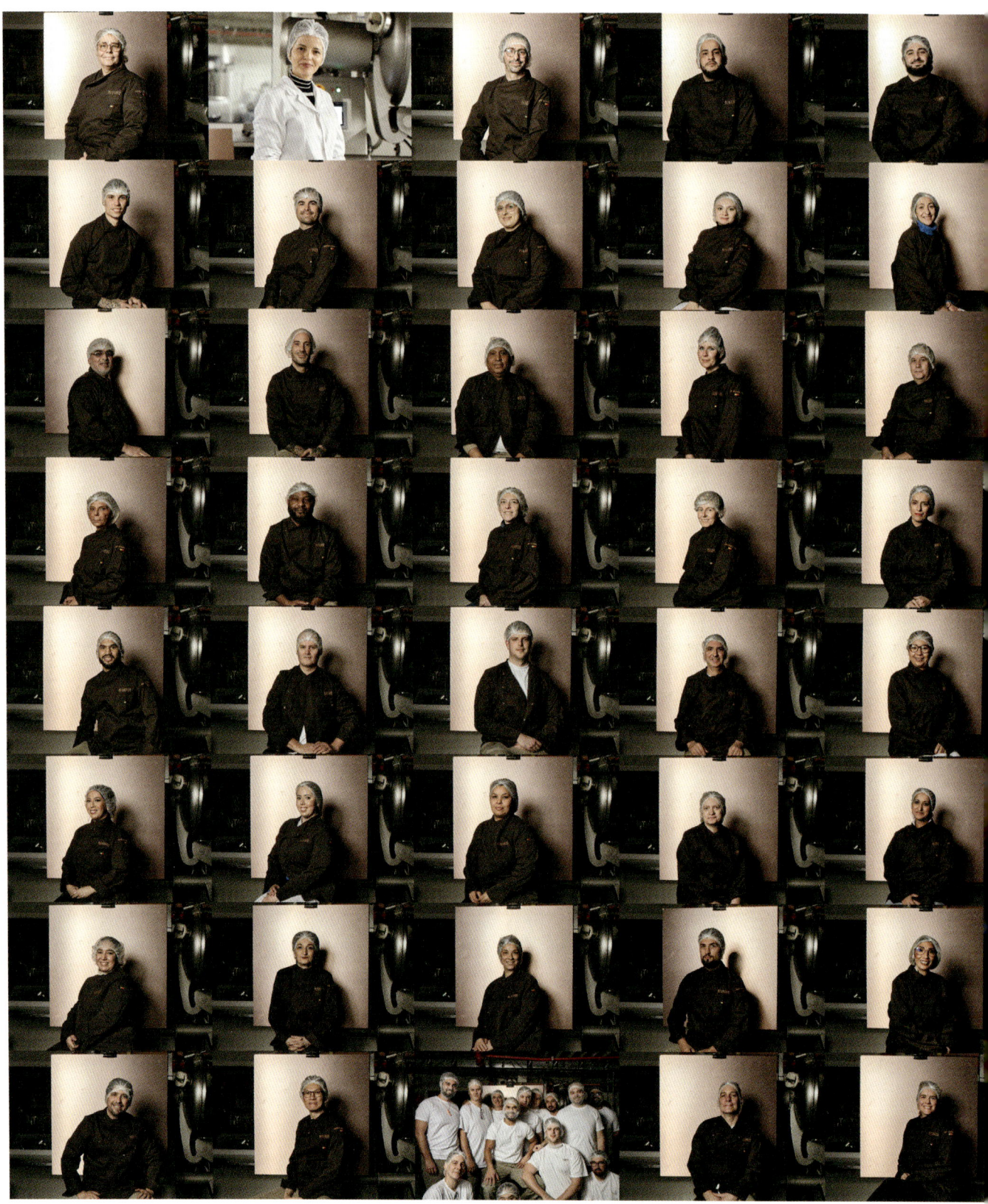

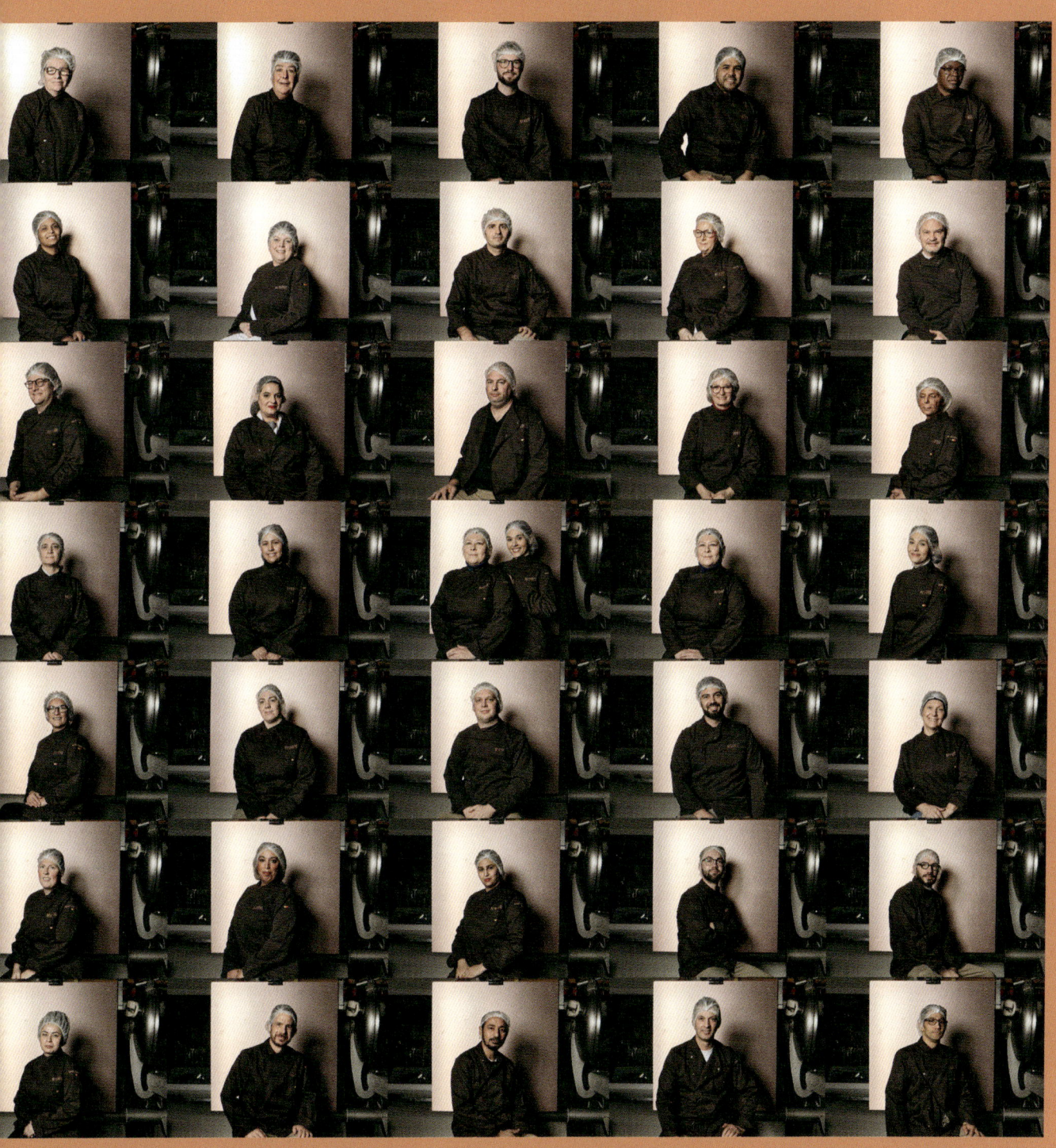

BEHIND EVERY NEUHAUS PRALINE, THERE IS A MOSAIC OF TALENT. THANK YOU TO ALL THOSE WHO WORK PASSIONATELY BEHIND THE SCENES TO BRING EXCELLENCE TO LIFE.

A NEW VISUAL IDENTITY FOR NEUHAUS

In 2017, Neuhaus undertook an overhaul of its visual identity, marking a strategic turning point aimed at modernising the brand's image while remaining true to its heritage. Annick Bastin recalls the painstaking process that led to this change. 'We had to think about what defines us and choose elements that made sense for the brand.'

One of the most emblematic choices in this transformation was the adoption of copper as the signature colour. 'Before, gold was omnipresent in our visual identity. But when we thought about it, we realised that it wasn't what best represented our expertise. ' Copper, on the other hand, directly reflects the craftsmanship and history of Neuhaus. In our workshops, we still use copper pans to work with the chocolate. This material embodies care, precision and tradition, while adding a touch of modernity.'

This change didn't stop with the packaging; it also influenced the shops and communication media. 'We wanted Neuhaus products to be immediately recognisable. The introduction of copper in our boxes, ribbons and graphic elements has made it possible to create a more consistent and impactful identity.'

Customers have wholeheartedly embraced this development. Annick Bastin concludes: 'The feedback has been very positive. People told us Neuhaus seemed more coherent, more elegant, while still respecting its history.'

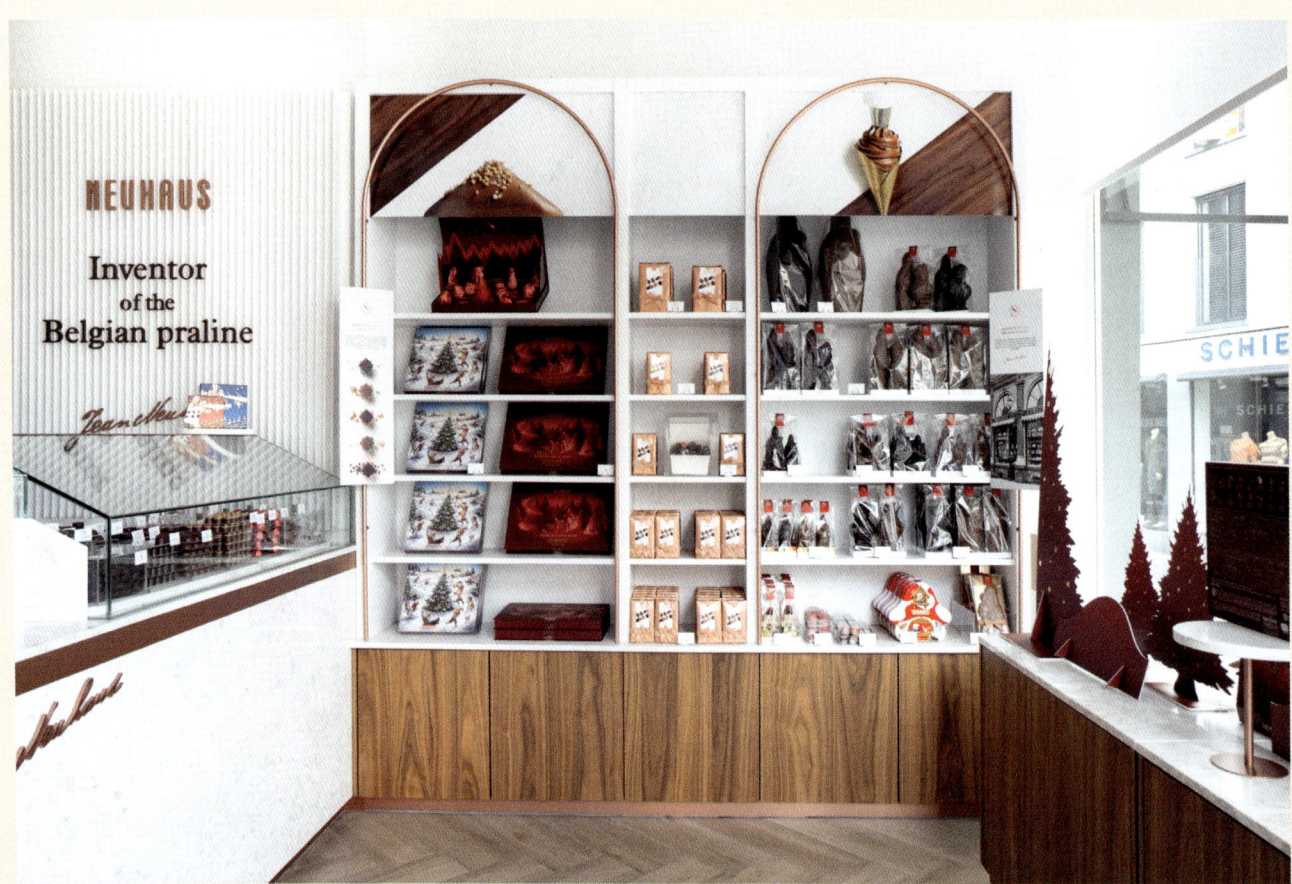

NEUHAUS

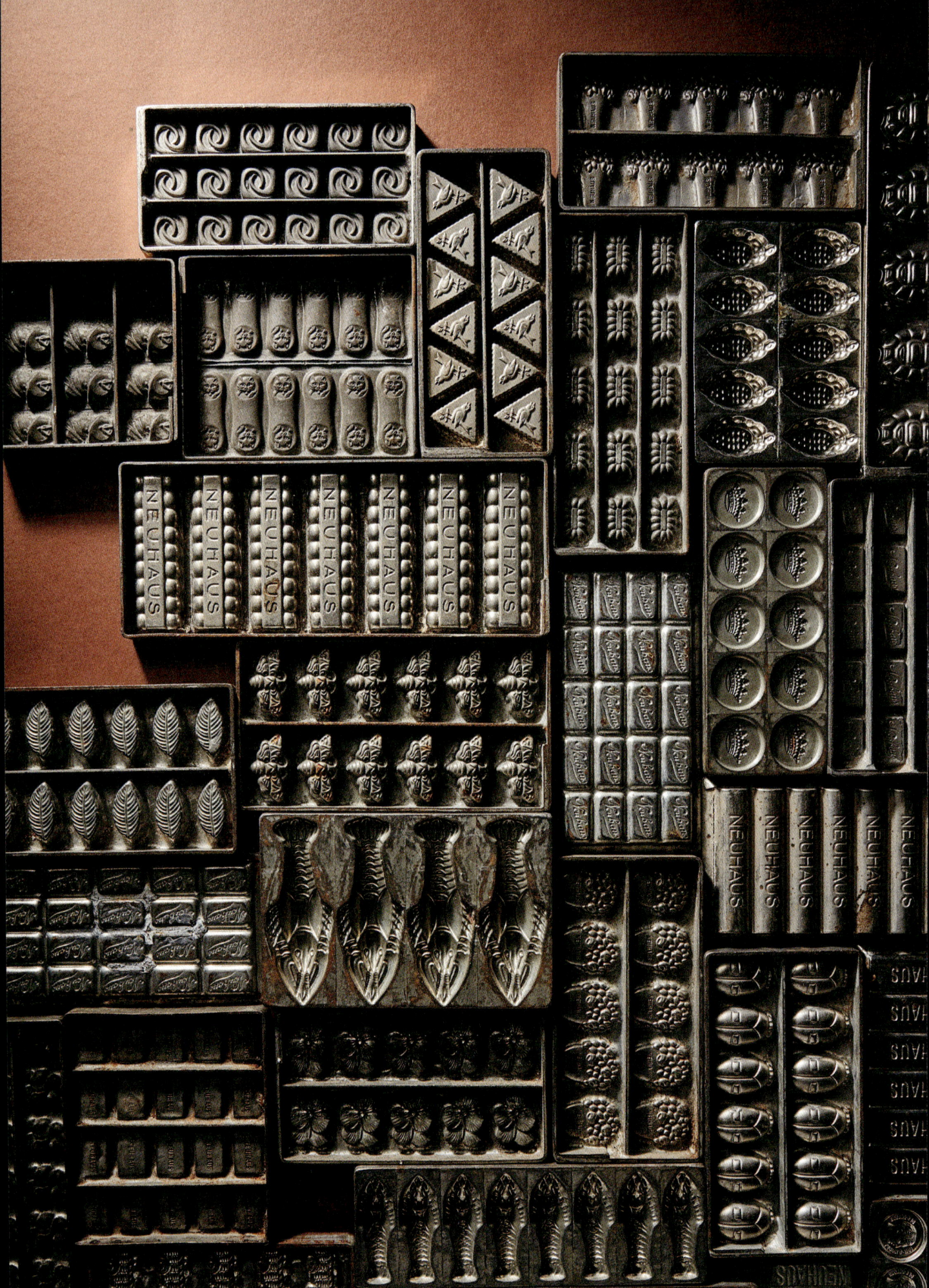

RECIPES

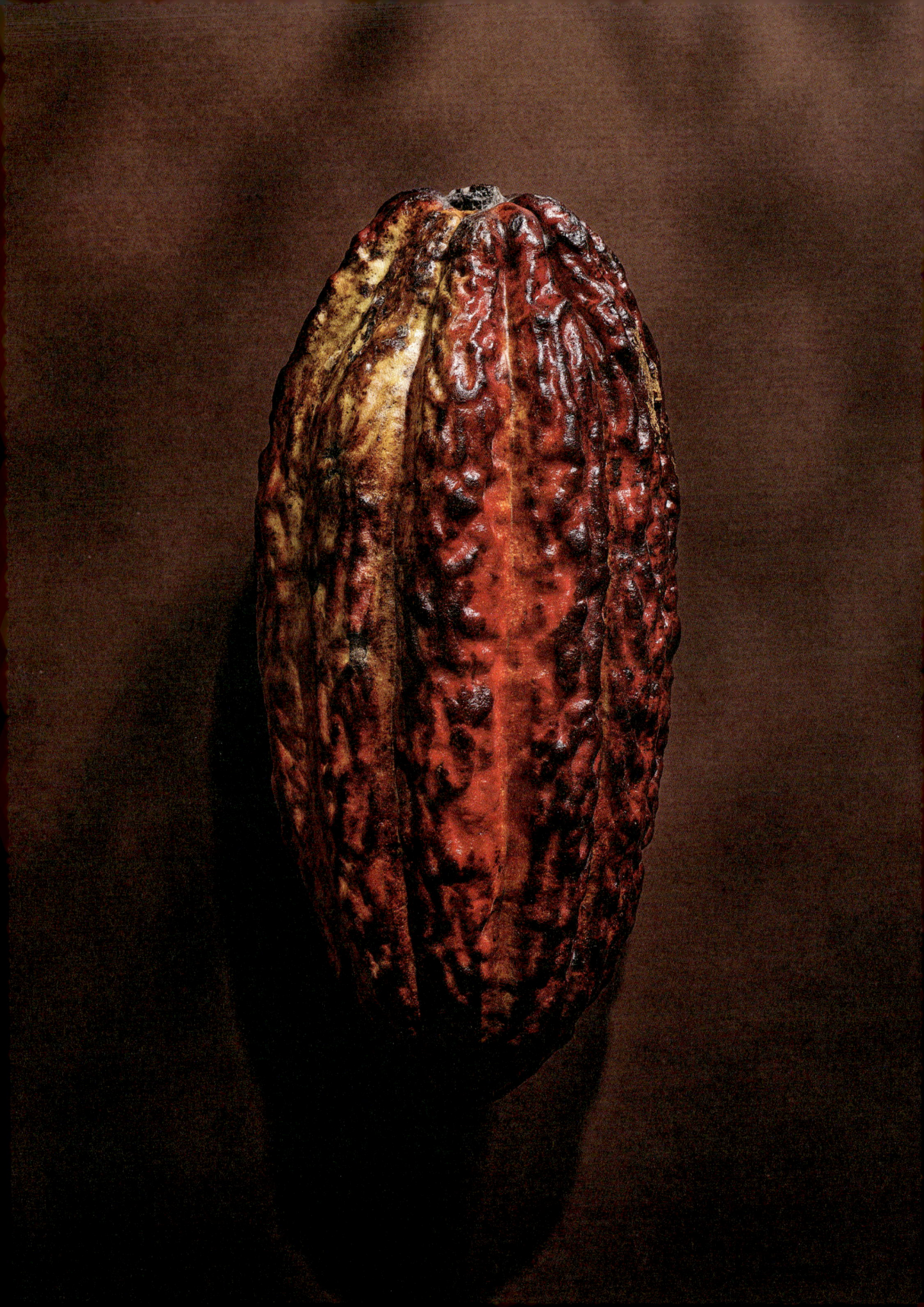

PART 1

THE MAÎTRE CHOCOLATIER'S LITTLE LEXICON

The razor-sharp definition of a praline provided by the Neuhaus master chocolatiers is 'A praline is a shell with a filling'. It captures the essence of a speciality representing Belgian chocolate-making's excellence. This apparent simplicity conceals a remarkable feat of precision, beginning with selecting raw materials and culminating in the expertise of the artisans who transform them.

The Belgian praline originated in 1912, when Jean Neuhaus Jr substituted his grandfather's chocolate-covered medicine with a gourmet filling encased in a chocolate shell. This innovation began a tradition featuring various textures and flavours: praline, ganache, gianduja, caramel, and crème fraîche. Each praline results from a delicate balance between the finesse of the chocolate and the richness of the filling, creating a unique taste experience.

OUTSTANDING RAW MATERIALS

The praline's main ingredient, chocolate, is derived from cocoa harvested in the world's finest plantations in tropical regions. The beans are primarily cultivated in the equatorial zone of West Africa, Central America, and Southeast Asia, where the warm, humid climate favours their growth.

There are three main bean varieties, most of which are harvested between September and March, each with distinct characteristics: Criollo, the rarest and most highly prized, is renowned for its delicate aromas and low level of bitterness. An eponymous praline in the Neuhaus range pays tribute to it. Forastero is the strongest and most widely grown, with a fuller-bodied, more intense flavour. Finally, Trinitario is a hybrid of the first two, combining aromatic finesse and resilience.

Neuhaus pralines derive their rich flavour not only from cocoa but also from other meticulously selected ingredients: California almonds, Piedmont hazelnuts, fresh cream, cocoa butter, Madagascar vanilla, and Belgian flower honey, each contributing to the sensory signature of these exceptional chocolates.

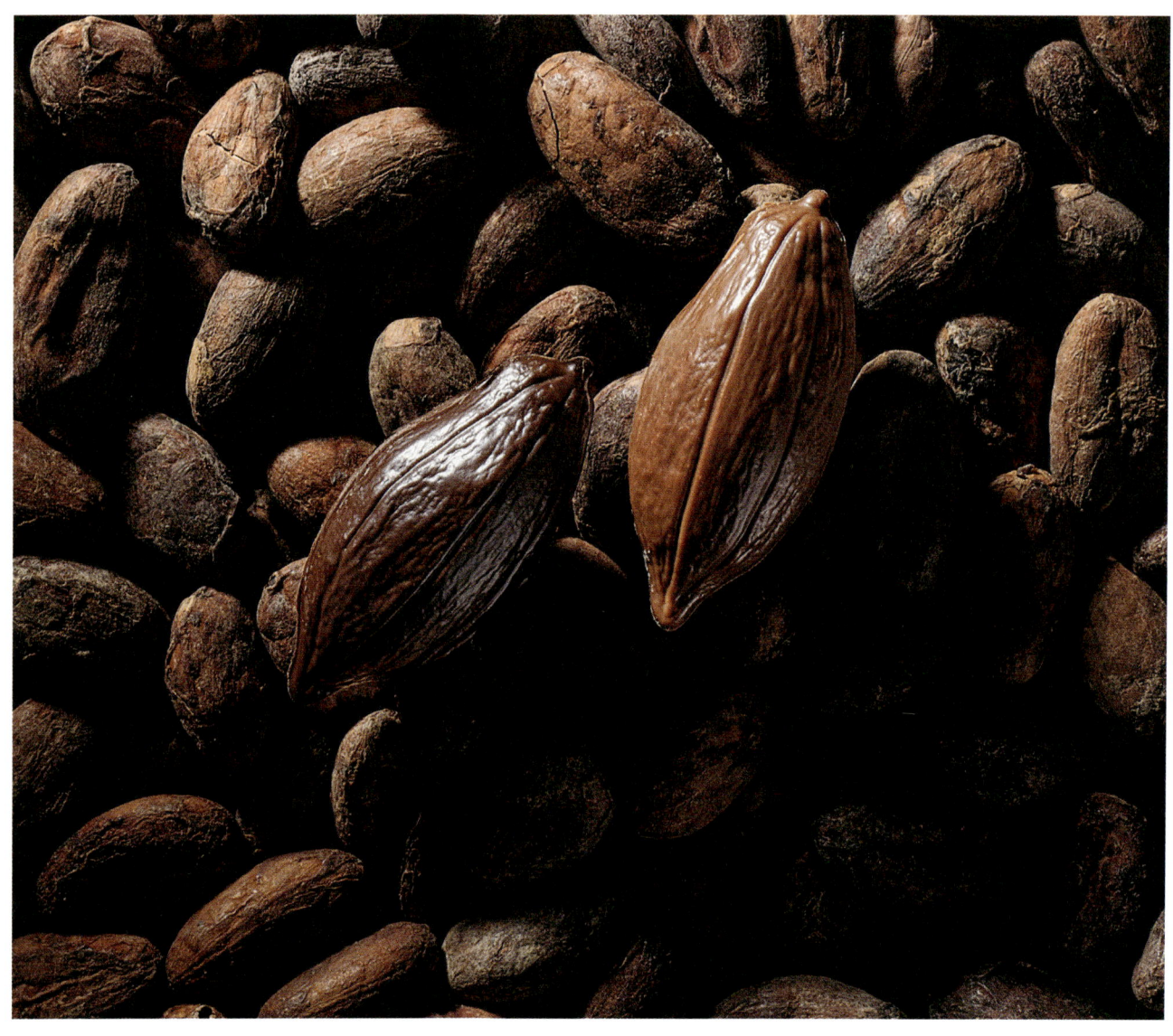

THE STAGES INVOLVED IN CHOCOLATE PRODUCTION

Before they are transformed into chocolate, cocoa beans undergo several essential stages.

HARVESTING AND FERMENTATION

After harvesting, the pods are opened to extract the beans, which ferment for five to seven days. This natural process enhances the chocolate's aromatic precursors.

DRYING

The beans are spread out in the sun or dried mechanically to reduce their moisture content, a crucial stage in preventing mould and ensuring their preservation.

ROASTING

Heated to approximately 120°C, the beans unveil their full spectrum of aromas and acquire their distinctive brown colour.

CRUSHING AND GRINDING

The roasted beans are crushed to extract the nibs (pieces of roasted and crushed cocoa beans, without sugar). These are then finely ground to produce a fluid paste: the cocoa liquor.

CONCHING

This lengthy brewing process at a controlled temperature (between 45°C and 80°C) refines the texture and softens the acidity of the chocolate.

TEMPERING

Melted chocolate is cooled and reheated cyclically in such a way as to ensure it remains shiny and crisp.

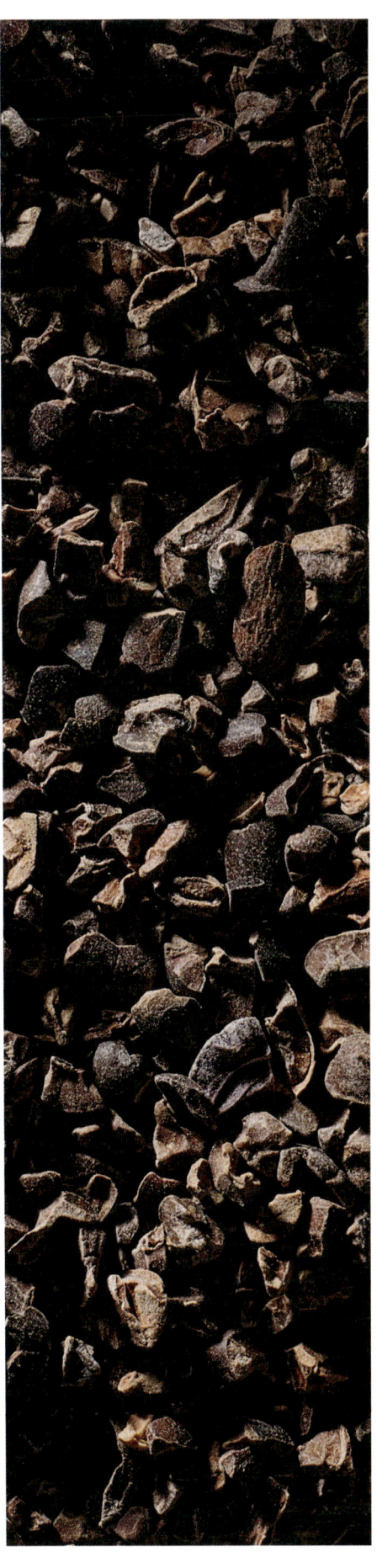

FUNDAMENTAL VOCABULARY

Here is a glossary of the technical terms most commonly used at Neuhaus to enhance understanding of the know-how and language of chocolate makers. From bleaching to vanilla, these words reveal the precision of the actions and the richness of the textures that make up the house's daily life.

Fatbloom

Occurs when chocolate is not stored at the correct temperature (between 15°C and 18°C). The vegetable fat in the cocoa then migrates to the surface, forming a white veil that alters the product's aesthetics without changing its taste.

Carame

Caramel is a sweet topping made by heating sugar until it melts and develops a distinctive flavour and a golden hue. It is often used in Neuhaus pralines for its intense yet comforting taste.

Coating

Coating covers a filling with a thin layer of tempered chocolate. This stage is crucial for giving the pralines a shiny, elegant finish.

Cocoa butter

Cocoa butter is a key ingredient in the production of chocolate. It is a vegetable fat derived from cocoa beans that imparts smoothness and texture. At Neuhaus, this ingredient is carefully selected to ensure exceptional quality.

Couverture

Couverture chocolate is a high-quality type of chocolate used by chocolate makers to coat their products. It has a higher cocoa butter content than conventional chocolate, which results in a smoother texture and a glossy finish after tempering.

Crystallisation

Crystallisation refers to the process by which cocoa butter molecules are organised stably and regularly as they cool. This precise structure, known as the 'V-shape', gives tempered chocolate its shine, crunchiness, and long shelf life. Well-controlled crystallisation prevents visual defects (whitening, stains) and ensures a perfect texture.

Feuillantine

This is a pastry preparation made from finely crushed crêpe dentelle flakes, used to add crunch to various sweet creations. Originally from Brittany, it is made by crumbling gavottes, ultra-thin crêpes rolled and baked until they become delightfully crumbly. Thanks to its delicate texture and slightly buttery flavour, feuillantine is often used in preparations that contrast melting and crunchiness.

Ganache

Ganache is a smooth mixture created by blending melted chocolate with cream (whipping cream, milk, or sour cream) or another liquid, such as tea, coffee, or alcohol. It is commonly used as a filling in various pralines and enhances the flavour of the chocolate.

Where does ganache come from? The story goes that an absent-minded apprentice pastry chef inadvertently spilt hot cream onto a chocolate preparation one day. His boss was furious; he first chastised him and called him a 'ganache' ('fool' in old French) before changing his mind after tasting the impromptu mixture.

Garnishing

Garnishing involves filling a chocolate shell with a filling, frequently utilising a piping bag to ensure even distribution.

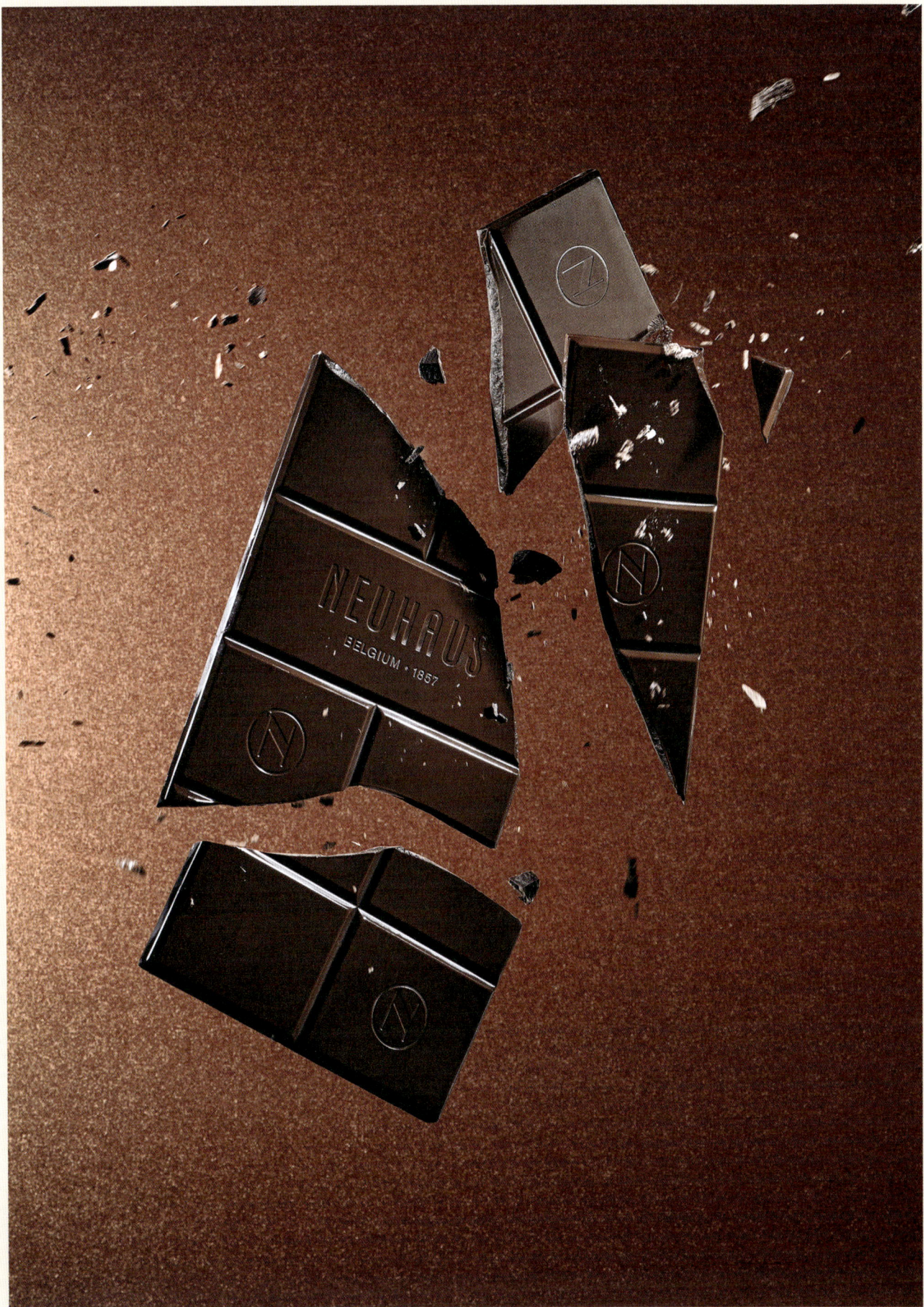

Gianduja

Like praliné, gianduja is a melting mixture of milk chocolate, hazelnut or almond paste (containing at least 20%, distinguishing it from praliné), sugar, and cocoa butter. Its creamy texture and rich flavour make it a preferred ingredient in artisan chocolate-making.

Where does gianduja come from? As the name suggests, it is a recipe of Italian origin, specifically from Piedmont, a region renowned for the quality of its hazelnuts. In the wake of Napoleon's cocoa blockade against Italy, Gianduja was created in the 19th century by Cafarelle. The name 'gianduja' originates from the fictional character Gianduja, who embodies the rural culture of Piedmont. He is an emblematic figure in the Turin carnival and the commedia dell'arte, often associated with greed and conviviality. Chocolates made from this chocolate paste are distributed during Carnival, which has contributed to its popularity.

Manon

A manon is an emblematic Belgian praline coated with white, dark or milk chocolate and featuring a creamy filling, often made from crème fraîche. It takes its name from the eponymous Neuhaus praline.

Marzipan

Marzipan is a solid paste consisting mainly of finely ground almonds and sugar. Its delicate flavour and slightly grainy texture make it a popular ingredient in certain Neuhaus pralines.

Mendiant

In pastry and confectionery, a mendiant is a thin slab of chocolate adorned with dried and candied fruit, often including almonds, hazelnuts, figs, and raisins. This speciality originates in the Provençal tradition of the four mendiants, emblematic elements of the thirteen Christmas desserts. Each dried fruit symbolises a religious order that has taken a vow of poverty: walnuts or hazelnuts for the Carmelites, dried figs for the Franciscans, almonds for the Dominicans, and sultanas for the Augustinians. The association of these fruits, which evoke sobriety and humility, has been perpetuated through confectionery, giving rise to mendicant chocolates, now available in various forms and fillings.

Moulding

Moulding involves pouring tempered chocolate into a mould to create a specific shape. This technique is used for various designs, such as shells, figurines, and pralines.

Nougatine

Nougatine is a crunchy preparation made from caramelised sugar and dried fruit (such as hazelnuts and almonds), often used to add a contrasting texture to pralines. Its production requires not only high-quality ingredients but also actual expertise. At Neuhaus, the master chocolatiers meticulously select the finest ingredients and prepare the nougatine by hand, adhering to a traditional recipe passed down within the company for many years. The process relies on a precise technique: the sugar is slowly melted in a copper vat before being baked in the oven, akin to a biscuit, to achieve this unique texture that combines crispness and crunchiness. This nougatine, the recipe for which is jealously guarded, is a key ingredient in some of Neuhaus' most emblematic pralines: the Irrésistibles. Their identity hinges on this subtle alliance between the delicacy of the chocolate and the gentle nougatine crunch.

Praliné

Praliné is a delicate blend of hazelnuts and/or roasted almonds with caramelised sugar and chocolate. It is one of the most iconic fillings in Neuhaus pralines, characterised by its creamy texture.

Where does praliné come from? The story goes that the chef to the Duke of Plessis-Praslin, Clément Jaluzot, inadvertently spilt some cooked sugar over a mixture of hazelnuts and almonds. Caught unawares when it came time to serve the dessert, the chef sent the caramelised mixture as it was. Enthusiastic, the duke and his guests found it so to their liking that the chef decided to name the recipe after the shrewd negotiator sent by Mazarin to negotiate with the Bordelais, who, during the reign of Louis XIV, were in insurrection against the royal power.

Rolling

Using a roller to roll out almond or gianduja paste to attain an even thickness, prepared for further work.

Soy lecithin

Soya lecithin is a natural emulsifier extracted from soya beans that aids in homogenising the texture of chocolate by facilitating the blending of cocoa butter with other ingredients.

Tempering

Tempering is a crucial technique in chocolate making that involves regulating the temperature of the chocolate to achieve a shiny, crunchy coating.

Truffle

A truffle is an irregularly shaped chocolate praline, often coated with cocoa powder or chocolate shavings. The filling is typically ganache-based and features an endless array of flavours.

Where does the truffle come from? This delicacy is named after the noble Perigordian tuber (Tuber melanosporum), whose rough shape and earthy appearance it adopts. It was created for the Christmas season in 1895 by Louis Dufour, a pastry chef in Chambéry, and was subsequently adopted by all chocolate makers.

Vanilla

Vanilla is a precious spice used to flavour many chocolate creations. Neuhaus favours Bourbon vanilla varieties from Madagascar and Mexico for their rich, complex aromas.

A REALM OF TEXTURES AND FLAVOURS

Contrary to popular belief, Neuhaus is not a chocolate manufacturer, but a creator of pralines. This nuance is essential: it's akin to a Michelin-starred chef who does not produce the flour or butter he uses, but carefully selects the finest ingredients to elevate his recipes. The quality of the fillings and raw materials ensures that the result is a delicious, refined, and elegant creation.

Each praline boasts a specific filling, each with its particular characteristics: praliné, a blend of finely ground caramelised hazelnuts or almonds; ganache, a combination of chocolate and cream that offers a melting texture and intense flavour; gianduja, a smooth hazelnut and chocolate paste, born in Piedmont and renowned for its sweetness; or caramel, both tender and flavoursome, created by heating sugar until it reaches an amber hue.

Three types of chocolate are used to coat the pralines: dark chocolate made from cocoa paste, cocoa butter and sugar (Neuhaus pure chocolate contains at least 55% cocoa); milk chocolate made from cocoa paste, cocoa butter, sugar and milk powder (this chocolate contains at least 35% cocoa); and white chocolate comprising cocoa butter, sugar and milk powder.

Each bite conceals a balance between technique and delicacy that makes the praline a true icon of Belgian chocolate. But what exactly is Belgian chocolate? It is chocolate whose entire blending, refining, and conching process has been conducted in Belgium.

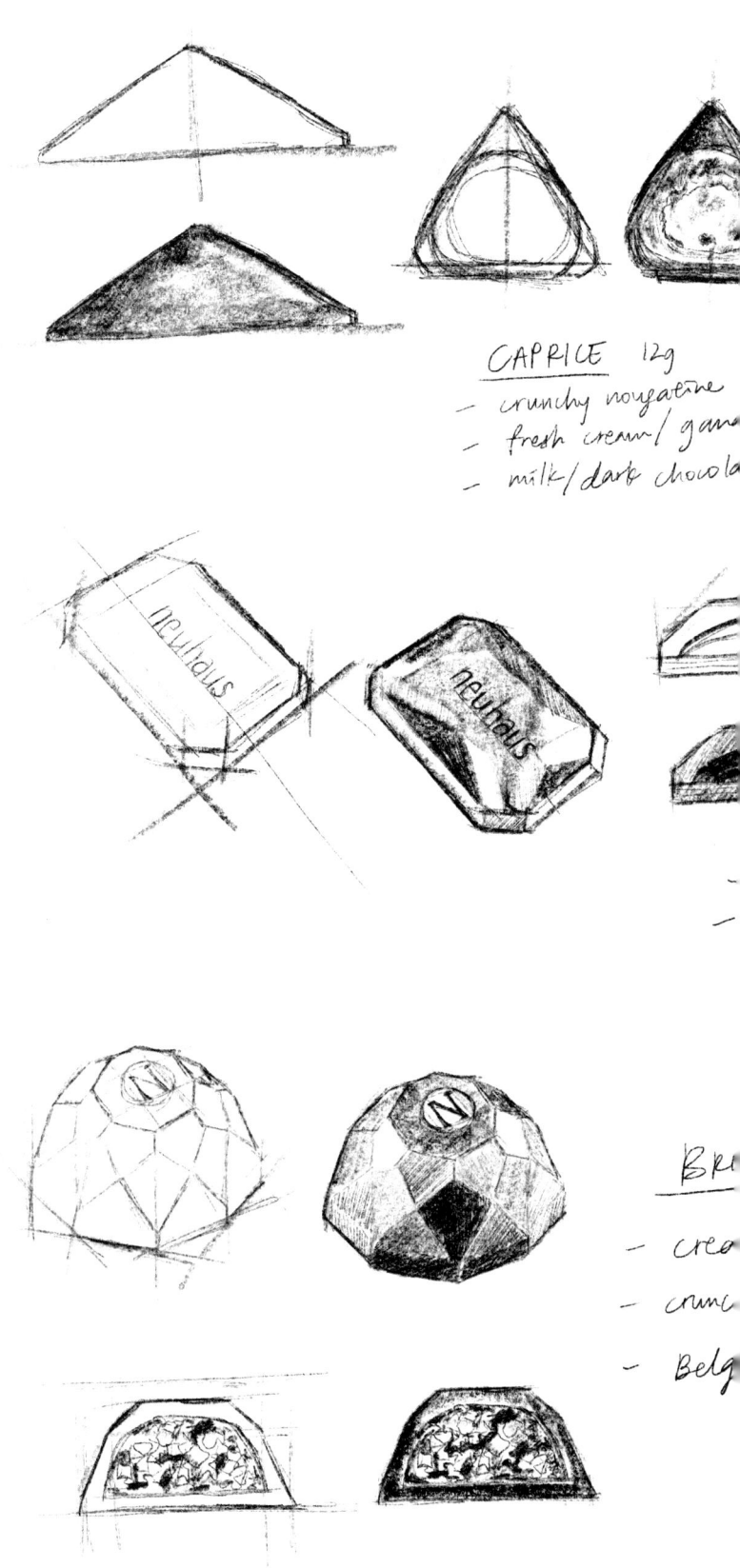

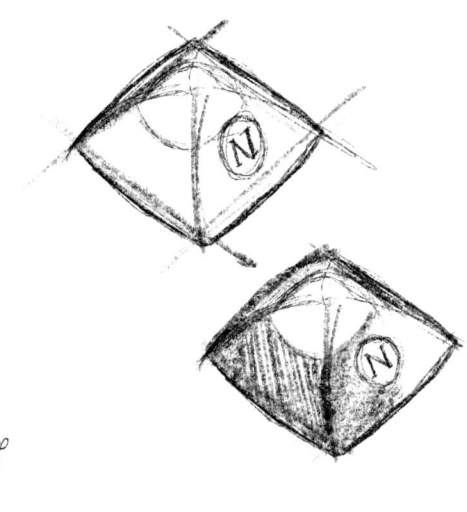

1857 12g
- Speuloos (cinnamon, ginger, cardamom, nutmeg)
- Milk chocolate coating

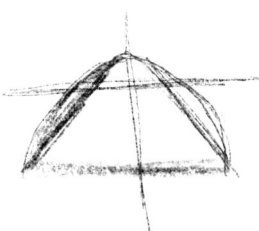
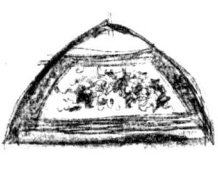

TERRE DE COLOMBIE N°3 12g
- Colombian chocolate filling (65% cocoa)
- samba tea
- orange pieces
- granduja
- dark Colombian chocolate

12g
citrusy chocolate
(72% cacao from ...gascar)

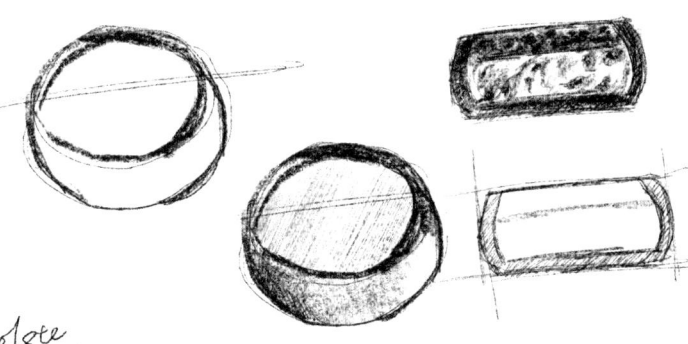

12g
nduja
chocolate

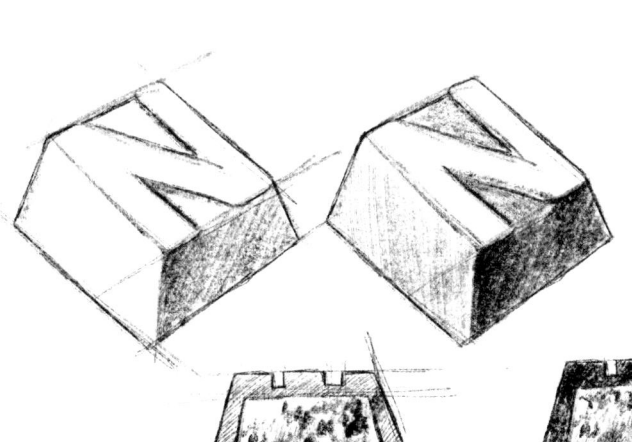

NEUHAUS LAIT 12g
- Almond praliné filling
- Milk chocolate coating

PART 2

THE MAÎTRE CHOCOLATIER'S BASIC SKILLS

Sculpting chocolate, understanding its secrets, and revealing all its nobility is the essence of a master chocolatier's expertise. Behind each exceptional praline lie precise gestures, techniques inherited and perfected over time, and subtleties that transform tasting into a unique sensory experience.

In the following pages, you'll discover the fundamental Neuhaus chocolate-making techniques that transform raw materials into edible works of art. Tempering, moulding, praline, ganache, caramel, or buttercream: each method is explained step by step, with precise advice on how to learn them at home. Whether you're an enlightened amateur or a curious professional, this compendium will help you understand the magic of chocolate better, master its subtleties, and enhance your practice.

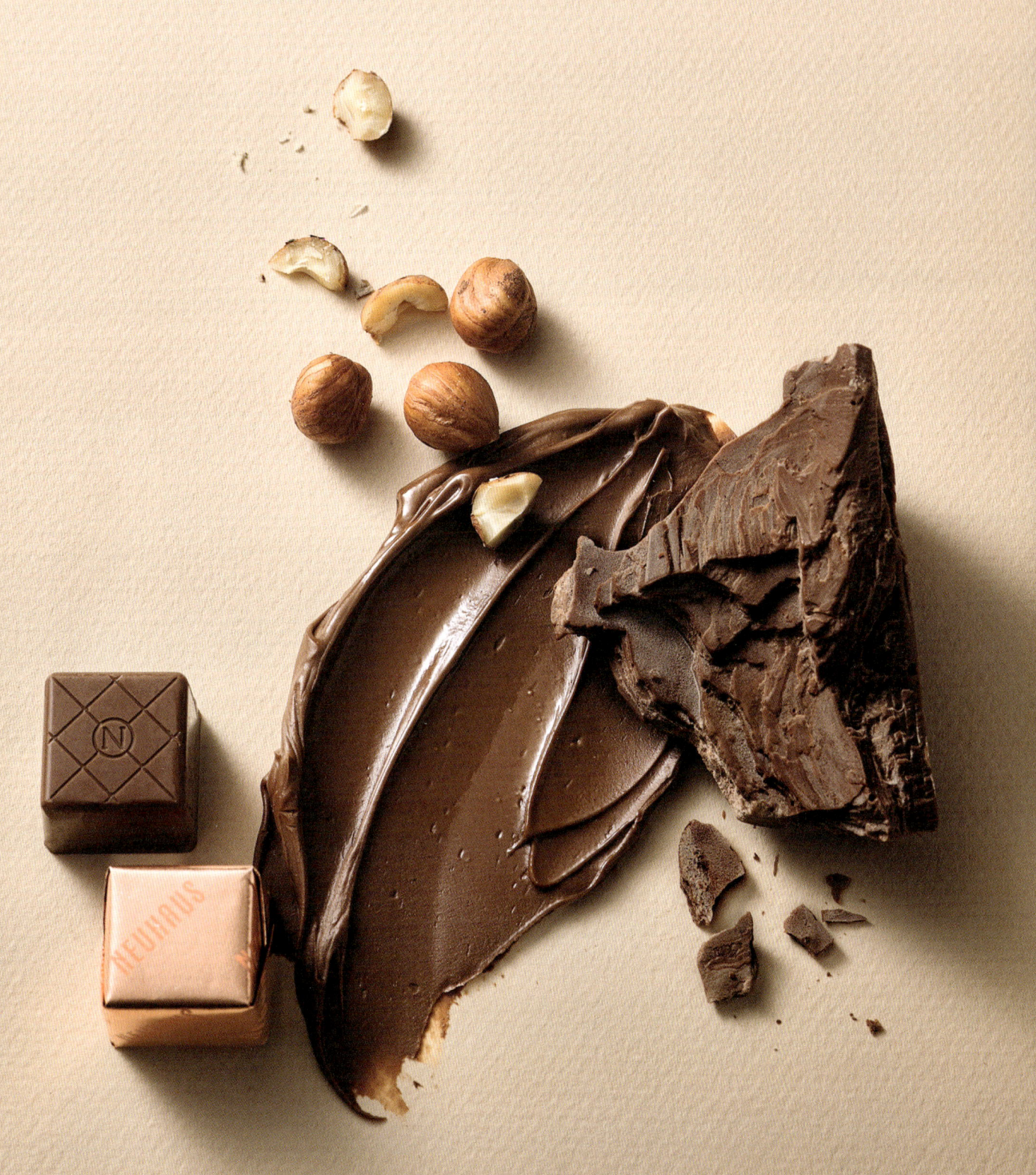

TEMPERING CHOCOLATE
THE FUNDAMENTAL FOUNDATION FOR FLAWLESS SHINE AND UNMATCHED CRISPNESS

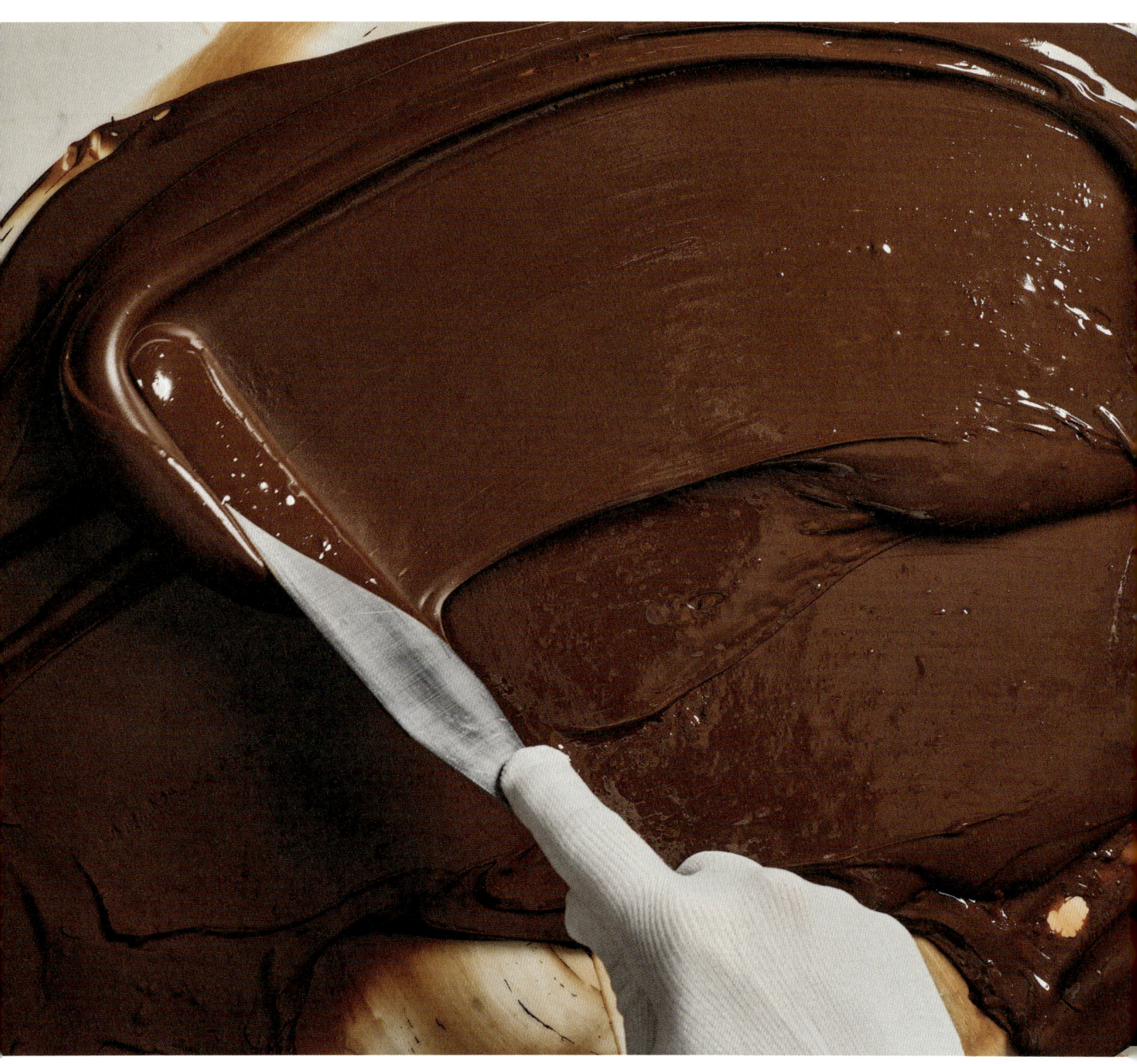

Mastering the art of tempering chocolate is the first step towards excellence. This process demands responsiveness and precision: the desired effects can be achieved in five to ten minutes, depending on the thickness of the chocolate. Tempering ensures a result worthy of the finest artisans—a perfect shine, a clean break, and a melting texture. It also ensures optimum stability: tempered chocolate remains smooth and homogeneous for several weeks, without whitening or melting prematurely, provided it is kept at room temperature (16 to 20°C), away from humidity and light. In short, tempering transforms a simple melt into a noble material, ready to enhance all your creations. Conversely, poorly tempered chocolate becomes dull, grainy, and unstable.

To achieve this, master chocolatiers employ two methods: tablage on marble and seeding.

Traditional method
Tabling on a marble slab

Tempering is crucial in moulding, enrobing, or constructing intricate decorations. It is a skill that demands patience and precision. This process involves melting the chocolate (at around 45°C, depending on the type), then cooling it by spreading it out on a marble surface with a spatula. The chocolate is worked back and forth to reduce its temperature to approximately 27°C, before being reheated slightly (up to 31-32°C for dark chocolate). This process allows the cocoa butter to crystallise properly, resulting in smooth, glossy, and brittle chocolate, with no white marks on the surface.

1. Melting the chocolate according to type (on the right).

To melt the chocolate, you may select from two options:

- Begin by bringing water to a boil in a large saucepan, taking care not to fill it to the brim. Chop the chocolate into small pieces and place them in a smaller saucepan. Position the smaller saucepan on top of the larger one. Reduce the heat and stir the chocolate occasionally until it melts and becomes fluid.

- Place a bowl of chopped chocolate in the microwave. Set the microwave to a temperature between 170° and 260° for gentle heat. Turn it off after 30 seconds, then again after 20 seconds, and once more after 10 seconds to check the consistency of the chocolate and stir it with a silicone spatula. This method accelerates and, more importantly, homogenises heat distribution. When the consistency appears correct, it is ready. This should take no longer than 3 to 4 minutes.

2. Pour two-thirds of the melted chocolate onto the marble slab and spread it using a spatula, moving it back and forth.

3. Reintroduce the cooled chocolate back into the remaining hot chocolate in the bowl.

4. Check the temperature and reheat the chocolate if necessary to reach the working temperature.

Advantages: This method allows for the tempering of large quantities and ensures optimal crystallisation.

Disadvantages: It necessitates skill and the use of a specific marble.

Accessible method
Seeding

This method involves adding unmelted chocolate to melted chocolate to trigger crystallisation.

1. Melt two-thirds of the chocolate at the suitable melting temperature (see above).

2. Incorporate the remaining third of finely chopped chocolate and stir until the appropriate crystallisation temperature is achieved.

3. Stir gently until smooth, and check the temperature before use.

Advantages: simplicity; no special equipment required.

Disadvantages: takes longer; crystallisation is less homogeneous than when tabling on marble.

ADVICE FROM THE MAÎTRE CHOCOLATIER

Always utilise a thermometer for utmost precision.

Avoid any contact with water, as the chocolate may set instantly.

Test the tempering by dipping a spatula into the chocolate; it is perfectly tempered if it sets within a few minutes with a shiny finish.

With these techniques, chocolate unveils all its brilliance and transforms into a truly noble material in your hands. Are you ready to play master chocolatier?

Ingredient (your choice)
- Dark chocolate
- Milk chocolate
- White chocolate

Utensils

- Heat-resistant bowl
- Microwave oven or bain-marie (for the most straightforward method)
- Marble worktop (for traditional tabling)
- Spatula (flexible silicone utensil) or scraper (rigid utensil in the shape of a rectangle or half-moon used to work the chocolate and scrape the work surface)
- An accurate food thermometer

Melting temperatures to be aware of
- **Dark chocolate:** melts at 50-55°C | crystallisation at 28-29°C | working temperature 31-32°C
- **Milk chocolate:** melts at 45-50°C | crystallisation at 27-28°C | working temperature 29-30°C
- **White chocolate:** melts at 40-45°C | crystallisation at 25-26°C | working temperature 27-29°C

MOULDING THE CHOCOLATE

BRINGING SHAPES TO LIFE AND ELEVATING CHOCOLATE TO NEW HEIGHTS

Moulding is an essential technique for master chocolatiers, allowing them to create precise and refined shapes, ranging from praline shells to figurines. The key to success lies in employing perfectly tempered chocolate and a clean, dry mould.

Steps for moulding

1. **Prepare the mould:** ensure the mould is clean, dry and at room temperature.

2. **Fill the mould:** pour the tempered chocolate into the mould until it is full.

3. **Eliminate air bubbles** by gently tapping the mould against a flat surface or using a vibrator to dislodge any bubbles that may affect the texture.

4. **Invert the mould and drain:** flip it over to remove any excess chocolate and create a thin shell.

5. **Leave to crystallise:** allow the chocolate to set at room temperature or refrigerate it for a few minutes to expedite crystallisation.

6. **Fill the shell:** once the shell has hardened, fill it with the filling of your choice, such as ganache, praline, caramel, etc.

7. **Seal the praline:** seal the praline by covering the filling with a thin layer of tempered chocolate.

8. **Careful unmoulding:** allow the chocolate to crystallise fully before gently inverting the mould and tapping lightly.

ADVICE FROM THE MAÎTRE CHOCOLATIER

Ensure the mould is clean and polished before use for perfectly shiny chocolate. Proper tempering guarantees easy removal from the mould and chocolate free from white streaks. With this technique, each moulding becomes a little work of art to be savoured. The rest is up to you!

Ingredient

Tempered chocolate (dark, milk or white)

Utensils

- Polycarbonate or silicone mould
- Chocolate spatula
- Food thermometer
- Shaker (optional, to eliminate air bubbles)

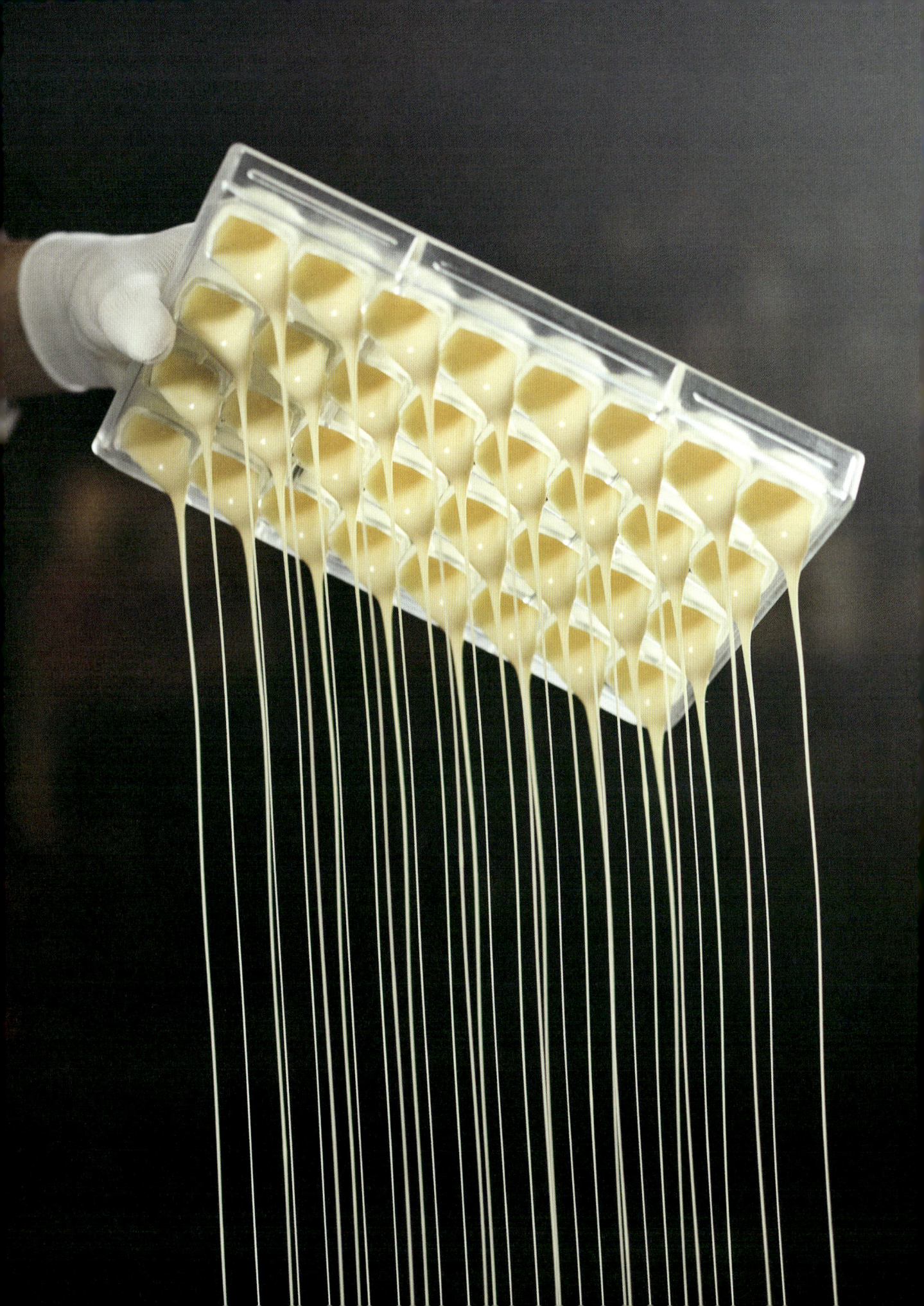

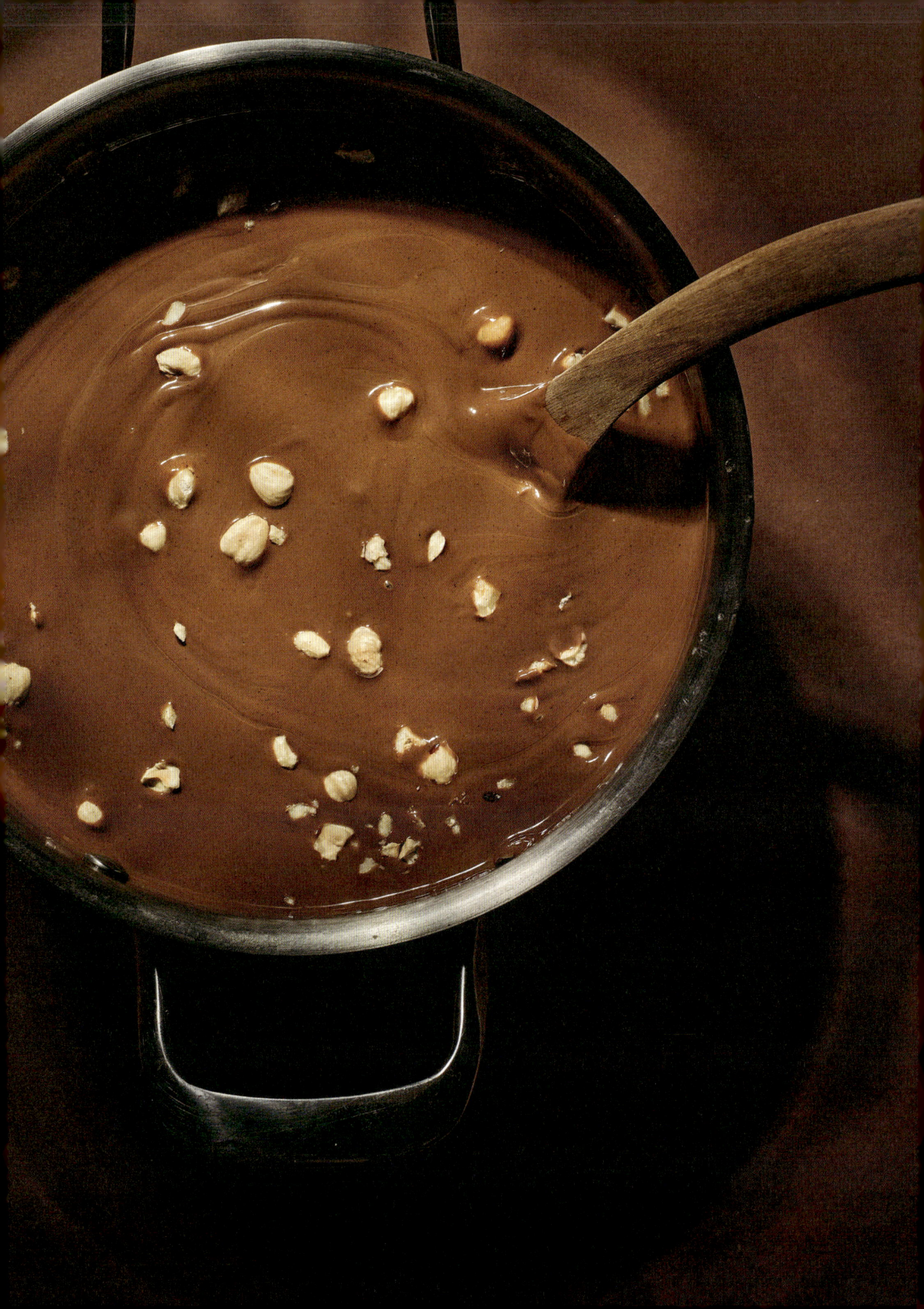

PRALINÉ

THE FOUNDATION FOR OUTSTANDING PRALINES

Praliné is a master chocolatier's emblematic creation. It is used as a filling for pralines, ganaches, or pastries. Traditionally made with hazelnuts, it can also be prepared with other nuts such as almonds, pecans, or a combination of varieties.

Preparation

1. **Roast the nuts:** place the hazelnuts (or other nuts) on a baking tray lined with greaseproof paper or a silicone mat and cook for 10 minutes at 180°C to increase their aromatic intensity.

2. **Peel off the skin:** remove the nuts from the oven and rub them with a tea towel to remove the skin. Be cautious not to burn yourself while the nuts are still hot!

3. **Prepare the dry caramel:** pour the sugar into a stainless steel saucepan and heat over medium heat until a golden caramel is reached. Do not stir to prevent crystallisation.

4. **Coat the hazelnuts:** Pour the hot caramel over the hazelnuts and allow them to cool completely until the caramel hardens.

5. **Blend gradually:** for a crunchy praline, pulse the ingredients until you achieve a crumbly texture. For a smooth, creamy praline, blend until the natural oils from the nuts are released, forming a homogeneous paste. Be careful not to overheat the blender.

6. **Incorporate the chocolate:** melt the milk chocolate at the correct melting temperature (see above) and mix it with the praline for a more delightful texture.

ADVICE FROM THE MAÎTRE CHOCOLATIER

Add a pinch of fleur de sel to enhance the aromas and balance the sweetness.

Test various combinations of nuts, including almonds from Valence, hazelnuts from Piedmont, or pecans, to create more complex flavours.

For a more intense flavour, substitute milk chocolate with fondant chocolate.

Whether as the garnish for a praline or as the foundation for chocolate desserts, homemade praliné is an essential hallmark of artisanal expertise. Get mixing!

Ingredients
(for approximately 300 g of praliné)

- 100 g hazelnuts (or almonds, pecans, etc.)
- 100 g caster sugar
- 100 g premium quality milk chocolate

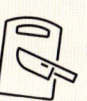

Utensils

- Bain-marie or microwave
- Stainless steel saucepan
- Powerful hand blender or food processor
- Baking tray
- Greaseproof paper or silicone mat
- Wooden spatula or scraper (utensil for scraping efficiently and incorporating delicate ingredients without breaking)
- Clean tea towel

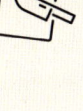

GANACHE

A FUNDAMENTAL FOUNDATION FOR ENHANCING PRALINES, ENTREMETS, AND DESSERTS

Ganache, the filling for pralines like Tentation and Art Nouveau 64 %, is a fundamental pillar of chocolate making and patisserie. This delicate emulsion combines intense flavour with a melting texture. It can be made with dark chocolate, milk chocolate, or white chocolate, thus offering an infinite palette of potential flavours and textures.

Preparation

1. **Warm the cream:** warm the cream and honey in a saucepan until bubbles form, taking care not to let the mixture boil, as this could alter its structure.

2. **Emulsify with the chocolate:** pour the warm cream over the chocolate in three stages. Mix with a scraper or spatula in circular motions until you achieve a homogeneous emulsion.

3. **Mix and incorporate the butter:** once the mixture is smooth and glossy, add the butter cut into cubes and stir until you achieve a perfectly fluid, velvety consistency.

ADVICE FROM THE MAÎTRE CHOCOLATIER

Substitute the cream with puréed fruits (such as raspberry, passion fruit, or mango) for a fruity, acidulated ganache.

To achieve refined aromatic notes, allow spices (such as vanilla, tonka bean, and cardamom) or fresh herbs (like basil, verbena, and lemon thyme) to infuse in the cream overnight in the refrigerator.

Top tip: toast the spices in a frying pan for a few minutes to enhance the flavours before pouring in the cream and allowing them to steep.

Choose plant-based alternatives like coconut cream, almond cream, or hazelnut cream for an exotic twist or praliné.

Incorporate caramelised nut slivers or cocoa nibs to enhance the crunch and create a play on textures.

Ingredients
(for about 1300 g of ganache)

- 500 ml heavy whipping cream (minimum 35% fat content)
- 450 g chocolate (dark, milk or white, depending on the desired intensity)
- 150 g unsalted butter
- 200 g honey from the Yucatan

Utensils

- Bain-marie or microwave oven
- Scale
- Plastic bowl
- Stainless steel saucepan
- Spoon
- Hand blender or powerful food processor
- A spatula or a scraper (a scraping tool appropriate for incorporating delicate mixtures · without making them curdle)
- Clean tea towel

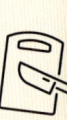
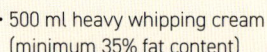

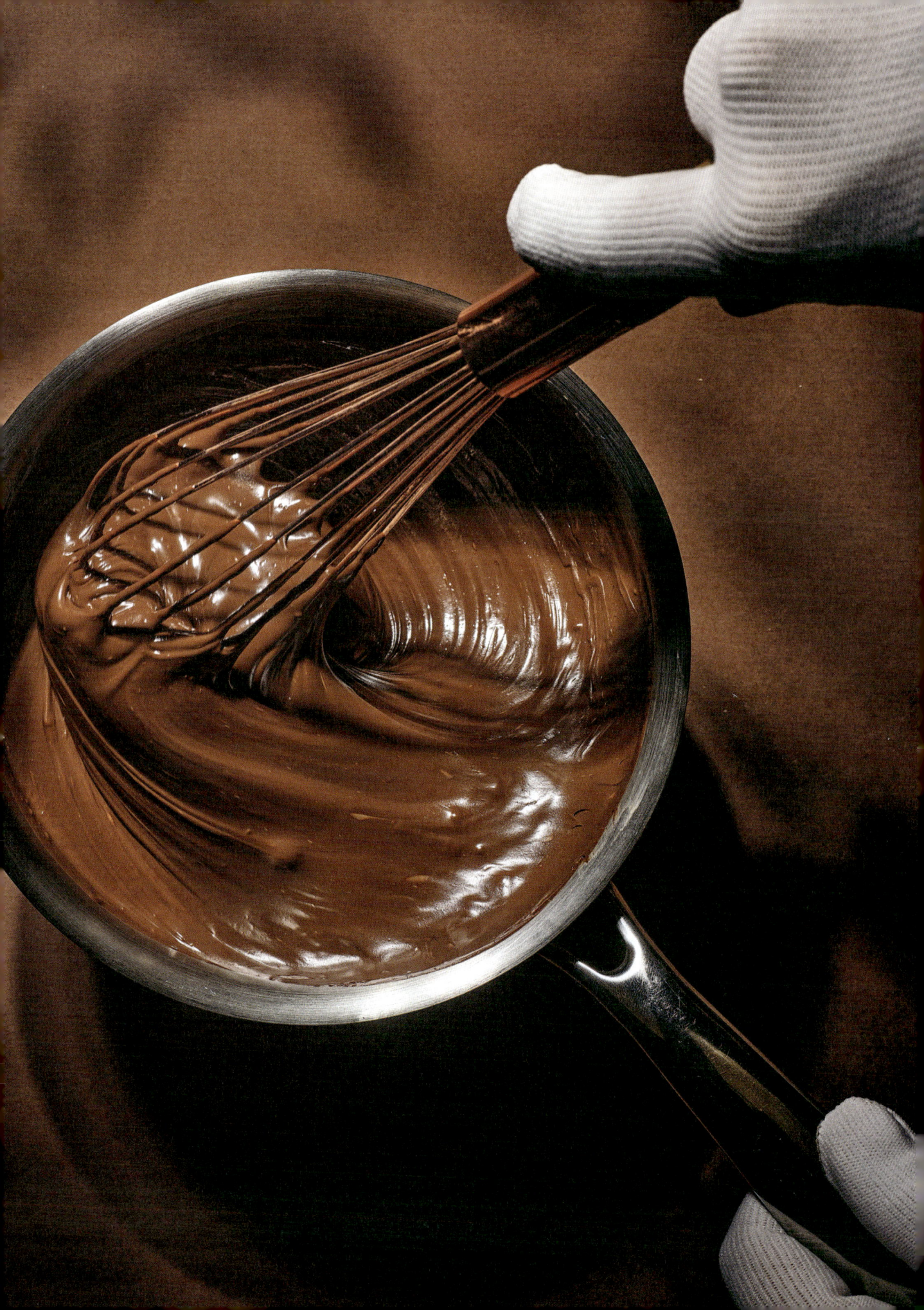

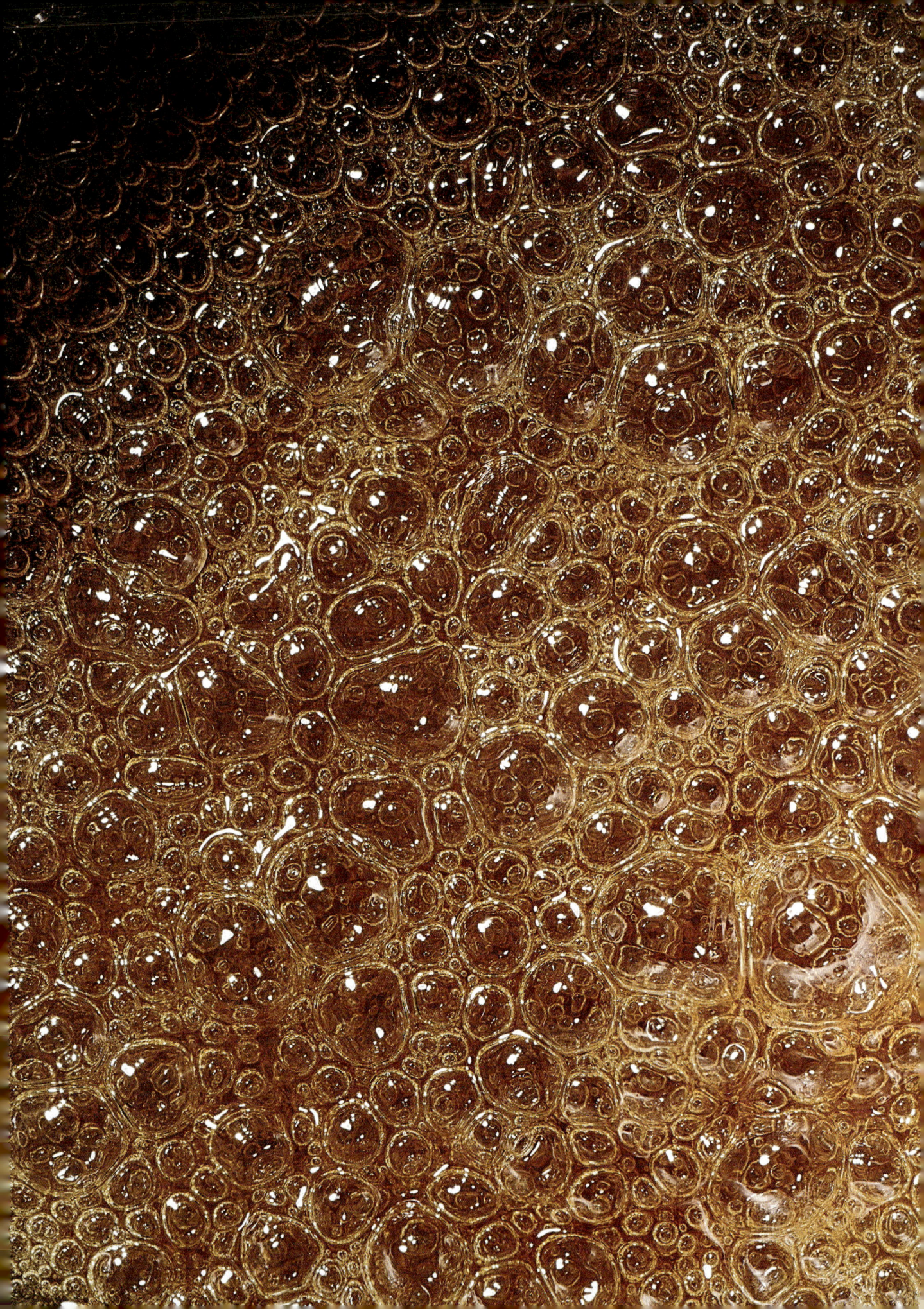

SALTED BUTTER CARAMEL

THE IDEAL BLEND OF SWEETNESS AND INTENSITY

Salted butter caramel is an iconic preparation with a creamy yet intense flavour. It is found in items such as Délice, a hand-filled praline, or Pierre, a tribute to Pierre De Gavre. It can garnish pralines, enhance a dessert, or add a luscious touch to a ganache. Its success relies on mastering the caramel and balancing sugar, salt, and fat.

Preparation

1. **To prepare the caramel,** boil the sugar and glucose in a heavy-bottomed saucepan. Allow it to cook, without stirring, until it reaches a beautiful golden colour.

2. **Stir in the cream:** off the heat, gradually add the previously heated cream (either in a microwave or in a saucepan at 45-50°C) along with the fleur de sel, mixing gently. Be cautious of splashes due to thermal shock.

3. **Blend:** return the saucepan to the heat and bring it back to the boil, stirring gently until the mixture becomes smooth.

4. **Finish:** remove from the heat and add the diced butter and chocolate; stir until entirely melted and combined.

5. **Allow to cool:** transfer the mixture to a bowl or glass jar and let it cool completely at room temperature before use.

ADVICE FROM THE MAÎTRE CHOCOLATIER

Infuse vanilla, coffee or spices such as cardamom into the cream for a refined flavour.

Tip: before infusing the vanilla, open the pod to remove the seeds and stir them into the cream. You can also infuse the vanilla pod in the cream overnight and heat the liquid to 45-50°C before straining.

Substitute the cream with coconut milk or vegetable cream for a more exotic version. Experiment with the texture: cook it longer for a thicker caramel or add more cream for a thinner texture.

Include a hint of melted chocolate fondant for an even more delicious and intense caramel.

Ingredients
(for about 1200 g of caramel)

- 200 g sugar
- 300 g glucose
- 500 ml heavy whipping cream (minimum 35% fat content), heated
- 6 g fleur de sel
- 100 g unsalted butter
- 100 g milk chocolate

Utensils

- Bain-marie or microwave oven
- Scale
- Plastic bowl
- Stainless steel saucepan
- Hand blender or powerful food processor
- Baking tray
- Wooden spatula or scraper
- Clean tea towel

BUTTERCREAM

ELEGANCE AND CREAMINESS
FOR HAUTE CHOCOLATERIE

Buttercream is a quintessential garnish and truly a Neuhaus signature. Its distinguishing feature? The absence of eggs. It is a component of the famous Manon pralines, imparting a light and fluffy sweetness, and of the iconic Caprice, which enhances the combination of chocolate and nougatine. Its melting texture results from a flawlessly controlled emulsion, the outcome of which is determined by the contribution of each ingredient.

Preparation

1. **Beat the diced butter** in small batches until a smooth, silky texture is achieved.
2. **Add the whipping cream,** coffee or vanilla, and caster sugar and beat until smooth. Transfer the mixture to a piping bag and pipe it onto a chocolate base. Allow it to cool and enrobe the Manon with the desired type of chocolate.

ADVICE FROM THE MAÎTRE CHOCOLATIER

To enhance the aromas and balance the sweetness, add a pinch of fleur de sel.

Substitute a portion of the butter with praliné for an even more delectable version.

Incorporate melted chocolate (dark, milk, or white) for an irresistible variation.

Liquors and spirits: a hint of rum, amaretto, or cognac can add ultimate refinement.

Get whipping; make way for refinement!

Ingredient
(for about 720 g of buttercream)

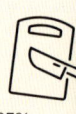

- 250 ml heavy whipping cream (minimum 35% fat content)
- 150 g caster sugar
- 300 g unsalted butter at room temperature for the vanilla version: 4 g powdered Madagascar vanilla
- for the coffee version: 20 g ground Arabica coffee (instant)

Utensils

- Bain-marie or microwave oven
- Scale
- Stainless steel saucepan
- Knife
- Hand blender or powerful food processor
- Cutting board
- Baking tray
- Wooden spatula or scraper
- Clean tea towel

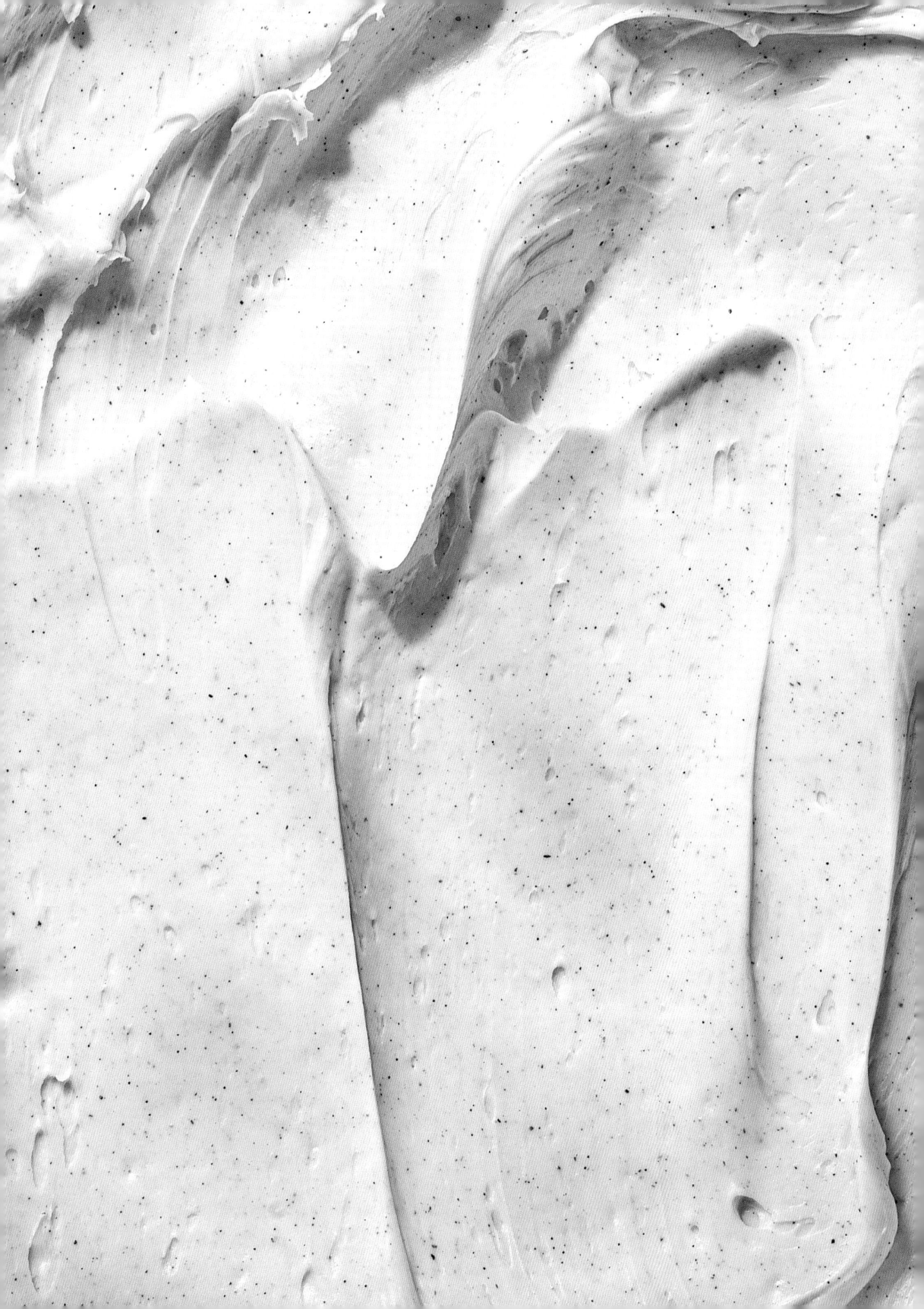

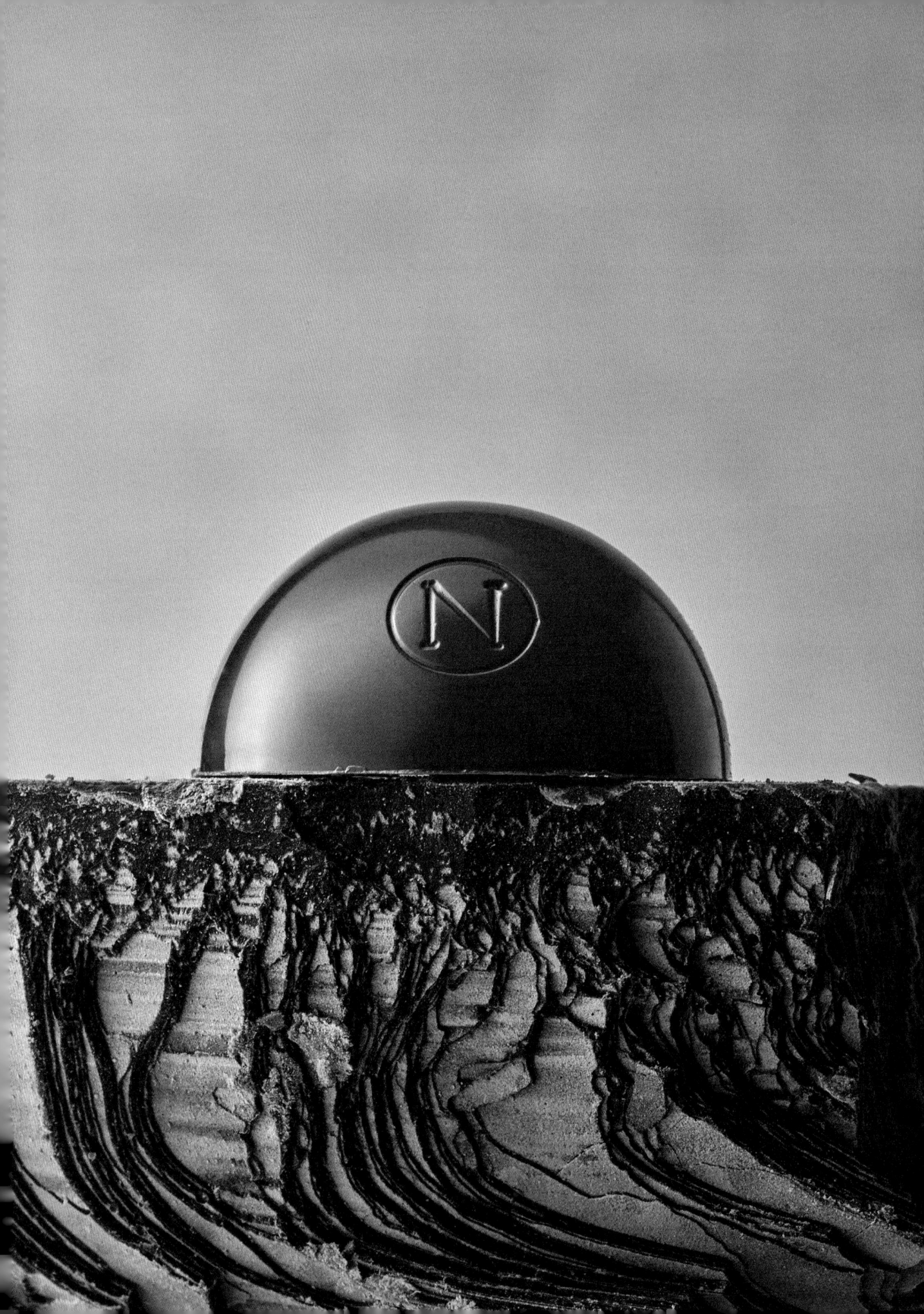

PART 3

THE MAÎTRE CHOCOLATIER'S PRALINES

If there is one art that Neuhaus masters with virtuosity, it is the art of praline. Since its invention in 1912, each creation expresses a subtle balance of textures, flavours, and refinement. Behind every bite lies a jealously guarded savoir-faire, a well-kept secret that signifies the Neuhaus House.

While the exact recipes for our emblematic pralines will remain a secret, we have created a few recipes inspired by this art to offer you the chance to try your hand at the craft of a master chocolatier. These recipes do not claim to reveal Neuhaus's unique alchemy, but they will help you explore the techniques and flavours that create the magic of the praline.

So don your apron, temper your chocolate, and unleash your creativity. While the perfection of a praline lies in the skill of the gesture, it ultimately boils down to passion.

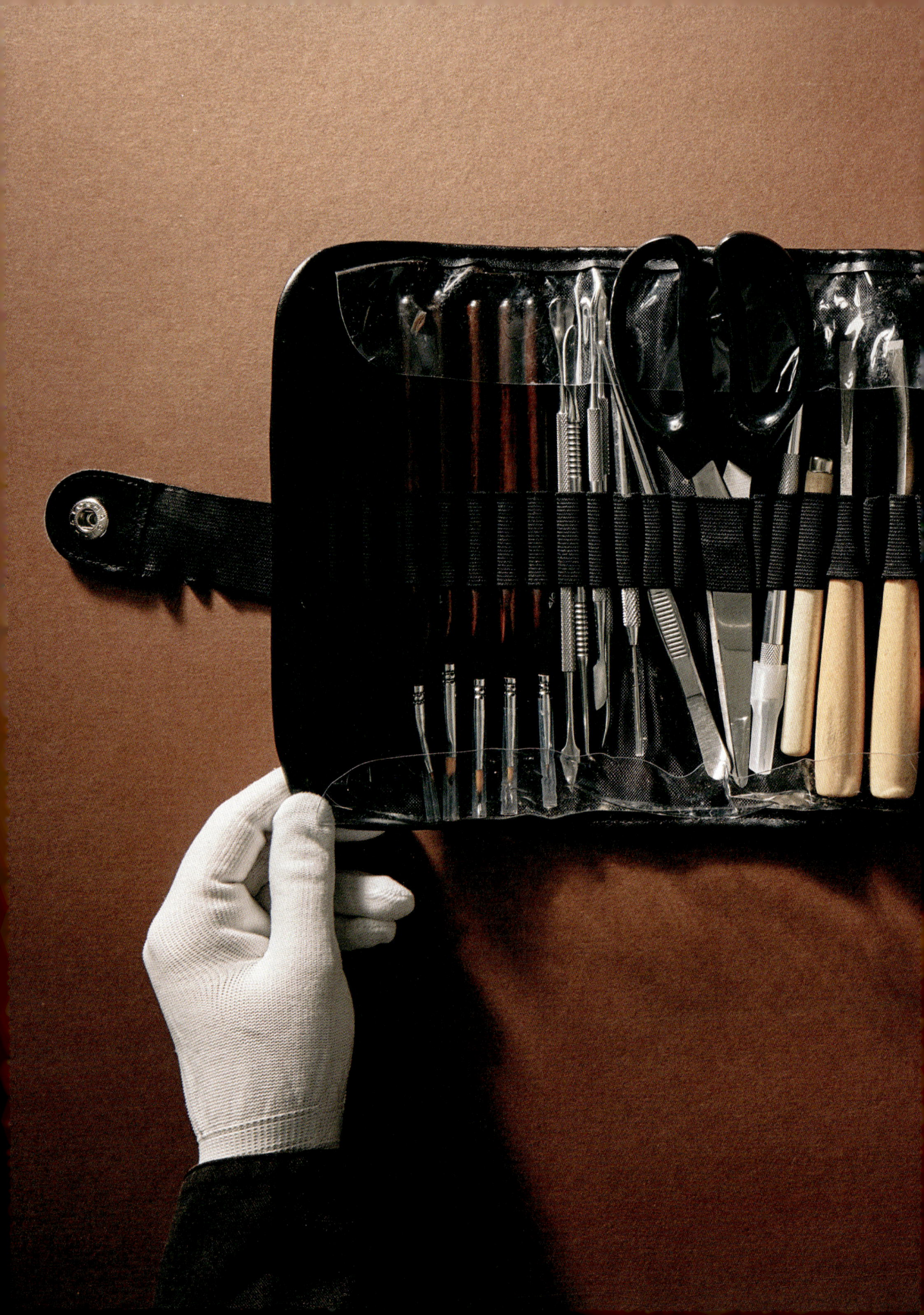

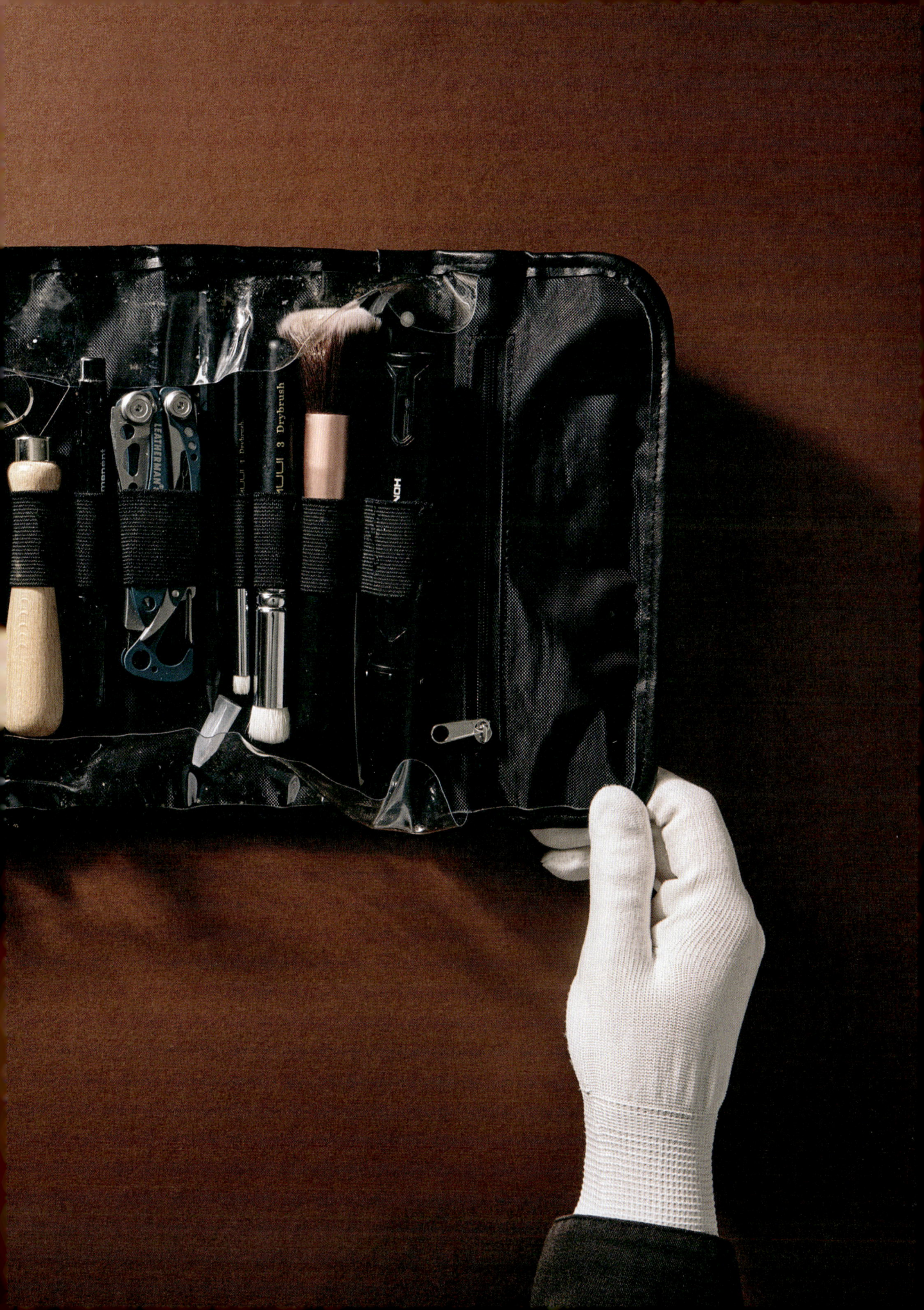

PRALINE WITH A GANACHE MADE FROM FONDANT CHOCOLATE AND HONEY

THE ELEGANCE OF MELTING GANACHE ENCASED IN A CRUNCHY CHOCOLATE SHELL

Its softness and creaminess are the qualities that make ganache one of the most popular fillings in the praline world. Its secret? The perfect emulsion of cream, chocolate, and butter creates a silky texture and an intense flavour.

Ganache pralines offer an irresistible blend of rich 70% fondant chocolate and sweet cream infused with honey from Yunnan. In the Neuhaus range, a praline like Caprice features a light buttercream, while Galerie offers an intense chocolate ganache, and Bonbon 13 presents a hazelnut and rum version.

Preparation

1. Temper the coating chocolate

Melt the dark chocolate in a bain-marie, a tempering machine, or a microwave oven set to reduced power (300-350 W) at the appropriate melting temperature (see below).

Ensure that all the chocolate is melted. Otherwise, crystallisation will remain incomplete. Pour two-thirds of the melted chocolate onto a marble slab and work it with a spatula, cooling it until it reaches 27°C.

Blend the cooled chocolate into the remaining third, which is still warm, mixing until it reaches 30-32°C.

Tip: ensure the moulds are at room temperature (at least 20°C) before pouring in the chocolate to prevent any thermal shock that could compromise the brilliance and adhesion of the moulding.

2. Mould the chocolate shells

Pour the tempered chocolate into the mould.

Flip the mould over and gently tap it to dislodge the excess chocolate.

Allow the mould to sit at room temperature (18-20°C) for 10 to 15 minutes, then place it in the fridge for 30 minutes to achieve optimal crystallisation

3. Prepare the ganache

Bring the whipping cream, sugar, and honey to a boil (100°C) in a saucepan, then remove it from the heat before it boils for too long.

Incorporate the diced butter and mix until it is fully melted.

Remove it from the heat and let it cool down to 40°C.

Incorporate the finely chopped fondant chocolate and mix gently until a smooth, homogeneous ganache is achieved.

When the ganache reaches 32°C, it is ready to fill the chocolate shells.

Ingredients
(for about 60 pralines)

- 50 g caster sugar
- 250 ml heavy whipping cream (minimum 35% fat content)
- 75 g unsalted butter
- 225 g dark chocolate 70%
- 15 g honey from Yunnan (or elsewhere)

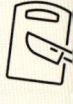

Utensils

- Bain-marie, chocolate tempering machine or microwave oven
- Saucepan
- Whisk or hand blender (for an even smoother texture)
- Polycarbonate mould
- Marble worktop
- Piping bag
- Chocolate spatula
- Silicone spatula or scraper
- Food thermometer

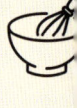

Summary of break times

Crystallisation of chocolate shells: 10 to 15 minutes at room temperature, followed by 30 minutes in the fridge.
The resting time of the ganache in the shells is 12 hours at room temperature.
Final crystallisation after closing the pralines: 2 hours at room temperature, followed by 30 minutes in the refrigerator.

4. Fill the shells with ganache

Transfer the ganache into a piping bag.

Fill the shells to three-quarters full, allowing space for the chocolate lid.

Allow to crystallise at room temperature for twelve hours to ensure a perfect texture.

5. Seal and unmould the pralines

Pour a thin layer of tempered chocolate into the mould to seal the pralines.

Level the excess using a spatula.

Allow the pralines to rest at room temperature for 2 hours, then refrigerate for 30 minutes.

Invert the mould and gently tap it to release the perfectly formed pralines.

ADVICE FROM THE MAÎTRE CHOCOLATIER

To achieve shiny, crunchy chocolate, ensure that the tempering is controlled and the moulds are clean and dry before filling them.

To achieve a melting, silky ganache, do not stir until it reaches 40 °C. Use a hand blender set at a low speed to avoid incorporating air bubbles.

To achieve perfect crystallisation, allow the pralines to rest at room temperature before refrigerating them, enhancing the formation of cocoa butter crystals.

To customise your ganache, infuse the cream with a vanilla pod, spices such as cardamom and cinnamon, or coffee.

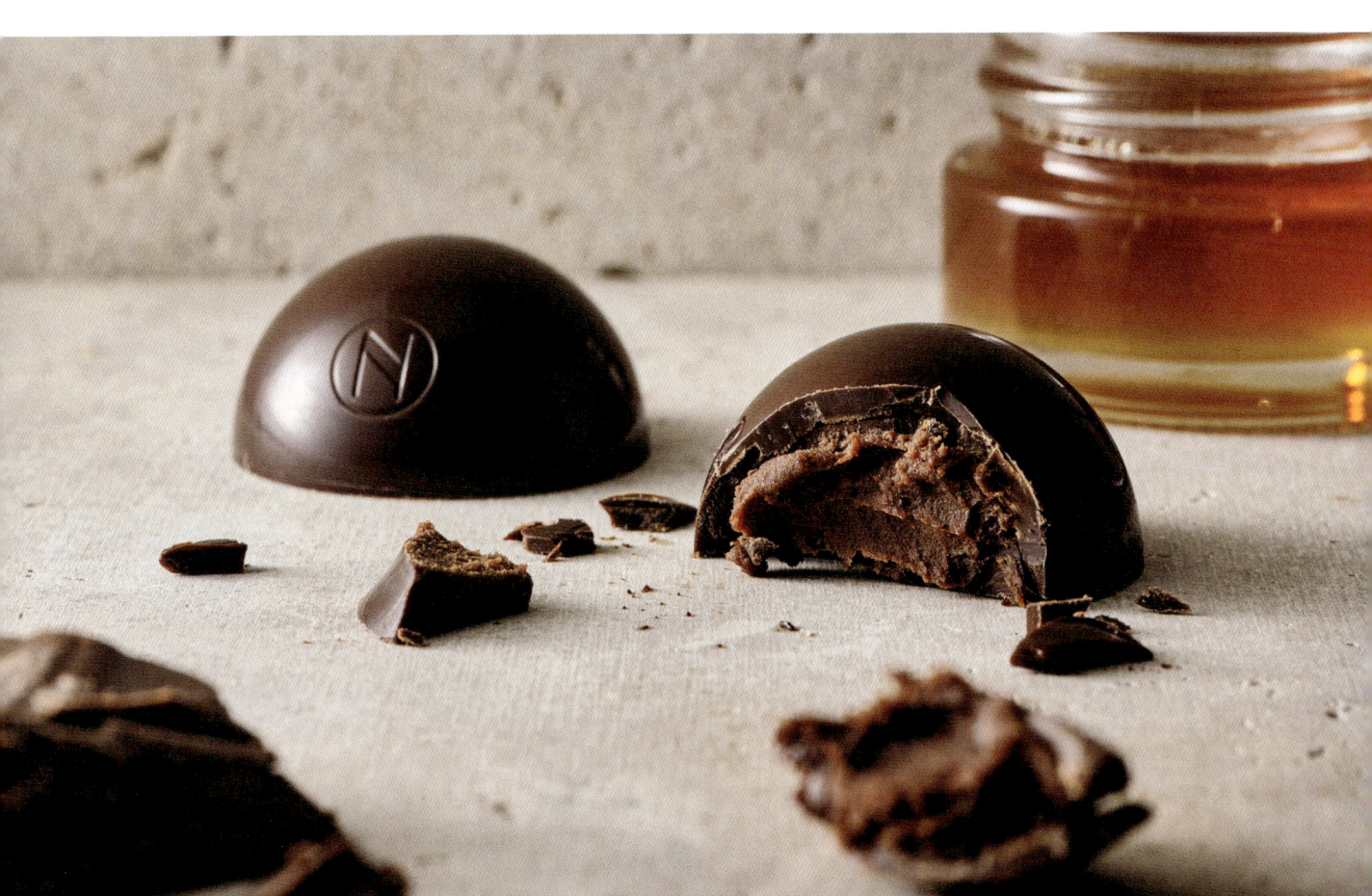

PRALINE FILLED WITH SALTED BUTTER CARAMEL

THE INTENSITY OF MELTING CARAMEL, ACCENTUATED BY A DELICATE CHOCOLATE SHELL

There's nothing quite as delicious as a perfectly balanced salted butter caramel: a touch of fleur de sel to enhance the depth of the caramelised sugar, a hint of milk chocolate to round everything off, and finally, a thin shell of chocolate for an irresistible contrast. Much like the Bonbon Salted Caramel or even Pierre or Délice, mentioned above, a salted butter caramel praline is an ode to the balance between sweetness and character, between fondant and crunch.

Preparation

1. Prepare the salted butter caramel

Heat the sugar and glucose in a thick-bottomed or copper saucepan over a medium-high heat, without stirring, until a golden blond caramel is achieved.

Meanwhile, gently heat the cream to 40°C in a different saucepan.

Take the saucepan off the heat and carefully pour the warm cream over the caramel, stirring continuously to avoid the formation of crystals. Be cautious of splatters!

Add the butter and fleur de sel. Stir until the butter is fully absorbed.

When the preparation attains 35°C, incorporate the melted milk chocolate at 32°C and stir until a smooth, homogeneous caramel is achieved.

Allow it to sit at room temperature until it reaches approximately 28°C; the caramel is ready to fill the chocolate shells.

2. Temper the coating chocolate

Melt the dark chocolate or milk chocolate in a tempering machine or a microwave oven set to a low power (300-350 W), until the appropriate melting temperature is reached (see above).

Ensure that all the chocolate has melted. Otherwise, crystallisation will remain incomplete.

Pour two-thirds of the melted chocolate onto a marble slab and work it with a spatula until it reaches a temperature of 27°c.

Include the cooled chocolate in the third part, which has remained warm, and stir until the mixture achieves a temperature of 30-32°c.

Top tip: Ensure that the moulds are at room temperature (minimum 20°c) before pouring in the chocolate, to prevent any thermal shock that could compromise its shine and moulding adherence

3. Shape the chocolate shells

Pour the tempered chocolate into the mould.

Invert the mould and gently tap it to remove the excess chocolate.

Leave the mould at room temperature (18-20°C) for 10 to 15 minutes, then refrigerate for 30 minutes to ensure optimal crystallisation.

Ingredients
(for about 120 pralines)

- 200 g glucose
- 300 g sugar
- 500 ml heavy whipping cream (minimum 35% fat content)
- 100 g unsalted butter
- 6 g fleur de sel
- 100 ml milk chocolate (to tone down the caramel)

Chocolate shells

600 g tempered dark or milk chocolate

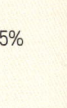

Utensils

- Bain-marie, tempering machine or microwave oven
- Two thick-bottomed or copper saucepans
- Polycarbonate mould
- Marble worktop
- Chocolate spatula
- Wooden spatula or scraper
- Food thermometer

Summary of break times

Crystallisation of the chocolate shells: 10 to 15 minutes at room temperature, followed by 30 minutes in the fridge.
Resting time for the caramel in the shells: 6 hours at room temperature
Final crystallisation after sealing the pralines: 2 hours at room temperature, followed by 30 minutes in the fridge.

4. Fill the shells with caramel

Pour the cooled caramel (approximately 28°C) into a piping bag.

Carefully fill the shells to three-quarters of their total height, allowing space for the chocolate seal.

Allow them to crystallise at room temperature for six hours to ensure a perfect texture.

5. Seal the pralines and remove them from the mould

Pour a thin layer of tempered chocolate over the mould to seal the pralines.

Utilise a spatula to remove any excess and smooth the surface.

Allow them to rest at room temperature for 2 hours, then refrigerate for 30 minutes.

Invert the mould and tap gently to release the perfectly formed pralines from the mould.

ADVICE FROM THE MAÎTRE CHOCOLATIER

To achieve a perfectly balanced, intensely flavoured caramel, allow it to brown lightly, but be cautious not to burn it.

Incorporate milk chocolate into the caramel to achieve a smooth, melting texture. This reduces the bitterness and achieves a silky finish.

Proper tempering guarantees easy unmoulding and a brilliant, crisp praline, ensuring your chocolate is shiny and crunchy.

Add a hint of vanilla or some grated tonka bean to customise the caramel.

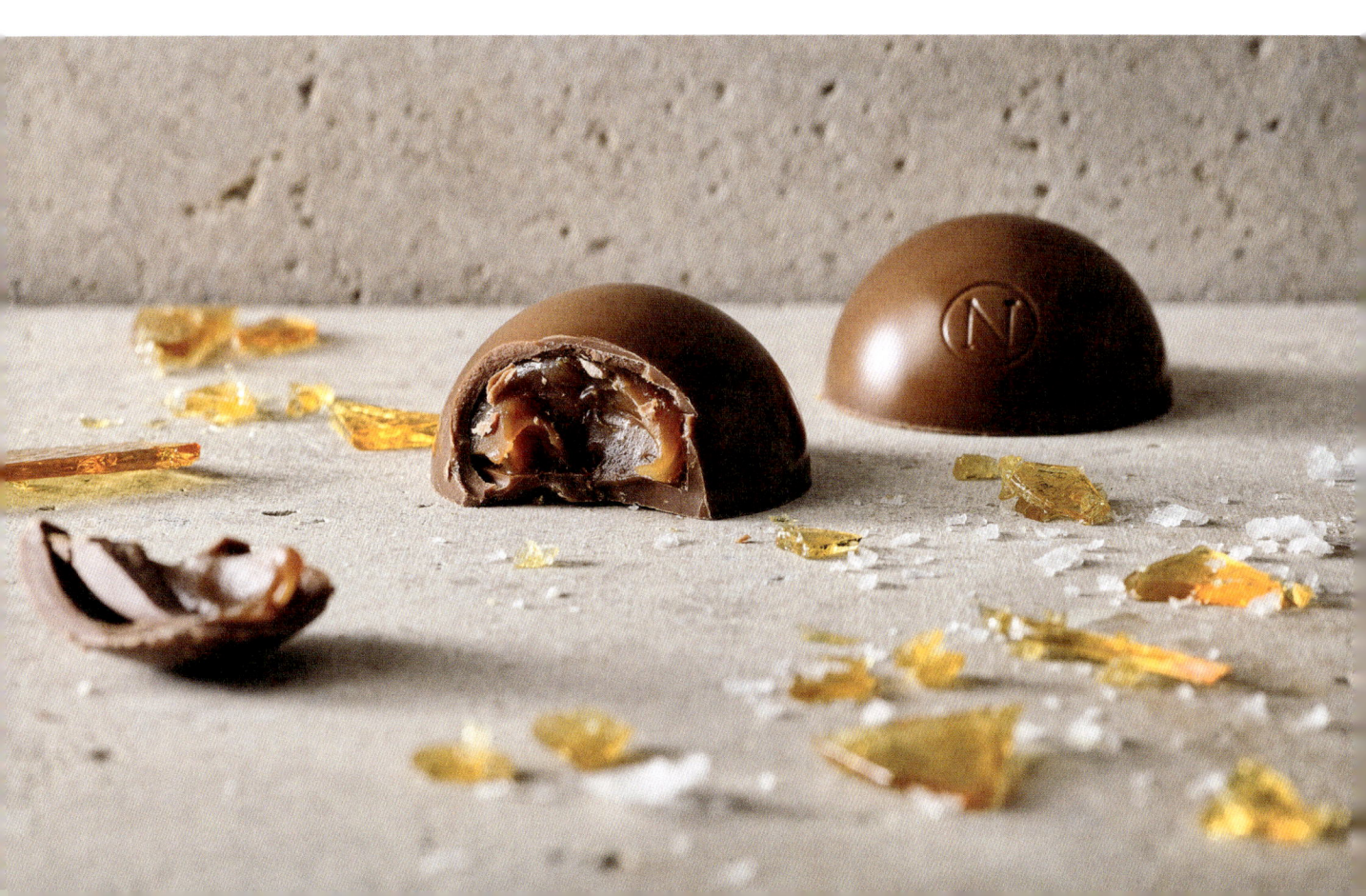

A GIANDUJA-STYLE PRALINE

THE ELEGANCE OF A HAZELNUT PRALINÉ

Gianduja, the creamy paste originating from Italy, is a crucial component in the world of chocolate. It is a finely ground mixture of roasted hazelnuts, sugar, and chocolate, resulting in an ultra-melting texture and an intensely indulgent flavour.

Making homemade gianduja, however, is quite challenging, as it necessitates a level of grinding that can only be accomplished with professional equipment. For this reason, we utilise PRA praliné, a professional praliné crafted from roasted and caramelised hazelnuts and almonds ground to a perfectly smooth paste, akin to gianduja.

This recipe can be used to make pralines moulded directly without a chocolate shell, or praliné bars to cut into smaller cubes for a rougher, more authentic presentation. The addition of whole hazelnuts to this recipe adds a delightful crunch to the praline.

You can find PRA praliné in specialist patisseries, chocolate shops, or online (it should contain at least 50% hazelnuts or almonds).

Preparation

1. Prepare the gianduja-praliné filling

Melt the milk chocolate in a bain-marie or a microwave oven set to a moderate power (maximum 350 W) until it reaches 45°C.

Stir gently to obtain a homogeneous texture.

Combine the PRA praliné with the milk chocolate and mix thoroughly using a scraper or spatula until a smooth, homogeneous paste is achieved.

2. Mould the pralines or form bars

Option 1. Moulded pralines

Place two hazelnuts into the mould for each praline.

Spread the chocolate paste over the nuts.

Smooth the surface with a spatula to remove excess and achieve a neat finish.

Allow to crystallise at room temperature for 2 hours before gently unmoulding.

Option 2. Bars to cut

Pour some hazelnuts into a ganache frame or a small rectangular mould lined with parchment paper. Pour the chocolate paste over the nuts.

Use a spatula to smooth the surface, ensuring a uniform bar.

Allow it to set in the fridge for 2 hours until the preparation is firm.

Remove from the mould and slice into squares or bars with a sharp knife.

Ingredients
(for about 100 pralines)

- 1000 g PRA praliné
- 200 g milk chocolate
- Some hazelnuts

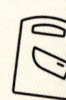

Utensils

- Bain-marie, tempering machine or microwave oven
- Polycarbonate mould or ganache frame to shape bars
- Parchment paper
- Chocolate spatula
- Wooden spatula or scraper

ADVICE FROM THE MAÎTRE CHOCOLATIER

To achieve perfectly melted gianduja, use only a professional-grade PRA praliné to ensure a smooth, grain-free texture.

Let the mixture rest before using it for optimal crystallisation. This allows it to congeal slightly and become easier to manipulate.

For an elegant finish, lift the gianduja squares with a fork and immerse them in tempered chocolate to achieve the appearance of a coated praliné.

For gourmet variations, include fleur de sel, dried fruit, hazelnuts, tea, or instant coffee…

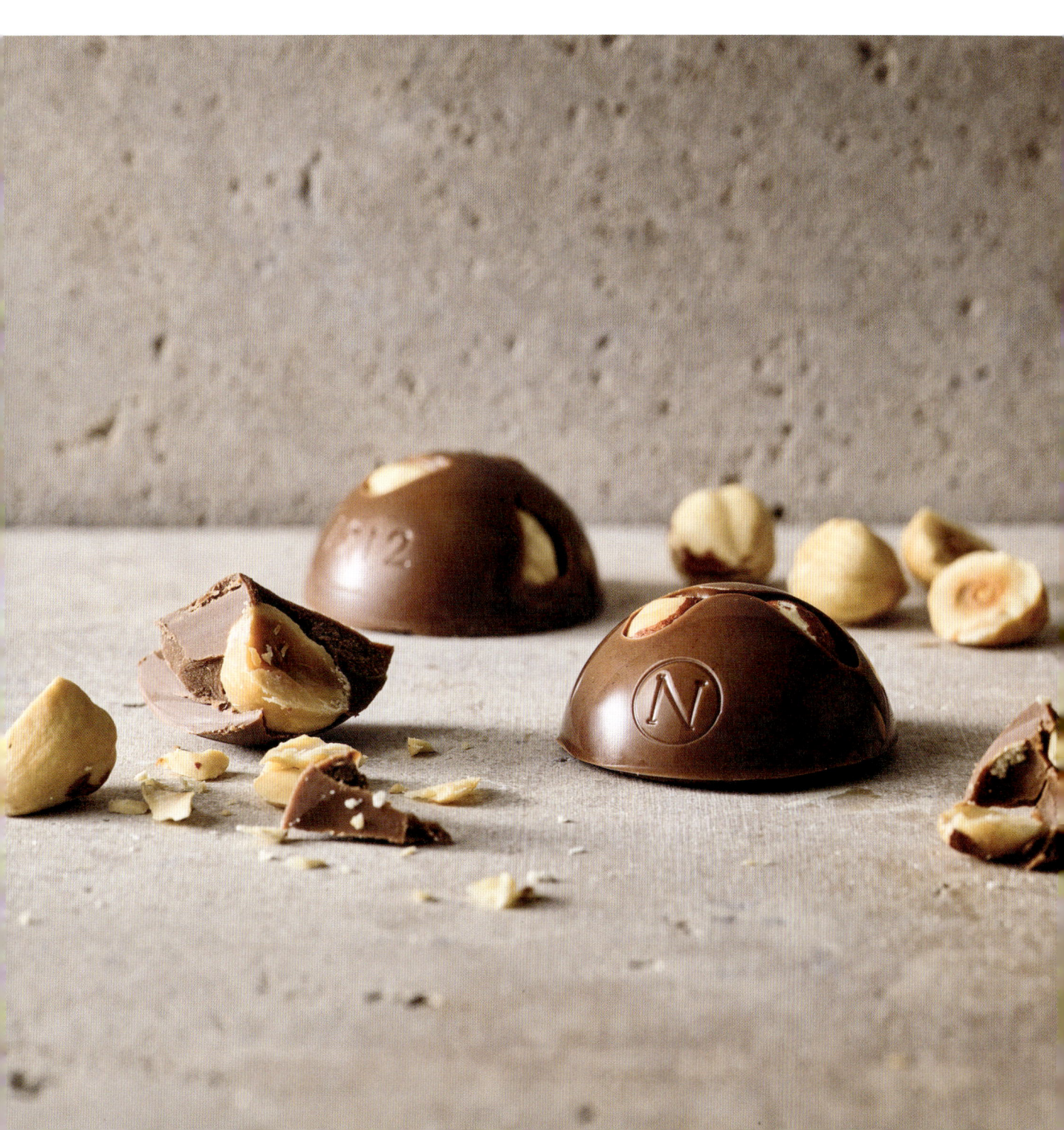

PRALINE FILLED WITH TRADITIONAL PRALINÉ AND SESAME SEEDS

THE INTENSITY OF PRALINÉ, HEIGHTENED BY THE SWEETNESS OF CHOCOLATE

The praline is a chocolate-maker's staple, and this sesame version, much like the delicious Dôme, offers a delicate alternative to the classic hazelnut or almond pralines. The roasted sesame adds a subtle bitterness and a crunchy texture, while the milk chocolate balances everything with its milky sweetness.

Preparation

1. Preparing the sesame praliné

Dry-roast the seeds in a frying pan on medium-high heat.

Add the sesame seeds and hazelnuts, stirring frequently until they turn golden and release a rich aroma (around 5 minutes).

Pour them straight onto a plate to stop cooking and prevent burning.
Heat the water, glucose, and sugar in a copper or stainless steel saucepan until a golden caramel is obtained.

To prevent crystallisation, refrain from stirring until the mixture develops an amber hue. While the pan is still hot, immediately add the hazelnuts and sesame seeds and mix well to coat them in caramel.

Pour the mixture onto a marble worktop, spread it out evenly, and let it cool for 30 minutes.

Once it has cooled, break it into pieces and place them in a food processor.

Blend gradually, using multiple pulses to prevent overheating, until a smooth paste is achieved. Add the fleur de sel and mix gently one more time.

2. Incorporate the chocolate and allow it to cool.

Melt the milk chocolate in batches in a bain-marie or a microwave (500 W).

Wait until it reaches 45°C, then let it cool to 30-32°C.

Add the melted chocolate to the praliné and stir until thoroughly combined.

Allow to rest in the fridge for 2 hours, permitting the texture to thicken slightly before use.

3. Temper the chocolate for the shells

Heat the dark chocolate or milk chocolate to the necessary melting temperature (see above).

Pour two-thirds of the chocolate onto a marble slab and use a spatula to work the mixture until it reaches 27°C (for the fondant chocolate) or 25°C (for the milk chocolate).

Use the spatula to gradually incorporate the cooled chocolate into the other third, stirring until the temperature reaches 30-32°C.

Ingredients
(for about 120 pralines)

- 160 g glucose (a thick syrup derived from starch)
- 100 g sugar
- 30 ml of water
- 250 g roasted hazelnuts
- 40 g white sesame seeds
- 400 g milk chocolate
- 8 g fleur de sel

Utensils

- Bain-marie, tempering machine or microwave oven
- Heavy-bottomed or copper saucepan
- Polycarbonate mould
- Cold plate or marble worktop
- Piping bag
- Roasting pan for the sesame
- Robotic cutter or powerful hand blender
- Wooden spatula or scraper
- Chocolate spatula
- Food thermometer

Summary of resting times

- **Crystallisation of the chocolate shells:** 10 to 15 minutes at room temperature, followed by 30 minutes in the fridge.
- **Resting time for the praliné garnish:** 2 hours in the fridge.
- **Final crystallisation after sealing the pralines:** 12 hours at room temperature.

4. Mould the chocolate shells

Pour the chocolate into the mould and tap it gently to remove any air bubbles.

Invert the mould to eliminate the excess chocolate.

To achieve optimal crystallisation, leave the mould at room temperature (18-20°C) for 10 to 15 minutes before refrigerating it for 30 minutes.

5. Garnish and seal the pralines

Transfer the sesame praliné to a piping bag.

Fill the shells to three-quarters full, allowing space for the chocolate sealing.

Allow to crystallise at room temperature for 12 hours.

Spread a thin layer of tempered chocolate over the mould to seal the pralines.

Eliminate the excess and even out the surface with a scraper.

Allow to rest at 18-20°C for 2 hours, then place it in the fridge for 30 minutes before unmoulding.

Tip: ensure that the moulds are at room temperature (at least 20°C) before pouring in the chocolate to prevent thermal shock, which could affect the gloss and adhesion of the mould.

ADVICE FROM THE MAÎTRE CHOCOLATIER

To achieve well-roasted sesame seeds, lightly toast them, ensuring they do not burn, to retain their aromas.

Mix gradually to achieve a smooth praliné, and do not hesitate to scrape the cutter's walls for a uniform texture.

Tempering chocolate properly is vital to achieving brilliant, crisp chocolate without turning white or becoming overly brittle.

For gourmet variations, add a hint of honey or ginger for an exotic twist.

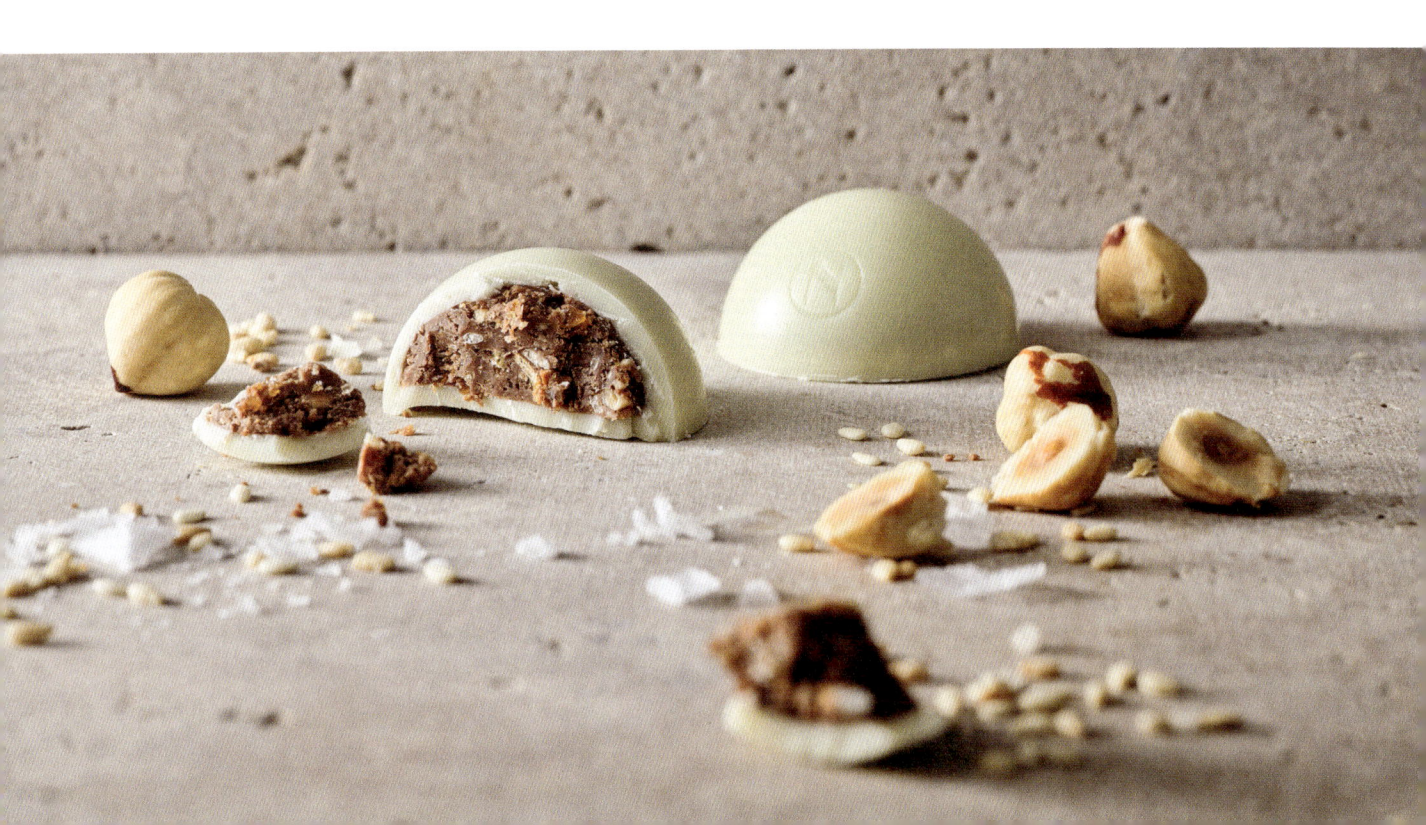

MANON-STYLE PRALINE

THE SOFT-CENTRED BELGIAN ICON

Among the most famous pralines produced in Belgium, Manon reigns supreme. Its history dates back to the periods of cocoa shortage in the 20th century, when chocolatiers had to compete in ingenuity to create recipes that were as delicious as they were refined. White chocolate, which requires less cocoa, emerged as a valuable alternative and gave rise to this praline, characterised by its light texture and subtly sweet taste.

The Manon has delighted palates with its perfect blend of creamy buttercream, melting praline, and a crunchy white chocolate shell. However, each company has crafted its interpretation, with variations ranging from coffee to praline, featuring hints of vanilla or caramel.

This version combines the sweetness of praliné with the intensity of a ristretto, creating a melting and airy texture, enhanced by a white chocolate coating.

Preparation

1. Prepare the coffee cream

Heat the whipping cream in a saucepan until it comes to a boil.
Add the ristretto and mix thoroughly.

Allow to cool at room temperature, then refrigerate for 30 minutes to allow it to thicken slightly.

2. Prepare the praliné buttercream

In a bowl, beat the softened butter and icing sugar until it is light and creamy.

Add the PRA praline and continue to beat until the mixture is smooth and homogeneous.

Gradually incorporate the cooled cream while whisking at a moderate speed.
Whisk the mixture until it becomes light and airy.

Refrigerate the praline buttercream for 1 hour to achieve the perfect consistency for use as a filling.

3. Preparing the chocolate bars (base of the manon)

Melt and temper 100 g of white chocolate (melt at 45°C, work at 27-29°C).

Use a piping bag or spoon to place small discs of white chocolate, measuring roughly 2.5 cm in diameter, onto a sheet of parchment paper.

Allow to crystallise for 15 minutes at room temperature.

4. Shape the pralines

Transfer the buttercream into a piping bag.

Pipe small balls of filling approximately 3 cm in diameter on a baking tray lined with parchment paper.

Chill in the fridge for 30 minutes to firm up.

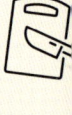

Ingredients
(for about 40 manons)

Buttercream and praliné filling
- 125 ml heavy whipping cream (minimum 35 % fat content)
- 110 ml ristretto (very strong)
- 1150 g unsalted butter
- 175 g icing sugar
- 1100 g PRA praliné (see explanation below)

Enrobage
- 400 g tempered white chocolate
- 100 g tempered dark chocolate (for garnishing)

PRA praliné is a high-quality professional praliné used by chocolatiers to ensure a smooth, homogeneous texture. Unlike homemade pralines, which are often grainy, PRA is ground exceptionally finely, making it ideal for creams, ganaches, and fillings. You will find it in specialist patisseries and chocolate shops.

If you cannot find PRA, you may use a well-mixed homemade praline; however, the final texture will be slightly different.

Utensils

- Bain-marie, tempering machine or microwave oven
- Saucepan
- Electric whisk or stand mixer
- Fork (for coating)
- Cooling rack
- Parchment paper
- Piping bag
- Spatula or scraper
- Food thermometer

Summary of resting times

Cooling the coffee cream:
30 minutes in the fridge.
Resting time for the buttercream:
1 hour in the fridge.
Final crystallisation following coating:
12 hours at room temperature.

5. Coating the pralines

Melt and temper the remaining white chocolate (melt at 45°C, work at 27-29°C).

Immerse each buttercream ball in the tempered white chocolate using a dipping fork.

Allow to drain slightly, then place on a cooling rack.

Set aside for 12 hours at room temperature, allowing the chocolate to set and become crunchy.

Fill a piping bag with tempered dark chocolate. Snip the end off the piping bag and use it to decorate with a fine line of chocolate.

ADVICE FROM THE MAÎTRE CHOCOLATIER

For a full-bodied coffee cream, a ristretto enhances the intensity and prevents the cream from becoming runny.

To achieve a light cream, beat the butter and sugar mixture for an extended period until it reaches a fluffy texture.

To achieve a perfect coating, dip the pralines swiftly to stop the white chocolate from setting too quickly.

To vary the flavours, add a hint of vanilla or substitute the white chocolate with milk chocolate for a milder version.

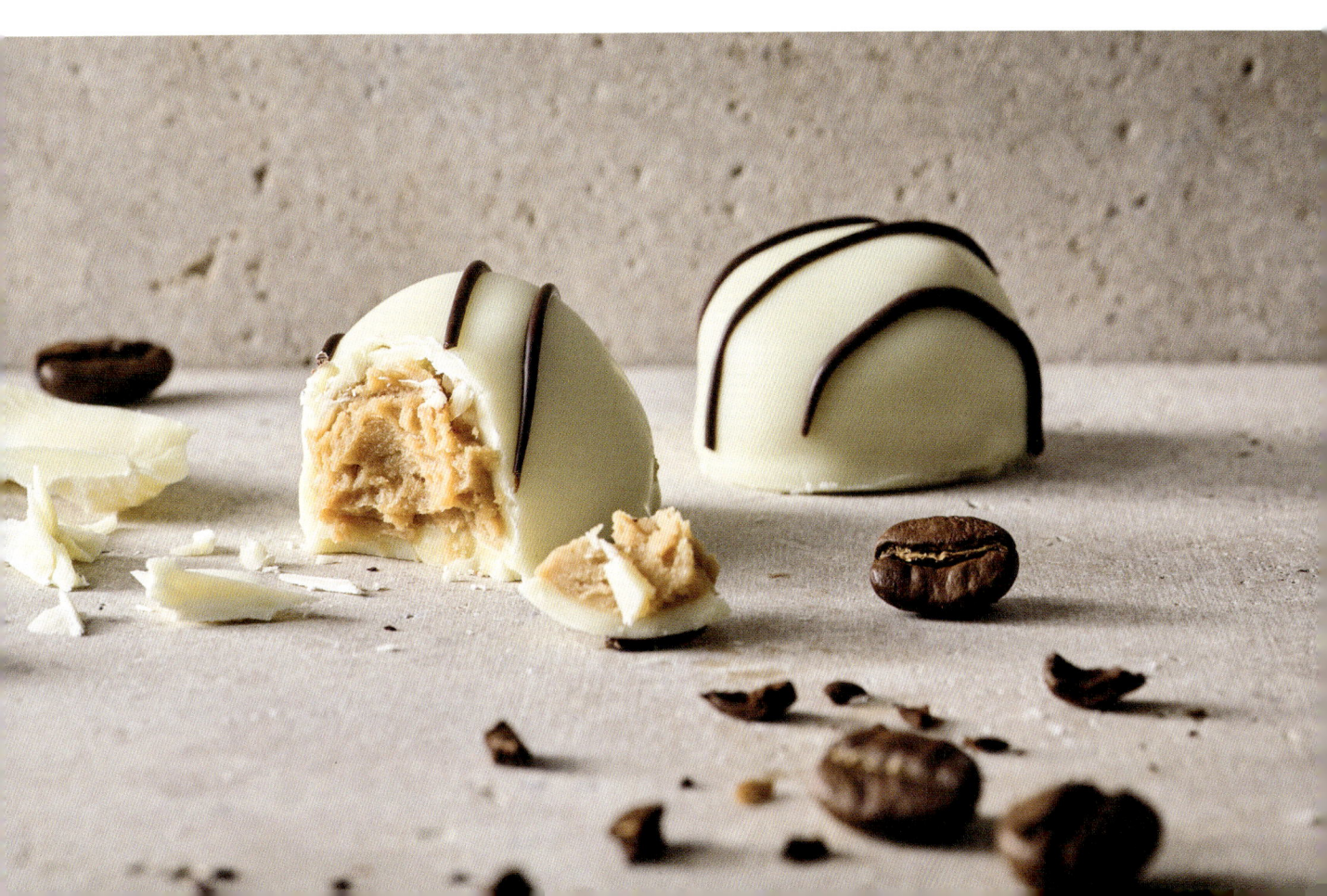

DARK CHOCOLATE TRUFFLES

A FONDANT DELIGHT

Chocolate truffles epitomise refinement and simplicity: a silky ganache, a crunchy coating, and a delicate layer of cocoa that enhances every bite. Their origins date back to the end of the 19th century, when a chocolatier is said to have mistakenly poured hot cream over melted chocolate, resulting in an incredibly melting texture.

In this recipe, we elevate the intensity of the chocolate fondant with a pinch of Guérande fleur de sel, which adds a subtle hint of iodine and enhances the flavours.

Preparation

Melt the chocolate in a double boiler and mix it with the cream and the pinch of salt.

Let the mixture cool in the fridge for 2 hours.

Shape small balls, either in the palm of your hand or using a piping bag. Place them back in the fridge for a few minutes.

Place each truffle on a fork, dip the fork into the melted chocolate, and then roll the truffle in cocoa powder.

ADVICE FROM THE MAÎTRE CHOCOLATIER

Tempering the coating chocolate stops the truffles from becoming sticky and provides them with a thin, crunchy coating.

Intense cocoa: unsweetened cocoa powder provides an elegant, powerful finish on the palate.

For something different, incorporate a dash of Espelette pepper, orange zest, or a hint of coffee into the ganache.

Enjoy!

Ingredients
(for about 70 truffles)

Fondant truffle
- 480 g dark chocolate
- 320 ml heavy whipping cream (minimum 35% fat content)
- 1 pinch of fleur de sel de Guérande

Coating
- 250 g tempered dark chocolate
- 200 g cocoa powder (unsweetened)

Utensils
- Bain-marie
- Saucepan
- Dipping fork
- Blender
- Piping bag (optional)
- Spatula or scraper

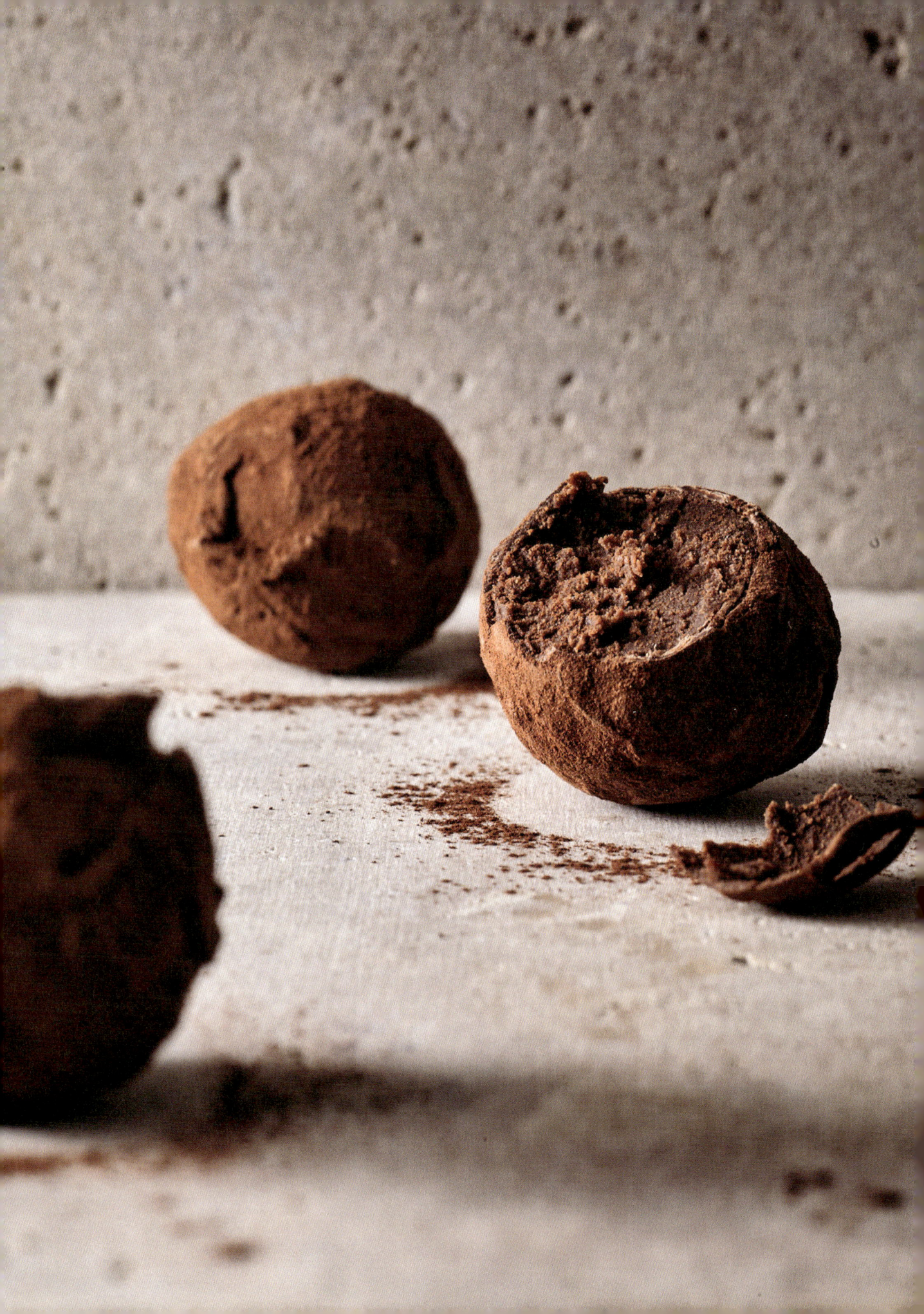

PARTT 4

THE MAÎTRE CHOCOLATIER'S DESSERTS

Some creations leave their mark on a story, a memory, an emotion. At Neuhaus, each praline is a signature, a harmony of textures and flavours that transcends simple sweet pleasure. Inspired by these chocolate masterpieces, the desserts presented here reinterpret the house's emblematic pralines, providing a new way to savour them.

From the delicacy of melting ganache to the crunch of caramelised nougatine, each recipe invites you to extend the Neuhaus experience and explore the contrasts and balance that create the magic of chocolate. In these creations, the expertise of the master chocolatier merges with that of the pastry chef, resulting in elegant, refined desserts designed to elevate the finest tables.

Whether for a special occasion or simply for the pleasure of recreating these iconic flavours at home, these recipes immerse you in Neuhaus's sensory and gourmet world. Are you ready to transform your kitchen into a haute chocolaterie workshop?

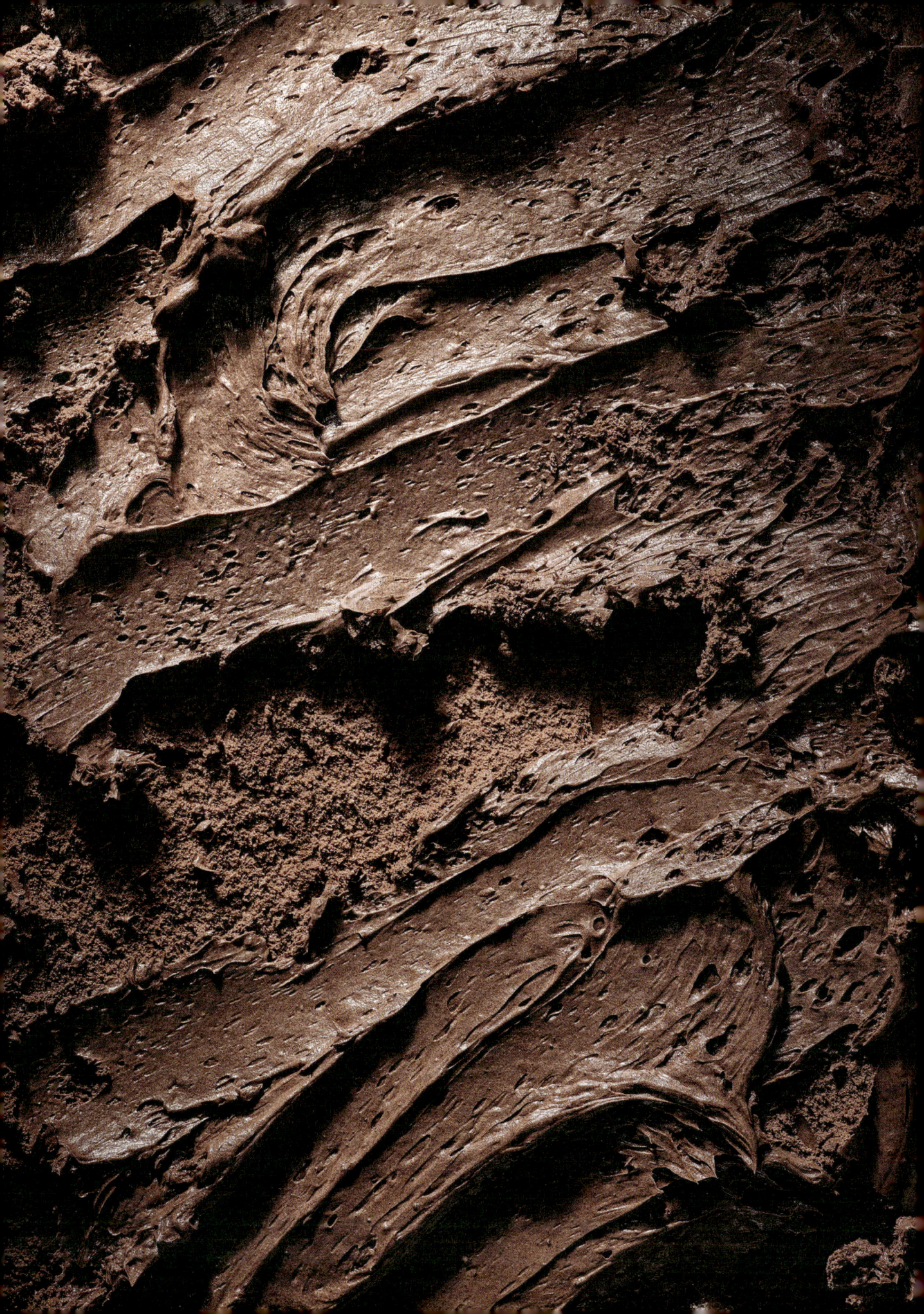

HOT CHOCOLATE
THE MAÎTRE CHOCOLATIER'S GOURMET ELIXIR

Hot chocolate is not merely a drink: it's an experience, an invitation to comfort, a chocolatey embrace for the senses. Inspired by the Neuhaus world, these recipes reinterpret hot chocolate in three variations, ranging from the most traditional to the most audacious, always honouring the expertise and quality of the ingredients. Whether you prefer the intensity of dark chocolate, the sweetness of milk chocolate, or a hint of spicy exoticism, these recipes celebrate the art of chocolate in its most comforting form.

DARK HOT CHOCOLATE
The pure intensity of chocolate, in a cup

Preparation

1. Infuse the vanilla

Bring the milk to the boil in a saucepan with the split and scraped vanilla pod (or use vanilla sugar).

Allow to infuse for 5 minutes off the heat, allowing the vanilla to release its aromas.

2. Stir in the chocolate

Take out the vanilla pod.

Return the milk to a low heat and add the broken pieces of dark chocolate.

Whisk gently until the chocolate melts and the mixture is smooth and velvety.

3. Adjust the consistency

Add 50 to 100 g of extra dark chocolate for a more indulgent texture, a thicker, creamier chocolate.

4. Serve and enjoy

Pour into pre-warmed cups to maintain warmth.

Optional: dust with cocoa powder or add a hint of cinnamon for an even more delightful treat.

Ingredients
(for two large cups or four small ones)

- 500 ml whole milk
- 200 g dark chocolate 80 %
- 1 vanilla pod
  (or two teaspoons of vanilla sugar)

Utensils

- Saucepan
- Fine-mesh sieve (optional)
- Cutting board and knife
- Whisk

Summary of preparation times

Infusion: 5 minutes
Blending and cooking: 5 minutes

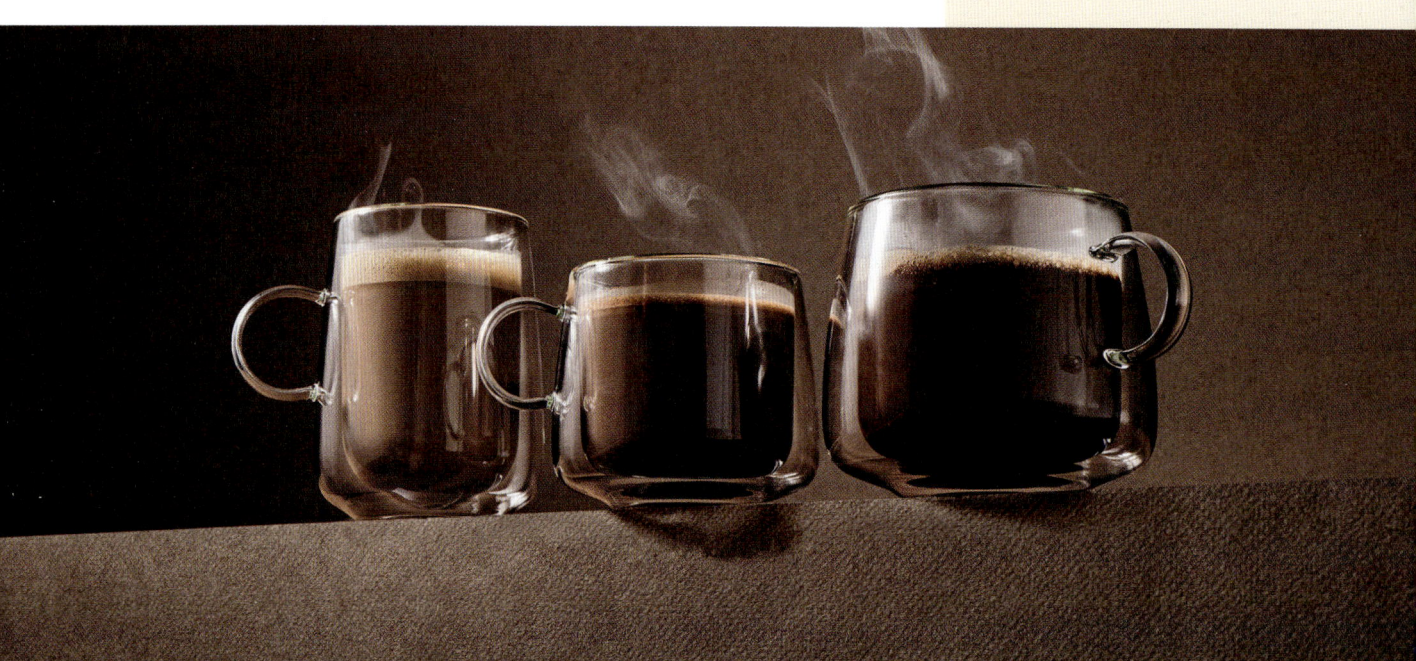

HOT CHOCOLATE PREPARED WITH MILK CHOCOLATE
The ideal harmony of smoothness and creaminess

Preparation

1. Infuse the vanilla

Bring the milk to the boil in a saucepan with the split and scraped vanilla pod (or the vanilla sugar).

Allow to infuse off the heat for 5 minutes.

2. Stir in the chocolate

Take out the vanilla pod.

Return the milk to the heat and add the milk chocolate, broken into small pieces.

Whisk gently until the chocolate has completely melted and the texture is smooth and velvety.

3. Adjust the consistency

Add 50 g of thicker, creamier milk chocolate for a more indulgent texture.

4. Serve and enjoy

Pour into pre-warmed cups to maintain warmth.

Optional: add a hint of whipped cream for an even more indulgent treat.

Ingredients
(for two large cups or four small ones)

- 500 ml whole milk
- 250 ml milk chocolate
- 1 vanilla pod
  (or two teaspoons of vanilla sugar)

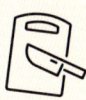

Utensils

- Saucepan
- Fine sieve (optional)
- Cutting board and knife
- Whisk

Summary of preparation times

- Infusion: 5 minutes
- Blending and cooking: five minutes

SPICED DARK HOT CHOCOLATE
A sensory exploration of power and exoticism

Preparation

1. Infuse the spices

Gently crush the lemongrass sticks to release their fragrance.

Bring the milk and coconut milk to the boil with the lemongrass and cayenne pepper.

Allow to infuse for 5 minutes away from the heat.

2. Stir in the chocolate

Take out the lemongrass.

Return the milk to the heat and add the broken pieces of dark chocolate.

Gently mix with a whisk until the chocolate fully melts and the mixture achieves a smooth velvety texture.

3. Filter and bring out the flavour

Strain through a fine sieve to remove lemongrass residues.

Serve immediately, preferably in a pre-warmed china cup to enhance the flavour experience.

ADVICE FROM THE MAÎTRE CHOCOLATIER

The choice of chocolate is crucial. For a rich hot chocolate, choose couverture chocolate with a high cocoa content (at least 70% for dark chocolate).

Avoid boiling the milk. Excessive heat can alter the chocolate's flavours and create a grainy texture.

Ingredients
(for two large cups or four small ones)

- 400 ml whole milk
  100 ml coconut milk
  200 g dark chocolate 80 %
  2 lemongrass stalks
  1,5 g cayenne pepper

Utensils

- Saucepan
- Fine sieve
- Cutting board and knife
- Whisk

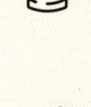

Summary of preparation times

Infusion: 5 minutes
Blending and cooking: 5 minutes

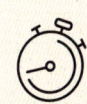

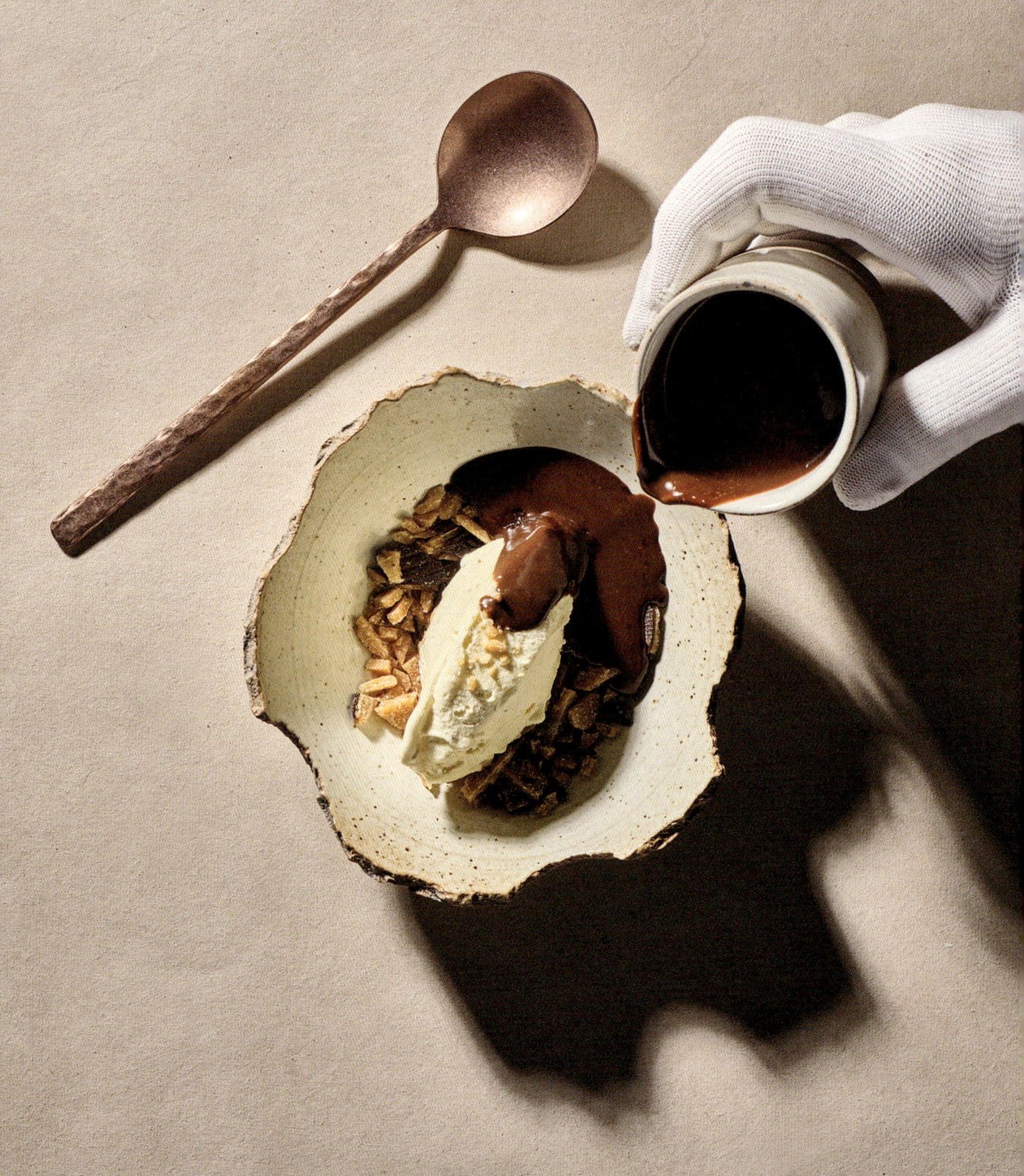

THE IRRESISTIBLE DAME BLANCHE

A HOMAGE TO THE CAPRICE

The legendary Dame Blanche dessert is reimagined here with a Neuhaus twist inspired by the Caprice praline. It perfectly balances the creaminess of homemade vanilla ice cream, the richness of chocolate sauce, and the irresistible crunch of a Neuhaus nougatine. At Neuhaus, nougatine is an art form. It imparts to the Irrésistibles pralines their distinctive and inimitable crunch. Here, it introduces a gourmet, textured element to this reimagined classic.

Homemade vanilla ice cream

The essence of a delightful frozen dessert

Preparation

1. Infuse the vanilla

Halve the vanilla pod and extract the seeds.

Place the seeds and pod halves in a saucepan with the milk, cream, and half the sugar.

Gently heat until just below a boil, then remove from the heat and allow it to infuse.

2. Blanch the egg yolks

Whisk the yolks with the remaining half of the sugar until you achieve a pale, thick mixture (called a 'ribbon').

3. Cook the custard

Pour half the hot milk over the egg yolks, continuously whisking.

Return the mixture to the saucepan and place it over low heat.

Heat to 80°C while stirring with a wooden spatula. Do not allow it to boil!

Spoon test: if you draw a line on the back of a spoon dipped in the cream and it remains clear, it's ready.

4. Allow it to cool and churn

Place the mixture in a bowl set in an ice bath and let it cool rapidly.

Refrigerate for at least 4 hours before using an ice cream maker to churn the ice cream.

Once the ice cream has set, place it in the freezer for at least 4 hours before serving.

Ingredients
(for 1 litre of ice cream)

- 300 ml whole milk
- 300 ml heavy whipping cream (minimum 35% fat content)
- 175 g caster sugar
- 5 egg yolks
- 1 vanilla pod (or a good quality natural vanilla essence)

Utensils

- Bowl for cooling with ice cubes
- Saucepan
- Whisk
- Ice cream maker (optional but recommended)
- Food thermometer

Summary of preparation times

Preparation: 15 minutes
Cooking: 10 minutes
Resting: 4 hours minimum
Blending: 40 minutes
Deep-freezing: 4 hours

Quick tip: If you're short on time, replace the homemade ice cream with a quality artisanal vanilla ice cream from a reputable manufacturer or a local producer.

Chocolate sauce

A wonderfully intense touch of charm

Ingredients
- 200 ml of heavy whipping cream (minimum 35% fat content)
- 50 g caster sugar
- 100 g high-quality dark chocolate (minimum 70 % cocoa)

Utensils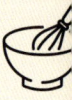
- Bol
- Balance
- Casserole
- Fouet
- Plaque de cuisson
- Thermomètre de cuisine

Summary of preparation times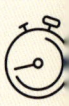

Preparation time: 5 minutes
Cooking: 5 minutes

Preparation

1. Heat the cream

In a saucepan, heat the cream until it simmers, but do not allow it to boil.

Add the sugar and stir until it has fully dissolved.

2. Incorporate the chocolate

Off the heat, add the chopped chocolate.

Stir gently until a smooth, shiny sauce is achieved.

3. Serve or preserve

Use right away for a creamy topping.

Store in the refrigerator for up to three days for later use.

Reheating: use a bain-marie or microwave oven on low power (300 W).

Crispy crunchiness. The signature Neuhaus mark

The element that makes the difference!

To add an irresistible crunchy texture, crush some Neuhaus Thins, pistachio, Guérande salt or speculoos. These are the same fine nougatines used in our Irrésistibles pralines to provide that inimitable crunchy, caramelised touch.

If you don't have any Thins to hand, you can make a homemade crisp. Crush some nougatine or hard toffee bits. Add some toasted, chopped hazelnuts for an even tastier treat.

Plating. The art of the irresistible Dame Blanche

Step 1: Place two generous scoops of vanilla ice cream in a bowl or soup plate.

Step 2: Generously cover with hot chocolate sauce.

Step 3: Sprinkle with crunch for an explosion of textures.

Step 4: (optional). To enhance the experience, add a finishing touch with a mint leaf or a few cocoa nibs.

ADVICE FROM THE MAÎTRE CHOCOLATIER

Serve in chilled bowls to slow down the melting of the ice cream.

Explore temperature contrasts: combining hot chocolate and ice cream creates an irresistible thermal shock.

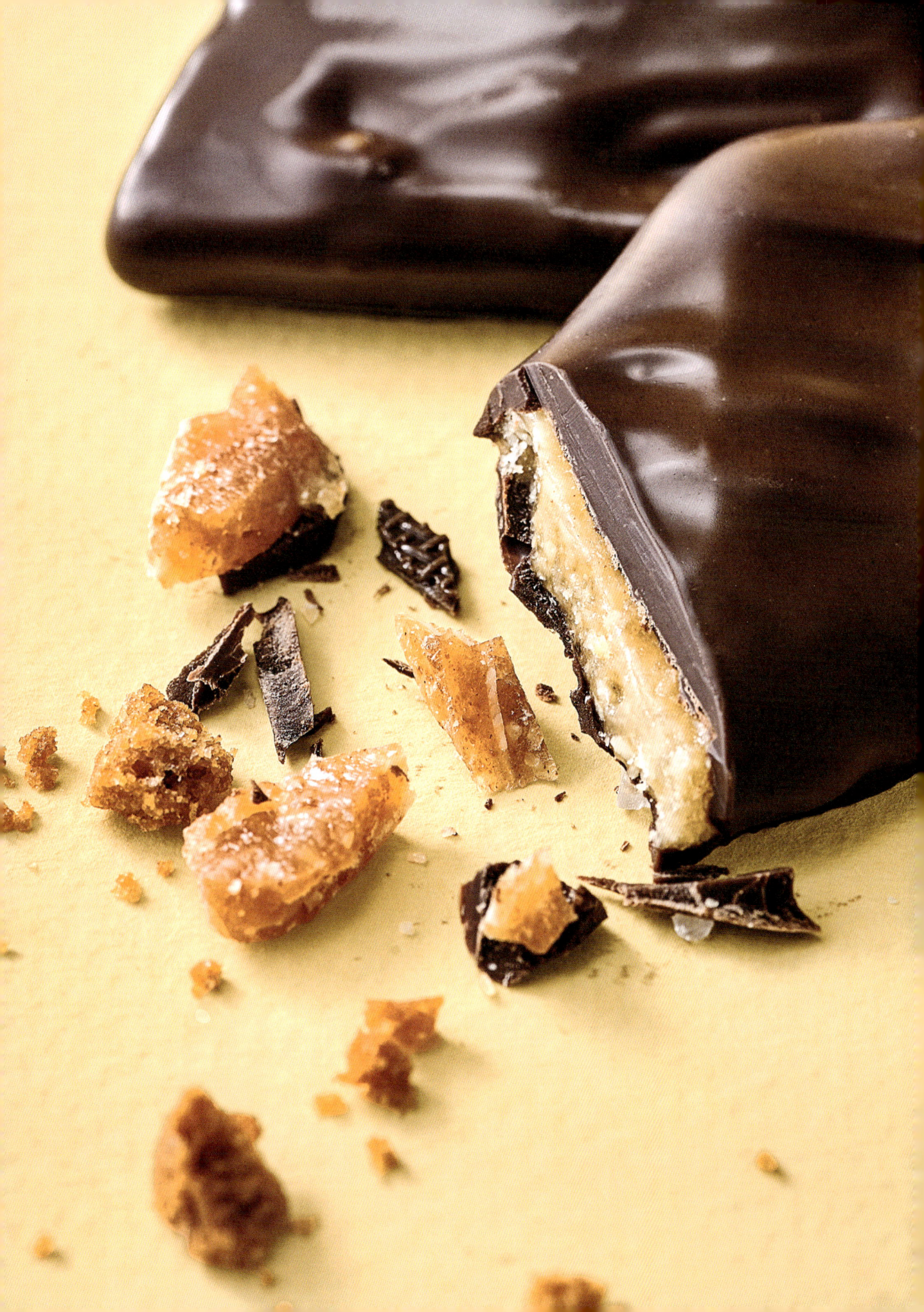

CHOCOLATE AND RASPBERRY TART

ODE TO THE SUZANNE

At Neuhaus, Suzanne de Gavre is more than just a name: she is a story, an inspiration. An opera singer and daughter of Jean Neuhaus Jr, she embodies elegance, passion, and pure emotion. Her first name has been given to an exceptional praline, reflecting her delicacy and intensity. This chocolate tart serves as a gourmet tribute to her timeless refinement.

The combination of a crisp shortbread pastry and a creamy chocolate fondant ganache reflects the perfect balance of the Suzanne praline. And for a touch of daring? A few fresh raspberries, akin to a fruity variation on the famous chocolate-hazelnut duo that characterises this iconic praline. A dessert that, like an outstanding performance, can be savoured in all its depth.

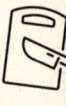

Ingredients
(for a 24 cm mould)

- 250 g flour
- 50 g icing sugar
- 30 ml of water
- 125 g diced cold butter
- 1 whole egg + 1 egg yolk
- 1 pinch of salt

Shortcrust pastry. The crunchy base

Preparation

Prepare the dough: combine the flour and butter using your fingertips until you achieve a sandy texture.

Add the icing sugar, egg yolk, cold water, and a pinch of salt.

Knead the dough only until it becomes a smooth ball. Avoid over-kneading, as this will result in excessive elasticity.

Cover the dough with cling film and let it rest in the fridge for 30 minutes.

Roll out the pastry on a lightly floured work surface and place it in a buttered tin.

Line a pastry with baking paper and cover it with weights, such as dried beans or baking balls. Bake at 180°C for approximately 15 minutes.

Remove the weights, brush the tart base with beaten egg, and return it to the oven for 5 minutes to seal.

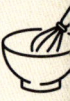

Utensils

- Scale
- Round tart mould
- Baking beans or dried beans
- Plastic bowl
- Knife
- Clingfilm
- Oven
- Parchment paper
- Rolling pin

Summary of preparation times

Preparation: 15 minutes
Resting: 30 minutes
Baking: 15 minutes plus 5 minutes

Dark chocolate ganache: a melting delight

Preparation

Warm the cream without allowing it to boil.

Pour the hot cream over the crushed chocolate fondant and blend until smooth and glossy.

Incorporate the butter while continuing to blend until you achieve a smooth ganache.

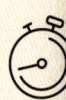

Ingredients

- 180 ml of cream
- 300 g dark chocolate
- 120 g butter

Utensils

- Scale
- Plastic bowl
- Saucepan
- Knife
- Whisk
- Blender
- Baking sheet

Assembly and presentation

Once the tart base has cooled, pour in the warm ganache. Ensure it is three-quarters full and that the layer of ganache is not excessively thick.

Leave to set in the fridge for 2 to 3 hours.

To decorate: include fresh raspberries for a fruity note that beautifully balances the intensity of the chocolate.

ADVICE FROM THE MAÎTRE CHOCOLATIER

For an even more refined finish, sprinkle a light dusting of cocoa over the tart before arranging the raspberries. A hint of grated tonka bean can also enhance the flavours of the chocolate fondant.

Savour chilled with an espresso or black tea for the ultimate chocolate experience.

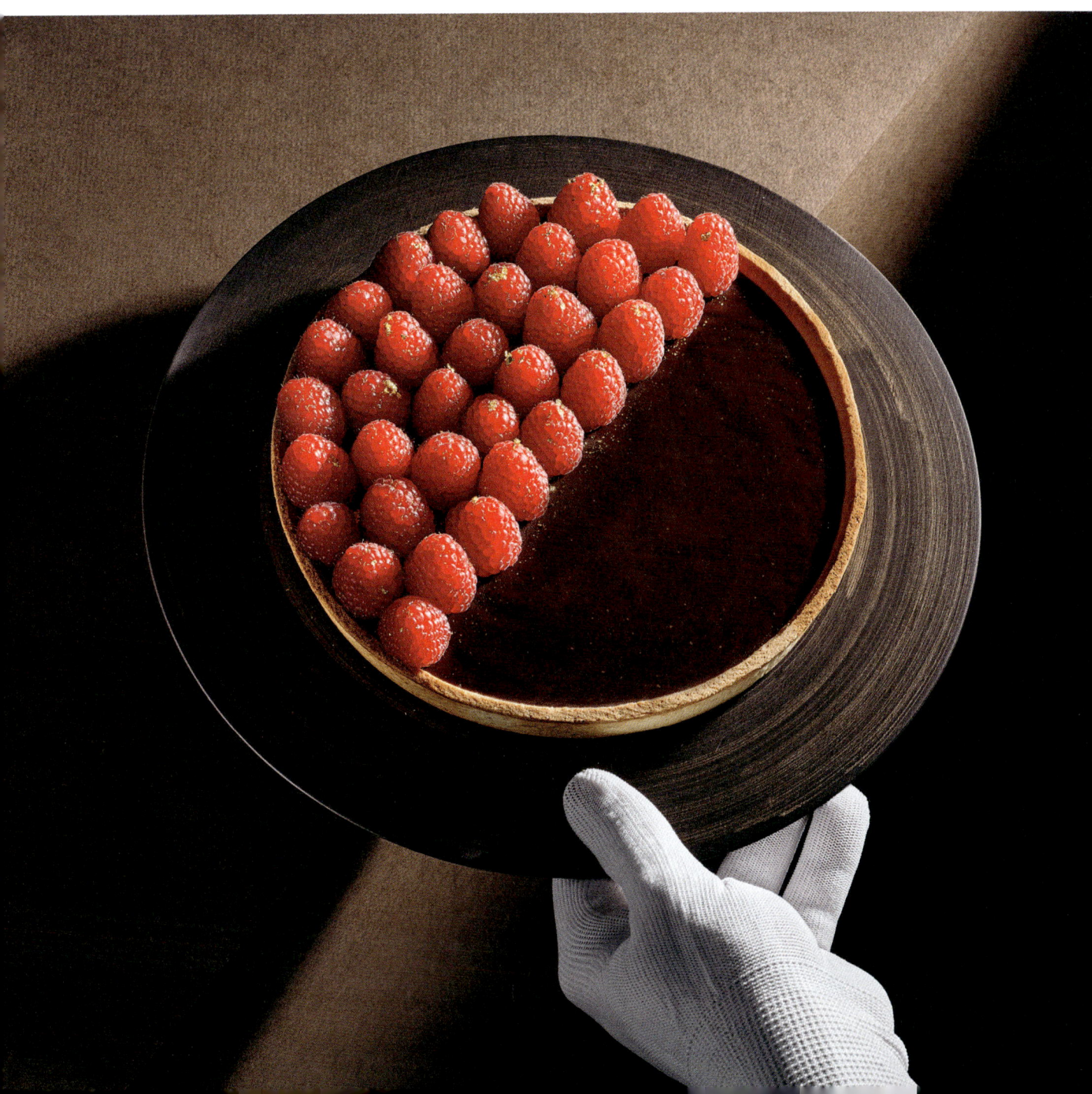

GOURMET COOKIE

AN ADDICTIVE TREAT

Inspired by the iconic Neuhaus pralines, such as N and Albert, this cookie reimagines the sweet treat with a touch of elegance and an irresistible interplay of textures. The secret? A generous dough, melting chocolate chips, and a refined finish of creamy praline and caramelised hazelnuts. A tribute to the classic Neuhaus pralines, delivering a generous and sophisticated version.

Cookie dough: the crunchy base

Preparation

Cream the butter, brown sugar, caster sugar, and fleur de sel until smooth and well combined.

Incorporate the eggs and continue churning for a few minutes.

Incorporate the flour and baking powder, mixing briefly until smooth and homogeneous.

Add the diced chocolate and mix for an additional 1-2 minutes.

Shape into small balls by hand or use an ice cream scoop.

Arrange the cookies on a baking tray lined with baking paper and bake at 180°C for 10 minutes, or until lightly golden brown.

Caramelised hazelnuts: a crunchy touch

Preparation

Bring the water and sugar to a boil in a saucepan until it reaches a temperature of 118°C.

Add the hazelnuts and salt, then stir gently over low heat with a wooden spatula for approximately 20 minutes, until the sugar has turned white and caramelised.

Pour the mixture onto a baking tray lined with paper or a silicone mat.

Spread a thin layer and allow to cool before using.

Ingredients
(for approximately 12 cookies)

- 300 g butter
- 200 g light brown sugar
- 100 g sugar
- 1 pinch of fleur de sel
- 2 eggs
- 400 g flour
- 14 g baking powder
- 300 g dark chocolate

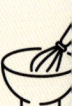

Utensils

- Scale
- Bowl
- Ice cream scoop (optional)
- Oven
- Blender
- Parchment paper
- Cutting board

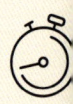

Summary of preparation times

- Preparation: 15 minutes
- Cooking: 10 minutes

Ingredients

- 300 g hazelnuts
- 200 g sugar
- 50 ml of water
- 1 g Guérande salt

Utensils

- Scale
- Plastic bowl
- Saucepan
- Baking tray
- Parchment paper or silicone mat
- Wooden spatula

Hazelnut praliné: utterly creamy

Preparation

Roast the hazelnuts on a tray lined with baking paper for 10 minutes at 180°c.

When they emerge from the oven, rub them with a tea towel to remove the skin.

Heat the sugar and water in a saucepan, without stirring, until you achieve an amber caramel.

Add the roasted hazelnuts to the caramel, coat them thoroughly, and cool on a baking tray.

Blend slowly until smooth.

Incorporate the melted milk chocolate and stir until thoroughly combined.

Plating and Finishing

Once the cookies have cooled, adorn them with caramelised hazelnuts and finish by piping a decorative stripe of hazelnut praliné.

ADVICE FROM THE MAÎTRE CHOCOLATIER

For an even more delightful touch, sprinkle a few flakes of fleur de sel onto the praline before indulging. This will intensify the flavours.

Serve with a black coffee for the perfect balance of sweetness and intensity.

Enjoy!

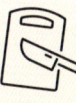

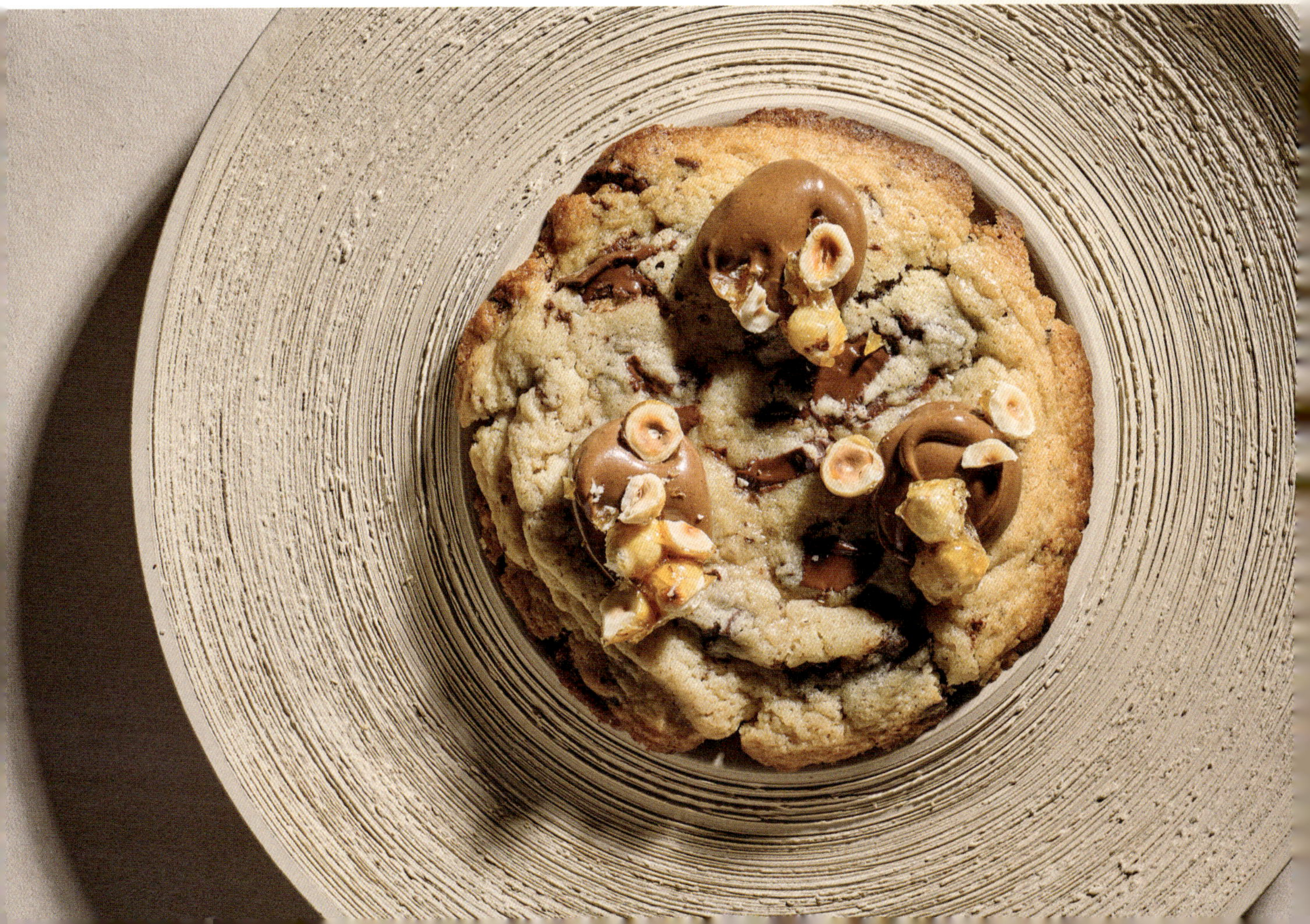

Ingredients
- 100 g hazelnuts
- 100 g caster sugar
- 100 g milk chocolate
- 20 ml of water

Utensils
- Scale
- Plastic bowl
- Saucepan
- Oven
- Blender
- Baking tray
- Parchment paper
- Silpat mat
- Wooden spatula
- Clean kitchen towel

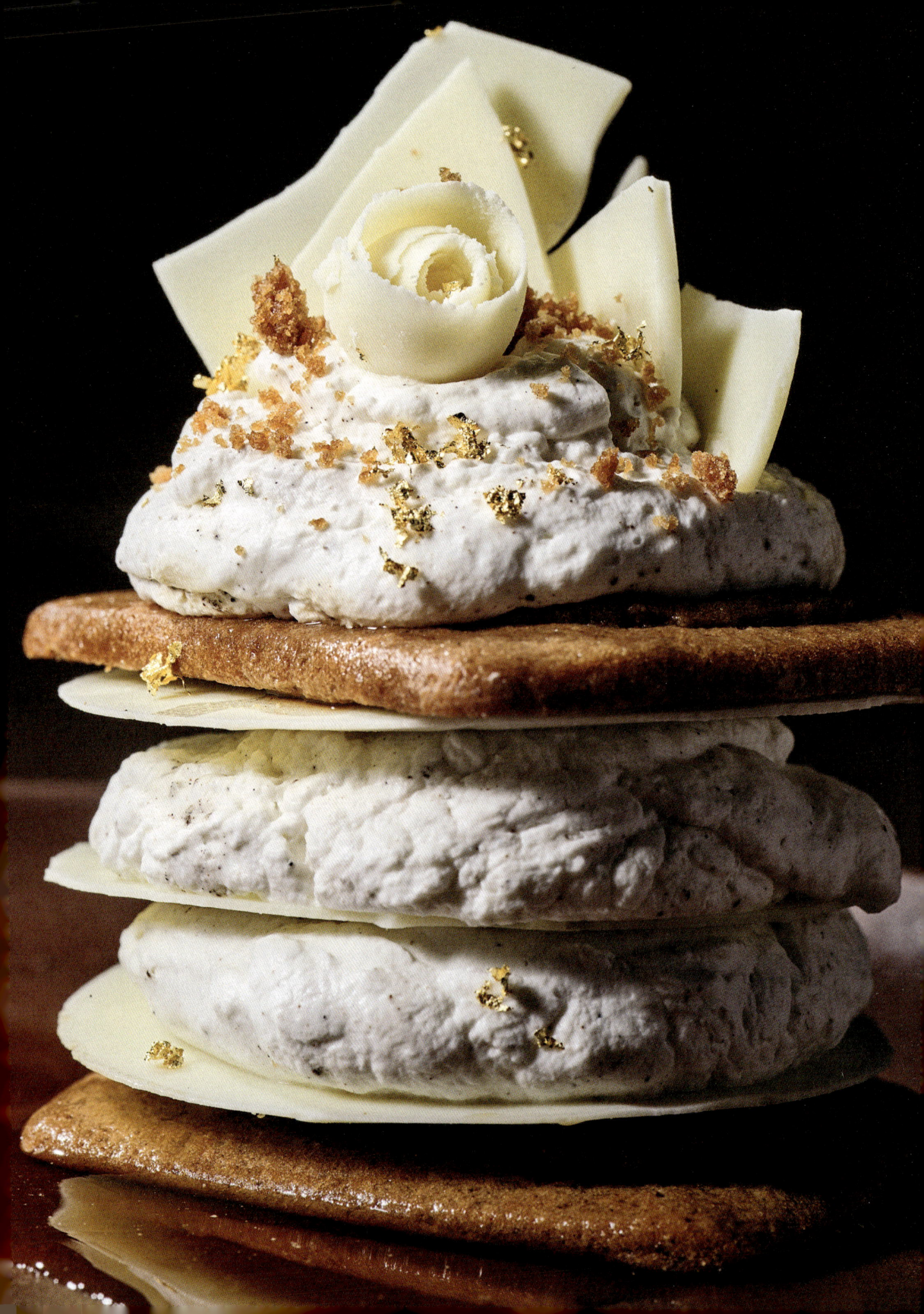

TIRAMISU, COFFEE, AND WHITE CHOCOLATE

A HOMAGE TO THE MANON CAFÉ

The coffee-flavoured Manon café is a legendary Neuhaus praline, embodying the perfect harmony between the intensity of coffee, the sweetness of white chocolate, and the smoothness of refined cream. Inspired by this essential delicacy, this reimagined tiramisu captures its iconic flavours by combining airy mascarpone, lightly crunchy Dandoy speculoos biscuits, and a gourmet touch of white chocolate shavings. This dessert should be prepared the day before for perfect texture and full-bodied flavours.

Preparation

Prepare the mascarpone cream

Separate the egg whites from the yolks.

Beat the egg whites until stiff, adding a pinch of salt when necessary. Set aside in a cool location.

In a large bowl, beat the yolks, brown sugar, and vanilla sugar until the mixture achieves a thick, creamy texture called a 'ribbon'.

Gradually fold in the mascarpone, gently incorporate the egg whites, and lift the mixture with a palette knife.

Prepare the assembly

Quickly dip the Dandoy biscuits in the strong coffee, taking care not to soak them too much to prevent disintegration.

Arrange a layer of soaked biscuits at the bottom of the dish.

Add a layer of mascarpone cream, then sprinkle with shavings of white chocolate.

Repeat the process, alternating biscuits, cream, and white chocolate until all the ingredients are used.

Plating and Finishing

Leave to rest in the fridge for 12 hours to allow the flavours to develop and achieve the perfect texture.

Before serving, add a final touch of white chocolate shavings and, for added contrast, sprinkle a pinch of cocoa or a crushed coffee bean on top.

Further presentation ideas

Individual version: serve the tiramisu in elegant drinking glasses.

Festive version: serve with a robust espresso and a small piece of white chocolate on the side.

ADVICE FROM THE MAÎTRE CHOCOLATIER

A strong coffee: a good espresso imparts all its intensity to this dessert.

Choose a white chocolate rich in cocoa butter for shavings that melt in your mouth.

Leaving the tiramisu to rest overnight is essential to achieve an ideal texture and a perfect marriage of flavours.

Ingredients
(serves six to eight)
- 3 eggs
- 100 g brown sugar
- 10 g vanilla sugar
- 250 g mascarpone
- 12 Dandoy biscuits (or artisanal Belgian speculoos)
- 200 ml of strong coffee
- 200 g shavings of white chocolate
- 1 pinch of salt

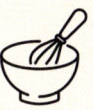

Utensils
- Scale
- Whisk or food processor
- Stainless steel bowl
- Scraper

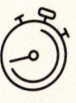

Summary of preparation times
Preparation: 20 minutes
Resting time: 12 hours

DARK CHOCOLATE FONDANT

THE INTENSITY OF THE CRIOLLO PRALINE

One of the rarest and most sought-after cocoa varieties, Criollo is a genuine treasure for connoisseurs. Grown in limited quantities due to its fragility, it is valued for its aromatic finesse, subtle notes, and delicate bitterness.

At Neuhaus, the Criollo praline pays homage to this exceptional variety with an intense and complex chocolate. Drawing inspiration from this iconic praline, the chocolate moelleux showcases the richness of an authentic chocolate fondant, featuring 80% Ugandan cocoa, which imparts both power and depth.

This dessert has an almost runny, melt-in-the-mouth texture, and is ideal just out of the oven for an explosion of chocolate on the palate.

Preparation

Break the chocolate into pieces and melt it over a bain-marie.

Gradually incorporate the diced butter and mix until smooth and glossy.

Sift the flour and icing sugar into a bowl.

Add the whole eggs and whisk until a smooth emulsion is formed.

Gently fold in the chocolate-butter mixture and combine using a pastry blender until smooth and well mixed.

Baking and Plating- Bake at 200 °C (pre-heated oven)

Grease and flour six individual moulds.

Pour the mixture into the moulds, filling them to three-quarters full.

Bake for 10 minutes at 200°C (fan oven).

Turn out straight away and serve warm for an irresistible melting centre.

Accompaniment and presentation

Serve alongside a vanilla custard or a scoop of vanilla ice cream.

Top with a few shavings of Criollo praline to emphasise the intensity of the cocoa.

ADVICE FROM THE MAÎTRE CHOCOLATIER

A powerful chocolate: 80% cocoa brings out the full authenticity of the Criollo, but you may also choose a slightly sweeter chocolate, depending on your preferences.

Controlling the baking process: Every oven is different, so it is advisable to monitor the baking to ensure the centre is slightly runny. Take it out a minute too late, and you'll end up with a more solid cake than a chocolate fondant should be.

Ingredients
(for six individual moelleux)

- 75 g flour
- 125 g icing sugar
- 175 g butter
- 250 g dark chocolate 80 % from Uganda
- 5 whole eggs

Utensils

- Scale
- Bowl
- Stainless steel bowl
- Saucepan
- Whisk
- Oven
- Scraper
- Baking paper
- Baking tray

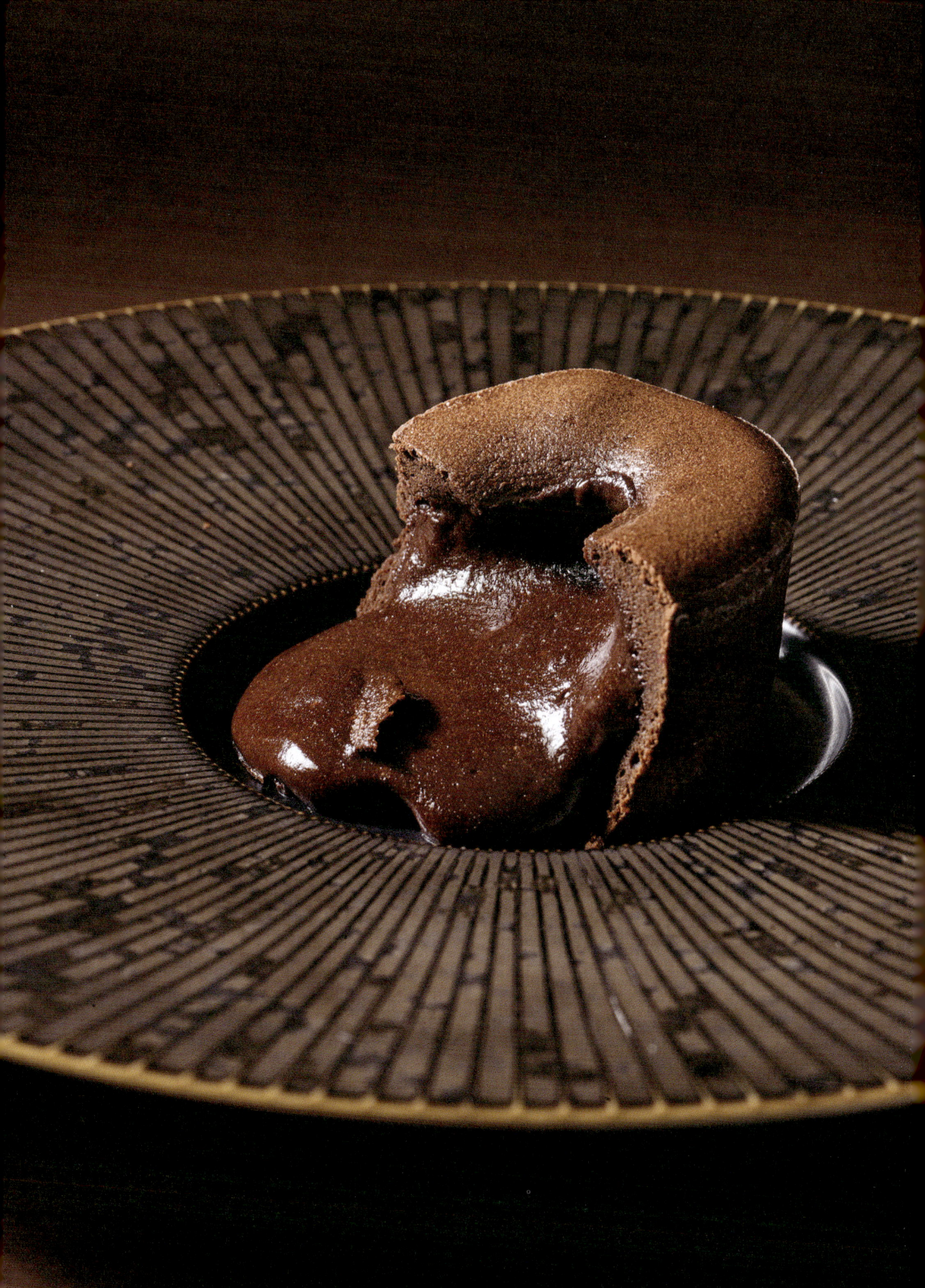

VEGAN CHOCOLATE, CARAMEL, AND PECAN NUT BROWNIE

100% PLANT-BASED PLEASURE

With its Vegan range, Neuhaus demonstrates that it is possible to reconcile the intensity of chocolate with a commitment to 100% plant-based ingredients without compromising on indulgence. Inspired by the richness of chocolate fondant and the crunch of dried fruit, this chocolate, caramel, and pecan brownie offers a soft, melt-in-the-mouth texture, enhanced by creamy caramel and caramelised pecans.

This recipe is free from eggs and dairy and features carefully chosen plant-based ingredients to ensure a rich and indulgent chocolate experience befitting a master chocolatier's expertise.

Chocolate brownie: a melt-in-the-mouth delight

1. Prepare the dough

Combine the flour, sugar, and baking soda in a bowl, then set it aside. Combine the liquid ingredients.

Melt the dark chocolate using a bain-marie.

Add the olive oil and plant-based milk, then mix thoroughly.

Pour this mixture into the bowl with the dry ingredients and stir until a smooth paste is achieved.

Finally, include the lemon juice and stir briefly.

2. Baking

Transfer the mixture into a greased mould.

Bake at 180°C (fan-assisted) for approximately 25 minutes.

Allow it to cool before removing it from the mould, then let it cool completely.

Vegan caramel: a hint of creaminess

Preparation

In a saucepan, heat the sugar with 30g of water over low heat without stirring until it reaches a golden honey colour.

Add the coconut oil and stir until thoroughly combined.

Stir in the soya cream, which has been heated to 40-50°C, along with the salt, then cook for a few minutes to thicken the texture.

Use either hot or cold. It keeps in the fridge for up to a week.

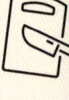

Ingredients
(serves six)

- 200 g flour
- 100 g sugar
- 1 level teaspoon of baking soda
- 150 g dark chocolate
- 100 ml olive oil
- 200 ml vegetable milk
- 10 g lemon juice (2 tablespoons)

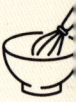

Utensils

- Scale
- Bowl
- Saucepan
- Spoon
- Whisk
- Oven
- Scraper
- Cake mould
- Baking sheet

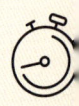

Summary of preparation times.
Preparation: 15 minutes
Cooking: 20 minutes
Resting time: 10 minutes

Ingredients

- 100 g sugar
- 50 ml coconut oil
- 75 ml soy cream
- 1 g salt

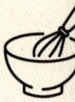

Utensils

- Scale
- Bowl
- Saucepan
- Scraper
- Microwave oven
- Baking tray
- Wooden spatula

Caramelised pecan nuts: the irresistible crunch

Preparation

Combine the sugar and salt in a small bowl.

Add the water and stir until a smooth paste is achieved.

Dry roast the pecans in a frying pan over high heat for approximately 3 minutes.

Lower the heat, add the sugar mixture, and mix thoroughly to coat the nuts.

Pour the mixture onto a baking tray lined with baking paper, allow it to cool, and break it up if necessary.

Plating and Tasting

Top the cooled brownie with the vegan caramel.

Include the caramelised pecan nuts for an added crunch.

For an elegant presentation, dust a light layer of cocoa or some cocoa bean nibs over the brownie to emphasise the intensity of the chocolate.

ADVICE FROM THE MAÎTRE CHOCOLATIER

For a robust flavour, use at least 70% dark chocolate.

Keep an eye on the cooking: the brownie should remain soft in the centre for a perfect texture.

Add a pinch of fleur de sel to the caramel for a delightful contrast.

An exquisite vegan brownie featuring a robust chocolate-caramel-pecan combination.

Ingredients

- 300 g pecan nuts
- 100 g cane sugar
- 50 ml of water
- 1 pinch of salt

Utensils
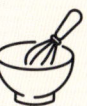
- Bowl
- Baking paper
- Baking sheet
- Frying pan
- Wooden spatula

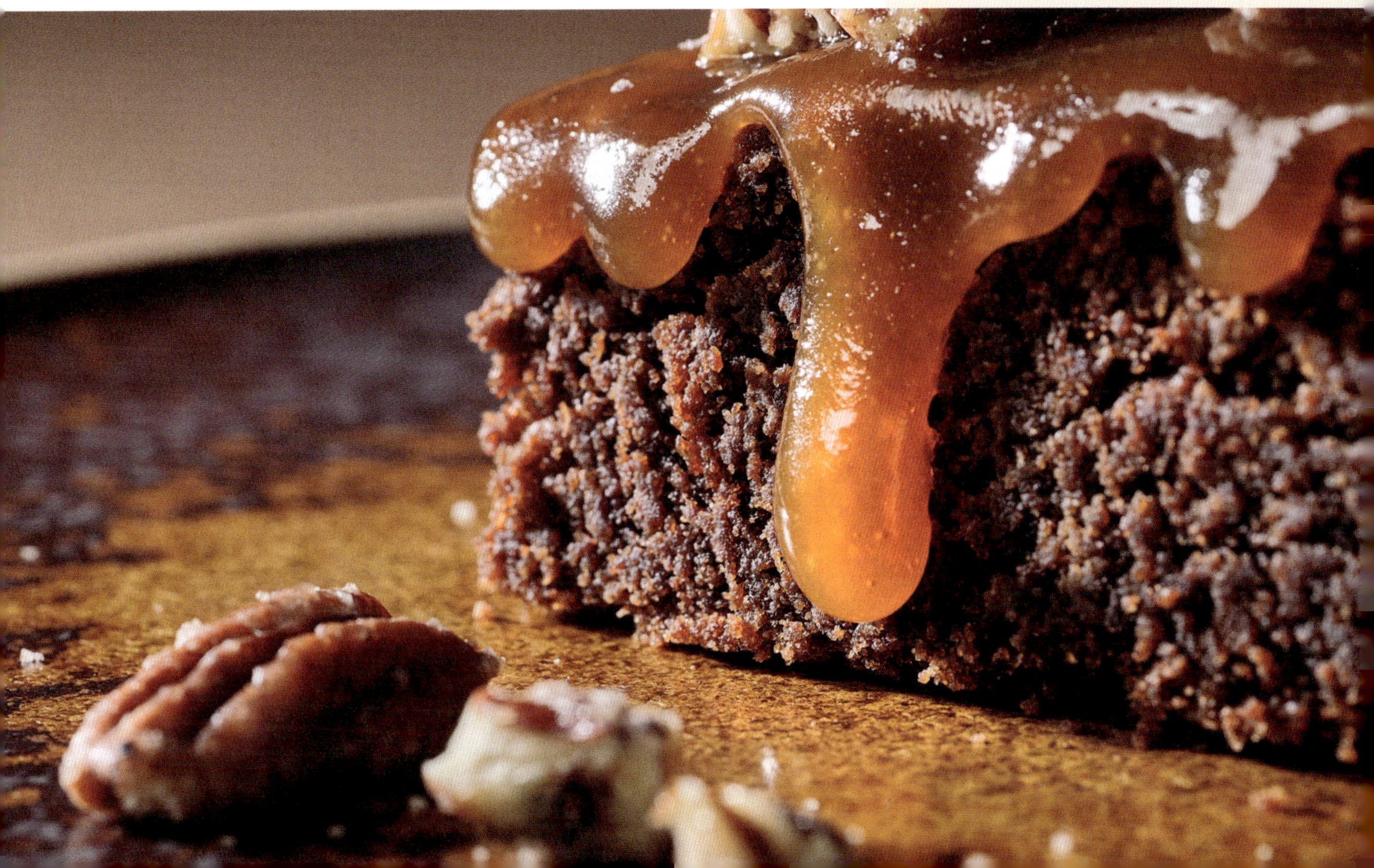

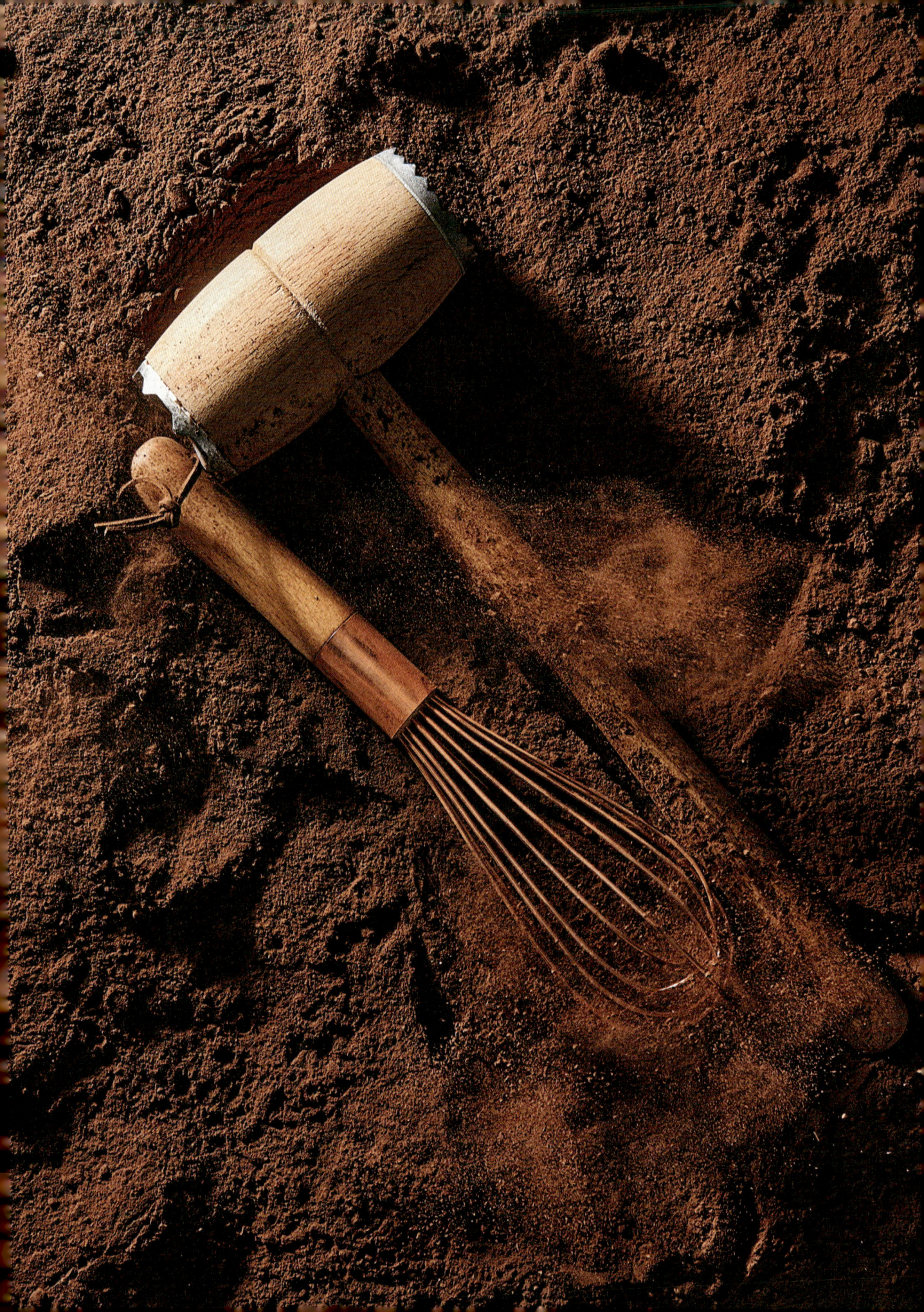

Credits and photo credits

© Antoine Melis, except for the following documents:
(t): top – (c): center – (b): bottom – (l): left – (r): right

Alamy: p. 15 (t)
Amélie de Wilde: p. 102 (t)
Choco-Story Bruges (Chocolate Museum): p. 10 (c)
Collection of Thierry Berlanger – LE MONDE DES CHOCOLATERIES BELGES: pp. 15 (l), 15 (b), 17, 18, 19
David Grimbert: pp. 68 (b), 69 (b)
Ecuadorcolat: pp. 33, 102 (b), 104
Go Forest: p. 105
Laurent de Kerchove: p. 108 (b)
Librairy of Congress, Washington: p. 13 (t)
Maximiliand Delvigne: p. 89
MIA Minesota: pp. 10 (t) and 11 (t)
Milestone Productions: pp. 70, 71
Museo Nacional del Prado, Madrid (Prado Museum, Madrid): p. 12
Musée des Beaux-Arts and d'Archéologie, Besançon (Museum of Fine Arts and Archaeology of Besançon): p. 14 (t)
Musée du quai Branly – Jacques Chirac, Dist. GrandPalaisRmn: p. 8
Neuhaus Archives: pp. 22, 25, 28, 29, 31, 32, 38, 39, 55, 58 (tr), 124, 125
Paris, Les Arts décoratifs: p. 14
Royal Library of Belgium: pp. 11 (b2), 13 (b)
Royal Museums of Art and History, Brussels: pp. 10 (b), 11 (b1)
Seppe Elewaut: pp. 23, 36, 43, 74, 99, 108 (t)
Styn: p. 76
VRT – Damon De Backer: p. 93

www.racine.be

Texts: Charlotte Huens and Pacôme Nasier
Translation: Anne Baudouin (except captions: Adele Palmeri)
Interior design and cover: Erik Lafontaine
Food design: Valérie Vermeeren
Photography: © Antoine Melis, except where otherwise credited

All rights reserved. No part of this publication may be reproduced, stored in a retrieval system, or transmitted in any form or by any means — electronic, mechanical, or otherwise — without the prior writtand permission of the publisher. Text and data mining (parts of) this publication is expressly not authorized.

All rights reserved, including rights relating to text and data mining, AI training, and similar technologies.

© Uitgeverij Lannoo nv, Tielt, 2025

D/2025/45/499
Legal deposit: October 2025
ISBN: 978-23-902-5354-9

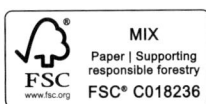